FINDING COMMON GROUND

U.S. EXPORT CONTROLS IN A CHANGED GLOBAL ENVIRONMENT

Panel on the Future Design and Implementation of
U.S. National Security Export Controls

Committee on Science, Engineering, and Public Policy

National Academy of Sciences
National Academy of Engineering
Institute of Medicine

NATIONAL ACADEMY PRESS
Washington, D.C. 1991

NATIONAL ACADEMY PRESS   2101 Constitution Avenue, NW   Washington, DC 20418

NOTICE: The National Academy of Sciences (NAS) is a private, self-perpetuating society of distinguished scholars in scientific and engineering research, dedicated to the furtherance of science and technology and their use for the general welfare. Under the authority of its congressional charter of 1863, the Academy has a working mandate that calls upon it to advise the federal government on scientific and technical matters. The Academy carries out this mandate primarily through the National Research Council, which it jointly administers with the National Academy of Engineering and the Institute of Medicine. Dr. Frank Press is President of the NAS.

The National Academy of Engineering (NAE) was established in 1964, under the charter of the NAS, as a parallel organization of distinguished engineers, autonomous in its administration and in the selection of members, sharing with the NAS its responsibilities for advising the federal government. Dr. Robert M. White is President of the NAE.

The Institute of Medicine (IOM) was chartered in 1970 by the National Academy of Sciences to enlist distinguished members of appropriate professions in the examination of policy matters pertaining to the health of the public. In this, the Institute acts under both the Academy's 1863 congressional charter responsibility to be an adviser to the federal government and its own initiative in identifying issues of medical care, research, and education. Dr. Samuel O. Thier is President of the IOM.

The Committee on Science, Engineering, and Public Policy (COSEPUP) is a joint committee of the National Academy of Sciences, the National Academy of Engineering, and the Institute of Medicine. It includes members of the councils of all three bodies.

This report is the result of the work of an independent panel appointed by COSEPUP, which has authorized its release to the public.

SPONSORS: Three agencies of the federal government provided principal support for the study: the Department of Commerce, the Department of Defense, and the Department of State. A limited amount of additional funding was provided by the Industry Coalition on Technology Transfer.

Library of Congress Cataloging-in-Publication Data

Finding common ground : U.S. export controls in a changed global environment / Panel on the Future Design and Implementation of U.S. National Security Export Controls, Committee on Science, Engineering, and Public Policy, National Academy of Sciences, National Academy of Engineering, Institute of Medicine.

    p.   cm.
    Includes index.
    ISBN 0-309-04392-1 : $34.95
    1. Export controls—United States.   2. United States—Commercial policy.   I. Committee on Science, Engineering, and Public Policy (U.S.). Panel on the Future Design and Implementation of U.S. National Security Export Controls.
HF1414.5.F56   1991
382'.64'0973—dc20   90-26801
                                                         CIP

Printed in the United States of America

Panel on the Future Design and Implementation of U.S. National Security Export Controls

ROLAND W. SCHMITT (*Chairman*), President, Rensselaer Polytechnic Institute; member, National Science Board of the National Science Foundation (former Chairman [1984–1988])

WILLIAM F. BURNS (*Vice Chairman*), Major General (retired), U.S. Army (former Director, U.S. Arms Control and Disarmament Agency [1988]; former Principal Deputy Assistant Secretary of State, Bureau of Politico-Military Affairs [1986–1988])

ARDEN L. BEMENT, JR., Vice President, Technical Resources, TRW; member, National Science Board of the National Science Foundation (former Deputy Under Secretary of Defense for Research and Engineering [1979–1981])

ASHTON B. CARTER, Professor of Public Policy, John F. Kennedy School of Government, and Director of the Center for Science and International Affairs, Harvard University

KENNETH W. DAM, Vice President, Law and External Relations, IBM Corporation (former Deputy Secretary of State [1982–1985])

HERBERT M. DWIGHT, JR.,* President, Superconductor Technologies, Inc.

JOHN L. ELLICOTT, Esq., Chairman, Management Committee, Covington & Burling

LINCOLN D. FAURER, Lieutenant General (retired), U.S. Air Force; President and Chief Executive Officer, Corporation for Open Systems (former Director, National Security Agency [1981–1985])

CHARLES GATI, Professor of Political Science, Union College

SEYMOUR E. GOODMAN,† Professor of Management Information Systems and Policy, College of Business and Public Administration, The University of Arizona

RUTH L. GREENSTEIN,* Vice President, Administration and Finance, Institute for Defense Analyses (until May 1990, Vice President and General Counsel, Genex Corporation) (former Associate/Deputy General Counsel, National Science Foundation [1981–1984])

BENJAMIN HUBERMAN, President, Consultants International Group, Inc. (former Deputy Director, White House Office of Science and Technology Policy [1978–1981]; former Senior Staff member, National Security Council [1978–1981])

---

*Former member of the National Academies' Panel on the Impact of National Security Controls on International Technology Transfer (also known as the Allen panel) [1986–1987]

†Former chairman, NRC Computer Science and Technology Board study on *Global Trends in Computer Technology and Their Impact on Export Control*, 1988

RAYMOND KLINE, President, National Academy of Public Administration (former Associate Administrator for Management Operations, NASA [1977–1979])

ROBERT LEGVOLD, Director, W. Averell Harriman Institute for Advanced Study of the Soviet Union, Columbia University

BOYD J. McKELVAIN, Manager, Corporate Export Administration Operation, General Electric Company; Chairman, Technical Advisory Committee on Implementation of the Militarily Critical Technologies List, Department of Commerce

JOHN L. McLUCAS,* Aerospace Consultant (former Secretary of the Air Force [1972–1975])

M. GRANGER MORGAN, Head, Department of Engineering and Public Policy and Professor, Engineering and Public Policy/Electrical and Computer Engineering, Carnegie Mellon

WILLIAM J. PERRY, Chairman, Technology Strategies & Alliances; Co-director, The Center for International Security and Arms Control, Stanford University; member, Defense Science Board (former Under Secretary of Defense for Research and Engineering [1977–1981])

O. M. ROETMAN, Vice President, Government and International Affairs, The Boeing Company

GASTON J. SIGUR, Distinguished Professor of East Asian Studies, School of International Affairs, The George Washington University (former Assistant Secretary of State for East Asian and Pacific Affairs [1986–1989]; former Special Assistant to the President for National Security Affairs [1982–1984])

JOHN D. STEINBRUNER, Director of Foreign Policy Studies, The Brookings Institution

PAULA STERN, President, The Stern Group (former Chair, U.S. International Trade Commission [1984–1986])

Staff

MITCHEL B. WALLERSTEIN, Project Director and Deputy Executive Officer, National Research Council

KARIN D. BERRY, Senior Consultant

JOHN R. B. CLEMENT, Staff Officer

DEBORAH J. MacGUFFIE, Project Assistant

EDWARD P. MOSER, Staff Consultant

JEAN M. SHIRHALL, Editor

THOMAS H. SNITCH, Staff Officer

---

*Former member of the National Academies' Panel on the Impact of National Security Controls on International Technology Transfer (also known as the Allen panel) [1986–1987]

Subpanel on Advanced Industrial Materials

ARDEN L. BEMENT, JR. (*Chairman*), Vice President, Technical Resources, TRW
NEIL AULT, Chairman, Technical Advisory Committee on Materials, Department of Commerce
PETER CANNON, President, Conductus Corporation
JAMES ECONOMY, Director, Materials Science and Engineering School, University of Illinois at Urbana-Champaign
RICHARD REYNOLDS, Technical Director, Hughes Research Laboratories
M. E. SHANK, Aeronautics Consultant
WILLIAM YEE, Manager, Materials and Processing Technology Division, General Dynamics

Staff

KARIN D. BERRY, Senior Consultant

Subpanel on Commercial Aircraft and Jet Engines

O. M. ROETMAN (*Chairman*), Vice President, Government and International Affairs, The Boeing Company
NEAL FRAZIER, Aerospace Management Consultant
RONALD KERBER, Vice President, Technology and Business Development, McDonnell Douglas Corporation
KENT McCORMICK, Senior Manager, International Trade and Government Relations, The Boeing Company
FRANK PICKERING, Vice President and General Manager, Aircraft Engines, Engineering Division, General Electric Aircraft Engines
ROGER SCHAUFELE, Vice President, Engineering, McDonnell Douglas Corporation

Staff

EDWARD P. MOSER, Staff Consultant

v

Subpanel on Computer Technology

Committee on Science, Engineering, and Public Policy

vii

Preface

The work of this panel has spanned a period of turbulent changes in the circumstances surrounding export controls. The study began in August 1989, when the transformations of Eastern Europe and the Soviet Union had just begun. The study was commissioned by a provision of the 1988 Omnibus Trade and Competitiveness Act and we were asked to examine all aspects of the U.S. national security export regime. The panel went beyond the scope of its predecessor, the Allen report, which concentrated "on national security export controls imposed on dual use technology." That report also "focused primarily on the Soviet Union and its Eastern bloc allies due to their central importance to the problem."

During the course of our study, we found that we could not address the most important issues of export controls today if we confined ourselves to that same scope. The reason is twofold. First, the different laws and regulations governing export controls now impinge strongly on one another, making it difficult to consider any one in isolation. Second, the structure of these laws and regulations was established in a world dramatically different from that of today. At that time, the principal targets of export controls were the Soviet Union, the countries of the Warsaw Treaty Organization, and the People's Republic of China. And the principal issue was to balance the military advantage to be gained from export controls against their damage to U.S. economic and industrial strength.

Today, both the nature of the threat and the balance of interests have changed while other threats of comparable if not greater importance have moved to center stage, i.e., the proliferation of weapons of mass destruction, as regional conflicts have taken on a more urgent cast.

Changes in the world today—not just in Eastern Europe and the Soviet Union, but also in Western Europe with the impending economic and political unification of 1992, and in Japan with its enormous economic power—are so dramatic and profound that they outstrip traditional thinking. Many of our policies are still rooted in the rubric of the 1970s and 1980s; the deep-seated views that have served us well for several decades are difficult to give up or change. But change they must if we are to respond to, and even lead in forming, the economic and political realities of the new world. And yet, in the midst of these changes, some of the old apprehensions remain: There continues to be an ominous array of weapons in the hands of forces that could once again become threatening. And new apprehensions grow: The spread of high-tech weapons, as well as the proliferation of nuclear, chemical and missile capabilities, change the calculus of national security.

One may ask if national security export controls haven't become moot. Can export controls still contribute significantly to our national security? We have answered this question, emphatically, "Yes"—not only in their continuing albeit dramatically altered role in East-West relations, but also in the realm of proliferation controls. The latter regimes, we conclude, must be brought fully under the rubric of national security. Export controls should neither be discarded in the glow of the moment nor retain the rigidity of the past.

As our panel has addressed these problems and tried to anticipate the future, we have constantly found that it was upon us. The changes have been so rapid that we have found it challenging to keep up with the present, let alone anticipate the future. Moreover, our conclusions and recommendations must fit into a future that will continue to change in directions that we cannot fully anticipate.

The report will be criticized by those who don't think we have gone far enough in abolishing export controls on East-West trade and, conversely, by those who think we have "caved in" to industrial interests. What we have attempted to do is to recommend not only policies and procedures appropriate for the circumstances at the time of writing but also processes that allow these policies and procedures to be changed to meet future circumstances. Thus, our goal has been to devise a system that can be responsive to the leadership of the President and Cabinet, a system more flexible and responsive than the present one has been and yet a system that is politically feasible both internationally and domestically.

Export controls have been a particularly troublesome corner of federal policy, as evidenced by the number of commissioned studies of them. The lineage of the present report traces back through the Allen and the Corson reports of the National Academies of Sciences and Engineering to the Bucy report of the Defense Science Board. The complexity of export control problems arises not only from the importance and intricacy of the competing interests—national security and industrial competitiveness—but also from the large number of federal agencies with an important and legitimate interest in them. In the past, the administration of the export control laws and regulations has been complex and cumbersome, leading to slow decisions that unduly impaired U.S. international competitiveness. Recently, the Departments of State, Defense and Commerce, under strong presidential guidance, have made great strides in the speed and effectiveness of their administration. They are to be commended for this. The changes that we recommend do not imply lack of significant progress toward improving the aim and effectiveness of export controls during the very recent past.

Nevertheless, we think that even greater strides are possible. Government should present as simple a face as possible to those being governed and regulated. In the case of laws and regulations as complex as export controls, it is especially important to do so. Even though large corporations have the resources and skill to deal with complexity in regulations, small firms and individuals do not. Today, many of our enterprises—for example, in the software industry—must become international at an early stage of their development. Because so much of the job creation and economic development of our nation depends on these small and mid-sized firms, we cannot burden them with excessively complex regulatory processes nor with policies that prejudice their ability to compete in world markets. Moreover, neither large nor small firms should have to bear the burden of jurisdictional overlap and the resulting controversies among executive agencies or congressional committees—or the fact that responsibilities have to be distributed to several different agencies or committees to assure the best expertise. We have tried to address these issues in a way that still preserves the legitimate interests and leading expertise of various federal agencies. We have attempted to keep control of policy where it belongs in the various agencies, while simplifying the routine administration of it. We see this simplified administrative process building on the positive steps already taken—and the potential revealed—by reforms recently initiated in the Department of State and the Department of Commerce.

An aspect of the emerging world that played heavily in our deliberations is the changing balance of importance between military and economic power and the changing position of the United States in this balance. Economies of other parts of the world are no longer as heavily tied to the fortunes of the U.S. economy as they once were. And yet for some of the tactics of the past to work, and even more so for others to work in the future, U.S. economic influence must be strong. With the emergence of Japan and Western Europe, and, increasingly, East Asia, as economic powers comparable to the United States, we will not have as much power to force others to follow our lead in imposing sanctions or controls as we have had in the past. We will have to seek much more concurrence with others in order to exercise even the leadership that our present, still-considerable economic strength gives us.

We did not go as deeply into problems with the foreign availability process as requested. We made this decision for two reasons. First, the emergence of even more urgent issues that had not been anticipated in the original charge, required that our efforts and resources be focused in other directions. Second, we came to realize that "foreign availability" was only a facet of the larger issue of "controllability."

Foreign availability is exceedingly difficult to ascertain in fact as well as in principle. With trading companies that are often no more than post office boxes, borders and ports that are open sieves, high-tech commodities that fit in pockets, software code that can be transmitted electronically, one would have to intercept and inspect a much higher fraction of world trade and communications than is feasible in order to determine the true extent of foreign availability.

Much technology that we might like to control has spread so widely, and is produced so extensively, that its control is no longer feasible. The reality of much of today's high-tech world—especially in computers and micro-electronics, somewhat less so in other areas like aircraft and engines—is that once a technology is used substantially in nonmilitary equipment, it may become by nature virtually uncontrollable. It is easier to determine "controllability" than "foreign availability," requires less bureaucratic apparatus to do so, and entails fewer fruitless delays by understanding and using specific criteria for "controllability" than by having to examine detail after detail of foreign manufacture and distribution. And, likely, there will be fewer errors.

The main panel and three subpanels assembled to carry out this study consisted of people from highly diverse backgrounds, and that was one of their strengths. Some were scholars with deep knowledge either of fields of technology or of regions of the world: the USSR, Eastern Europe, and the Pacific Rim. Others were industrial people with intimate knowledge of how our system of export controls works and how it affects industry. Still others were people with military or diplomatic backgrounds relevant to the issues we studied. And the legal profession, too, was represented by individuals fully engaged with the systems we studied. Various members of our panel had served in the Departments of State, Defense, and Commerce, as well as the White House. Moreover, the outlook of various members of the panel was diverse. But, as the study proceeded, the varied sets of views, experience, and knowledge converged on the conclusions given in the report. The fact that this broad base of experience and outlook came to a unanimous report is, we think, significant in itself. We believe that the report is impressively free of ideological taint in any direction and that it represents the best efforts of a group that dedicated itself to a dispassionate examination of the issues.

As such, we hope it will be a singularly useful report to those in Congress and the Administration that have to deal with these complex issues.

The staff assembled by the National Research Council to support the panel was also outstanding in its knowledge and its dedication to the success of the study. Substantial drafting was performed by Mitchel Wallerstein (Chapters 1, 2, 4, 5, 7, and executive summary), Karin Berry (Chapters 6, 7, and 8), John Clement (Chapters 1, 2, and 3), Ed Moser (Chapters 6 and 9), and panel member Granger Morgan (Chapter 10). The staff went through draft after draft after draft of the report in an unending quest to capture the essence of the panel's thinking and make it intelligible to the future reader. They truly have been patient and forbearing heroes in the entire process with substantive contributions of both word and thought throughout the report. We also wish to acknowledge the important contributions of Deborah MacGuffie, who kept both panel and staff well organized and who worked tirelessly to produce the multiple drafts noted above, and Jean Shirhall, who meticulously edited the drafts into proper English.

Finally, we should thank the participating government agencies for their assistance and cooperation, and especially the panel's liaison representatives. Many individuals and organizations—both U.S. and foreign—provided briefings and information to the panel and we are indebted to them all.

ROLAND W. SCHMITT
President—Rensselaer Polytechnic Institute
Chairman

WILLIAM F. BURNS
Major General—U.S. Army (Retired)
Vice Chairman

December 1, 1990

Contents

BRIEF OVERVIEW 1

1 INTRODUCTION 5
Mandate and Background of the Study, 5
Scope of the Panel's Work, 8
Focus of the Study in a Rapidly Changing Environment, 9
Organization of the Report, 11

**2 THE NEED FOR EXPORT CONTROLS IN A
CHANGED GLOBAL ENVIRONMENT** 12
Military and Political Changes in the Soviet Union and
    Eastern Europe, 13
Growing Economic and Technological Challenges for the
    United States, 14
New Threats to International Security, 15
Redefinition of U.S. Policy, 15

**3 THE IMPACT OF EXPORT CONTROLS ON
U.S. INDUSTRY** 18
Areas of Concern to U.S. Industry, 19
The Effect of Export Controls on Specific U.S. Industrial
    Sectors, 20
Summary, 25

**4 EVIDENCE ON THE ACQUISITION OF SENSITIVE
WESTERN TECHNOLOGY** 26
Soviet and WTO Technology Acquisition Efforts Prior to
1990, 27
Changes in the Nature and Patterns of Soviet and WTO
Technology Acquisition Since the Beginning of
1990, 31
Soviet Utilization of Acquired Western Technology, 33
Acquisition of Technologies of Proliferation Concern, 35
The Role of the Intelligence Community in the Export
Control Policy Process, 36
Implications of the Intelligence Evidence, 36
Recommendations, 37

**5 THE CHANGING CALCULUS OF U.S. NATIONAL
SECURITY INTERESTS** 39
Growing Economic and Technological Challenges, 40
Changes in the Traditional Sources of Physical Threat, 43
The Advent of New Sources of Physical Threat, 53

**6 THE U.S. AND MULTILATERAL EXPORT CONTROL
REGIMES** 61
Development of the Export Control Regimes, 61
Specific Characteristics of U.S. Export Controls, 72
Basic Problems of the U.S. Export Control Regimes, 86

7 ELEMENTS OF A NEW RESPONSE: U.S. POLICY 106
The Need for Export Controls in the New Era, 107
A New Approach to East-West Export Controls, 111
New Targets for National Security Export Controls, 112
Limitations on Certain Types and Uses of Export
Controls, 114

**8 ELEMENTS OF A NEW RESPONSE: MULTILATERAL
CONTROL REGIMES** 118
CoCom: A New Direction, 118
CoCom: A New Environment, 120
CoCom: Administration and Management, 126
Proliferation Controls: The Need for Collective
Security, 128

9   ELEMENTS OF A NEW RESPONSE: THE U.S.
    CONTROL REGIME 138
    Policy Process Goals, 138
    Policy Formulation, 139
    Policy Execution, 143
    Other Changes Relating to Proposed Reforms, 146
    Enhancing Industry Participation, 151

10 IMPROVING METHODS FOR LIST CONSTRUCTION
    AND REVIEW 154
    Redesigning List Construction and Review for East-West
        Controls, 156
    Generalization to Other Control Regimes, 162
    Controllability, 162

11 KEY FINDINGS AND CONCLUSIONS OF THE
    PANEL 165
    The Need for Export Controls in a Changed Global
        Environment, 165
    The Impact of Export Controls on U.S. Industry, 166
    Evidence on the Acquisition of Sensitive Western
        Technology, 167
    The Changing Calculus of U.S. National Security
        Interests, 168
    The U.S. and Multilateral Export Control Regimes, 171
    The Need for Export Controls in the New Era, 174
    New Targets for National Security Export Controls, 174
    Limitations on Certain Types and Uses of Export
        Controls, 175
    CoCom: A New Direction, 175
    CoCom: A New Environment, 175
    CoCom: Administration and Management, 176
    Coordination of Current Nonproliferation Regimes, 177
    Changes to the U.S. Control Regime, 178

12 SUMMARY OF RECOMMENDATIONS OF THE
    PANEL 181
    Reshape U.S. National Security Policy in Response to the
        Changing Calculus of U.S. National Security
        Interests, 181
    Develop New U.S. and Multilateral Export Control
        Regimes, 183

APPENDIXES

A. Report of the Subpanel on Advanced Industrial Materials, 199
B. Report of the Subpanel on Commercial Aircraft and Jet Engines, 222
C. Report of the Subpanel on Computer Technology, 248
D. Panel Foreign Fact-Finding Mission Reports, 266
E. Congressional Request for the Study, 304
F. COSEPUP Charge to the Panel, 306
G. The Evolution of U.S. Export Control Policy: 1949–1989, 308
   Mitchel B. Wallerstein with *William W. Snyder, Jr.*
H. Judicial Review Under the Export Administration Act of 1979: Is It Time to Open the Courthouse Doors to U.S. Exporters?, 321
   Franklin D. Cordell for *John L. Ellicott*
 I. A Proposal for Increased Use of Industry Technical Expertise in the U.S. Export Control Process, 336
   Paul Freedenberg
J. Some Details on the Proposed Method for List Construction and Review, 349
K. Glossary, 356
L. List of Acronyms, 362
M. List of Briefers, Contributors, and Liaison Representatives, 366
N. Biographies of Panel Members, 371

INDEX 379

Brief Overview*

This study addresses two fundamental questions: (1) How should U.S. export control policies be organized in a post-Cold War world? (2) Are U.S. export control policies formulated in a manner consistent with, and supportive of, the full scope of U.S. interests? The conditions that determined the feasibility and effectiveness of national security export controls† since World War II have now changed dramatically, and the nature of the Western security alliance seems likely to change as well. The Warsaw Treaty Organization (WTO), also known as the Warsaw Pact, has lost its meaning as a threatening military alliance. The dissolution of the WTO, particularly when combined with obligations assumed under the Treaty on Conven-

---

*A detailed *Executive Summary* has been published separately and is available from the Committee on Science, Engineering, and Public Policy, National Academies of Sciences and Engineering.

†*National security export controls* are procedures designed to regulate the transfer of items from one country to another in such a way as to protect militarily important technologies from acquisition by potential adversaries (see Section 5 of the Export Administration Act (EAA) of 1979, as amended). These are contrasted in the report with *foreign policy export controls*, which are restrictions imposed on the export of general classes of items to one or more specified countries in order to further the foreign commitments and interests of the United States or to fulfill its international obligations (see Section 6 of the EAA).

1

tional Forces in Europe (CFE), means that a forward-based, Soviet strategic offensive capability in Central Europe is no longer possible.

Thus, on the basis of the agreed reductions in Soviet and East European military forces (assuming that they are completed in good faith), the dissolution of the WTO, and the emerging defensive Soviet military posture in Asia, the panel concludes that a new paradigm for the application of West-East export controls is now required. **The panel recommends that the United States and the other nations of the Coordinating Committee for Multilateral Export Controls (CoCom) change the basis of their technology transfer and trade relationships with the Soviet Union and the East European countries from the "denial regime" that has existed for more than 40 years to an "approval regime" based on multilaterally agreed and verifiable end-use conditions.**

In contrast to the reduced threat posed by the Soviet Union and the former WTO countries, there are growing concerns about the acquisition by certain countries and political organizations of technologies contributing to nuclear, chemical, and biological weapons, missile delivery systems, and advanced conventional weapons. Proliferation of these technologies could be a decisive factor in the expansion to a global scale of conflicts initiated by regional powers, the exacerbation of intraregional instabilities, and the further spread of extremist violence and state-sponsored terrorism.

The most important distinction between traditional East-West and proliferation controls is that the United States is not in a position to exercise the same level of influence over the suppliers of proliferation technologies. Indeed, some of the potential suppliers of weapons of mass destruction also are the *targets* of current control regimes. **Moreover, to be effective, such control regimes *must* include participation by the Soviet Union and the People's Republic of China. With the end of the Cold War, the possibility of such comprehensive multilateral cooperation may now exist.**

The panel notes that proliferation of weapons of mass destruction and their delivery systems is a U.S. national security concern and should be treated as such in U.S. law and policy. Proliferation control regimes must be tailored to the particular circumstances or threats, but some of the policy responses are likely to include properly fashioned export controls. **The choice of policy responses— including the appropriate mix of export controls—for** managing proliferation risks is a complex and difficult problem that requires far more careful and extensive study than this panel or any other group has yet been able to conduct.

U.S. POLICY

Carefully tailored and/or refashioned export controls can be appropriate and viable in support of the following U.S. policy objectives: (1) constraining access by the *Soviet military* to technology and end products that contribute significantly and directly to the improvement of weapons capabilities, (2) constraining access by certain countries to technology and end products that contribute significantly and directly to the development of advanced weapons systems, (3) constraining access by countries of proliferation concern to nuclear, biological, chemical, and missile delivery technologies and know-how, and (4) imposing multilaterally agreed sanctions for violations of international agreements or norms of behavior.

THE COCOM REGIME

The continued credibility of CoCom now depends on the willingness of its members to recognize and respond to the new political, economic, and military realities by developing a flexible and adaptive strategy. **The panel finds that the traditional CoCom objective of retarding the qualitative progress of Soviet military capabilities could be preserved while simultaneously allowing for expanded trade by shifting the focus from a denial regime, based on an embargo of controlled goods and technology, to an approval regime, based on a sharply reduced CoCom Industrial List and contingent on verifiable end-use conditions *approved by CoCom*.**

PROLIFERATION REGIMES

There are currently insufficient linkages between the multilateral arrangements established to address nuclear, chemical, and missile technology exports and the CoCom control regime. Further, issues pertaining to international arms trade, and trade in high-technology weapons, require more coherent multilateral attention than they now receive. Given the great complexity of proliferation problems, and the many actors who are involved, the panel believes that high-level leadership and policy coordination will be needed from a small number of countries, including at least the United States, the United Kingdom, the Soviet Union, France, Germany, Japan, and China. This should be combined with a mechanism or set of mechanisms for developing and maintaining coordinated international regimes to which all interested states can be parties. In applying export controls to proliferation problems, care must be taken to make them narrowly targeted and as fully multilateral as possible.

THE U.S. CONTROL REGIME

The U.S. government should develop a new policy process in which all interests are fully and clearly expressed so that presidential leadership can drive decisions in a balanced and timely fashion. At present, line agencies with conflicting missions are often unable to integrate the various national security, economic, and foreign policy issues and give executive authorities a balanced, coherent view of the key issues. As a result, a disproportionate amount of bureaucratic resources are expended in resolving disputes, rather than administering and enforcing the export control system. The resulting confusion has on some occasions caused additional delay and expense for U.S. exporters. To resolve these difficulties, the panel recommends that clear policy guidance be established by the President in a national security directive; that an interagency policy coordinating process be established to formulate and review proposals and recommendations in full consideration of all relevant national interests; and that all routine administrative activities undertaken within the established policy guidelines be consolidated in a *single* administrative agency, with clear instructions as to when issues should be referred to the interagency policy coordinating process.

Note to readers: A complete statement of the key findings and conclusions of the panel is presented in Chapter 11 of this report, and a summary of the panel's recommendations is provided in Chapter 12.

1

Introduction

MANDATE AND BACKGROUND OF THE STUDY

This study was mandated in Part I, Section 2433, of the Omnibus Trade and Competitiveness Act of 1988, in which the Congress requested that the National Academies of Sciences and Engineering "conduct a comprehensive study of the adequacy of the current export administration system in safeguarding United States national security while maintaining United States international competitiveness and Western technological preeminence."* The legislative request for the study came more than a year before the opening of the Berlin Wall and all the other extraordinary political and economic changes that have occurred in Eastern Europe and in the Soviet Union itself, the consequences of which are being played out across the world.

Congress asked the National Academy complex† to undertake the study on the basis of its past record of accomplishment in the general subject area. In 1982, for example, the Academy complex's Committee on Science, Engineering, and Public Policy (COSEPUP) convened a special panel to determine whether U.S. national security interests were being compromised by the open communication of the results of basic research. The resulting report,

---

*Appendix E contains the complete language used in Part I, Section 2433, of the Omnibus Trade and Competitiveness Act of 1988, which was signed by the President on August 23, 1988.

†The National Academy complex includes the National Academy of Sciences, the National Academy of Engineering, and the Institute of Medicine.

Scientific Communication and National Security[1] (known as the Corson report after its chairman, Dale R. Corson), released in September 1982, laid the basis for the development in 1985 of National Security Decision Directive 189, which restated the importance to the national interest of maintaining open communication of "fundamental" research within the constraints imposed by security classification or other existing law.

At the time of its report, the Corson panel indicated that there was another major dimension to the export control problem, which it did not have the opportunity or mandate to examine in depth—namely, that of technology transferred as part of or in association with commercial activities. In 1985, COSEPUP undertook this second study, when it appointed the Panel on the Impact of National Security Controls on International Technology Transfer, chaired by Lew Allen, Jr. The report of this study, *Balancing the National Interest: U.S. National Security Export Controls and Global Economic Competition* (known as the Allen report), was released in January 1987.[2] The Allen report stated clearly for the first time that it was necessary to take account of U.S. economic vitality and competitiveness in formulating export controls on strategic technology, and it urged that U.S. policy move toward complete multilateralization of the formulation and implementation of export control policy.

Most recently, the National Research Council's Computer Science and Technology Board established a committee to assess trends in computer science and technology as they affect and are affected by export controls. From that assessment came the report *Global Trends in Computer Technology and Their Impact on Export Control*,[3] released in December 1988, which made recommendations for export control based on the committee's conclusions about the intrinsic controllability of computer technologies and the interplay among controls, technology development, and prospects for the U.S. computer industry.

In response to the current congressional request, COSEPUP established the Panel on the Future Design and Implementation of U.S. National Security Export Controls. The composition of the panel was the result of a careful search by the presidents of the National Academies of Sciences and Engineering designed to ensure a panel with balance, depth of expertise, and objectivity. The panel included many individuals who have had substantial experience in government at the most senior levels pertaining to national security affairs, a number of others who have held senior posts in or contributed advice to the intelligence community, and still others who possess substantial legal expertise from work on strategic trade issues. Many others hold (or have held) leadership positions in high-technology industries. Three members of the panel also served on the earlier Allen panel.

The congressional request also called for the Academies to examine the impact of any recommended conceptual approach to export controls in several industrial sectors. COSEPUP considered those industries subject to export controls in which U.S. exports are dominant or strong competitors. Industrial sectors for which, at the outset of the study, export controls were known to be under executive branch review (e.g., machine tools and telecommunications) were excluded from consideration. COSEPUP appointed separate subpanels, representing sectors with a range of product life cycles, on (1) computer technology (hardware and software), (2) advanced industrial materials, and (3) civilian aircraft and jet engines. Each subpanel was connected to the main panel through its chairperson, who was a member of the main panel. Like the members of the main panel, those appointed to the three subpanels were chosen after a careful search, primarily on the basis of recognized expertise in the particular field of technology. The computer hardware and software subpanel comprised members of the Computer Science and Technology Board study committee that had previously produced the *Global Trends* report.

Section 2433 of the Omnibus Trade and Competitiveness Act of 1988 set out five specific tasks for the Academies' study. After carefully examining the terms of the legislation and consulting with the relevant federal agencies, COSEPUP developed a five-point charge to the panel* that incorporated all of the major issues raised in the legislative request: (1) consider various existing and alternative conceptual approaches to the design of national security export controls, including methodologies for determining which end products and technologies are likely to make a significant difference in the military capabilities of controlled countries; (2) develop a set of dynamic and implementable principles for determining which technologies should be subject to control; (3) demonstrate how the principles would be applied to a few selected technological sectors; (4) clarify in operational terms the meaning of "foreign availability" and rationalize and harmonize the U.S. and CoCom (Coordinating Committee for Multilateral Export Controls) procedures for dealing with identified cases of foreign availability; and (5) to the extent warranted, develop proposals for new procedures and organizational arrangements to ensure more timely, predictable, and effective decision making on national security export controls.

The charge to the panel was prepared by COSEPUP in early 1989 and accepted by the panel at its organizational meeting in August of the same year. The study itself began in the fall of 1989 and ended in late 1990. During that period, international developments reshaped the global political landscape, with marked consequences for the agencies of the U.S. government responsible for export control matters, for the leadership of the executive branch, and for the deliberative and policy oversight committees of the Congress.

---

*The complete COSEPUP charge to the panel is contained in Appendix F.

Due to the dramatic changes in the context and circumstances of its work, the panel found itself repeatedly having to reexamine its charge. Inevitably, some of the original emphases of the study have shifted, and the relative importance of various elements of the original charge has changed. In particular, the panel expanded its examination of export controls beyond dual use technologies (i.e., technologies that have military and commercial applications) to consider technologies of proliferation concern: advanced conventional weapons, missile delivery systems, and nuclear, biological, and chemical weapons. The panel also broadened its consideration of ways to change export control policies as the Soviet Union and its former Warsaw Treaty Organization (WTO) allies, traditional adversaries of the United States, evolve internally and become more fully integrated into the global political and economic system. Finally, the panel examined shifts in the sources of threat in the new global context—a shift dramatically highlighted by the explosion of regional conflict in the Middle East in 1990. These changes in emphasis notwithstanding, the panel believes it has remained faithful to the original charge of the study.

SCOPE OF THE PANEL'S WORK

The panel and its professional staff pursued an ambitious scope of work that included briefings, foreign fact-finding missions, and commissioned research papers. First, the staff collected and analyzed public literature and classified documents made available by government agencies. The panel also held discussions with representatives of all the federal agencies involved directly in the formulation or implementation of national security export control policy (and related topics)—namely, the Departments of Defense, Commerce, State, Treasury (U.S. Customs Service), and Energy; the National Aeronautics and Space Administration; and the White House's Office of Science and Technology Policy. In addition, the panel heard classified briefings by the Technology Transfer Intelligence Committee, an interagency group of the intelligence community, and a special subcommittee of the panel heard a number of additional briefings at high levels of classification. The panel also had extensive contact with and heard briefings by representatives of affected sectors of U.S. high-technology industry. (Appendix M provides a list of the briefers and contributors to the panel and their affiliations.)

Three foreign fact-finding missions constituted the second element of the study. In February 1990, a delegation of the panel visited five Asian countries: Hong Kong, Japan, Macao, South Korea, and Taiwan. In May 1990, a second delegation visited five European countries: Belgium, France, Germany, Switzerland, and the United Kingdom; this trip also included a stop at CoCom headquarters in Paris. Also in May 1990, a third delegation of the panel visited Canada. In each country, panel members held confidential, frank meetings on national security export control matters with government officials, industry leaders, academic experts, and other informed observers. (Summary reports describing the panel's foreign fact-finding missions are included as Appendix D.)

A third element of the study involved the commissioning of a series of research reports prepared by outside consultants and by the panel's professional staff. Some of these reports developed new information; others reexamined existing problems from new perspectives. (Three of these reports are included as Appendixes G, H, and I. Four additional papers prepared for the panel are available on request.*)

Finally, each of the three appointed subpanels held a series of meetings and subsequently reported its findings to the main panel, in writing and through its respective chairperson. The subpanels' views provided valuable input for the analysis that follows. The complete reports of the subpanels are included as Appendixes A–C.

FOCUS OF THE STUDY IN A
RAPIDLY CHANGING ENVIRONMENT

In addressing its charge, as noted earlier, the panel confronted a special challenge due to the unprecedented political changes that were occurring while the study was in progress. On the one hand, it is impossible to predict with certainty the permanence or eventual success of the democratization process in the East European countries or of *glasnost, perestroika*, and other politico-military changes in the Soviet Union. On the other hand, it is equally impossible to ignore these new realities, or the new and growing threats from nontraditional sources, given that they condition the need for and design of national security export controls. Ultimately, the panel made what it believed were reasonable and prudent judgments about Soviet military capabilities and doctrine, the technological requirements for Soviet military systems, and the overall nature of the threat—both current and prospective—posed by the Soviet Union and its former WTO allies. In its analysis and its findings and recommendations, the panel endeavored to develop an approach to export controls that would (1) facilitate flexible and positive responses to further improvement in East-West relations, (2) continue to protect the security of the United States and its allies during this highly uncertain period of political and economic transition, (3) minimize the adverse impact of export controls

---

*The following papers are available through the Publications-on-Demand program of the National Academy Press: Donald Goldstein, *Japan's Strategic Trade Controls: A New Era*; Joel Hellman, *The State of Perestroika: A Survey of U.S. Specialists on the Soviet Union*; International Business-Government Counsellors, Inc., *National Security and Foreign Policy Export Controls*; and Wolfgang Reinicke, *Recent Developments in Eastern Bloc Countries and Their Effects on CoCom: West German and European Perspectives*.

on economic competition in the global marketplace, and (4) be responsive to new threats from countries that raise concerns about proliferation.

The assumptions built into and the limitations imposed on the study are to some extent similar to those of the previous COSEPUP study, the Allen report. But they also differ in several important respects. The similarities and differences include the following:

- *Means of strategic technology transfer*   Like the Allen report, this analysis focuses on problems associated with the direct or third-party diversion—or in some cases, legal sale—of technology considered important to the military systems of potential adversaries. It does not address, except in a general way, the problem of military or industrial espionage, against which export controls are largely ineffective.

- *Deficiencies in the U.S. defense industrial base and military procurement process*   Because maintaining Western military capabilities requires developing and fielding new technology, as well as denying technology to potential adversaries, issues relating to the U.S. industrial base and procurement process are highly relevant. However, as did the Allen panel, the panel determined that the complex problems associated with maintaining the U.S. defense industrial base and/or rationalizing the military procurement process were beyond the terms of the congressional request.

- *Use of export controls to protect short supplies and U.S. markets*   The panel chose to set aside the application of export controls to prevent the short supply of certain strategic commodities. It also did not address more recent proposals to impose (or reimpose) export controls to promote U.S. economic competitiveness, for example, in situations in which another nation is selling products or services (e.g., space launches) on the international market at heavily subsidized prices. The panel determined that the treatment of such policy issues also exceeded its charge.

- *Economic and technological impact of export controls*   The Allen report was concerned exclusively with the impact of export controls on the United States and other non-Communist countries. Although that remains a primary focus of the current study, the dynamic political situation in Eastern Europe and recent progress on arms control negotiations make the situation today vastly more complicated. Among cooperating Western countries, the need for virtually license-free trade with each other is now taken almost as a given. But the constraining impact of controls on countries newly converted to democracy and to market economics was—and properly so—a subject of concern to this panel as well.

- *Broadened focus of controls*   The Allen panel focused exclusively on the control of dual use goods and technology, primarily as implemented under Section 5 of the Export Administration Act of 1979, as amended, and it chose explicitly not to address issues associated with munitions controls or foreign policy controls. **This panel decided to address these issues because in the new political and economic environment, maintaining these often artificial distinctions has tended to impede rational policy-making. This is particularly true with respect to the initiation or maintenance of controls on exports to countries of proliferation concern. Although currently treated as a foreign policy or munitions issue, proliferation may pose the most urgent national security threat to the United States and to other countries interested in maintaining a stable world order.**

ORGANIZATION OF THE REPORT

Chapter 2 examines the need for export controls in the changed global environment, following which Chapter 3 examines the impact of export controls on U.S. industry. Chapter 4 discusses evidence on the acquisition of sensitive Western technology by the Soviet Union and its former WTO allies and by countries of proliferation concern. Chapter 5 rounds out the overview of changing conditions with an examination of transformations in the calculus of U.S. national security interests.

Chapter 6 describes the history, development, and operation of the current U.S. and multilateral export control regimes. The next four chapters address the components of the panel's proposed response to changing national security conditions, beginning with an examination of U.S. policy considerations (Chapter 7), followed by discussion of multilateral regimes (Chapter 8), and concluding with two chapters on the U.S. export control regime. Chapter 9 examines details of the policy process, and Chapter 10 addresses the formation and management of U.S. control lists.

Two final chapters summarize key findings and conclusions (Chapter 11) and the recommendations (Chapter 12) of the study.

NOTES

1. National Academy of Sciences, *Scientific Communication and National Security* (Washington, D.C.: National Academy Press, 1982).
2. National Academy of Sciences, National Academy of Engineering, and Institute of Medicine, *Balancing the National Interest: U.S. National Security Export Controls and Global Economic Competition* (Washington, D.C.: National Academy Press, 1987).
3. National Research Council, *Global Trends in Computer Technology and Their Impact on Export Control* (Washington, D.C.: National Academy Press, 1988).

2

The Need for Export Controls in a Changed Global Environment

Since World War II, the United States and its CoCom (Coordinating Committee for Multilateral Export Controls) allies have been engaged in an effort to deny certain Western technology to the Soviet Union and its principal allies. This effort has limited the access of Soviet bloc countries to technology and products that could otherwise have upgraded their military capabilities. Although this denial effort has not prevented the Soviets from fielding capable and effective weapons systems, it has caused them to rely on less sophisticated technological approaches, and it has forced them to invest enormous resources in military-related research and development that might otherwise have been dedicated to civilian purposes. Now, for a variety of reasons, perhaps including the very success of national security export controls,* significant changes have occurred in the nature of the threats that export controls are

---

*The term *national security export controls* is used throughout this report as it is defined in statute (see Section 5 of the Export Administration Act of 1979, as amended). It refers to procedures designed to regulate the transfer from one country to another of items that would make a significant contribution to military potential that could prove detrimental to the United States. The report, however, extends the reach of national security export controls to include broader threats to national security, such as the proliferation of nuclear, chemical, biological, and advanced conventional weapons and missile delivery systems. Control of exports related to some of these threats has traditionally been dealt with through foreign policy export controls, which are restrictions imposed on the export of general classes of items when necessary to further the foreign commitments and interests of the United States or to fulfill declared U.S. international obligations (see Section 6 of the Export Administration Act of 1979, as amended).

intended to address and in the definition of ''national security'' under which the controls are implemented.

For 40 years a broad consensus has existed among the United States and its Western allies with regard to the source and nature of the threats to common security interests. In such circumstances, export controls could be imposed not only on technologies the transfer of which would immediately threaten security (e.g., weapons systems), but on other technologies that could, over a longer period, contribute to the military strength of a potential adversary (e.g., machine tools or critical electronics technology). In the new environment, in which the traditional East-West threat has significantly changed and proliferation concerns have become of major significance, target countries, activities of concern, and other aspects of the national security threat are likely to change, sometimes rapidly, and it may often be difficult to form an effective, enduring, and broad international consensus. In this new setting, export controls may have more limited utility in achieving national security objectives. More emphasis may have to be placed on items with particular end uses that pose immediate or near-term threats.

MILITARY AND POLITICAL CHANGES IN THE SOVIET UNION AND EASTERN EUROPE

Although the Soviet military threat has not disappeared, it has changed, and the threat posed by the former Soviet allies in the Warsaw Treaty Organization (WTO) is sharply reduced and qualitatively different. The surprising aspect of these developments is that the threat is diminished, not because of significant reductions in the number or capability of weapons possessed by the Soviets (although some reductions have occurred and more are promised), but because of changes in the political structures and processes that govern the use of those weapons.

During 1990, democratic forces in the Soviet Union greatly strengthened their position, although the depth of the crises facing the leadership continues to make further progress uncertain. In addition, as described in Chapter 5, the nations of Eastern Europe have moved away from their commitment to WTO force deployments, and Soviet military leaders regularly speak of a new defensive orientation. Thus, even though Soviet military force deployments have not changed as dramatically as other operational and organizational factors, and the Soviet strategic capability remains largely unchanged, the West has an opportunity to influence democratic forces and the evolving military posture in the Soviet Union and Eastern Europe. Indeed, it now appears to be in the interest of the West to encourage investment, aid, and technology transfer to the East European countries in order to accelerate their integration into the Western economic system.

Economic necessity is drawing the Soviet Union toward market principles and closer economic contact with the West. Although major obstacles remain and the time required is uncertain, movement toward eventual integration of the Soviet economy into the global market also seems likely.

Changing global political circumstances—including most recently the crisis in the Persian Gulf—are drawing the Soviet Union into closer political and, in some cases, military cooperation with the West as well. It would be premature to suggest that Soviet and Western interests and policy objectives have converged, but there is closer consultation and, occasionally, direct cooperation. This trend is likely to continue as both superpowers struggle with the problem of regional conflicts.

GROWING ECONOMIC AND TECHNOLOGICAL CHALLENGES FOR THE UNITED STATES

The operative definition of U.S. national security has also changed. Years of staggering trade deficits, declining market shares and competitiveness in world trade, and loss of technological leadership in many fields have forced the United States to contemplate the prospect of a changed position in the global order.

Among the growing economic and technological challenges facing the United States (discussed in detail in Chapter 5) are the following factors:

- The changing structure of the global economy
- The increasingly rapid global diffusion of technology
- Declining U.S. technological and manufacturing preeminence
- Growing technological and manufacturing sophistication in Japan and the newly industrializing countries
- Increasing U.S. concern about the defense industrial base, including a growing dependence on commercial and foreign technology
- The changing distribution of global economic and financial power
- The growing importance of exports to U.S. economic vitality
- Continuing U.S. domestic problems

Moreover, even if the United States is not, as some have claimed, a "declining hegemonic power,"[1] policymakers are coming to recognize that **(a) a strong military alone is not sufficient to protect U.S. interests or to influence world events; (b) failure to maintain a vigorous economy can also threaten fundamental security interests; and (c) an alliance strategy can only be effective if all participants are committed to finding multilateral solutions to common problems.**

The rationale for any new export control policy must include the recognition that the United States needs to maintain a successful, vigorous role in the global economy. Early entry into, and sustained participation in, global markets by U.S. exporters are key elements of such a role.

NEW THREATS TO INTERNATIONAL SECURITY

From the beginning of the Cold War, U.S. policy implicitly assumed that the Soviet Union and its allies were relentless opponents of U.S. interests, the political philosophy and structure of the Soviet Union were impervious to democratic processes, and the Soviet economic structure was immutable. Thus, U.S. national security depended principally on the balance of weapons within a fundamentally unchanging political and economic context. The primary strategy for maintaining U.S. national security was to seek significant reductions in the weapons posing physical threats while maintaining technological superiority. Although this approach has achieved many successes, as noted, the United States today is still far from the goal of a relatively safe and secure world. New and growing concerns have arisen about the behavior and intentions of various countries and political organizations beyond the traditional Cold War adversaries, concerns related to the acquisition of missile technologies and advanced conventional, nuclear, chemical, and biological weapons.

The new, proliferation-related threats could potentially manifest themselves in ways quite different from the traditional East-West military confrontation in Europe. These ways include expansion of conflicts initiated by regional powers, regional instabilities exacerbated by the availability of advanced weapons and technologies of proliferation concern, and extremist violence and state-sponsored terrorism. They reflect the emergence of stronger military forces, and an accompanying proliferation of high-performance weaponry and weapons of mass destruction, in many parts of the world that have not previously been a focus of security concerns. Managing these threats will require different kinds of policy approaches than those developed to respond to the threat posed by the Soviet bloc.

REDEFINITION OF U.S. POLICY*

Export controls, sharply reduced in number and fully multilateral, are a necessary and appropriate policy instrument for responding to any remaining threat posed to the United States by the Soviet Union and the other former WTO countries, but a new policy approach must be developed if export controls are to remain an effective policy instrument

---

*In this and subsequent chapters, formal findings and conclusions of the panel are printed in boldface type; recommendations of the panel are preceded by an asterisk(*) and printed in boldface type.

under the changed national security conditions. Given the new realities, export controls will be viable only if they enable the United States and other nations that share common objectives to (a) remain vigilant and prepared during the period of economic and political transformation now under way within the Soviet Union and Eastern Europe; (b) facilitate (rather than obstruct) the pursuit of important political and economic objectives, such as further democratization and the development of market economies in the Soviet Union and Eastern Europe; and (c) address flexibly new types and sources of national security challenges, such as those derived from growing proliferation threats or the threat of terrorism, as they emerge.

Because of the enormous uncertainties* inherent in the current situation, a new and clearly more sophisticated approach to export control policy is required, one that could be adapted and modified to a range of future conditions. Among its principal features would be the following interactive goals:

• Maintaining a qualitative edge in U.S. military systems as a deterrent against threats of aggression, including those posed by Soviet and Soviet-allied forces.

• Preventing or retarding the proliferation of items† that could directly and immediately enhance the conventional or strategic capabilities of countries that may now or in the future pose a threat to the physical security or vital interests of the United States and other nations that share common objectives.

• Preventing or retarding the proliferation of items for use in acts of terrorism or other political violence against the interests of the United States and other nations that share common objectives.

• Preventing or retarding the proliferation of items that may be destabilizing to global or regional political structures and power alignments.

• Avoiding negative impacts on economic competitiveness and the overall viability of the free market economies that participate in global trade.

• Promoting further political democratization and economic development in the Soviet Union, Eastern Europe, and elsewhere.

---

*Discussion of anticipated political and economic developments covers, as of this writing, a remarkably broad range of scenarios. For the Soviet Union, for instance, these extend from fragmentation of the Soviet republics, through radical changes in leadership, to an accelerated pace of democratization and a rapid transition to a market economy.

†As used throughout this report, the term *items* refers to systems, individual products, critical components, unique or exotic materials, associated test and calibration equipment, software, and technical data and know-how that have both military and commercial applications.

• **Encouraging conversion (or closure) of military industrial facilities in the Soviet Union and Eastern Europe to the manufacture of products for civilian consumption.**

• **Maintaining harmony with U.S. allies and cooperating countries in the administration of export control measures.**

• **Improving the structure and administration of export controls to increase efficiency and lessen adverse effects on the private sector.**

NOTE

1. Paul Kennedy, *The Rise and Fall of the Great Powers: Economic Change and Military Conflict from 1500 to 2000* (New York: Vintage Books, 1989).

3

The Impact of Export Controls on U.S. Industry

As the global demand for goods and services has expanded since the end of World War II, the U.S. position as the world's foremost producer and exporter has come under increasing challenge. Export controls are one of a number of factors that collectively contribute to the competitive difficulties of the United States. Experts are unable to measure, and disagree about, the relative contribution of most of these factors, but it is clear that export controls can, in some circumstances, impose significant burdens on the economy. **Unlike some other factors, however, export controls are largely modifiable by changes in U.S. policy, and hence, their negative impact can be ameliorated, if not entirely eliminated.**

The three subpanels for this study worked in parallel with the main panel to, among other things, assess the effect of export controls on specific industrial sectors. The export-sensitive, high-technology areas selected—advanced materials and composites, commercial aircraft and jet engines, and computers (both hardware and software)—reflect a range of structural features that can alter the way export controls affect competitiveness. Some of the effects and areas of concern are common to much of U.S. industry; others are industry specific.

Before examining the specific effects of export controls on the industrial sectors that were the subject of detailed study, this chapter briefly describes three general areas of concern to U.S. industry. These issues are discussed further in Chapter 5, and recommendations for change in the export control policy process are presented in Chapters 7–9.

AREAS OF CONCERN TO U.S. INDUSTRY

In general, U.S. industry has three primary concerns about the U.S. implementation of export controls: the unilateralism of U.S. export control policy, the lack of selectivity in developing and managing lists of controlled items, and the lack of fairness and efficiency in the administration of export controls.

Unilateralism

The negative economic impact of export controls on the U.S. economy has stemmed almost entirely from the unilateral aspects of U.S. policy, including restrictions and control practices not followed by U.S. allies and partners in the Coordinating Committee for Multilateral Export Controls (CoCom).

Significant unilateral features of the U.S. control system include the following:

- controls on reexports of U.S. items to third countries and the requirement for written assurances regarding end use and reexport;
- controls on U.S.-owned foreign entities;
- controls on foreign products that use (or are made with) technologies of U.S. origin;
- controls on foreign products that have U.S.-origin components in them;
- control of some dual use items as munitions that other CoCom nations regulate less restrictively as dual use products;
- selective imposition of unilateral product and technology controls;
- more burdensome and complex licensing regimes; and
- more stringent enforcement mechanisms.

Except in those increasingly less frequent cases in which the United States has a functional monopoly on items in question, unilateral U.S. controls do not significantly affect the availability of items to proscribed nations. In fact, the major export control problems have involved West-West, rather than East-West, trade. As a result, the costs of export controls in the past have largely derived, not from the loss of specific sales to customers in proscribed countries, but from the loss of sales in nonproscribed countries because of pragmatic concerns by importers in those countries about the unilateral features of U.S. controls.

Unilateralism disadvantages the U.S. economy and can rarely be justified in a competitive world economy by security concerns. Unilateral features should be eliminated from U.S. national security export controls except in those rare instances in which such a unilateral action would be effective or holds the prospect of changing the position of other countries within a relatively short time.

Lack of Selectivity in Developing and Managing Control Lists

For much of the recent past, multilateral controls have been applied to a broader range of goods and technologies than appears to have been warranted by the facts, or for which there was a real consensus within CoCom.

The June 1990 CoCom High-Level Meeting produced two significant achievements: (1) the number of controlled-item categories was reduced by approximately one-third and (2) a commitment to further reductions was made through the *ab initio* creation of a "core list" of controlled items. **Thus, the problem of overinclusiveness appears to be in the process of remediation; it should not be permitted to recur.**

Lack of Fairness and Efficiency in the U.S. Export Control Process

Although routine licensing has become more efficient and routine processing times have been reduced, requests for export licenses involving first entry into a new market, or those that require more detailed examination for other reasons, can still be substantially delayed. Moreover, it can be difficult to get information about the cause of any delay and the prospects for its resolution. The U.S. export control system is viewed as overly complex, and process information can be hard to obtain. Reports from other CoCom countries suggest that private industry in those countries has much better access to information about the ongoing export control process. Here again, U.S. companies may be substantially disadvantaged with regard to "first entry" licenses that may open export markets.

THE EFFECT OF EXPORT CONTROLS ON SPECIFIC U.S. INDUSTRIAL SECTORS

Advanced Materials*

The Subpanel on Advanced Industrial Materials noted that while U.S. export controls apply only to a limited portion of worldwide trade in advanced materials, their estimated impact on U.S. competitiveness is substantial. The

---

*The complete report of the Subpanel on Advanced Industrial Materials is included as Appendix A.

effect of export controls on the materials industry derives from controls on both the advanced materials and the end products incorporating the materials. The subpanel also noted that some circumstances peculiar to the materials industry figure in the impact of export controls on the industry. For example, advanced materials are not militarily critical of themselves. It is the design, fabrication, and application technology that are critical for strategic applications.* If a material is patented for commercial use without provisions preventing detailed disclosure, the formula and most effective fabrication method may also be specified in the patent, thereby undercutting the effect of export controls.

Another distinctive feature of the materials industry is that most applications of advanced materials are commercial, but military funding typically drives research and development (R&D) efforts. Advanced materials require a long lead time between R&D and application. As a result, a number of materials that were developed under Department of Defense (DoD) contract have not yet been incorporated into weapons prototypes or systems, but they are nonetheless controlled for export. Further, controlling materials on the basis of military specification of performance characteristics assumes that the same performance characteristics are not necessary or useful for commercial applications. A recent Department of Commerce study stated, however, that high-performance, advanced materials figure prominently in those emerging technologies with the greatest potential for commercial application and for advancing production and quality levels.[1]

Cuts in military spending and the high cost of investment capital, combined with continued export restrictions on advanced materials with high commercial potential, could suffocate the U.S. technology base and severely limit incentives for investment in R&D. The Department of Commerce study referred to above also indicated that the United States is currently behind Japan, and likely to continue losing ground, in advanced materials and emerging technologies that are highly dependent on advanced materials. At the same time, many small U.S. materials companies are being bought by multinational firms, which results in an ''export'' of technology.

These facts limit the ability of the United States to control access to, and the diffusion of, advanced materials, and they presage problems for U.S. defense capabilities because these same technologies figure prominently in the long-term strategy for maintaining the qualitative superiority of U.S.

---

*Canopies for jet fighter planes are an illustration of this fact. The canopies themselves are controlled as munitions items. They are made from a certain quality polycarbonate sheet, which is also controlled. It is the process for forming the sheet into the canopy, however, that is complicated and protected, even in the United States, for security and proprietary reasons. Without the process know-how, the polycarbonate sheet has no critical value.

weapons systems. Thus, instead of protecting the qualitative superiority of U.S. weapons systems, export controls on advanced materials may contribute to the weakening of U.S. defense capabilities.

Commercial Aircraft and Jet Engines*

The Subpanel on Commercial Aircraft and Jet Engines found that export controls, and in particular foreign policy controls, have a generally pernicious effect on the export sales of the U.S. commercial aerospace industry. The decision to purchase U.S. or foreign aircraft is often a very close call. Although many factors are involved in the loss of a sale, repeated U.S. experience has shown that the long-term ability of U.S. firms to provide spare parts and product support can be a determining factor in the purchase. Variable and unpredictable U.S. foreign policy controls that can affect product support have had a significant impact on U.S. exports. Further, unilateral embargoes on exports to numerous countries not only make sales impossible but actually encourage foreign competitors to develop relationships with the airlines of the embargoed countries. By the time the U.S. controls are lifted, those foreign competitors may have established a competitive advantage.

Each lost export sale, in turn, generates further long-term effects. According to a generally accepted industry rule of thumb, for every aircraft sold, at least three more will be sold to the same customer in the future. Once an airline has chosen a particular producer, it may continue in some instances to buy airplanes from that producer over several decades; the same is obviously true for engine purchases. Thus, the loss of one sale due to export controls can bring about the loss of an entire export market.

The negative impact of export controls is heightened by particular characteristics of the aerospace industry. The aircraft business is volatile. It involves great risk in the introduction of new products and continual changes in technological leadership among the major companies. Very long lead times are required to develop and introduce new transports and engines and to recoup massive investments of capital and skilled labor. Export controls heighten the risk that such investments will not pay off. In addition, aircraft and jet engine technology is a perishable commodity; much know-how diffuses rapidly throughout the industry through sales, licensing arrangements, and competitive R&D.

The challenges faced by U.S. aerospace firms occur against a backdrop of ever-increasing foreign competition. Although the U.S. commercial aircraft and jet engine industry has prospered in recent years, and despite the fact that the United States is still the overall leader in R&D, German, French,

---

*The complete report of the Subpanel on Commercial Aircraft and Jet Engines is included as Appendix B.

British, and Japanese firms are becoming increasingly competitive and/or are pulling ahead in many areas of technological application. Moreover, foreign competitors, such as the European Airbus Industrie consortium, receive government support. Airbus is gaining market share and is working to reduce the proportion of U.S. components and subsystems in their aircraft. At the same time, a continuing trend toward internationalization of large-scale projects and supplier bases makes controls by any single nation generally ineffective.

Computers*

The Subpanel on Computer Technology found no good quantitative assessments of the costs of export controls to the U.S. computer and microelectronics industries. Export controls are, at best, only a secondary factor in the overall decline in the international competitive position of U.S. firms in this sector. Controls have hurt U.S. competitiveness in specific instances, however, and an argument can be made that relatively strict U.S. interpretation of controls has contributed to a significant loss of business for U.S. firms.

The U.S. and global computer industries are heavily influenced by the nature of the technologies involved. Although the most spectacular of its products are large and complex machines, the industry's volume and global importance are due to the pervasive abundance of small, increasingly inexpensive, modular components that are easily interconnected. Computers and other electronic devices can be assembled anywhere in the world, given moderate technical skills, an entrepreneurial spirit, good organization, and an adequate supply of components. To an increasing extent, components are being manufactured all over the world, especially in the newly industrializing countries of the Far East. In the past, when the United States dominated the global computer technology industry, all international computer technology buyers needed U.S. components and subsystems, and export controls had no adverse impact on U.S. firms. The situation is much changed today, however. Components and subsystems to integrate equipment of significant computing power are available from numerous suppliers in and outside of CoCom. Under intensive competitive pressure, marginal supplier disadvantages can lead to significant losses in market position, and it is just such marginal disadvantages that can be introduced by export controls.

Disadvantages that are frequently mentioned by manufacturers include the time it takes to get export licenses, in particular for first international shipments; the perception that U.S. policy on exports is variable, and thus, that a component that is freely usable today may be unavailable for export to-

---

*The complete report of the Subpanel on Computer Technology is included as Appendix C.

morrow; and the perception of risk of eventual denial of access to components if, for instance, a component of U.S. origin is found to be part of a system ultimately diverted to a proscribed nation. None of these disadvantages is a major obstacle by itself; but in combination they can reduce a U.S. supplier's competitive edge.

A principal cause of problems for the computer and microelectronics industries in the past has been the failure to decontrol items in a timely fashion. As technology improves capabilities and reduces the size and cost of components and full systems, many items formerly at the technological forefront move into the mainstream. New suppliers for the same items arise, often in overseas markets. In some instances, components and even end products have become so inexpensive or so widely available as to reach commodity status. Export control lists, however, have failed to keep up with these rapid technological changes; as a result, controls continue to be imposed on products that are available from overseas producers or are so inexpensive and portable as to be effectively uncontrollable. The problem is currently being addressed through the establishment of a much-reduced CoCom core list of controlled items, but it will unquestionably threaten to recur in the future. As the 1988 report on *Global Trends in Computer Technology and Their Impact on Export Control* stated, "quick and expert review of the appropriateness of the control status is essential if the potential for U.S. market success is to be maximized and the risk to national security minimized. Anecdotal evidence, however, casts doubt on the ability of the current system to provide sufficiently rapid and expert review."[2]

The existence (and unilateral enforcement) of reexport controls is another source of problems. The extraterritorial nature of such controls makes them politically distasteful; they are difficult to enforce; and if trading partners are relatively less effective in enforcing them, they can become in effect unilateral controls.

The recent changes in the Soviet Union and Eastern Europe can be expected to have a significant effect on indigenous computer industries and the prospects for trade with those countries. East European computer industries are selling their assets to, or establishing joint ventures with, Western companies, and they are expected to produce higher quality computers for Eastern Europe and the Soviet Union. On the other hand, many more channels for the legitimate transfer of Western machines and technology to these countries have been opened (e.g., relaxation of CoCom controls, dissemination of Western computer journals, increased travel by Soviet programmers, and contracting Soviet research institutes or "software cooperatives" to develop software for Western systems). One consequence has been the decreased demand for indigenous machines, often functional duplicates of now-obsolete Western systems.

One of the most visibly affected sectors of the computer industry is that of high-performance computers, or supercomputers, a technology indigenous to the United States and for which significant Japanese competition now exists. Supercomputers as a class have been subjected to rigorous and cumbersome end-use controls for several years.

The establishment of performance levels that define supercomputing has been problematic. In the past, controls on the export of supercomputers have been invoked at performance levels that remained relatively static over time. Advances in technology have been rapid, however, and the performance of many mainframe, and even work-station, computers has come to exceed the performance threshold for supercomputers. The static definition of supercomputer control levels has meant that controls are being applied to many machines that are far below the state of the art and to a much broader range of machines than necessary.

Decisions at the June 1990 CoCom High-Level Meeting redefined control levels for computers, but they did not address control levels for supercomputers. Industry concern with this problem will likely remain strong for the long term as high-performance architectures and machines proliferate and as definitions of what is a ''supercomputer'' evolve.

SUMMARY

No single factor explains the decline of U.S. global competitiveness. Export controls are only one of a number of factors, but in some cases they can be significant. It is important to examine control policies carefully, to guard against situations in which modifiable policies diminish the capacity of exporters to compete. To a large extent, loss of competitiveness due to export controls can be avoided or minimized by ensuring that controls are *multilateral, highly selective*, and *fair and efficient*.

Balancing the national interest between security and competitive opportunity is, more than ever, a necessary goal. Chapter 5 analyzes the changing policy forces that shape export controls, and Chapter 6 examines current U.S. and multilateral export control processes. In those chapters, as well as in discussions in later chapters on policy processes, the analysis includes consideration of both the concerns of industry and national security issues in balancing the national interest.

NOTES

1. U.S. Department of Commerce, Technology Administration, *Emerging Technologies: A Survey of Technology and Economic Opportunities* (Washington, D.C.: U.S. Government Printing Office, 1990).
2. National Research Council, *Global Trends in Computer Technology and Their Impact on Export Control* (Washington, D.C.: National Academy Press, 1988), p. 233.

4

Evidence on the Acquisition of Sensitive Western Technology

In this period of rapid political change and uncertainty in East-West relations, the role of intelligence has become increasingly critical to informed policymaking. Yet, just at the time when intelligence is urgently needed as the basis for difficult and important decisions, its availability and reliability have been affected by the political upheavals in Eastern Europe and the Soviet Union. At the same time, the changing types and sources of threat to U.S. national security require the near-term redirection of limited intelligence resources.

This chapter sets forth the results of the panel's examination of the intelligence evidence, including some at high levels of classification, on the acquisition of sensitive Western technology, principally by the Soviet Union and its (former) Warsaw Treaty Organization (WTO) allies. This analysis has two major limitations, however. First, the evidence available from the intelligence community* as of the end of 1990 still focused primarily on the traditional agents of technology acquisition—namely, the Soviet Union, the countries of Eastern Europe, and the People's Republic of China (PRC), and it provided only a limited basis on which to describe how patterns of behavior might now be changing, particularly among those countries that have turned

---

*The *intelligence community* is a collective term denoting the director of central intelligence, the Central Intelligence Agency, the intelligence and counterintelligence elements of the Army, Navy, Air Force, and Marine Corps, the Defense Intelligence Agency, the National Security Agency, the intelligence elements of the Departments of Defense, State, Energy, and the Treasury, and the counterintelligence element of the Federal Bureau of Investigation.

dramatically away from communism. Second, the evidence presented here is limited regarding the technology acquisition activities of countries of proliferation concern, in part due to its highly classified nature. As a result, the treatment of this dimension of the problem in this chapter may underrepresent its actual importance as a source of current threat to the national security of the United States.

Given the constraints just noted, this chapter first provides an update of the evidence presented in the 1987 Allen report on Soviet and WTO technology acquisition efforts *prior to the beginning of 1990*. It then considers probable *changes* in the nature and pattern of (primarily) Soviet technology acquisition since the beginning of 1990 in the wake of the profound political changes that have taken place, and it analyzes the capacity of the Soviet Union to utilize the Western technology that it has acquired or may acquire in the future. After a limited treatment of the acquisition of technologies of proliferation concern (for the reasons noted above), the chapter examines the role of the intelligence community in the export control policy process and concludes by identifying major implications and making specific recommendations.

SOVIET AND WTO TECHNOLOGY ACQUISITION EFFORTS PRIOR TO 1990

Since 1981, the collection and analysis of intelligence pertaining specifically to decision making on national security export controls has been the responsibility of the Technology Transfer Intelligence Committee (TTIC). The TTIC is an interagency committee, under the aegis of the director of central intelligence, composed of representatives of the various intelligence-gathering agencies as well as other relevant federal agencies, such as the Department of Commerce and the U.S. Customs Service. It has coordinated the collection and analysis of information on foreign efforts to acquire controlled technology and end products and integrate them into military systems. Until recently, the TTIC's work has focused predominantly on the technology acquisition efforts of the Soviet Union, the other former WTO members, and the People's Republic of China.

The TTIC is not a regulatory or decision-making body. Its function is to gather, analyze, and disseminate to appropriate government agencies the most accurate and current intelligence relevant to a particular case, export control list, or policy review decision. Such analyses can then be considered, along with other political and economic factors, in reaching a final government position.

Given the momentous political changes in Eastern Europe that were dramatized in November 1989 by the opening of the Berlin Wall, it is useful to focus on the year 1990 as a point of demarcation in evaluating the nature and extent of Soviet and other WTO technology acquisition efforts in the West. Prior to 1990, the intelligence services of the Soviet Union and the other WTO countries acted largely in concert to target, acquire, and pass on to the Soviet military a wide range of specific high-technology products, keystone equipment,* plans, blueprints, and technical data developed and produced in the West.

The determination of specific acquisition requirements under this reportedly massive effort† was (and continues to be) directed by the Military-Industrial Commission (VPK) in concert with the Soviet intelligence services, principally the Committee on State Security (KGB), the Chief Directorate of Military Intelligence (GRU), the State Committee for Science and Technology (GKNT), and the Ministry of Defense.[1] Once a list of acquisition requirements was established, the next steps were to target potential sources of supply, usually in the private sector, and to identify possible channels and methods of acquisition. The latter typically involved a variety of mechanisms, including (a) espionage, (b) illegal sales, (c) diversions from the originating country and via reexport through third countries,‡ and (d) legal acquisition through purchases in third countries.

Espionage

Espionage in this context was (and is) covert activity intended to obtain information about end products and technologies pertinent to military systems. Espionage has continued to be a major source of concern to the United States and the other members of the North Atlantic Treaty Organization (NATO), despite the political changes within the Warsaw Pact. There have been a series of well-publicized ''spy scandals'' since 1986, some of which reportedly did serious damage to U.S. and Western security. While some covert collection was directed at obtaining design plans or technical data— or, in some cases, individual or limited numbers of pieces of militarily critical hardware—the bulk of the effort was targeted directly at obtaining infor-

---

*The term *keystone equipment* was developed in the 1976 report of the Defense Science Board Task Force on Export of U.S. Technology, also known as the Bucy report after its chairman, J. Fred Bucy.[2] The term is used to denote critical technological equipment, such as sophisticated machine tools, necessary to manufacture other products.

†The Academies' Allen panel reported that ''during the Tenth Five-Year Plan (1976–1980), the Soviet acquisition program satisfied more than 3,500 specific collection requirements for hardware and documents for the 12 Soviet industrial ministries. Of the items acquired in the West, the Soviets estimated that approximately 70 percent were subject to national security export controls. This proportion was apparently much the same during the Eleventh Five-Year Plan (1980–1985). . . .''[3] Evidence reviewed by this panel suggests that this collection effort continued unabated during the most recent five-year plan (1985–1990) as well.

‡*Third countries* are nonproscribed countries that are not part of CoCom.

mation regarding U.S./NATO military systems, cryptological practices, and/ or military plans of operation.*

There was no definitive evidence in 1990 to indicate that the Soviet Union had changed the level of overall resources or manpower it devotes to intelligence collection by means of espionage. And there is little basis to assume that the Soviets will cease to use espionage for the foreseeable future as one means of acquiring strategic technology. **But the underlying point is that export controls cannot—and are not designed to—prevent this type of acquisition effort. Rather, they are designed to restrict sales (direct or indirect) of strategic technology and equipment.**

Illegal Sales

Illegal sales occur in situations in which a manufacturer, its agent, or a subsequent buyer conspires to sell—or has immediate knowledge of the sale of—a controlled item directly to a targeted country. Although there may be some instances in which an illegal sale takes place entirely without an export license, in most cases export licenses are sought but the technical parameters and capabilities of the equipment and/or the final destination are purposely misrepresented. Neither the intelligence community nor export licensing officials have precise information on the frequency of illegal sales in recent years, but it appeared that the advent of improved export licensing practices (including increased penalties) in the major CoCom (Coordinating Committee for Multilateral Export Controls) countries, together with heightened awareness on the part of manufacturers and resulting efforts to improve internal compliance procedures, limited the number of cases.

The so-called Toshiba-Kongsberg case,† the most widely publicized (and perhaps most damaging from a national security standpoint) illegal sale of the 1980s, was a sobering reminder to manufacturers of the likely consequences of being tied to an illegal sale. In fact, the case resulted in the inclusion of language in the Omnibus Trade and Competitiveness Act of 1988 directing that companies convicted of selling CoCom-proscribed items

---

*One of the more recent and well-documented cases of espionage involved John Walker and family. For nearly two decades, until his arrest and conviction in 1985, Walker provided his Soviet handlers with thousands of classified documents and Top Secret encryption codes on sensitive U.S. Navy operations.

†In late 1983 and early 1984, the Soviet Union acquired several numerically controlled, high-precision, nine-axis milling machines from Japan's Toshiba Machine Company. A Norwegian firm, Kongsberg Vaapenfabrikk, supplied the critical numerical controls for the Toshiba machines and developed sophisticated software to enable the machines to mill complex shapes. These machines were used by the Soviets to mass produce advanced, low-noise naval propellers. The deployment of these propellers substantially decreased the ability of the United States to detect and track Soviet submarines and surface combatants, thereby affecting U.S. national security interests both strategically and tactically.

to controlled countries without a license were to lose their export privileges to the U.S. market for a minimum of two years and a maximum of five years.

Diversion

Another and probably more common channel for acquiring controlled technology was diversion of exported items, either with or without the direct knowledge of the manufacturer. In this situation, an item is exported legally to a purchaser in a nonproscribed destination (sometimes in another CoCom country) and then reexported to a proscribed destination, often through a series of intermediate nonproscribed destinations. In some cases, exporters or their brokers in CoCom and/or third countries actively participate in diversions, usually by constructing elaborate networks of "front companies" and mail drops to obscure the export paper trail.

A more common situation, however, is the legal export of an item to a bona fide purchaser in a third country, who either immediately reexports it to a proscribed country—sometimes without ever "landing" the item in the third country—or "adds value" to the item, often by incorporating it as a component, and then reexports it to a proscribed country.

As the result of diplomatic pressure from the United States, the CoCom countries have made continuing efforts under the Third Country Cooperation initiative, modeled on U.S. bilateral agreements, to convince third countries to cooperate with CoCom export control policies by preventing reexports of CoCom-controlled items. **However, evidence reviewed by the panel, which was corroborated by information collected during the panel's fact-finding missions in Asia and Europe,* indicated that such diversion practices continued through 1990.** There are many reasons for this, among the most important of which have been that (1) the bureaucratic machinery of many third-country governments has been technically ill-prepared and insufficiently financed to undertake adequate enforcement, (2) there has been a notable absence in these countries of monetarily significant penalties for violation, (3) many of these countries have been nonaligned and some have not shared the threat perceptions of the CoCom countries, and (4) illegal reexport trade can be highly lucrative. Thus, despite continuing efforts by the United States, other countries—both in and outside CoCom—have countenanced, if not actively facilitated, the diversion of technology.

---

*See Appendix D.

Legal Sales

With the growing diffusion of technology and technical and manufacturing know-how beyond the advanced industrialized countries, it was no longer necessary in some cases for a proscribed country to resort to any of the mechanisms and channels described above to acquire certain types of strategic technology. For example, even prior to the 1990 CoCom decision to decontrol most personal computers, it was readily possible to make legal purchases of personal computers manufactured entirely in countries such as Taiwan or South Korea (unless the machine contained controlled U.S. components). Evidence from a wide variety of sources indicates that the Soviet Union and other proscribed countries are fully aware of and have exploited these opportunities.

There are obvious limits to what the United States or the CoCom countries together can do to constrain third countries from exporting indigenously manufactured, and in some cases indigenously designed, products. Moral and economic pressure has been successful with some third countries— particularly, for example, the industrialized neutral countries of Europe— but less so with others.

Based on the sum of the evidence that it reviewed, both from classified and published sources, the panel was unable to identify any overall change *in the late 1980s* in the efforts by the Soviet Union and its WTO allies to acquire technology in the West for incorporation into military systems.

CHANGES IN THE NATURE AND PATTERNS OF SOVIET AND WTO TECHNOLOGY ACQUISITION SINCE THE BEGINNING OF 1990

Despite the urgent need on the part of the Soviet Union for advanced technology to speed the process of economic modernization, and in some cases the transformation to a market economy, it is too soon to assess the characteristics of the post-Cold War technology acquisition "problem." Nevertheless, some clear indications can be identified.

Because so much of the modern technology and equipment needed by the Soviets is now dual use, by 1990 diversions and legal sales in third countries had become the predominant acquisition methods and accounted for the majority of successful acquisition efforts. The role of diversions and legal sales is likely to increase, relative to espionage, in the future.

One factor may be a net loss to the Soviets of a significant amount of the cooperation they previously received from the intelligence services of some of their former allies, principally Czechoslovakia, Hungary, and Poland. A second factor may be that, specifically with regard to the acquisition of dual use items, as opposed to military information and/or hardware, other channels and methods of acquisition simply may have become easier and cheaper, given the diffusion of technology and sources of supply.

Among the most significant changes associated with the end of the Cold War and the dissolution of the WTO as a military alliance is the partial disbandment of the state security apparatus in Poland, Hungary, and Czechoslovakia, as well as the total dissolution of the *Stasi* in the former German Democratic Republic. In fact, the newly democratic governments in those countries have indicated a willingness to establish barriers against the reexport (i.e., diversion) to the Soviet Union of technology that is needed for East European economic modernization and development. The disbandment of these intelligence-gathering organizations removes much of the non-Soviet Warsaw Pact (NSWP) government-sponsored capability to acquire strategic technology, either through espionage or diversion. Thus, as noted above, even though the Soviet Union is continuing active collection efforts, it is apparently no longer able to call upon the active, official cooperation of its former allies.

On the other hand, there are countertendencies even within the NSWP countries. First, there is what the panel considers may be a short-term phenomenon: the potential for continued collection efforts by former employees of disbanded intelligence services, either on a free-lance basis or under the sponsorship and direction of the Soviet intelligence services. It will take some time to dismantle fully a system—and indeed, a means of livelihood for thousands of people—that has been in place for more than 40 years. **For the time being, these "free-lance" collection efforts, which could operate largely detached from national political processes, are a continuing source of concern.** A second countertendency is that growing business pressures, as the NSWP countries attempt to integrate themselves into the global market, may create incentives to permit (if not condone) active programs of industrial espionage.

Soviet intentions and practices in the post-Cold War era are far more difficult to determine, again in part because it is simply too soon for new patterns to have emerged. In fact, on the basis of the quantity and quality of the evidence it reviewed, the panel found it impossible to draw any valid conclusions about either positive or negative changes. The available evidence is anecdotal in nature and must be interpreted in light of the possibility that there has been some (perhaps temporary) loss of human intelligence sources as a result of the dissolution of the formerly Communist regimes in Eastern Europe. On the other hand, some of the disruption in human intelligence channels, to the extent that any has occurred, may be offset by the increase in and ready availability of information provided by emigres from the Soviet Union and the East European countries.

SOVIET UTILIZATION OF ACQUIRED WESTERN TECHNOLOGY

As noted previously in the Allen report, the intelligence community continues to find it difficult to determine the nature and extent of the impact of technology obtained in the West on the development of Soviet military systems. Unfortunately, no further sources of information have become available on an unclassified basis that are comparable to the "Farewell papers,"* which provided a unique inside look at the fulfillment of the individual needs of Soviet defense manufacturing ministries.

In some respects, it appears that the chaos and disruptions associated with *perestroika* in the Soviet Union have exacerbated the difficulties the Soviets have long had in overcoming internal barriers to effective diffusion and application of technology obtained in the West. Yet, the Soviets have continued to be successful at obtaining one or more copies of a particular item, which in some cases may have removed key manufacturing bottlenecks in their military industry (e.g., access to the Toshiba-Kongsberg numerically controlled, multiaxis machine tools) or may have given them confidence that a specific design approach had been successful in the West. It is also likely that the opening of the Soviet economy to Western investment may facilitate more transfers of technology to Soviet military industries.

In general, however, the Soviet effort to acquire Western technology has *not* succeeded in reducing the West's technology lead, according to Defense Department and intelligence community estimates. As suggested by the data in Tables 4-1 and 4-2, the United States held a superior position in 15 of 20 militarily related technology areas in 1990, compared with 13 of 20 areas in 1986 (as reported by the Allen panel). Although the more recent data indicate that the Soviets have for the first time attained superiority in two technology areas, an analysis of net change by sector indicates an overall increase in the U.S. technological advantage. On average, the Soviet Union continues to remain at least 5 to 10 years behind in most key technology areas. The situation remains different, however, for *fielded* military systems, regarding which the strong Soviet emphasis on the development and production of military hardware has resulted in many effective weapons systems.

In all likelihood, the Soviet Union will continue to maintain—and more important, to modernize—its strategic forces, albeit at a somewhat reduced size, despite recent and prospective arms control agreements. The situation

---

*"Farewell" was the code name for a KGB officer who gave the West detailed information in 1981 on the plans, organization, and financing of Soviet efforts to target and acquire Western technology. This information was later released by the Department of Defense in 1985 as part of an unclassified white paper, *Soviet Acquisition of Militarily Significant Western Technology: An Update* (see note 1).

TABLE 4-1   Relative U.S. Versus USSR Standing in 20 Militarily Related Technology Areas, 1986

Basic Technologies	USSR Superior	U.S./USSR Equal	U.S. Superior
Aerodynamics/fluid dynamics	X		
Computers and software			X→
Conventional warheads (including all chemical explosives)	X		
Directed energy (laser)	X		
Electro-optical sensors (including infrared)	X		
Guidance and navigation			X
Life sciences (human factors/biotechnology)			X
Materials (lightweight, high strength, and high temperature)			←X
Microelectronic materials and integrated-circuit manufacturing			X
Nuclear warheads	X		
Optics	X		
Power sources (mobile—includes energy storage)	X		
Production/manufacturing (includes automated control)			X
Propulsion (aerospace and ground vehicles)			←X
Radar sensors			←X
Robotics and machine intelligence			X
Signal processing			X
Signature reduction			X
Submarine detection			←X
Telecommunications (including fiber optics)			X

NOTE: This list is in alphabetical order. Relative comparisons of technology levels depict overall average standing only; countries may be superior, equal, or inferior in subcategories of a given technology. Arrows indicate that relative technology levels are changing significantly in the direction shown.

SOURCE: *The FY1987 DoD Program for Research and Development* (Report by the Under Secretary of Defense for Research and Engineering to the 99th Congress, Second Session, 1986).

with respect to the modernization of conventional forces is somewhat harder to predict, given the current economic and political disruptions within the Soviet Union and the external pressures that now exist as a result of the successful completion of the Treaty on Conventional Forces in Europe. In modernizing either strategic or conventional forces, however, the Soviet Union will for the foreseeable future continue to remain dependent on certain Western technology that it cannot produce itself or could produce only at inordinate expense.

TABLE **4-2**   Relative U.S. Versus USSR Standing in 20 Militarily Related
Technology Areas, 1990

Basic Technologies	USSR Superior	U.S./USSR Equal	U.S. Superior
Aerodynamics/fluid dynamics			←X
Computers and software			X→
Conventional warheads	X		
Directed energy (laser)		X	
Electro-optical sensors		X	
Guidance and navigation			X
Life sciences			X
Materials (aerospace)			X
Materials (armor)	X		
Microelectronics			X→
Optics		X	
Power sources (pulse power)			X
Production/manufacturing			X→
Propulsion			←X
Radar sensors			←X
Robotics and machine intelligence			X→
Signal processing			X
Signature reduction			←X
Submarine detection			←X
Telecommunications			←X

NOTE: This list is in alphabetical order. This assessment compares U.S. and Soviet capabilities in each technology area as of mid-1990. The arrows indicate any ongoing changes in the technological standing of one country relative to the other. Comparisons are based on *overall* capabilities; either the United States or the Soviet Union may excel in specialties within each technology area.

ACQUISITION OF TECHNOLOGIES OF PROLIFERATION CONCERN

Within recent years, the intelligence community has begun to devote increased attention to monitoring and analyzing the acquisition of proliferation technologies—namely, advanced conventional weapons, missile delivery systems, and technologies associated with nuclear, chemical, and biological weapons—by countries considered to represent potential national security threats to the United States and to international security. In some respects, the development of such data is even more difficult than in the case of Soviet acquisition efforts due to (a) the multiplicity of areas and actors that potentially require attention, (b) the difficulty of developing reliable sources of human intelligence, and (c) the ease with which the acquisition and use of some of these technologies are justified for commercial purposes or can be misrepresented or hidden entirely.

A good generic example of such covert development is chemical weapons. It is often difficult to determine with certainty that commercially available chemicals used in agriculture are instead being diverted as precursors to the manufacture of chemical weapons. Similarly, a commercially justifiable interest in space launch technology can mask the development of a ballistic missile delivery capability. Despite such difficulties, much is known about the evolving nature of the threat in each proliferation area.

THE ROLE OF THE INTELLIGENCE COMMUNITY IN THE EXPORT CONTROL POLICY PROCESS

Intelligence has played an important continuing role in the export control policy process since the early days of the effort after World War II, and particularly since the 1981 founding of the Technology Transfer Intelligence Committee. In this regard, one of the most valuable contributions of the intelligence community has been to develop "red side" methodological approaches that have made it possible to examine Soviet technology acquisition efforts from the standpoint of *Soviet*, rather than Western, military needs and capabilities. **Such "red side" thinking is not yet sufficiently institutionalized in the intelligence community's support for U.S. export control policy, however. As a result, policy analysis for export controls has tended to continue to use "mirror image" assumptions regarding Soviet requirements for Western technology, based on *Western*, instead of Soviet, military systems and capabilities.**

In this period of rapid change and uncertainty within the Soviet Union and Eastern Europe, of conflicting desires in the West to advance these countries technologically in order to help them economically (while not increasing the military risk to the West), and of growing proliferation threats from other sources, the quality, accuracy, and timeliness of intelligence information are ever more critical. The obstacles to the collection of such information by overt and covert means are not insignificant. **The panel took note of the continuing paucity of reliable data on changes in the nature and pattern of Soviet technology acquisition efforts since 1989. It also found an even more serious lack of reliable data on the scope and extent of technology acquisition in the West by countries that are the focus of proliferation concern.**

IMPLICATIONS OF THE INTELLIGENCE EVIDENCE

- The end of the Cold War and the opening of *both* sides to access by nationals of the other, together with new interest in market economics and industrial modernization on the part of many former WTO countries, create the opportunity for an increase of military and industrial espionage. Under these circumstances, the application of appropriate analytic resources is required in order to obtain an accurate assessment of Soviet technology needs and thus be in a position to undertake a responsive calibration of the U.S. export control program that blends the twin goals of strategic technology protection and economic cooperation.

- In the past, Soviet and other WTO technology acquisition efforts in the West were driven almost exclusively by military needs and requirements that were unattainable (or attainable only at great expense) within the bloc. Today, however, because the Soviets may seek to acquire technology for commercial as well as military reasons, there is a need for more thorough assessments of Soviet requirements so that the West can differentiate between various motivations for technology acquisition and can apply more appropriate policy responses.

- The demands on the intelligence community in the "new era" regarding acquisition of Western technology by traditional and new potential adversaries have increased and are likely to continue to do so for the foreseeable future. Some of these new responsibilities likely will require either the reallocation of existing human and financial resources or supplemental resources. It is also likely, however, that insofar as the Soviet and former WTO countries are concerned, the intelligence community can take advantage of the increased ease of access to develop a better understanding of the planning dynamics that condition their efforts to acquire and apply Western technology.

RECOMMENDATIONS

* The intelligence community should expand its efforts to develop reliable assessments of changes in the nature and pattern of *current* Soviet technology acquisition efforts—and current patterns of Soviet utilization of the technology it acquires—and should make this information available to the relevant agencies of the U.S. government and to the countries participating in CoCom.

* The intelligence community should continue and expand its recent efforts to develop an analytic capability to examine Soviet technology acquisition and utilization *from the standpoint of the actual state of Soviet technology progress*, both civilian and military, and the internal dynamics of technology diffusion within the Soviet Union and East European countries.

* The executive branch should give serious consideration to reallocating resources—and/or identifying additional resources—to develop better information about the acquisition and utilization of

sensitive Western technology by countries of proliferation concern.*

NOTES

1. U.S. Department of Defense, *Soviet Acquisition of Militarily Significant Western Technology: An Update* (intelligence community white paper) (Washington, D.C., September 1985).
2. U.S. Department of Defense, Office of the Director of Defense Research and Engineering, *An Analysis of Export Control of U.S. Technology—a DoD Perspective* (Report of the Defense Science Board Task Force on Export of U.S. Technology) (Washington, D.C.: U.S. Government Printing Office, 1976).
3. National Academy of Sciences, National Academy of Engineering, and Institute of Medicine, *Balancing the National Interest: U.S. National Security Export Controls and Global Economic Competition* (Washington, D.C.: National Academy Press, 1987), pp. 42–43.

---

*A recent study by the Defense Science Board, *Scenarios for American Defense: Implications for Intelligence and for the Defense Technology and Industrial Bases* (Washington, D.C.: U.S. Department of Defense, 1990), reaches a similar conclusion.

5

The Changing Calculus of
U.S. National Security Interests

The current U.S. national security export control regime, and indeed the entire multilateral control framework embodied in the Coordinating Committee for Multilateral Export Controls (CoCom), is an artifact of the Cold War, which has now ended. It was relatively simple during that period to identify potential adversaries and to respond to the threat with an appropriate mix of military, economic, and diplomatic initiatives. Today, the external challenges to U.S. national security are more complex.

First, many of the most difficult and urgent challenges, rather than being purely military in nature, are now often economic and technological. Although the United States is still by far the largest national economy, its international economic and technological position is far less commanding than it was a decade ago.

Second, the military challenge posed by the Soviet Union is reduced and substantially less offensively oriented. On the one hand, the size and configuration of the Soviet Union's strategic nuclear arsenal and its continuing modernization, together with still sizable Soviet conventional ground forces—until their removal over the next few years—require that the United States and its allies remain vigilant. On the other hand, because of progress on arms control and other aspects of U.S.-Soviet relations, as well as the dramatic internal political changes in the Warsaw Treaty Organization (WTO) countries, the United States and the North Atlantic Treaty Organization (NATO) have declared the Cold War to be at an end.[1] The Western alliance is thus left in the ambiguous position of responding to the reduced threat through expanded East-West cooperation and defense spending reductions, while at the same time needing to guard against the remaining Soviet military threat.

Third, in contrast to the dramatic political changes in Europe and the improved East-West climate, significant and troubling challenges remain in other geopolitical areas, particularly a generally heightened potential for regional hostilities. Some of these regional problems—such as the recent crisis in the Persian Gulf—represent a direct threat to U.S. and international security; others threaten to spill over into broader international contexts. Many of these problems are driven or exacerbated by the proliferation of advanced munitions and dual use technologies related to nuclear, chemical, and biological weapons and to missile delivery systems.

GROWING ECONOMIC AND TECHNOLOGICAL CHALLENGES

The economic and technological challenges facing the United States have been widely analyzed for many years.[2] As noted in Chapter 2, the following are among the most significant of these challenges.

• *The changing structure of the global economy*   The revolution in information and telecommunications technologies has facilitated the development of integrated multinational corporations that operate in worldwide markets. Multinational firms now have a much broader range of choices regarding the siting of research and development (R&D) and manufacturing facilities. This broader field of opportunity has also led, in some cases, to a relative loss of capacity in the United States in key technology areas (e.g., D-RAM semiconductors) as manufacturers have moved their operations off shore, or in some cases have left the sector entirely. A second result has been a blurring of the specific national identity of technologies and multinational firms, thereby potentially raising additional complications from the standpoint of nationally based export controls.

• *The increasingly rapid global diffusion of technology*   The search for new external markets, the siting of research and operating facilities abroad, and the growing strength and sophistication of technology development in other nations have accelerated the global diffusion of technology. Multinational companies constantly must transfer massive amounts of information to control and develop their international business. Moreover, technology transfer—frequently by license—to the host country also may be a condition of doing business. Such diffusion, however, also increases the difficulty of implementing effective export controls at the national level.

• *Declining U.S. technological and manufacturing preeminence*   In recent years, as the unique postwar period of unchallenged U.S. economic dominance has further receded, there has been widespread concern about declining U.S. economic competitiveness. The enormous infrastructural and other advantages uniquely enjoyed by the United States following the end of World War II have now diminished. In fact, parts of the U.S. R&D and manufacturing infrastructure are now aging and in need of significant new capital infusions. Growth in productivity, at least outside of manufacturing, has been sluggish.

Some believe that the economic union of Europe, combined with the political union of Germany, will create another economic juggernaut across the Atlantic, similar to that in the Pacific. In consumer electronics, for which the United States developed most of the breakthrough technologies, Japanese and European companies have largely displaced U.S.-owned manufacturing. Intensive international competition is beginning to emerge in almost every sector, including such advanced high-technology sectors as supercomputers, in which U.S. superiority was once unchallenged.

- *Growing technological and manufacturing sophistication in Japan and the newly industrializing countries*   In a series of industries—steel, automobiles, semiconductors, consumer electronics—foreign companies, in particular East Asian firms, have seized major shares of the U.S. market. Japan's high rate of industrial innovation, emphasis on process technologies to nurture manufacturing, and a tax system and import control regime that encourage long-term growth over short-term profits have brought it rapidly to the status of an economic superpower. The May 1989 report of the Department of Defense on critical military technologies stated that the United States had fallen behind Japan in key areas of semiconductors and microelectronics.[3] Indeed, the involvement of the Defense Advanced Research Projects Agency in the SEMATECH semiconductor consortium reflects, in part, concerns about U.S. performance vis-à-vis Japan in the key area of semiconductor manufacturing.

The so-called newly industrializing countries (NICs)—Hong Kong, Singapore, South Korea, and Taiwan—are now becoming industrialized countries. They have transformed their one-time dependency on aid and trade preferences—and reliance on low-cost, low-technology exports—into high-technology partnership and competition with American industry. The NICs have achieved impressive success in emulating the postwar Japanese example by focusing on the development and enhancement of indigenous R&D and manufacturing capabilities.

- *The changing distribution of global economic and financial power*   The United States became the world's leading debtor nation in 1986. Seven of the world's 10 largest banks are now Japanese.[4] The United States continues to suffer large negative trade balances with Japan, South Korea, Taiwan, and some of its other major trading partners. The net effect of these and other changes has been a redistribution of economic and financial power.

• *The weakening of the U.S. defense industrial base** Many defense officials have become concerned about the decline in the U.S. defense industrial base, which they argue can and already has led to certain vulnerabilities resulting from dependence on foreign (albeit cheaper) sources of supply. The Department of Defense has had increasing difficulty obtaining at reasonable cost U.S.-made goods and technologies needed to maintain its qualitative edge in weapons. Low profits, disincentives in the federal procurement system, and other government regulations, among other factors, are causing small-to-medium-sized U.S. companies to leave the defense sector in large numbers,[5] and this trend is being accelerated by cuts in defense spending resulting, in part, from improved U.S.-Soviet relations. And the Defense Science Board has stated that the Defense Department and U.S. defense industry alone can no longer supply the military's needs.[6]

Moreover, in the past few years, numerous government studies have documented that the U.S. defense establishment is becoming increasingly dependent on civilian technologies. In the March 1990 Defense Department *Critical Technologies Plan,*[7] 17 of the 20 technologies cited were judged critical to both commercial and military applications. Indeed, in a reversal of past technology flow, innovations are now often "spinning on" from the commercial sector into the defense sector.

• *The growing importance of exports to U.S. economic vitality* The United States remains the world's largest international trader, with manufactured exports of $289.7 billion and total exports of $363.9 billion in 1989.[8] Exports have assumed growing importance to the U.S. economy, in particular to U.S. producers of manufactured goods. The United States is becoming nearly as dependent on exports as its major competitors, and therefore, its economy is becoming more vulnerable to the negative effects of export controls.

Finally, the position of the United States in the emerging world order also is affected by domestic problems. These include (a) the continuing budget deficit, (b) low rates of personal savings, (c) high volume of credit-financed personal consumption (relative to most other industrialized countries), and (d) systematic underinvestment in the modernization of manufacturing infrastructure.

Taken together, these challenges—problems with the defense industrial base, the shift from defense- to commercially driven innovation, the emergence of Asian and European industrial competitors, and the increased importance of exports to the U.S. economy—all have led to a

---

*The term *defense industrial base* refers to the complex of industries, skilled personnel, and technologies needed to manufacture today's—and tomorrow's—sophisticated weapons systems.

growing realization that economic factors must be given increased weight in the formulation of U.S. national security policy.

CHANGES IN THE TRADITIONAL SOURCES OF PHYSICAL THREAT

While the economic and technological challenges facing the United States continue to multiply, the older problem of East-West conflict, featuring various types of Soviet military threat, has been reduced dramatically. The Soviet Union remains the only country capable of destroying the United States with nuclear weapons. While it still retains vast conventional arms and large standing armies, buffeted as they have been by ethnic turmoil in the Soviet Union and change in Eastern Europe, mutual force reductions agreed to under the 1990 Treaty on Conventional Forces in Europe (CFE), if implemented in good faith, mean that forward-based Soviet forces in Europe will be reduced to conditions of rough parity with those of the NATO countries. Moreover, the political context within the Soviet Union surrounding these residual strengths no longer bears any resemblance to the earlier circumstances of the Cold War, and trends under way promise further reductions in the external power and influence of the Soviet military, although it is likely to remain a substantial factor for some time to come.

Changes in the Soviet Union and Eastern Europe

The most far-reaching changes have come in Eastern Europe, where countries once in the thrall of the Soviet Union have destroyed, one after another, a Soviet-imposed political order and set about to create new democratic and market-based systems. It is a historic process whose timing owes much to the vast changes remaking the political face of the Soviet Union itself. For without the tolerance, and in some instances the apparent encouragement, of the Soviet leadership, the crumbling of the old regimes would not necessarily have been so early nor so swift.

The shattered status quo in Eastern Europe has had two major consequences. First, the cohesion, indeed, the political foundation of the Warsaw Pact has been undone. German unification has eliminated the outer salient of the pact. Already the freedom of maneuver of Soviet forces in Germany is severely constrained, and by 1994 the forces are to be withdrawn entirely. In the meantime, Poland, Hungary, and Czechoslovakia, the core of the WTO, have all obliged the Soviet government to withdraw forces from their territory by the middle of 1991.

Second, throughout Eastern Europe, even in countries such as Romania or Bulgaria, where the pace of democratization has failed to match that under way elsewhere, governments have adopted independent defense postures no longer responsive to Soviet bidding. **As a result, it is reasonable to assume that the WTO has lost its fundamental meaning as a military alliance and for all practical purposes no longer makes possible a forward-based, Soviet strategic offensive capability in Central Europe. Indeed, trends in Europe soon will foreclose the very possibility of stationing Soviet forces outside the borders of the Soviet Union.**

In addition, Soviet leaders, including the military command, have been thrown into doubt over where the borders will be behind which Soviet forces must withdraw. The Soviet Union has become a maelstrom of change. As its leaders struggle to overcome a deepening economic crisis and launch the country on the path of thorough-going economic reform, and as they strain to manage the now seemingly inexorable fragmentation of the Soviet federation, the nature of the Soviet challenge changes for those on the outside. No longer is the Soviet Union a cohesive, stable, disciplined entity. Nor will it soon be again. No longer does its considerable military power rest on a secure economic base and a political order capable of reliably mobilizing human and material resources. No longer does the Soviet Union preside over a docile, working military alliance.

An equally important factor is that Soviet foreign policy under Gorbachev has, by all indications, undergone a radical transformation. From the arms control agreements it has concluded (and others that are under negotiation), to the cooperation it has provided in dealing with regional conflicts, the Soviet leadership appears to be approaching the core issues of the historic East-West conflict in a fundamentally different and more constructive fashion. Behind this satisfying evolution in Soviet behavior, there appears to lie a deeper rethinking (at least among the national civilian leadership) of the Soviet role in the world, the meaning and utility of military power, the nature of alliances and the basis on which they should be built, the place of multilateral cooperation and the contribution of international institutions, and the relations between the Soviet economy and the international economic order.

As a practical matter, in the narrower sphere of immediate concern to this report, these changes have altered the intelligence and verification challenge facing the United States and its Western allies. In Eastern Europe, the transformation is almost total; most governments have largely severed their formal intelligence cooperation with the Soviet Union and have offered guarantees of nondiversion of technology to the Soviet Union and indicated a willingness to permit intrusive end-use verification.* **The panel recognizes that German reunification may give the Soviet Union access to some technologies that it would otherwise have been denied, as refurbished former East German firms honor standing contracts, but it also believes that the larger pro-**

---

*For further discussion of these issues, see Chapter 4.

cesses at work are sure to erode the Soviet ability to acquire technology throughout the region.

In the Soviet Union, too, the closed character of the society and the political system has undergone significant change. As a result of new on-site verification regimes embodied in recent arms control accords, including the 1987 Intermediate-Range Nuclear Forces treaty and the prospective Strategic Arms Reduction Talks (START) agreement, together with the explosion of technical, business, and private contacts with the outside world, **the Soviet Union is becoming a far more transparent and penetrable society, which has important implications for the West's estimation of its security concerns.**

The Soviets have themselves begun to discuss the possibility of assurances against diversion of dual use items to the military. Although it is difficult, if not impossible, to trace the movement within countries of certain dual use items, such as microcircuits, the Soviet need for Western help in converting some military plants to civilian production—a trend the West should encourage—may well provide an opening to test various mechanisms for end-use assurance.

Preventing war, primarily by political means, is now said to constitute the central objective of Soviet security policy.[9] This new formulation both requires and enables a substantial reduction, disengagement, and restructuring of Soviet military forces. The offensive threat to Western Europe, inherent in the WTO's military doctrine and force posture, has been both disavowed by the Soviet leadership[10] and undone by the political revolution in Eastern Europe, by successful completion of the CFE treaty, and by the expanded emphasis on the CSCE process. The military's traditional preparations for a counteroffensive are to be sharply contained, and military forces will not be expected to carry the sole or even the primary burden of Soviet state security. The prevention of war, the defense of the integrity of the Soviet Union, and the pursuit of Soviet international interests are to be accomplished primarily by political means.

Soviet leaders now have increased credibility when they claim to seek a deliberate dissolution of the prevailing alliance confrontation and its replacement with cooperative security arrangements. Rather than conducting its security in confrontation with a coalition of all the industrial democracies, the Soviet Union is attempting a cooperative approach to the problem of mutual security with this coalition. In this regard, it has accepted the implication that this will require strict adherence to defensive military objectives. Given the vast scale of the economic and political problems facing the Soviet Union, whatever the evolution of its internal politics, any Soviet leadership will find it difficult to reverse these adaptations. But the ultimate success of this change in policy also will depend substantially on the continued support of the Soviet military.

The same security logic extends to the other members of the dissolving WTO as well. Though the East European countries' swift progress toward democracy remains uncertain, their commitment to cooperative security policies does not. Whatever the character of the political systems that ultimately emerge, these countries are virtually compelled by circumstances to rely for their basic security on international arrangements for limiting military capabilities in Central Europe strictly to those required for the defense of national territory. They do not have the resources or the technical base to create independently competitive military establishments, and any effort to do so would conflict seriously with their efforts to work out productive economic relations with the West. The United States and other Western governments can assume reliably a powerful and enduring impulse in Eastern Europe for close, constructive cooperation on matters of security.

As this report is completed, these changes in Soviet and East European policies have not yet been fully implemented. Until that occurs, Western responses appropriately will contain an element of caution. Nonetheless, these policy changes have been articulated clearly enough and are motivated sufficiently by compelling background circumstances that they already alter radically the context for Western policies on technology transfer, weapons export, and regional conflict. Whatever inclination the Soviets may retain to acquire Western technology (through both legal and illegal means) to support military programs, that objective clearly will have receded in relative priority. Moreover, it will diminish in significance for the West as the Soviet military establishment becomes further restricted and more defensively configured.

As these changes occur, substantial opportunity exists for exercising direct Western influence on Soviet security policy through mechanisms of cooperation. **It now appears possible to establish and maintain a distinction between commercial and military applications in considering technology trade with the Soviet Union. Cooperation in regulating general weapons exports also appears feasible in this new context, as do mutually supportive policies on regional conflict. This relief from traditional concerns and the expansion of constructive opportunities enable a shift in Western export control policy from one emphasizing general denial to one focusing on positive behavioral change. In other words, the West can move from an export control regime characterized by negative sanction to one characterized by positive inducement.**

Soviet Defense Doctrine and Military Force Deployment

A separate concern from the broad societal changes sweeping the Soviet Union and Eastern Europe is the philosophy and doctrine that underpin Soviet military planning and their impact on current Soviet force deployments.

Although final force dispositions and supporting doctrine are likely to be partially shaped by the evolving political and military situation in Europe, including the course of future arms control negotiations, fundamental changes are inevitable. Faced now with the prospect of no longer being able to defend forward, of having also to defend inside Soviet borders, and of having to do so with shrinking resources, the Soviet military is compelled to devise a new military posture.

It would be naive to assume that the Soviet Union is any more likely than the United States to move to a *strictly* defensive military posture. As a great power, it undoubtedly will retain its ability to project force when it believes that its vital national interests or those of its allies are threatened. But Soviet military leaders speak regularly of a new defense doctrine, which they claim will be evident in their troop deployments, weapons development, exercises, and training manuals. Soviet forces are to be organized to provide the basic requirements of strategic deterrence and to ensure the defense of home territory against any threat of invasion by conventional forces.

Comparisons of overall *conventional force deployments* in Europe continue to reveal quantitative imbalances—albeit of a reduced size—between NATO and Soviet forces in Europe.[11] Because the WTO is no longer functioning as an effective military alliance, current analyses compare NATO forces with Soviet forces in Europe, excluding the East European countries that are still nominal members of the WTO.

At the same time, although current Soviet capabilities remain great, the rapid pace of change in the Soviet politico-military posture has led to substantial and ongoing alterations in force deployments. The Soviets have already announced publicly—and largely carried out—a series of unilateral force reduction measures that are to be completed by early 1991. These include the following:

• *Personnel*: 500,000 troops are to be cut from the Soviet armed forces, of which 50,000 will come from outside the Soviet Union. The 450,000 troops to be demobilized inside the Soviet Union will include 190,000 from the European part of the Soviet Union, 60,000 from the south, and 200,000 from Asia.

• *Force Structure*: *Tanks*—10,000 tanks are to be removed from the European USSR and Eastern Europe. *Artillery*—8,500 artillery systems are to be removed from the European USSR and Eastern Europe. *Aircraft*—800 aircraft are to be removed from the European USSR and Eastern Europe.[12]

Under agreement with the new Czechoslovak government, all Soviet forces are to be withdrawn by June 1991. Indeed, Czechoslovak officials announced at the end of August 1990 that more than half of these forces (37,000 troops) already had been removed. Soviet forces are also scheduled to be out of

Hungary and Poland by the middle of 1991 under a similar formal agreement.[13]

The WTO countries themselves collectively are committed to reducing conventional forces by more than 581,000 troops, nearly 13,000 tanks, and about 1,000 aircraft *without* reciprocal reductions by NATO.[14] Moreover, the announced terms of the CFE treaty call for an equalization of weaponry in Central Europe and substantial Soviet troop withdrawals,[15] thereby virtually eliminating the possibility of a successful surprise attack. Indeed, the asymmetrical reductions called for in the CFE treaty would make the initiation of any major offensive action by the Soviet Union unlikely.

In the Asian theater, the Soviets have begun to implement Gorbachev's stated commitment to withdraw 120,000 troops, including the demobilization of a substantial number of obsolete ships, tanks, and planes. Soviet force deployments have been reduced in Mongolia and along the Chinese border.[16] At the same time, however, there is some evidence that the limited withdrawal of troops and equipment from Europe may have permitted a concurrent modernization of Soviet forces in Asia.

Soviet force deployments in Asia have, in general, been more defensively configured and have not displayed the potential for preemptive offensive operations that the Soviet forces in Europe maintained prior to the recent change in political circumstances. It is significant, in this regard, that a recent Japan Defense Agency white paper details the actual reduction in Soviet land, sea, and air forces and concludes for the first time that Soviet aggression against Asian countries is now unlikely.[17]

A comparison of relative U.S.-Soviet strength in *strategic nuclear forces* reveals a more balanced picture than current conventional force comparisons.[18] As has been the case for at least two decades, current strategic force deployments provide both sides with ample capability for implementing any of the various theories of deterrence that have been argued in doctrinal discussions of the subject. The modernization programs now under way on both sides will not radically improve these capabilities, nor will the reductions envisaged in the draft START treaty meaningfully diminish them. Current and projected strategic force deployments will amply support, moreover, the traditional objective of extended deterrence—that is, a credible retaliatory capability against a conventional ground attack. Since these basic deterrent and extended deterrent capabilities are not likely to be decisively affected by technical improvements or changes in deployment levels, and since trade in directly associated technology is not contemplated at any rate, the strategic balance has relatively minor immediate significance for export control policy.

On the basis of the announced reductions in Soviet and East European military forces—assuming that they are completed in good faith—the apparent dissolution of the WTO as a military alliance, and the emerging, defensive Soviet military posture in Asia, the panel accepts the conclusion

drawn by the Department of Defense that there is *no* credible scenario in which the Soviet Union could mount a theater-wide conventional attack against the West in either the European or Asian theaters with less than 18 to 24 months preparation.[19] Indeed, even if there were to be a change of leadership in the Soviet Union, it would take a very long time for a legitimate conventional offensive threat to be remounted, and such a mobilization would be easily observable by national technical means. **There is a continuing concern, however, about Soviet capabilities to launch local attacks within regions near the Soviet border with as little as 90 days mobilization.**

Economic Exchange with the East

The question that arises is whether the West should use its considerable leverage—namely, trade, aid, direct investment, and technology transfer—to try to *accelerate* desired changes in Soviet and East European behavior and whether such measures would elicit a positive response. Even before the recent dramatic changes, the East European and Soviet countries were becoming increasingly vulnerable to the pressures of the international economy, and recent developments will make them even more susceptible to external economic forces.

Most of the East European countries are attempting to transform themselves into market economies. Poland has embarked on a laissez-faire course. Hungary and Czechoslovakia are approaching economic reform at a more measured pace, but they will still face the transitional costs of factory layoffs and higher prices. Eastern Germany has been absorbed into the dynamic, market-driven economy of a reunited Germany.

Companies from Western Europe, the United States, and Japan are increasing their commercial contacts with Eastern Europe and the Soviet Union. Although short-term prospects for economic growth in these countries are constrained by severe structural problems, many companies are now laying the groundwork for potentially lucrative future operations. Large enterprises, like Fiat and General Electric, are building new facilities in these countries. As of June 1990, the number of registered joint ventures between Western companies and Soviet partners had risen to 1,754 (as compared with 685 in June 1989), and about 350 joint ventures had been formed between Western enterprises and East European countries. Of the Soviet joint ventures, 541 (approximately 31 percent) were actually operating or producing goods and services, and another 162 ventures (approximately 9 percent), while not producing, were at least paying workers. Thus, it is reasonable to conclude that, as of mid-1990, a total of 703 Soviet joint ventures (approximately 40 percent) had tangible existence.[20]

Despite wariness by the United States and the United Kingdom, Western economic aid to Eastern Europe and the Soviet Union is significant and growing. The Group of 24 industrialized countries has pledged $14 billion in loans, direct aid, and technical assistance to Poland and Hungary, and it will provide additional help to Czechoslovakia, eastern Germany, Bulgaria, and Yugoslavia. The European Bank for Reconstruction and Development will direct its initial capital of $12 billion to private and state enterprises throughout Eastern Europe. Even the notion of targeting large-scale assistance to the Soviet Union has now become an acceptable subject of debate among the Western allies.

The argument advanced for increased aid and economic intercourse with the East European countries and the Soviet Union is essentially threefold. First, aid and trade can act as catalysts to bring about or facilitate further desirable economic and social changes. Second, economic assistance and trade agreements can function in a more political context as a direct quid pro quo for specific concessions. Third, doing nothing—that is, *failing to grant aid or permit trade*—risks further serious deterioration of the internal political, economic, and social fabric of these countries, the consequences of which would be unpredictable and, most likely, undesirable. Instability in Eastern Europe (or the Soviet Union) is not in the West's interest; the orderly transformation of the economic and social systems of these countries is most definitely to the West's advantage.

Events are inexorably drawing Eastern Europe into the economic orbit of the West. There is already discussion in the European Community about its evolving into a three-tiered system of current members, European Free Trade Association countries, and the nations of the former Soviet bloc. The implication is that Eastern Europe will become, at least economically, *part* of the West. **The likely result of large-scale Western economic assistance will be greater East European (and, to a lesser extent, Soviet) integration with the West and a greater Western stake in the success of the economic and political reforms now under way in these countries.**

At the same time, debate will continue over where to draw the line in imposing East-West export controls. It is now in the West's security interest to permit the flow to Eastern Europe and the Soviet Union of dual use technology, apart from a few highly critical items. Indeed, the liberalization of controls could be part of a broad strategy to encourage the process of political and economic reform in Eastern Europe and the Soviet Union, thereby strengthening that region's stability and security.

The PRC as a National Security Threat

The panel did not devote as much consideration to the People's Republic of China (PRC) as a "traditional" source of threat to U.S. national security as it did to the Soviet Union and the other WTO countries, primarily because the Chinese have not posed the same degree of direct threat to the United States as have the WTO countries. Indeed, the decision of the United States in the early 1980s to assist China with its efforts to modernize signaled the fact that the United States no longer considered China a direct or immediate threat to its security interests. This was reflected in a substantial relaxation within CoCom of the restriction on strategic technology exports to China, generally known as the "China Green Line."

At the same time, however, China has emerged as a powerful regional actor in Asia. It is now a strategic nuclear power with a well-developed ballistic missile delivery capability. China also maintains a significant conventional military capability that potentially could be used to threaten the vital interests of a number of close U.S. allies, including Japan, Taiwan, and South Korea, or to further other political objectives in the Asian and Pacific region. Moreover, the PRC continues to produce missiles and other weapons for international sale, and it has so far been willing to accept only limited constraints on its munitions export prerogatives.

China apparently still sees the major threat to its national security as coming from the Soviet Union. It is unlikely to change that perception as long as substantial Soviet nuclear and conventional forces remain deployed at or near the northern Chinese border. Sino-Soviet arms control negotiations are now under way and may help to reduce further threat perceptions on both sides of the border.

The current leadership is doing everything possible to bolster the flagging Chinese belief in communism. But China's internal situation is likely to remain inherently unstable as the struggle for power goes on, at least until a new generation of leaders emerges. In the meantime, however, the recent emphasis on economic modernization can be expected to continue. Thus, contacts and economic ties with the industrialized nations are likely to grow, despite the political uncertainties. At the same time, those in China who advocate a more open and pluralistic political system also will increase in number, again despite the repression of the post-Tiananmen environment.

Under these uncertain and evolving internal conditions, the West is likely to maintain its wait-and-see posture before undertaking any further trade liberalization with China. **Among other reasons, a cautious policy is warranted by the impending generational change in leadership, with its associated potential for further political upheaval. But it is also in the interest of the United States to nurture a deeper and more cooperative relationship with the current Chinese regime, including further efforts to convince China to participate more fully in the major nonproliferation regimes.**

Ultimately, establishing a certain degree of symmetry between the export control regime for China and the new rules that are under de-

velopment for the democratizing East European countries and the Soviet Union may be desirable. As in the case of the former WTO countries, however, the rate of further change in U.S. and CoCom export controls for the PRC is likely to be governed by the stated foreign and domestic policies and actual practice of the Chinese government.

Summary Findings and Recommendations on the Traditional Threat

The threat presented by Soviet military capabilities has fundamentally changed. Conventional capabilities in Europe have been reduced and limited by the CFE treaty, and the possibility of surprise conventional attack in Central Europe has been virtually eliminated. The possibility of a fully mobilized attack has been dramatically reduced. Conventional capabilities in other theaters, such as the Pacific, also are being reduced. Nuclear weapons capabilities are essentially unaltered, but the potential for new reduction agreements appears to have increased.

Together with United States, the Soviet Union is now attempting to move beyond the traditional paradigm of alliance confrontation to establish a new security relationship. The Soviets also have indicated their intention to integrate their economy with the international economy, based at least in part on market principles.[21]

In Western Europe in particular, the calculation of the need for export controls has changed as a result of the dramatic political events that have taken place since late 1989. The result is that support in Europe for the continuation of dual use export controls beyond the short term is disappearing rapidly. The continuation of viable controls even for the next few years will require a major reduction in the scope of the control list—at a minimum, to the level of the "core list" that was under negotiation within CoCom during the latter half of 1990—and a shift in the policy governing dual use export controls to allow controlled items to be exported to the Soviet Union if they are verifiably for civilian (i.e., commercial) end use.

The foregoing factors are part of a larger process of rethinking U.S. security policy, including possible fundamental changes in defense policy. The export control dimension of this new policy prescription is a mixed strategy: Encourage change and make further relaxation of export controls contingent on evidence of additional change. This policy should keep in mind the following elements:

* **Continue to constrain access by the *Soviet military* to technology and end products that contribute significantly and directly to the improvement of weapons capabilities.**

* Ensure that export controls do not impede the permanent conversion (or closure) of Soviet military industrial resources to the manufacture of products for the civilian sector.
* Encourage further positive changes in the security policy of the Soviet Union, including additional force demobilizations and redeployments.
* Encourage stable political and economic transition in the Soviet Union through a broadened process of democratization and economic reform.
* Maintain consensus with U.S. allies on the coordination of further liberalization of export controls on trade with the Soviet Union.
* Move progressively toward the removal of export controls on dual use items to the Soviet Union and the East European countries for commercial end uses that can be verified.

THE ADVENT OF NEW SOURCES OF PHYSICAL THREAT

During the past two decades, the attention of the United States, its allies, and indeed the rest of the world has been drawn increasingly (and often violently) to a range of complicated new politico-military challenges outside the East-West context. Some of these problems represent direct national security threats to the United States and the international community; others are of concern due to their potential to "spill over" into a broader international arena. Their common characteristics are that (a) they are exacerbated—or made potentially more dangerous—by the availability of certain types of dual use technology and munitions and (b) they are not dealt with effectively by existing *multilateral* control regimes. Among the most notable of these developments are the following:

• *Expansion of regional conflicts initiated by regional powers*   The danger has long existed that regional conflicts could escalate into broader international military engagements. But ready access to foreign-made munitions and new indigenous design and manufacturing capabilities have contributed to a growing threat that regional powers might attempt to take unilateral action on the basis of a perceived short-term military advantage over their neighboring rivals. The danger in this case is that the alliance commitments or overriding politico-economic interests of the United States and/or other international actors would draw them into the conflict.

Many aspects of this scenario occurred recently in the case of the Persian Gulf. There seems little doubt that Iraq was emboldened in its decision to invade and annex Kuwait by the size, quality, and armament level of its army in comparison with those of Kuwait and the other regional powers likely to oppose its aggression. The response of the United States and the international community to the Iraqi invasion demonstrates clearly the chain of events that can result in a broadened international involvement.

• *Regional instabilities exacerbated by the availability of technologies of proliferation concern* The proliferation of technical know-how and process equipment necessary to manufacture chemical and nuclear weapons and weapons delivery systems has increased the danger that long-standing regional rivalries in the Middle East, the Indian subcontinent, Southeast Asia, and South America could result in widespread loss of human life. Here as well, the United States and/or other nations could be drawn into such regional conflicts, presumably in an effort to prevent weapons of mass destruction* from being used and to protect their foreign nationals and financial investments in the country. Thus, a regional conflict that threatened to involve weapons of mass destruction could well endanger the broad national security interests of the United States and other countries.

• *Extremist violence and state-sponsored terrorism* The diffusion of certain types of dual use technology (e.g., plastic explosives and sophisticated digital timing devices) and technical know-how, much of it available "off the shelf" and entirely legally, has heightened and expanded the danger that all countries face from terrorist violence by internal and external extremist organizations—some of them operating with the direct or indirect support of other governments. There is also the added (and growing) danger that terrorists could acquire weapons of mass destruction or smart/advanced weapons from countries that do not have well-developed mechanisms to protect their stockpiles of such weapons, or whose national politics supports the goals and objectives of terrorist violence, or that are seeking simple monetary gain.

Regional Instability

The end of the Cold War has led to a greater focus on regional conflicts potentially threatening to U.S. interests. Even before the collapse of the Warsaw Pact, many military analysts had judged that the likelihood of war in Europe had lessened considerably. In fact, this perception had generated calls for a major shift in the mission and structure of the U.S. armed forces toward the development of units light enough for swift movement to distant trouble spots (such as the Persian Gulf) and flexible enough to deal with the challenges of low-intensity conflicts.

Although a detailed analysis of this issue is beyond the scope of this study, these anticipated changes in the U.S. military mission are related to the

---

Weapons of mass destruction are defined for the purposes of this study as nuclear explosives, nuclear-capable missiles, and chemical or biological weapons, including those delivered by missile.

heightened concerns about regional arms proliferation. Many regions of concern are also areas where weapons proliferation is most acute and involve countries toward whom the major powers often have differing export policies. An important adjunct of this intersection with the problem is state-sponsored terrorism, against which trade restrictions may have deterrent or punitive value.

Although better relations between the United States and the Soviet Union have been accompanied by some progress toward reducing regional conflicts in southern Africa and Central America, other areas have been marked by greater tensions between regional powers. Throughout the Cold War, the Middle East was thought the most likely region to trigger a superpower conflict. With the substantial improvement in U.S.-Soviet relations—and with the decrease of military and financial support for certain Arab states by the Soviet Union and the East European countries—this particular specter has diminished considerably, although conflict in that region remains a major security concern. The fruits of this change were evident in the close consultation and cooperation between the United States and the Soviet Union during the early part of the Persian Gulf crisis.

On the other hand, the Iraqi invasion of Kuwait and the Palestinian uprising in the Israeli-occupied territories have severely strained relations and heightened tensions among countries in the region and beyond. The fact that nuclear and chemical weapons and missile delivery systems are now part of the Middle East security calculus only adds to the danger posed to U.S. bases and allies in the region.

The Indian subcontinent also has been threatened recently by the outbreak of large-scale hostilities. India and Pakistan, which have fought a series of wars since independence over still-disputed land on their borders, are upgrading their advanced military capabilities, such as short- and medium-range missiles. India has a proven ability to manufacture nuclear weapons, and there is growing concern that Pakistan may be in the process of adapting its nuclear energy program for military purposes.

In East Asia, fears about weapons proliferation have added to the peril of continuing confrontation. Korea remains divided as a result of lingering Cold War antagonisms, and even as the United States withdraws some forces from South Korea and Japan, it is concerned about reports that North Korea is pursuing a vigorous program of nuclear weapons development.

New forms of regional instability also could arise out of the disintegration of the Soviet Union, if that were to occur. Already, a serious and violent conflict exists between Armenia and Azerbaijan and, less directly, between Kirghizia and Uzbekistan. Moreover, not only is there a continuing risk of conflict between republics of the Soviet Union, but a further danger also exists that these tensions might spill over current Soviet borders and embroil neighboring countries.

Tensions in areas *outside* Central and Eastern Europe, the region traditionally of greatest Western concern, are being exacerbated by the spread of weapons of mass destruction and high-performance weapons. This trend adds to the need for a close reexamination and restructuring of existing nonproliferation regimes.

Proliferation of Nuclear, Missile, and Chemical Technologies

During the past 15 years, technologies useful in the construction of nuclear weapons, chemical/biological weapons, and missile delivery systems have been diffused to a number of additional nations. There is substantial evidence that India, Iraq, Israel, Pakistan, and South Africa may now or soon possess nuclear weapons capabilities. And the Iran-Iraq war provided graphic evidence of the use of missiles and chemical warfare on both sides. These capabilities in the hands of so many nations pose a direct threat to the security of the United States.

There has been a steady diffusion of scientific knowledge, technical and engineering talent, and manufacturing ability in all areas of proliferation, and a concentrated group of nations have acquired the new capabilities. In fact, the most disturbing development has been the potential for expanded negative impacts created when countries acquire *both* the means of mass destruction and long-range delivery vehicles, such as ballistic or cruise missiles. Especially to the extent that this trend overlaps with increased concerns about regional instability, proliferation poses new threats to national and global security.

NUCLEAR PROLIFERATION

Efforts to control the spread of nuclear weapons to additional states have probably been the most successful of efforts in the three major areas of proliferation. Indeed, President Kennedy's expectation in 1962 that over 20 nations would develop nuclear weapons by the late 1970s did not come to pass. But trends toward development or expansion of nuclear capability in a number of countries require continuing efforts to strengthen the nuclear nonproliferation regime.

While much of the information about nations attempting to move forward with efforts to develop nuclear weapons is classified, a number of published reports detail the nuclear activities of the "problem" countries.[22] As noted, Pakistan is on the threshold of a nuclear weapons capability. South Africa reportedly is also close to or already possesses a nuclear weapons capability. It has been estimated that Israel has between 60 and 100 nuclear devices. Brazil and Argentina continue to operate unsafeguarded nuclear facilities. More recently, North Korean activities at its Yongbong nuclear facility have caused some concern. Although North Korea signed the Nuclear Non-Proliferation Treaty, it has not concluded an International Atomic Energy Agency safeguard arrangement for its nuclear program.

It is noteworthy that each of these nations has been engaged to some degree in regional conflicts. The pairings of traditional enemies or competitors, such as Pakistan and India or Iraq and Israel, create the possibility in the event of open hostilities for escalation to a nuclear exchange.

MISSILE DELIVERY TECHNOLOGY

The proliferation of nuclear weapons capability has been accompanied by the spread of missile delivery technology. The Iran-Iraq war focused worldwide attention on the dangers of such capabilities, and although many of the missiles exchanged during that conflict came from or were developed on the basis of technology supplied by either the Soviet Union or China, the ability to produce such missiles indigenously is rapidly becoming the norm, rather than the exception, in regional conflicts.

The United States, the Soviet Union, China, and France have been the primary suppliers of missile technology. In almost every case, missiles were first obtained from outside suppliers, often under the guise of developing a national space program, and then modified by the acquiring country to upgrade the delivery system's capability. Earlier generations of missiles were highly inaccurate. Now, however, there have been substantial technical improvements in accuracy and range capabilities that pose a heightened threat to U.S. national security interests.

CHEMICAL WEAPONS

Prior to the Iran-Iraq war, chemical weapons were viewed largely in the context of East-West superpower stockpiles. The widespread use of chemical weapons in that conflict highlighted the growing global diffusion of these weapons. Allegations that Libya used chemical weapons in Chad and the revelation of involvement by West German companies in Libya's Rabta chemical facility also focused worldwide attention on the problem.[23]

More than a dozen nations besides the United States and the Soviet Union are thought to have access to chemical weapons. At least 11 other nations are suspected of trying to acquire such weapons, and another 11 are alleged to have attempted to obtain chemical weapons, although no official sources have corroborated such allegations. Table 5-1 lists the chemical weapon status of developing countries as of August 1989.

Of the three types of proliferation technologies that have been discussed, chemical weapons have the highest probability of use because their design and production require a lower level of technical sophistication. In addition,

TABLE 5-1   Chemical Weapons Status of Developing Countries

Known	Probable	Possible	Alleged
Iraq	Burma	Angola	Afghanistan
	China	Argentina	Chad
	Egypt	Cuba	Chile
	Ethiopia	India	El Salvador
	Iran	Indonesia	Guatemala
	Israel	Laos	Jordan
	Libya	Pakistan	Mozambique
	North Korea	Somalia	Nicaragua
	Syria	South Africa	Peru
	Taiwan	South Korea	Philippines
	Vietnam	Thailand	Sudan

SOURCE: Aspen Strategy Group, *New Threats* (Lanham, Md.: University Press of America, 1990), p. 72.

the widespread diffusion of such weapons raises the probability of their falling into the hands of terrorist groups.

Work on creating an international chemical weapons treaty has been under way for a number of years at the United Nations Conference on Disarmament in Geneva. Although progress has been slow, this activity has been useful in working to "delegitimize" the use of chemical weapons. A binding international treaty is probably still several years away. Nevertheless, the international community has been sensitized to the horrors of chemical weapons, and this in turn has provided momentum for continued negotiations.

Summary Findings and Recommendations on the Proliferation Threat

During the past two decades there has been a continued proliferation of nuclear weapon related technology and missile delivery systems around the world, as well as a relatively rapid diffusion of capability to produce chemical weapons. Taken together, the growing capacity of many nations to develop and employ weapons of mass destruction poses new security threats to U.S. forces overseas and to the international community and, in turn, requires new and innovative policy responses.

Such responses will require the creation of new multilateral regimes, or strengthening of existing regimes, involving both the Soviet Union and China. There will be little chance for long-term success if these two key players are not officially included in all proliferation control regimes at the earliest opportunity. Without comprehensive multilateral regimes, the chances for effective control of proliferation threats are critically weakened.

With this in mind, the panel makes the following recommendations:

* **Proliferation of weapons of mass destruction, their delivery systems, and advanced conventional weapons is a U.S. national security concern and should be treated as such in U.S. law and policy.**
* **The principal focus should be on those proliferation problems— nuclear weapons, chemical and biological weapons, and missile delivery systems—that, in combination, have the potential to create expanded negative impacts.**
* **Control regimes should be tailored to the particular circumstances of specific proliferation threats and, to be effective, should be as fully multilateral (i.e., involve the maximum number of suppliers) as possible. Some of these regimes are likely to rely, at least in part, on properly fashioned export controls. Such controls should be targeted only on those technologies or products directly essential to the development and/or manufacture of weapons of mass destruction.**

NOTES

1. "Final Declaration of NATO Summit Leaders," *Associated Press*, London, July 6, 1990.
2. See, for example, U.S. Congress, Office of Technology Assessment, *Holding the Edge: Maintaining the Defense Technology Base* (Washington, D.C.: U.S. Government Printing Office, 1989); U.S. Congress, Office of Technology Assessment, *Making Things Better: Competing in Manufacturing* (Washington, D.C.: U.S. Government Printing Office, 1990); Michael L. Dertouzos, Richard K. Lester, and Robert M. Solow, *Made in America: Regaining the Productive Edge* (Cambridge, Mass.: The MIT Press, 1989); U.S. Department of Defense, *Bolstering Defense Industrial Competitiveness* (Report to the Secretary of Defense by the Under Secretary of Defense (Acquisition) (Washington, D.C., 1988); National Academy of Sciences, National Academy of Engineering, Institute of Medicine, and National Research Council, *Industrial R&D and U.S. Technological Leadership* (Washington, D.C.: National Academy Press, 1988); Richard M. Cyert and David C. Mowery (eds.), *The Impact of Technological Change on Employment and Economic Growth* (Cambridge, Mass.: Ballinger, 1988); and Council on Competitiveness, *America's Competitiveness Crisis: Confronting the New Reality* (Washington, D.C., 1987).
3. U.S. Department of Defense, *Critical Technologies Plan* (Report to the Committees on Armed Services, U.S. Congress) (Washington, D.C., 1989).
4. "The World's One Hundred Largest Banks," *Wall Street Journal*, September 21, 1990, p. R29.
5. U.S. Congress, Office of Technology Assessment, *Arming Our Allies: Competition and Cooperation in Defense Technology* (Washington, D.C.: U.S. Government Printing Office, 1990).
6. U.S. Department of Defense, Office of the Under Secretary of Defense (Acquisition), Defense Science Board, *Task Force Report on Defense Semiconductor Dependency* (Washington, D.C.: U.S. Government Printing Office, 1987).
7. U.S. Department of Defense, *Critical Technologies Plan.*
8. Data from International Trade Administration and Bureau of the Census, U.S. Department of Commerce, 1990.

9. Statement of Soviet President Gorbachev at the 27th Congress of the Communist Party, February 1986; see also "Political Report of the Central Committee," *Pravda*, February 2, 1989.

10. Dimitri T. Yazov, *Pravda*, July 27, 1987.

11. U.S. Department of Defense, Office of the Secretary of Defense, *Soviet Military Power, 1990* (Washington, D.C.: U.S. Government Printing Office, 1990), pp. 72–102.

12. Data adapted from *Jane's Defense Weekly*, November 11, 1989; U.S. Department of Defense, Office of the Secretary of Defense, *Soviet Military Power, 1989* (Washington, D.C.: U.S. Government Printing Office, 1989), p. 62; *Soviet Military Power, 1990*, p. 96.

13. U.S. Department of Defense, Office of the Secretary of Defense, *Soviet Military Power, 1990*, p. 96.

14. U.S. Department of Defense, Office of the Secretary of Defense, *Soviet Military Power, 1989*, p. 62.

15. See "U.S.-Soviet Accord on Europe Armies is Reported Near," *New York Times*, October 4, 1990, p. A1; "Arms Control Catching Up," *New York Times*, October 5, 1990, p. A7; and "Soviets Said to be Removing Arms from Europe Before Treaty," *Washington Post*, October 5, 1990, p. A20.

16. U.S. Department of Defense, Office of the Secretary of Defense, *Soviet Military Power, 1990*, pp. 97–99; Allan Romberg, "The Future of U.S. Alliances with Japan and Korea," *Critical Issues* (New York: Council on Foreign Relations, 1990), p. 9.

17. "Defense White Paper Says 'Soviet Threat' Fades," Tokyo, Kyoto News Service (Reported in *Foreign Broadcast Information Service*, FBIS-EAS-90-181, September 18, 1990, p. 10).

18. U.S. Department of Defense, Office of the Secretary of Defense, *Soviet Military Power, 1990*, pp. 63–71.

19. Statement of Secretary of Defense Richard Cheney at the White House, September 17, 1990.

20. Alan B. Sherr, unpublished data in personal communication, Center for Foreign Policy Development, Brown University, November 29, 1990.

21. See, for example, references to the so-called "500 days" speech by Soviet President Gorbachev in "500 Days to Shake the World" and "Russia Meets the Market," *The Economist*, September 15, 1990, pp. 13–14, 93–94; and "The Union of the States," *The Economist*, September 22, 1990, pp. 53–55.

22. See, for example, Leonard S. Spector, *The Undeclared Bomb: The Spread of Nuclear Weapons, 1987–1988* (Cambridge, Mass.: Ballinger, 1988); Leonard S. Spector, *Going Nuclear* (Cambridge, Mass.: Ballinger, 1987); and Janne E. Nolan and Albert D. Wheelon, "Third World Ballistic Missiles," *Scientific American*, vol. 263, no. 2 (August 1990), pp. 34–40.

23. Regarding alleged Libyan use of chemical weapons in Chad, see Elaine Sciolino, "U.S. Sends 2,000 Gas Masks to the Chadians," *New York Times*, September 25, 1987, p. 4, and Michael Gordon, "U.S. Thinks Libya May Plan to Make Chemical Weapons," *New York Times*, December 24, 1987, p. 1. For German involvement in Libyan chemical weapons facilities, see Serge Schmemann, "Bonn Will Tighten Curb on Export of Deadly Goods," *New York Times*, January 11, 1989, p. 1.

6

The U.S. and Multilateral Export Control Regimes

DEVELOPMENT OF THE EXPORT CONTROL REGIMES

In 1940, following the outbreak of war in Europe, Congress gave the President authority to control the export of "militarily significant" goods and technology, as well as arms. Following World War II, U.S. export control policy began for the first time to assume important peacetime dimensions.* It is significant that national security during this period was being defined largely in terms of the importance of conserving supplies of critical materials, rather than in strategic, ideological, or other terms.

The Cold War Response

By late 1948, the United States had begun for the first time to impose licensing requirements on exports to the Soviet bloc, and Congress formally recognized the need for continuing peacetime controls in the Export Control Act of 1949. By the early 1950s, U.S. and North Atlantic Treaty Organization (NATO) strategy was firmly rooted in the need to contain Communist expansionism (now including China) and to maintain the political and territorial integrity of the West (which by this time included Japan). In 1955, the NATO alliance was formally opposed by the newly established Warsaw Pact.

---

*See Appendix G for a more detailed discussion of the evolution of U.S. export control policy.

The primary objective of the export controls authorized in the Export Control Act then became to prevent or delay improvements in Warsaw Pact (and Chinese) military capabilities that could be accomplished or facilitated through the acquisition of Western technology and end products. This objective derived in large measure from a recognition that, for political and economic reasons, it was neither possible nor even desirable for the West to maintain numerical equality with the mobilized troop strength or fielded conventional weaponry of the Warsaw Pact countries. This recognition led to the "force multiplier" strategy of maintaining technological superiority over potential adversaries. An inevitable outgrowth of this strategy was the control of exports of goods and technology that had commercial, as well as military, applications. Thus, the NATO decision in the early 1950s to rely on force multipliers also locked the alliance into an active policy of controlling the export of militarily significant goods and technology, including arms and so-called dual use* items, which has continued until the present day.

The Coordinating Committee for Multilateral Export Controls (CoCom),† was established in 1949 as an informal forum associated with NATO to coordinate national export control policies and review potential exports to the Soviet Union and other proscribed destinations.

U.S. Export Control Policy

The Cold War strategy was translated in the United States into laws governing trade in arms and goods with significant military utility. The Arms Export Control Act (AECA) of 1976, which succeeded the Battle Act of 1954, authorized the President to control the export and import of defense articles and services. Although preventing Cold War adversaries from acquiring military items is a function of export controls on defense articles and services or munitions items, the stated rationale for munitions controls is to further U.S. foreign policy, world peace, and security. The Export Control Act of 1949 was superseded by the Export Administration Act (EAA) of 1969 and 1979. The objectives of the Export Administration Act of 1979, as amended, are threefold:

• *The short supply objective* "To restrict the export of goods where necessary to protect the domestic economy from the excessive drain of scarce materials and to reduce the serious inflationary impact of foreign demand."

---

*A dispute has continued over how to distinguish between exports to be controlled as arms or munitions and exports to be controlled as "dual use," that is, items not inherently military in character.

†The CoCom participants currently are Australia, Belgium, Canada, Denmark, France, Germany, Greece, Italy, Japan, Luxembourg, the Netherlands, Norway, Portugal, Spain, Turkey, the United Kingdom, and the United States.

- *The national security objective* "To restrict the export of goods and technology which would make a significant contribution to the military potential of any other country or combination of countries which would prove detrimental to the national security of the United States."
- *The foreign policy objective* "To restrict the export of goods and technology where necessary to further significantly the foreign policy of the United States or to fulfill its declared international obligations."[1]

To implement the national security objective, Section 5 of the EAA requires the President to establish a list of countries and a list of commodities and technologies controlled for reasons of national security. The decision on targeted countries for national security purposes must take into account several factors, including (1) the extent to which a particular country's policies are adverse to the national security interest of the United States; (2) whether the nation is Communist or non-Communist; (3) the nation's current and potential bilateral relationship with the United States, other countries that are friendly with the United States, and countries that are hostile to the United States; (4) the nation's nuclear weapons capability and its record of compliance with nuclear weapons agreements (e.g., the Nuclear Non-Proliferation Treaty, NNPT) to which the United States is a party; and (5) any other factors that the President may deem appropriate. With respect to trade with CoCom countries and countries cooperating with CoCom, the act directs the President to certify those countries whose export control programs meet certain standards outlined in the law. With limited exceptions, the export of goods to certified countries may not be controlled. To date, the executive branch has not certified any countries as meeting the standards in the law. Section 5 of the EAA, as amended in 1988, also states that no unilateral national security controls can be maintained, except on items for which it is determined there is no foreign availability.

Section 6 of the EAA concerns the foreign policy objective. The denial of exports, or in some cases, the offer of renewed access, as a source of political influence or leverage has been an attractive instrument in the conduct of U.S. foreign affairs for many years. This has been increasingly true as other traditional foreign policy instruments, such as the threatened or actual use of military force, have become less viable in some circumstances. The denial of exports is a prerogative jealously guarded by the administration and the Congress, and it is employed in support of an enormously broad range of policy objectives: from emphasizing the seriousness of human rights violations to addressing the proliferation of nuclear and chemical weapons. Few of the remaining foreign policy controls are significantly related to East-West tensions.

A distinctive feature of foreign policy export controls is that they may be applied with extraterritorial features and without corresponding action in other countries. As a result, they have caused serious damage both to the reputation of the United States as a reliable trading partner and to the competitiveness of U.S. companies whose major foreign competitors are not similarly constrained.*

The EAA renewal in 1979 added a provision requiring all foreign policy controls to be reviewed annually. The President must certify annually the need and justification for continuing foreign policy controls. The President's ability to apply foreign policy controls was also modified by the 1985 Export Administration Amendments Act, which required that the President consult with Congress and American business organizations before imposing foreign policy controls. The Congress also specified that, prior to imposing such controls, the President should determine that reasonable efforts have been made to employ diplomatic or other alternative means to achieve the purpose of the proposed controls.

In the event that foreign policy controls are imposed, the President is directed to "take all feasible steps" to secure the cooperation of other governments in establishing comparable export controls. Exports that fulfill contracts or agreements entered into prior to the date on which the President announces the intention to impose foreign policy controls may not be restricted unless the President determines that the export would constitute a breach of the peace or a direct contribution to the situation posing the threat.

CoCom

The NATO response to the Cold War through CoCom has evolved since its inception in 1949, and CoCom has undergone major organizational and political changes in the past five years. The increasing ability of newly industrializing countries to produce CoCom-controlled goods has necessitated either decontrolling all goods not produced exclusively in CoCom countries or including those third countries within the control process. In addition, the highly publicized Toshiba-Kongsberg illegal sale of high-precision, multiaxis milling machines (see Chapter 4) focused attention on each member's political commitment to CoCom and the effectiveness of the group as a whole. Although the operational environment and political attention to the organization have changed over time, the fundamental rule of decisions by consensus,†

---

*This fact was substantiated by information collected on the panel's European, Asian, and Canadian fact-finding missions.

†Decision by consensus requires that no member dissent from the decision, not necessarily that every member express unconditional support for the decision. This rule of consensus applies to all CoCom decisions.

which applies to list review, case review, and the determination of proscribed countries, remains unchanged.

CoCom Methodology

CoCom maintains an International Munitions List (IML), an International Atomic Energy List (IAEL), and an International Industrial List (commonly referred to as the Industrial List, or IL). The three lists are reviewed completely on a four-year cycle, but the Industrial List is given primary attention. In June 1990, CoCom members agreed to overhaul the list of controlled items by creating a new "core list" to replace the current Industrial List. The core list exercise is expected to be completed in the spring of 1991.

CoCom members collectively determine proscribed destinations. They also collectively review all applications to export IL goods at the "general exceptions" level (i.e., the level of goods for which a general embargo is assumed and approvals, while possible, are the exception). For some IL entries, "favorable consideration" parameters have been established for items that may be approved for export to appropriate destinations and end uses, and "administrative exception notes" have been established for items that the members consider warrant national control, but not collective review.

CoCom itself has no independent methodology for constructing the lists of items to be controlled, because the lists are based on national submissions of items for control or decontrol. CoCom did, however, identify in 1978 criteria for "strategic" items as guidance for national systems. The strategic criteria include (1) materials, equipment, and technology specifically designed for and used in national military systems; (2) unique technology that, if acquired, would be of significant assistance to an adversary's military capability; and (3) materials, equipment, and technology regarding which proscribed countries are so deficient that, in the event of war, the gap could not be closed within a reasonable period of time. The IML contains items meeting the first criterion; the IAEL and IL contain dual use items meeting the second and third criteria.

The CoCom list of proscribed countries has remained virtually unchanged since the organization's inception, with one notable exception. In 1985, the United States initiated a change in the status of the People's Republic of China (PRC) as a controlled destination, which was accepted by CoCom. As a result, the technical parameters for goods requiring CoCom review for export to the PRC are less restrictive than for other proscribed countries. This threshold for CoCom review is known as the "China Green Line." In addition, CoCom agreed in June 1990 to extend special treatment in limited areas to Czechoslovakia, Hungary, and Poland and to extend broad special treatment eventually to countries that represent a lesser strategic threat and have adopted appropriate safeguard systems to protect controlled technology imports.

THIRD COUNTRY COOPERATION

The original goal of the Third Country Initiative, now called Third Country Cooperation (TCC), was to encourage third countries to adopt five essential elements outlined by CoCom as constituting an effective control program. The essential elements are as follows:

1. Acceptable import certificate and delivery verification documents (IC/DV)
2. Control over reexports of CoCom-origin, controlled goods
3. Control over indigenous exports of CoCom-controlled goods
4. Cooperation in prelicense and postshipment checks
5. Enforcement cooperation (includes cooperation in policing transshipments and free-trade zones)

CoCom partners agreed on primary and support assignments to approach a number of newly industrializing countries concerning cooperative agreements. A permanent working group, the Third Country Cooperation Working Group, was established to track progress in completing cooperative agreements. CoCom members are committed to support agreements reached with third countries and to use the control mechanisms installed in such countries.

Some CoCom countries have been reluctant to engage third countries in formal negotiations, primarily because they are uncomfortable with the extraterritorial nature of the TCC requirements. This lack of effort has been largely overlooked by the United States, in part because U.S. officials doubted the commitment of CoCom partners to negotiate agreements containing all five elements.

All CoCom countries use the IC/DV documents available from cooperating third countries to some degree. The real discrepancy in practice is in the area of reexports. Unlike the United States, other CoCom members expect that any general export control program put in place in a cooperating country will sufficiently cover reexports of CoCom-origin goods. **Thus, no other CoCom partner requires the type of authorization for reexport out of a CoCom or cooperating country required by the United States. The end result is a serious disadvantage for U.S. economic interests.**

Section 5(k) of the Export Administration Act requires that cooperating countries, or countries with export control systems comparable in practice to those in place in CoCom countries, be given preferential licensing treatment similar to that for CoCom countries and distinct from that for other nonproscribed countries. The preferential treatment, called 5(k) benefits, consists of the special or general license practices that automatically apply to CoCom members. U.S. officials have considered the 5(k) benefits as negotiating tools with third countries and have promised to grant the benefits incrementally in accordance with progress in implementing the five essential CoCom elements.

Nine distinct licensing benefits are available to third countries, although two of the provisions (G-Com and G-CEU) are outdated and are being eliminated. (Table 6-1 identifies the types of licenses available to specific cooperating third countries.) **Given the current licensing guidelines and processing times for most third countries, however, the only benefits of any significant value are the enhanced distribution license, permissive reexport exceptions, the broad general license for CoCom (G-CoCom), and the new general license for intra-CoCom trade (GCT).*** No country outside CoCom currently is eligible for GCT, although Switzerland and Finland receive all the other benefits, and Austria was expected to receive the same package by the end of 1990.

There are no CoCom-wide economic benefits to third countries for co-operation and no real penalty for noncooperation. In reality, most CoCom partners rarely restrict trade in CoCom-controlled goods with noncontrolled countries, except for trade in munitions and proliferation-related items. Further, most CoCom partners do not have the licensing resources to distinguish among nonproscribed destinations and may not even offer any special licensing privileges for exports to other CoCom countries.

A COMMON STANDARD OF LICENSING AND ENFORCEMENT;
INTRA-COCOM TRADE

In January 1988, an ad hoc working group on the "common standard level of effective protection" was established to improve harmonization of export controls. The establishment of this working group followed several special and high-level meetings to "reenergize" CoCom.

The "common standard" working group identified the elements of effective licensing and enforcement systems, which were then approved by the CoCom Executive Committee. All members were requested to submit analyses of their systems based on the agreed elements. The working group reviewed the submissions and summarized the basic areas for improvement. Members agreed at the June 1990 High-Level Meeting to comply fully with all elements by April 1991.

Members have repeatedly stated that while equally effective measures are essential, identical measures are not necessary. Thus, it is difficult to identify

---

*For a complete description of these provisions, see Sections 770, 773, and 774 of the Export Administration Regulations.

TABLE 6-1   Date of Receipt of 5(k) Export Licensing Benefits, by Country

Benefit	Austria	Finland	Singapore	Sweden	Switzerland
G-Com[a]	12-1-87	8-26-87	10-21-87	7-17-87	8-28-87
GCG[b]	12-1-87	11-15-88	10-21-87	7-17-87	8-28-87
G-CEU[c]		11-15-88		7-17-87	8-28-87
15/15 day[d]	3-1-88	8-26-87			8-28-87
PRC reexport[e]	12-1-87	11-15-88			8-28-87
Enhanced DL[f]		11-15-88			6-20-86
G-CoCom[g]		7-11-89			7-11-89
Reexport to CoCom[h]		7-7-89			7-7-89
GCT[i]					

NOTES: The dates indicate the day on which a *Federal Register* notice appeared granting the benefit to the country.

South Korea signed a Memorandum of Understanding with the United States in 1987, but the agreement was not ratified by the Korean parliament until 1989. South Korea was scheduled to receive GCG and 15/15 day licensing benefits in late 1990. Further benefits are predicated on implementation of the agreement.

[a] General license for CoCom and cooperating countries, G-Com, authorizes exports under general license of administrative exception note items (not advisory notes for the People's Republic of China, PRC) to countries listed in Part 771.18 of the Export Administration Regulations (EAR). G-Com was almost entirely subsumed in general license free-world, GFW, as expanded by the Omnibus Trade and Competitiveness Act of 1988.

[b] General license for cooperating governments, GCG, allows for export under general license of all controlled national security items to government agencies of countries designated as cooperating in Part 771.14 of the EAR.

[c] General license for certified end users, G-CEU, authorizes the export under general license of all national security controlled items, except supercomputers, to any entity that is "controlled in fact" by the government of the cooperating countries listed in Part 771.20 of the EAR.

[d] The "15/15" benefit requires that license applications for countries listed in Part 770.14 of the EAR be processed within 15 days after receipt, unless an extension is requested, in which case the government has an additional 15 days to complete the license processing.

[e] PRC permissive reexport allows countries listed in Part 774.2(j) of the EAR to reexport goods below the PRC "Green Line" to the PRC without prior approval from the U.S. government.

[f] The enhanced distribution license, DL, benefit makes a higher threshold of goods eligible for export under the distribution license for countries listed in Supplements 2 and 8 to Part 773 of the EAR.

[g] General license for CoCom, G-CoCom, authorizes the export under general license of items that require only notification to CoCom (not full review), including items below the PRC "Green Line" as of August 1988, to countries listed in Part 771.24 of the EAR.

[h] Permissive reexport to CoCom authorizes the reexport of all national security controlled items, with limited exceptions, to and among countries listed in Part 774.2(k) of the EAR without prior U.S. government authorization.

[i] General license for intra-CoCom trade, GCT, was not in final form as of December 1, 1990, but was published for comment in June 1990. GCT would authorize exports under general license of all national security controlled items, with limited exceptions, to CoCom countries.

SOURCE: U.S. Department of Commerce, Bureau of Export Administration.

specific deficiencies in any system since judgments of its effectiveness are subjective.

Another working group, this one on intra-CoCom trade (ICT), was established to review export control practices among members. This working group considered a number of options to reduce the burden of licensing practices for trade among members while minimizing the risk of diversion. The initial proposals involved the exchange of multiple copies of customs documents between exporting and importing governments and some combination of exporter and importer registration with their respective governments. The proposal that was ultimately accepted was a joint U.S.-Canadian scheme that retains a paper trail and some responsibility on the part of both the exporter and importer, while virtually eliminating government involvement.

Beyond these elements, CoCom members have not yet agreed on the scope of a new ICT system. This includes both the goods and the destinations that are eligible for license-free treatment. The United States supports the exclusion of a limited list of items from license-free treatment until all common standard elements are in place, as well as the eventual extension of license-free treatment to cooperating countries. All CoCom members have accepted, in principle, the exclusion of some items from license-free treatment until the target date for complete implementation of the common standard. However, members do not agree on the need for a common or joint list, opting instead for national exclusion lists. Most members also favor independence in determining destinations eligible for license-free treatment.

The Proliferation Challenge

The challenges to U.S. security interests posed by the proliferation of chemical and nuclear weapons and advanced missile delivery systems are addressed through the Export Administration Act, the Arms Export Control Act, and the Atomic Energy Act, as amended by the Nuclear Non-Proliferation Act. Many of the laws are directly related to U.S. obligations internationally.

NUCLEAR WEAPONS

The Nuclear Non-Proliferation Treaty of 1968 formed an agreement between the nations that possessed nuclear weapons in 1968 and those that did not. The nuclear "haves" pledged to work toward nuclear disarmament and to share peaceful nuclear technology with the "have nots." In return, the other signatory nations pledged not to attempt to acquire nuclear weapons.

The NNPT currently has over 140 signatories.* In addition, regional agreements exist that preclude the placement of nuclear weapons in Latin America, outer space, the seabed, the South Pacific, and Antarctica.

U.S. export controls on nuclear-related items were originally based on authority in the Atomic Energy Act of 1954. The Nuclear Non-Proliferation Act of 1978 updated the Atomic Energy Act and is the principal authority for the control of nuclear, dual use items. Although the NNPT does not specifically obligate signatories to institute and practice broad export controls, such controls are implicit in treaty commitments. In 1974, a group of countries signed a letter of agreement prohibiting the export of certain items to "non-weapon" states without a pledge of "no explosive use" and acceptance of International Atomic Energy Agency (IAEA) safeguards. The list of items triggering the need for assurances and IAEA safeguards became known as the "trigger list," and the group became known as the Zangger Committee,† after its first chairman, Claude Zangger.

In 1978, another group of countries committed themselves to similar, but more comprehensive export guidelines in support of nonproliferation goals and added technology and technical assistance to the "trigger" list. This group is known as the Nuclear Suppliers Group (NSG),‡ or London Suppliers Group (the group originally met in London).

MISSILE TECHNOLOGY

U.S. missile technology controls were implemented on July 31, 1987, by both the Departments of Commerce and State for items under their respective control, as part of the multilateral Missile Technology Control Regime (MTCR). The MTCR was developed in response to the challenge of missile proliferation and the ensuing threat to the security of its members and to world peace. The arrangement developed from the conventional arms talks of the 1970s into a formal arrangement in 1987 among France, Germany, Japan, Canada, the United Kingdom, Italy, and the United States. Australia, Spain, the Netherlands, Belgium, and Luxembourg have since joined the organization.

---

*Countries of proliferation concern that have not signed the NNPT are Argentina, Brazil, India, Israel, Pakistan, and South Africa. Among countries of concern that have signed the treaty are Iran, Iraq, and North Korea.

†The members of the Zangger Committee are Australia, Canada, Czechoslovakia, Denmark, Finland, the Federal Republic of Germany, the former German Democratic Republic, Greece, Hungary, Italy, Japan, Luxembourg, the Netherlands, Norway, Poland, Sweden, Switzerland, the United Kingdom, the United States, and the Soviet Union. (France, although not a signatory to the NNPT or to the letter in question, agreed to abide by the letter's guidelines.)

‡The members of the Nuclear Suppliers Group are Belgium, Canada, Czechoslovakia, France, the Federal Republic of Germany, the former German Democratic Republic, Italy, Japan, the Netherlands, Poland, Sweden, Switzerland, the United States, the United Kingdom, and the Soviet Union.

The MTCR's purpose is to restrict the export of goods and technology that could be used to produce a missile capable of carrying a nuclear payload. The parameters of control are missiles with ranges greater than 190 miles and payloads of more than 1,100 pounds (300 kilometers/500 kilograms). The MTCR includes guidelines for participants and an annex of items to be controlled, but national export decisions are not subject to group review or consensus. Exports of munitions items on the annex are to be denied to nonmembers, but dual use items can be exported with "appropriate assurances" from the government of the importing country. Multilateral cooperation is based on an agreement not to undercut the export denials of other members and to share intelligence on "projects of concern."

CHEMICAL WEAPONS

Twenty nations, under the leadership of Australia, have joined what has come to be known as the Australia Group.* The Australia Group identifies chemical precursors that could be significant in the development of chemical weapons and are being sought for such purposes. The Australia Group is meant to be an interim arrangement in anticipation of the Chemical Weapons Convention (CWC) currently being negotiated as part of the Conference on Disarmament.

The Australia Group has no formal basis and does not specify required conduct by its participants. Export controls or appropriate restrictions are recommended for trade in the chemicals identified as weapons precursors. Intelligence is shared among the participants on suspected chemical weapons development, and Iran, Iraq, Libya, and Syria have been identified as official targets of export controls. There are no collective sanctions for end-use violations.

Country-Specific Objectives

In addition to the East-West national security controls, nuclear proliferation controls, and other, foreign policy based proliferation controls, the United States targets a number of individual countries for specific export restrictions. Authority for these specific types of controls is found in Section 6 of the EAA and in the Trading with the Enemy Act of 1917, as amended by the International Emergency Economic Powers Act (IEEPA) of 1977. Before imposing controls under the IEEPA, the President must determine that a situation constitutes a national emergency or an "unusual and extraordinary

---

*The Australia Group consists of Australia, Austria, Belgium, Canada, Denmark, France, Germany, Greece, Ireland, Italy, Japan, Luxembourg, the Netherlands, New Zealand, Norway, Portugal, Spain, Switzerland, the United Kingdom, and the United States.

threat.'' The President invoked the IEEPA in 1990 when Iraq invaded Kuwait in order to authorize the trade embargo against Iraq. Export controls targeted at Cuba, Vietnam, North Korea, and Cambodia are grandfathered under the Trading with the Enemy Act, and controls targeted at Libya and Iran are maintained under the IEEPA, with corresponding controls under Section 6 of the EAA.

Section 6 of the EAA was used to impose extraterritorial foreign policy controls on oil and gas equipment to the Soviet Union in 1982. These controls had a particularly negative effect on U.S. trade relations because several West European countries had already signed contracts to participate in the construction of a Soviet gas pipeline to Western Europe. The uncompromising stance of the United States on the pipeline and its extraterritorial application of export restrictions damaged long-standing commercial relationships and directly contributed to the perception of the United States as an unreliable trade partner and supplier.

If U.S. exports to a specific destination are already controlled, an embargo or increased trade restrictions may be imposed through an executive branch directive to deny, delay, or ''closely review'' licenses. This type of country-specific restriction was put in place with respect to the People's Republic of China following the Tiananmen Square demonstrations in June 1989. Items subject to U.S. munitions controls can be blocked to destinations without invoking specific regulations.

The United States is not the only country to impose export restrictions outside a multilateral regime. A number of countries control items covered by the United Nations arms embargo against South Africa for anti-apartheid reasons, including the European Community (EC) and the Nordic countries. A number of countries restrict the export of military-related equipment to areas either engaged in conflict (e.g., Iraq-Kuwait) or where conflict is imminent. The EC collectively and the United States, the United Kingdom, Japan, France, Canada, Italy, and the Federal Republic of Germany individually ban sales of military equipment to Libya.

SPECIFIC CHARACTERISTICS OF U.S. EXPORT CONTROLS

Control List Management

Like CoCom, the United States separates controlled items into lists of munitions, industrial, and nuclear-related items. The U.S. lists are, respectively, the Munitions List (ML), the Commodity Control List (CCL), and the Nuclear Referral List (NRL). The Department of State (in consultation with Defense) generates and administers the Munitions List. The Department of Commerce, in consultation with Defense and other agencies, generates and administers the Commodity Control List. The Departments of Commerce and Energy, with assistance from the Nuclear Regulatory Commission and the national research laboratories, draw up the Nuclear Referral List,* which is incorporated in the CCL. By law, the CCL is to be reviewed annually. The law does not provide for periodic reviews of the Munitions List, and there is no established review cycle for the NRL.

Although the U.S. control lists are similar to the CoCom lists, they are not identical. For example, the U.S. Munitions List (defense articles and services maintained under the AECA) covers more items than the International Munitions List, and it is maintained for broader purposes than traditional CoCom objectives. The U.S. Munitions List also controls a number of dual use items that are on the CoCom Industrial List. The United States controls "nuclear-related" or dual use items through its Nuclear Referral List, whereas the International Atomic Energy List consists of items specifically designed or prepared for nuclear use.†

EAA NATIONAL SECURITY

The management of lists of items controlled for reasons of national security under the EAA is a complex process involving extensive technical review, policy input, internal dispute resolution, and negotiation of the U.S. position in CoCom (see Figure 6-1). The development of a CoCom core list during the second half of 1990 was handled differently from the usual U.S. list construction process. Prior to the CoCom High-Level Meeting in June 1990, the President directed the Joint Chiefs of Staff to conduct a study of the impact of increased access to Western technology on militarily critical Soviet mission areas. The results of that study figured prominently in the initial U.S. core list proposal to CoCom in June. It is unclear how the list construction process will be modified as a result of the core list exercise, but changes will be necessary, at least to reflect the new categories of controlled goods.

Construction and review of the national security aspects of the CCL begin with a reference document known as the Militarily Critical Technologies List (MCTL). The EAA directs the Defense Department to develop a list of militarily critical technologies, in particular:

- arrays of design and manufacturing know-how,
- keystone manufacturing, inspection, and test equipment,

---

*The list of specially designed nuclear equipment, materials, and facilities is found in 10 C.F.R. and is maintained by the Nuclear Regulatory Commission.

†The trigger list associated with the NNPT identifies nuclear items for control to "have-nots" under the NNPT and to nonsignatories. The CoCom IAEL identifies nuclear items for control to CoCom-proscribed destinations, many of which are signatories to the NNPT and possess nuclear weapons capability.

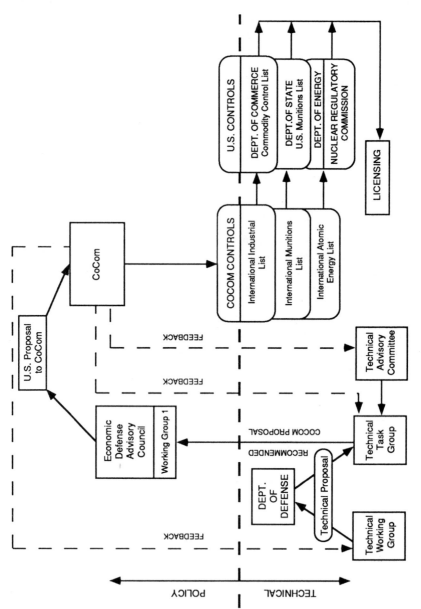

FIGURE 6-1 U.S. process for generating CoCom proposals

- goods accompanied by sophisticated operation, application, or maintenance know-how, and
- keystone equipment that would reveal or give insight into the design and manufacture of U.S. military systems that are not possessed by, or available from sources outside U.S.-controlled countries, and that, if exported, would permit a significant advance in a military system of any such country.[2]

The Department of Defense (DoD) contracts the task of drawing up the list to the Institute for Defense Analyses (IDA). Primary technical inputs are obtained through a series of technical working groups (TWGs), established and managed by IDA, which are composed of representatives from industry, academia, and government.

Interagency technical task groups (TTGs) devise proposed entries for the CoCom Industrial List using information from the MCTL, the existing list, and recommendations from concerned agencies. The TTGs are made up of government experts from the Departments of Defense, Commerce, State, and occasionally, Energy and the intelligence community; industry representatives may serve in an advisory role. The TTGs also receive input from a number of technical advisory committees (TACs), which are made up of industry and government experts and authorized by the EAA. The TTGs forward control list proposals to the Economic Defense Advisory Council (EDAC) Working Group I. This working group, led by the State Department, then communicates the U.S. position to CoCom.

The EAA also explicitly calls for the consideration of foreign availability in the list construction and review process. As defined in Section 5 of the EAA, "foreign availability" exists when any good or technology is available in fact from a non-U.S. source(s) in sufficient quantity and of comparable quality to make the requirement of a validated license ineffective. The Commerce Department's Office of Foreign Availability is responsible for assessing the foreign availability of controlled items in response to claims from industry or the TACs, or on its own initiative. The results of a formal assessment may be either positive or negative; a positive finding indicates that all the criteria for determining foreign availability were met, and a negative finding indicates that they were not. A positive finding may lead to decontrol of the item in question, unless the foreign source(s) agrees to control the item. The results of foreign availability assessments, as well as information from the assessment itself, are ordinarily injected into the list review process by the Department of Commerce.

A committee structure exists to resolve disputes over the list construction process for national security controls. The first level for resolving disputes over the control list is also the last level of operational review—EDAC Working Group I. It is chaired by the State Department and may include representatives of the Defense, Commerce, and Energy Departments, the National Aeronautics and Space Administration (NASA), and the intelligence community. Disputes that are unresolved in Working Group I may be referred to the EDAC itself, which is also chaired by the State Department and includes representatives at the deputy assistant secretary level from the Defense and Commerce Departments, along with other agencies as required.

Disputes that are not resolved through the EDAC structure usually reflect disagreements in interpreting basic U.S. policy rather than arguments over matters of a technical nature. The resolution of policy disputes is handled through two policy coordinating committees (PCCs) reporting to the National Security Council (NSC). The PCC on Technology Transfer handles CoCom-related issues at the under secretary level and is chaired by the NSC. The PCC on Non-Proliferation is chaired by the State Department's under secretary for security assistance, science and technology, with an observer from the NSC. It deals with trade issues relating to the spread of nuclear and chemical weapons and missile delivery capabilities. Disputes that the PCCs cannot resolve are forwarded through appropriate channels to the President, which seldom happens.

EAA Foreign Policy

Although the Nuclear Non-Proliferation Act is the principal authority for nuclear export controls, controls on items that are not specially designed for nuclear use but which could be of significance for nuclear explosive purposes are implemented under the EAA. Since nuclear controls are not aimed at traditional national security targets, they often are considered foreign policy controls. In fact, they are covered under Section 17 of the EAA, rather than either Section 5 or Section 6.

Four lists identify items controlled for purposes of nuclear nonproliferation: (1) the trigger lists maintained by the Zangger Committee and the Nuclear Suppliers Group; (2) the Nuclear Referral List maintained by the Departments of Commerce and Energy, which is made up of items that are not specially designed or prepared for nuclear uses but that could be of significance for nuclear explosive purposes; (3) 10 C.F.R. 110, which consists of specially designed nuclear equipment, materials, and facilities; and (4) 10 C.F.R. 810, which identifies controlled technology and technical assistance. The Zangger Committee and NSG lists are essentially the same, except that the Zangger list is more specific and the NSG list includes technology. These two lists correspond to 10 C.F.R. 110 and 810.

The annex to the multilateral Missile Technology Control Regime identifies two categories of items that could contribute significantly to the development of nuclear-capable missiles. Category 1 of the annex contains munitions items, and most of category 2 covers dual use items. This annex has been translated into various entries on the U.S. Munitions List and Commodity Control List. Most of the items listed in the annex fall on the Munitions List.

Chemical agents or chemical weapons are controlled under the authority of the Arms Export Control Act, and chemicals that may be precursors of chemical weapons are considered dual use and are controlled under the Export Administration Act. The Australia Group has identified a core list of 11 chemical weapons precursors and a warning list of 39 precursors. The Department of Commerce administers these controls.

MUNITIONS LIST

The Arms Export Control Act is the basis for the International Traffic in Arms Regulations (ITAR), which contain the U.S. Munitions List. According to the 1976 AECA, "The President is authorized to designate those items which shall be considered as defense articles and defense services." Four considerations are listed in the ITAR for determining whether something is a defense item:

1. Whether an item "is deemed inherently military in character."
2. Whether an item "has a predominantly military application."
3. The fact that an item has military and civil uses "does not in and of itself determine" whether it is classified as a defense article.
4. "Intended use . . . is also not relevant" to an item's classification.[3]

The AECA and, in turn, the President give the State Department complete authority to determine whether an item is a defense article.

The list construction process for the Munitions List is not nearly as lengthy or involved as for the CCL because the ML does not contain the same degree of detail on performance parameters or the technical characteristics of controlled items as found in the CCL. Moreover, a large part of the ML construction process is dynamic in that categories, rather than performance parameters, of items are listed and control determinations often are made on the basis of individual interpretations.

Regulations

Each October, the Department of Commerce publishes the Export Administration Regulations (EAR),[4] which state how the Export Administration Act is to be implemented. Changes are published in the *Federal Register* to update the EAR during the year. Changes in existing regulations or new regulations are first circulated for interagency review and comment; the Office of Management and Budget also reviews the regulations. Public comments are usually sought and are ordinarily summarized with publication of the final regulation in the *Federal Register*.

The EAR describes items subject to export control and the requirements for their export to various destinations. It also details the potential penalties for violations of the Export Administration Act.

The regulations divide the various types of export licenses required into three categories: general licenses, special licenses, and individual licenses. General licenses, with some exceptions, do not require prior government approval, but they must be noted on a Census Bureau Shippers Export Declaration, which is filed with U.S. Customs when an item is exported. Both special and individual licenses require prior government approval, but special licenses allow for multiple and continuing transactions under one validation, whereas individual licenses must be validated on a case-by-case basis.

As of December 1990, the destinations listed in the EAR as targeted by the United States for national security purposes were the Soviet Union, Eastern Europe, and the embargoed countries of North Korea, Vietnam, Cuba, and Cambodia.

The following is a descriptive listing of the various U.S. foreign policy and nonproliferation controls outlined in the Export Administration Regulations.

• *Crime control*[5]   An individual license is required to export crime control and detection instruments and equipment and related technical data to any destination *except* NATO members, Japan, Australia, and New Zealand. The purpose of the control is to ensure that U.S.-origin police equipment is not exported to countries whose governments do not respect internationally recognized human rights standards and to distance the United States from human rights violations.

• *Antiterrorism*[6]   Certain countries are designated by the Secretary of State as supporting terrorism, including North Korea, Cuba, Iran, Libya, Syria, and the People's Democratic Republic of Yemen. An individual license is required to export all national security controlled goods, as well as some aircraft, to these destinations in order to prevent contributions to their ability to support acts of international terrorism.

• *Regional stability*[7]   The objective of regional stability controls is to deny military items to certain regions of the world where conflict and tension prevail and thereby limit the possibility that American equipment will contribute to the destabilization of such regions. Regional stability controls apply to exports to all destinations, *except* NATO countries, Australia, Japan, and New Zealand. Commodities subject to individual license requirements include military vehicles and certain equipment used to manufacture military equipment.

• *Embargoed countries*[8]   There is a presumption of denial for virtually all exports to Cuba, Cambodia, North Korea, Vietnam, and Libya. Controls are also maintained by the Treasury Department under the Trading with the

Enemy Act. The objective of the embargo is to demonstrate the unwillingness of the United States to maintain normal trade relations with embargoed countries until they take steps to improve relations and/or change their political behavior.

• *South Africa*[9]   The United States maintains controls, with the presumption of denial, on the export of all national security controlled commodities and technical data to South African military and police entities. Munitions are controlled to all entities pursuant to the United Nations arms embargo of South Africa. In addition, the export of aircraft, helicopters, crude oil, refined petroleum products, and computers and software to any end user in South Africa requires an individual license.

• *Biological organisms*[10]   The United States maintains controls on the export of certain viruses and bacteria to all destinations except Canada. These controls are intended to prevent the development of weapons for biological warfare.

• *Nuclear nonproliferation*[11]   Nuclear controls are maintained by the United States for reasons of nonproliferation. License requirements are imposed on commodities and technologies that could be significant for nuclear explosive purposes. Products and technologies affected include, in addition to those contributing directly to nuclear explosives, those that could be used in the production of special nuclear material or equipment. In addition, all commodities and technical data are controlled to sensitive nuclear production facilities in all countries.

• *Missile technology controls*[12]   This section of the EAR lists certain types of equipment and related technical data that require an individual license for export to all destinations except the United Kingdom, France, the Federal Republic of Germany, Canada, Italy, Spain, Japan, and the Benelux countries. The primary factors for consideration in licensing decisions also are listed.

• *Chemical weapons*[13]   The United States maintains individual license requirements on the export of 50 precursor chemicals that could be used in the manufacture of chemical weapons. Currently, there is a presumption of denial for exports to Libya, Iran, Iraq, and Syria and to any other destination if there is reason to believe that the chemicals will be used in the production of chemical weapons or otherwise be devoted to chemical warfare purposes.

License Processing

National Security Cases

Three agencies are most prominently involved in national security license processing and review. In the Commerce Department, the Bureau of Export Administration (BXA) administers the licensing process for items on the

Commodity Control List. The State Department's Center for Defense Trade, Office of Defense Trade Controls, formerly the Office of Munitions Control, and its parallel policy arm, the Office of Defense Trade Policy, process licenses for items on the Munitions List.

The Defense Department's Defense Technology Security Administration (DTSA) reviews cases referred to it by both the State and Commerce Departments. Although DTSA has no specific statutory export control authority, Section 10(g) of the EAA authorizes a consulting role for the Defense Department in license review, and a 1985 executive order gives DTSA review responsibility for certain dual use exports to noncontrolled destinations that may pose a risk of diversion to a proscribed destination. DTSA also reviews most dual use exports to proscribed destinations. License applications for items controlled under the ITAR may be referred to the Defense Department and other appropriate agencies as necessary.

According to data provided by the Center for Defense Trade, approximately 54,000 licenses, with a total value of $57 billion, were processed in FY 1989. The average processing time for munitions cases dropped from 61 days in 1987 to 49 days in 1989, for roughly the same case load. Based on a two-month sample, a further significant decline in processing times was expected for 1990 (see Table 6-2).

The State Department reorganized the munitions licensing function under the Center for Defense Trade early in 1990 due, at least in part, to repeated complaints from industry of unnecessary time delays and general incompetence. Additional personnel, resources, and automated licensing equipment have been acquired and continued expansion is planned.

According to data provided by the Commerce Department, BXA processed close to 81,000 individual cases, with a value of more than $132 billion, in 1989 (see Table 6-3). Of those cases, 92 percent were approved (valued at more than $122 billion). An additional $34 billion is estimated to be exported under U.S. distribution licenses. The average processing time for all individual cases dropped from 28 days in 1985 to 17 days in 1989. The 1989 processing times for cases that Commerce handled without referral to other agencies ranged from 4 days for exports to CoCom to 28 days for exports to the Soviet Union and East European countries. Processing times in 1989 for cases that required referral to other agencies, either for reasons of national security or foreign policy, ranged from 49 days for exports to CoCom to 129 days for exports to the PRC. This includes the time required for CoCom to review PRC and Eastern bloc cases. CoCom and U.S. review of exports to the PRC, for example, has been slow since June 1989 (see Table 6-3). Exports to CoCom and other nonproscribed countries that require referral are likely to be very sensitive.

The Commerce Department is required by law to issue quarterly reports to Congress on cases pending beyond statutory licensing time limits. These

TABLE **6-2**   License Processing by Center for Defense Trade, Department of State, FY1987–FY1989

Fiscal Year	Munitions Licenses Processed	Average Processing Time
1987		
Number	52,879	61 business days
Value (billions)	$40.3	
1988		
Number	51,823	49
Value (billions)	$39.9	
1989		
Number	53,780	49
Value (billions)	$56.5	

Breakdown of Average Processing Time, April 1–May 31, 1990

	Number of Cases	Number of Business Days
Nonreferred	6,797 (71%)	4
Referred	2,654 (28%)	36
Weighted average		13

NOTE: Processing time for a license begins when a case is logged in at the Department of State and ends when a licensing determination is forwarded to the exporter.

SOURCE: U.S. Department of State, Center for Defense Trade.

reports indicate that the large majority (usually 70 percent or more) are held pending further interagency review or dispute resolution. Many delayed cases also may be awaiting government-to-government assurances or the results of prelicense checks. Nonetheless, the cases pending beyond statutory deadlines generally represent less than 1 percent, by volume, of all cases received during the quarter (see Table 6-4).

Two additional steps should further expedite the licensing process. First, the Defense and Commerce Departments reached an agreement in 1990 whereby Commerce licenses national security exports to the Soviet Union and Eastern Europe at the administrative exception level without DoD review. Second, the new GCT, or general license for intra-CoCom trade, eliminates many requirements for validated licenses for exports to CoCom members.

The Export Administration Review Board (EARB) exists for resolution of disputes over U.S. national security licenses under the EAA.* The lowest

---

*A revision of the EARB dispute resolution process was in progress at the time of publication. It is anticipated that the revision will expand the role of the EARB to cover foreign policy cases, as well as national security cases.

TABLE **6-3**   Department of Commerce License Processing Times (in business days), 1989

	1985	1986	1987	1988	1989
All cases					
Average	28	25	21	17	17
Nonreferred	17	14	10	8	8
Referred	98	59	59	61	67
Nonreferred cases					
Free world[a]	16	13	9	7	7
CoCom	14	10	5	5	4
China	31	23	18	16	21
Eastern bloc	40	45	27	16	28
Referred cases					
Free world[a]	59	38	41	50	50
CoCom	35	26	19	42	49
China	172	172	169	126	129
Eastern bloc	151	146	111	82	83

Disposition of Licenses Processed in 1989

Approved	74,905 =	$122.88 billion
Returned w/o action	5,677 =	9.08
Rejected	484 =	0.40
Total	81,066 =	132.36

NOTE: Processing time for a license begins when a case is assigned to a licensing officer at the Department of Commerce and ends when a licensing determination is made.

[a]Department of Commerce designation for all nonproscribed, non-CoCom countries.

SOURCE: U.S. Department of Commerce, Bureau of Export Administration.

level of the EARB is the Operating Committee, which reviews agency positions on U.S. licenses for export to proscribed destinations and to the PRC. It is chaired by the director of BXA and consists of representatives at the level of office director from the Defense and State Departments, among other participants. Disputes unresolved at this level may go to the Advisory Committee on Export Policy, an assistant-secretary-level body. The third and highest level is the cabinet-level EARB itself. The board is chaired by the secretary of commerce, and the secretaries of defense and state are members. High-ranking intelligence officials and other agency representatives may be asked to attend, as appropriate.

The Export Administration Act places certain time limits on case review. EARB guidelines attempt to manage dispute resolution within those time frames. Once the Commerce Department has received licensing recommendations from other agencies and made a preliminary licensing decision, other departments are given 10 days to either accept the decision or take the matter

TABLE 6-4   Department of Commerce License Cases Pending Beyond
Statutory Deadlines

| | | | Reasons for Pending Cases | | |
Period	Cases Completed[a]	Over Deadline	Interagency Review[b]	Awaiting Government Assurances	PLCs[c]
First quarter 1989	21,688	911	754	145	134
Second quarter 1989	21,136	775	578	69	163
Third quarter 1989	21,610	797	595	51	137
Fourth quarter 1989	20,783	816	555	48	162
First quarter 1990	17,523	375	299	32	28

NOTE: In addition to the reasons outlined above, cases also may be pending receipt of responses to negative consideration (denial) letters or being held without action at the exporter's request. Some cases may be pending for more than one reason.

[a]The number of cases does not include cases referred to the Subgroup on Nuclear Export Control, cases for export to CoCom or fully cooperating countries, or special license cases.

[b]Either currently under interagency review or have required interagency review.

[c]Prelicense checks or investigations.

SOURCE: U.S. Department of Commerce, Bureau of Export Administration.

to a higher level of review. If the Commerce Department does not receive a letter within this time requesting escalation of the case, it proceeds with the license.

FOREIGN POLICY CASES

As previously noted, a number of different controls are maintained for foreign policy or nonproliferation purposes. The Department of Commerce administers the dual use licensing program for each of the different foreign policy controls, with guidance from the Departments of State, Defense, and Energy and the intelligence community.

Basic U.S. trade policy with respect to items related to nuclear and chemical weapons and missile technology is handled by the Policy Coordinating Committee on Non-Proliferation. This PCC, as noted, is chaired by the under secretary of state for security assistance, science and technology and includes representatives at the under secretary level from the relevant government agencies. The committee deals with such issues as the fundamental goals of U.S. controls on items related to proliferation, U.S. efforts to gain international cooperation in controlling certain items, and the executive branch position on legislation related to proliferation activities.

Nuclear

The Nuclear Regulatory Commission issues licenses for nuclear research, power plants, special equipment and materials, and items associated with nuclear reactors. The Department of Energy authorizes the provision of technical assistance and information for nuclear technology, as well as any subsequent arrangements for previously exported U.S. nuclear items. The Center for Defense Trade licenses items related to nuclear weapons. The United States currently is the only country that officially maintains controls on a number of nuclear-related dual use items.

Department of Commerce individual licenses are required for exports of dual use, Nuclear Referral List items for certain countries, end uses, or end users. An individual validated license is required for the export of *any* item for which the exporter ''knows or has reason to know'' that the item will be used in sensitive nuclear activities. There is a presumption of denial of all items to unsafeguarded nuclear facilities. The United States also restricts sales of nuclear-related items to safeguarded facilities if they are in countries where all facilities are not subject to safeguards.

Applications to export NRL items are reviewed by the Commerce Department with assistance from the Energy Department. If the Department of Energy deems it necessary, the application is sent to the Subgroup on Nuclear Export Coordination (SNEC). The SNEC is chaired by the State Department's Bureau of Oceans and International Environmental and Scientific Affairs and includes representatives from the Defense, Energy, and Commerce Departments, the Nuclear Regulatory Commission, and the Arms Control and Disarmament Agency (ACDA). The SNEC forwards its licensing recommendations to the Commerce Department. Disputes on the appropriate licensing action may be referred to the EARB or the PCC on Non-Proliferation, as appropriate.

Missile Technology

License applications for munitions items that are also subject to missile controls are reviewed based on the stated country of destination and end use. The State Department's Center for Defense Trade may seek recommendations from DoD, ACDA, and the intelligence community in making a licensing decision. License applications for dual use items that are subject to missile controls are reviewed based on the factors listed in Part 776.18 of the EAR as follows:

- assessment of the end use;
- significance of the export in terms of the potential development of missiles capable of delivering nuclear weapons;

- capabilities and objectives of the missile and space programs of the recipient country;
- nonproliferation credentials of the importing country; and
- types of assurances or guarantees against use for nuclear weapons delivery purposes or proliferation given in a particular case.

The Commerce Department initially reviews license applications to determine the potential contribution of the items to missile development and the sensitivity of the end use and end user based on information from the intelligence community. Applications for items that could make a significant contribution and are destined to countries identified as being of potential concern are referred to the interagency Missile Technology Export Control (MTEC) group, chaired by State's Bureau of Politico-Military Affairs (PM), Office of Weapons Proliferation Policy.

The PM bureau chairs MTEC meetings on U.S. export licensing decisions and foreign sales to missile-related programs on alternate weeks. The Commerce and Defense Departments, ACDA, NASA, and the intelligence community are represented in these interagency meetings. Licensing recommendations, including provisions for certain conditions or government-to-government assurances, are forwarded to Commerce. If government-to-government assurances are necessary, they are requested by State from the recipient government on behalf of Commerce. Disputes on the appropriate licensing action may be referred to the PCC on Non-Proliferation.

Chemicals

The United States requires an individual license for export of core list chemicals to any destination, except other Australia Group members; exports of chemicals on the warning list to Libya, Syria, Iran, or Iraq require an individual license. There is a presumption of denial for applications to export chemicals on the core or warning lists to Libya, Syria, Iran, or Iraq. Applications to export chemicals on the lists to other destinations identified by the intelligence community as being of potential concern are referred by Commerce to State's Economic Bureau. Disputes on the appropriate licensing action may be referred to the PCC on Non-Proliferation.

Enforcement

The U.S. Customs Service and BXA's Office of Export Enforcement share responsibility for export enforcement functions. The Customs enforcement program covers all export control laws, including the Export Administration Act, Arms Export Control Act, Atomic Energy Act, and Trading with the Enemy Act, as well as other, unrelated laws. Interdiction efforts related to the Export Administration Act are carried out by approximately 100 Customs inspectors, about 300 criminal investigators, and efforts at international cooperation through 19 overseas offices. The Customs enforcement program involves random inspections of exports at ports of exit, industry outreach, and investigations of potential violations. Potential criminal cases are forwarded to the Department of Justice for prosecution. Cases for civil penalties under the EAA must be forwarded to the Department of Commerce. Although the Arms Export Control Act contains provisions for civil penalties, the State Department has no mechanism for adjudicating contested penalties.

The Commerce Department's Office of Export Enforcement focuses solely on enforcement of the Export Administration Act. It has eight domestic offices and two overseas posts. Enforcement operations include industry outreach and a number of preventive measures, such as license screening and prelicense checks of the stated end use and end user. The Office of Export Enforcement also investigates potential export control violations. The Commerce Department may either forward cases to the Department of Justice for criminal prosecution or levy civil penalties for violations, or both. The Commerce Department also may deny export privileges to both national and foreign parties by placing them on the "Table of Denial Orders" (TDO). Parties denied export privileges on the TDO may not take part in any way in any export-related transaction.

Among the positive developments in export enforcement are the steps Customs has taken toward an automated data entry system for shipping and trade documents and a greater emphasis by both agencies on industry outreach and on violations of controls on nuclear, missile, and chemical items. The Commerce Department has also upgraded its enforcement training programs to include comprehensive training on the Export Administration Act.

BASIC PROBLEMS OF THE U.S. EXPORT CONTROL REGIMES

Multiplicity of Statutes, Agencies, and Regimes

Export controls are issued under a multiplicity of statutes with differing objectives and criteria (see Tables 6-5 and Figures 6-2–6-4).[14] The statutes themselves were not coordinated at the time they were written and come under the supervision of different congressional committees. Over a dozen agencies, plus the military services, are engaged in administering controls and apply distinct regulatory provisions that often overlap and conflict. The lead agencies in constructing export control policy hold strongly diverse positions corresponding to their separate interests. As a result, these disparate agencies are often unable to integrate the various national security, economic, and foreign policy issues and give executive authorities a balanced, coherent view of the key issues.

As part of its evaluation of the export control system, the panel asked the Congressional Research Service (CRS) to examine other issue areas in the government characterized by shared authority among multiple regulatory agencies. **The CRS was unable to find an analogous area with a comparable number of differing bureaucracies and regulatory categories.**

A number of solutions to this problem have been suggested in draft legislation and by industry observers, ranging from the creation of a new agency, to consolidation of all functions in one agency, to elimination of all export controls. The objective of any new organizational scheme should be to simplify the administration of export controls and minimize interagency redundancy.

Jurisdictional Disputes

In many instances it is unclear which administrative agency has jurisdiction over a particular category of items. Neither the trade laws nor the implementing regulations of the various agencies provide clear standards for determining the correct authority covering the export.

Fundamental disagreements among the various agencies as to the appropriate working definitions of basic terms that determine jurisdiction, such as "defense article," "militarily critical," and even "national security," have crippled the system and led to acute interagency in-fighting. **A disproportionate amount of bureaucratic resources are thus expended in resolving disputes, rather than administering and enforcing the export control system.**

Broad interpretation of the term "defense article" has resulted in the inclusion on the U.S. Munitions List of many dual use items that are either on the CoCom Industrial List or are not multilaterally controlled at all. As a result, a range of commercially used items, from metal fasteners to air conditioning units to civilian aerospace equipment, are unilaterally controlled as munitions items by the United States.

There is no cross-referencing between the Commodity Control List and Munitions List and very little public guidance for exporters on how to determine which regime applies to their exports. Although the International Traffic in Arms Regulations contain a procedure for establishing commodity jurisdiction whereby the Office of Defense Trade Controls determines (on written request and in consultation with the State, Commerce, and Defense Departments) whether the item in question is contained on the Munitions List, there is no effective opportunity for the Department of Commerce to have an equal voice in this process, and there are no accepted criteria for making a decision. This situation has generated calls for making operationally

TABLE 6-5 Matrix of National Security Controls

Control Purpose	Agency	Legislation[a]	Scope of Controls	Control Regime
Prevent acquisition of militarily critical items by Soviet bloc countries	Commerce, Bureau of Export Administration (BXA)	Export Administration Act (EAA)	Militarily critical civil goods and technology	CoCom (Industrial List)
	State, Center for Defense Trade (CDT)	Arms Export Control Act (AECA)	Defense articles and services	CoCom (International Munitions List)
	Nuclear Regulatory Commission (NRC)/ Energy	Atomic Energy Act/ Nuclear Non-Proliferation Act (AEA/NNPA)	Nuclear weapons design and test equipment	CoCom (International Atomic Energy List)
Nuclear proliferation	Commerce (BXA)	EAA/NNPA	Dual use products; nuclear technology;[b] sensitive nuclear uses[c]	None
	State (CDT)	AECA	Nuclear weapons design and test equipment	Nuclear Non-Proliferation Treaty
	NRC	AEA/NNPA	Nuclear power generation, nuclear material, and fuel-cycle equipment and technology	Nuclear Suppliers Group (NSG)/Zangger Committee
	Energy	AEA/NNPA	Technical assistance and subsequent arrangements	NSG

	Agency	Legislation	Items	Regime
Chemical weapons proliferation	Commerce (BXA)	EAA	Chemical weapons precursors	Australia Group
	State (CDT)	AECA	Chemical weapons agents	None
Biological weapons proliferation	Commerce (BXA)	EAA	Biological weapons precursors	Biological Weapons Convention
	State (CDT)	AECA	Biological weapons agents	Biological Weapons Convention
Missile system proliferation	Commerce (BXA)	EAA	Designated commodities and technology	Missile Technology Control Regime
	State (CDT)	AECA	Missiles, launch facilities	Missile Technology Control Regime
Conventional weapons proliferation	State (CDT) and DoD (Defense Security Assistance Agency)	AECA	Defense articles and services	None
"Emergencies"	Commerce (BXA)	Trading with the Enemy Act (TWEA)/ International Emergency Economic Powers Act (IEEPA)	Export embargoes	None
	State (CDT)	AECA	Defense articles and services	None
	Treasury, Office of Foreign Assets Control	TWEA/IEEPA	Transaction prohibitions	None

[a] See text note 14 for relevant excerpts of the legislation cited.
[b] Items that could be of significance in nuclear applications, but are not specially designed or produced for nuclear applications.
[c] Any export of a good or technology that the exporter knows, or has reason to know, will be used in a sensitive nuclear activity.

90

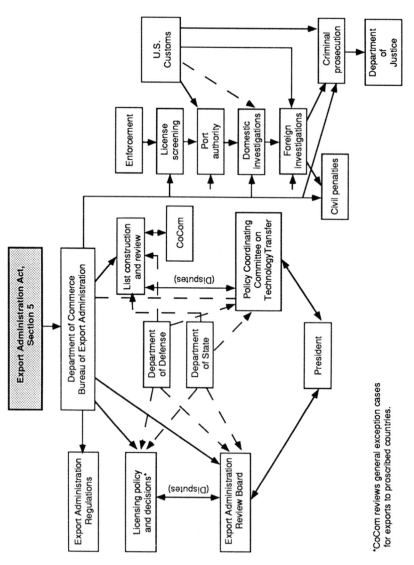

FIGURE 6-2 National security export control process

*CoCom reviews general exception cases for exports to proscribed countries.

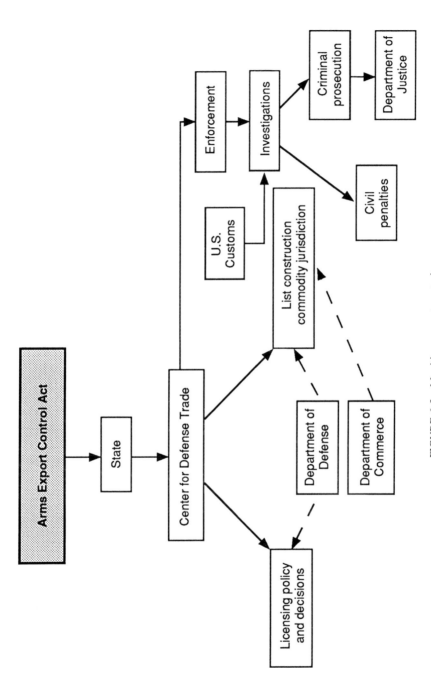

FIGURE 6-3 Munitions export control process

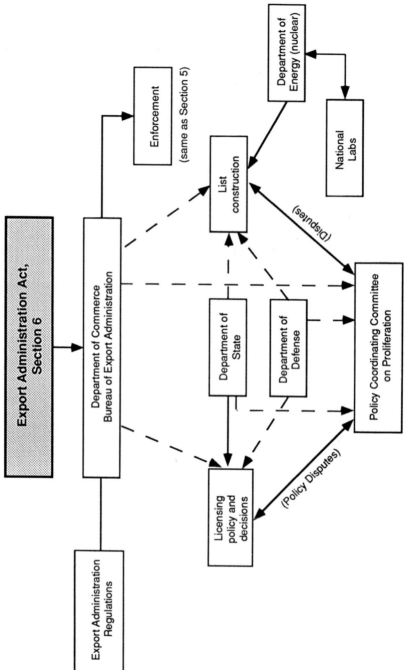

FIGURE 6-4 Foreign policy export control process

useful distinctions between defense articles controlled under authority of the Arms Export Control Act and items controlled under the Export Administration Act. Jurisdictional disputes also arise over Defense Department authority to review exports to nonproscribed destinations for national security purposes, Defense Department authority to review cases controlled for foreign policy reasons, and Department of Energy review of dual use goods controlled for purposes other than nuclear nonproliferation.

The confusion over which law and which set of agency regulations pertain to particular items has caused delay and expense for U.S. exporters. The working definitions and interpretations of various key terms should reflect overall U.S. goals with respect to specific export control programs and should be clearly understood by all agencies with implementation responsibilities. Although presidential executive orders and national security directives outlining basic export control objectives and establishing some dispute resolution mechanisms have been issued periodically, there has been too little explicit guidance on the priorities, interpretations, and jurisdiction of export control policies.

Licensing Complexity

A complex pattern of overlapping and sometimes conflicting regulations must be understood by exporters even though no single agency's responsibilities span more than one set of regulations. The license process for items under the International Traffic in Arms Regulations is considerably different from that for items under the Export Administration Regulations. The system is further complicated by different licenses being introduced under the EAR for the purpose of relaxing controls at different levels of West-West trade, as well as different levels of control and license conditions for proscribed countries and proliferation concerns. For example, as of late 1990, there were three general licenses for trade with CoCom: GCT, G-CoCom, and G-Com (refer to Table 6-1). Distinctions are also made between Hungary, Poland, and Czechoslovakia and the rest of Eastern Europe and the Soviet Union in terms of goods eligible for export without full CoCom review. Although a controlled item might be eligible for export under a general or special license to a certain destination for national security purposes, the export of the same item to the same destination might require an individual validated license for a foreign policy purpose.

Processing of licenses may take several months, especially for shipments to China, the Soviet Union, or Eastern Europe, and this does not include the time spent in preparing the license application or determining that a license is required. Foreign-based multinational corporations that use U.S.-origin goods and technology find compliance requirements very difficult, and most find it necessary to employ U.S. consultants or law firms to keep track of the system. Small and medium-sized companies, both U.S. and foreign majority-owned, that lack the resources necessary to make sense of U.S. export laws often simply give up the effort to seek new international markets for U.S.-manufactured products.

Overlapping Enforcement

Domestically, overlapping jurisdiction and lack of communication between Customs and the Commerce Department Office of Export Enforcement have sometimes resulted in their working on the same case without each other's knowledge. The Export Administration Act, as amended, states that the Customs Service and the Commerce Department can conduct—separately or mutually—EAA-related investigations within the United States. At borders or ports of entry, the Commerce Department must give the Customs Service prior notice of its investigation. Outside the United States, the jurisdictional lines blur. Neither the Department of Commerce nor the Customs Service actually "investigates" overseas; rather, they coordinate with overseas law enforcement agencies to obtain evidence needed for U.S. domestic cases. Commerce enforcement agents must obtain Customs concurrence to travel abroad.

According to the Commerce Department's International Trade Administration, "to ensure their effective cooperation in export control, Commerce and Customs will routinely and promptly exchange licensing and enforcement information, including advising as to the opening and closing of investigations."[15] Despite this guidance, the Customs Service and BXA's Office of Export Enforcement have not been able to establish an official, working mechanism to coordinate enforcement activities.

As for sanctions, the levels of sanctions for violations and the circumstances that must be established for their imposition vary from statute to statute. Sanctions have developed over the years through ad hoc legislation, and no effort has been made to assess and systemize them. A critical decision as an investigation progresses is whether to recommend criminal prosecution, civil penalties, or both. Depending on the nature of the violation, civil penalties might be a more effective deterrent than criminal prosecution and vice versa. There is, however, no agreed, interagency standard for cases that warrant criminal prosecution as opposed to cases that should be addressed through civil penalties. Moreover, consultation between Commerce and Customs on the appropriate action is limited.

In the administration of civil penalties, the Commerce Department makes use of an administrative law judge and judicial review.* Although the Arms

---

*An issue in this procedure deserving further study is that the Commerce Department, which lacks the same degree of independence as an administrative law judge, has the power to modify the decisions of an administrative law judge.

Export Control Act provides for civil penalties, the State Department does not have a comparable system. Both the Customs Service and the Treasury Department's Office of Foreign Assets Control use what can be characterized as a primitive "show cause" civil penalty process without an administrative law judge. The use of a denial order is peculiar to the Export Administration Act,* and a number of export control statutes, including the Trading with the Enemy Act and the Atomic Energy Act, lack civil enforcement provisions.

Another area of enforcement overlap involves U.S. and foreign enforcement activities. Although the denial order as applied to foreign parties has proven to be an effective enforcement tool, it is generally regarded abroad as an illegitimate exercise of U.S. authority. Also controversial is denial of U.S. import and government contracting privileges to foreign parties not abiding by U.S. or multilateral export control measures. Such denials now apply only to foreign exports in violation of multilateral security controls, but they have been proposed for other situations. **Unilateral U.S. adoption of extraterritorial sanctions such as these may seriously undermine U.S. efforts to achieve effective export control cooperation.**

Despite the need for multilateral action, Customs and BXA officials report that while other CoCom governments are generally cooperative in assisting U.S. investigations, they seldom initiate their own investigations or request information from the United States on the credibility of end users. Some CoCom countries use the U.S. Table of Denial Orders as a list of potentially unreliable end users, but other CoCom countries do not recognize that list at all. Further, there is no CoCom-wide mechanism for identifying suspicious parties or parties that have been proven unreliable.

Outdated and Confusing Control Lists

The system of U.S. list management suffers from a lack of clear definitions and criteria for control and decontrol, as well as the widely varying formats and structures that exist in domestic and international lists. The Militarily Critical Technologies List is supposed to be the basis for U.S. proposals for items on the CoCom Industrial List and U.S. Commodity Control List. However, many items that are not on the MCTL remain on the CoCom and U.S. lists, and the United States has not proposed their removal. A recent report by the Institute for Defense Analyses evaluated the CoCom Industrial List on the basis of control parameters in the MCTL. Of 115 controlled categories examined, the report recommended additional controls for 17 percent of the categories, no change for 13 percent, deletion for 10 percent, and some decontrol of *60 percent* (69 categories).[16] **The fact**

---

*The provision for a denial order under the AECA might be redundant since every munitions case is reviewed on an individual basis and may be denied if the parties involved are not reliable.

that an item is taken off the MCTL does not necessarily lead to U.S. action to delete it from the CoCom or U.S. control lists.

Further, the dissension and confusion surrounding the definition of "militarily critical" for items under national security control have resulted in outdated U.S. control lists. Despite repeated calls to "balance" military criticality with economic concerns, the only balancing factor explicitly recognized in the list construction process is the foreign availability, or controllability, of items. Of the 14 foreign availability assessments completed since the Omnibus Trade and Competitiveness Act was passed in 1988, 10 resulted in positive findings. Of those 10, 1 was referred to negotiations with the foreign source, 1 resulted in approved licenses, 5 resulted in decontrol, and the others are awaiting action. The average time from the initial claim to final action for those items that were decontrolled was more than seven months (see Table 6-6). **The foreign availability assessment process that was established to determine the controllability of items on the Commodity Control List has proven largely ineffective. Although data from the foreign availability assessments are used in list review, the assessment process itself is costly and contentious and has rarely resulted in timely decontrol.**

The extensive decontrol of certain CoCom-controlled categories at the June 1990 High-Level Meeting provides an instructive case study of the policy process for list construction and review. In only a few months, CoCom agreed to the complete elimination of 30 control categories (out of 116) and to partial elimination of 13 more (favorable consideration practices were outlined for certain East European destinations). It focused revisions on three key areas—computers, machine tools, and telecommunications—and called for swift development of a "core list" of critical technologies.

Prior to this decontrol, a series of streamlining efforts to reduce the control list were perceived as largely ineffective. It took a foreign catalyst—communism's collapse in Eastern Europe and the resulting pressures on CoCom for loosening restrictions—to bring about, temporarily, a workable process for decontrol. The U.S. interagency review was propelled by the need to formulate a position in time for the June 1990 CoCom meeting and, indeed, to avert a feared collapse of CoCom if certain of its members judged the resulting decontrol insufficient. **The President was able to present a coherent decontrol plan to CoCom only by short-circuiting the existing process. Continued White House pressure on the participating agencies was necessary to bring about significant loosening of restrictions.** Advice from the Joint Chiefs of Staff, who conducted a threat assessment prior to the decontrol, proved especially useful. Because the White House policy aim—wide-ranging decontrol—was made clear and constantly reiterated, the types of interagency disputes that have often blocked the process were minimized. Although the United States succeeded in presenting an acceptable plan of action to CoCom in June 1990, subsequent U.S. proposals on specific

TABLE **6-6**   Results of Foreign Availability Assessments Under the Omnibus Trade and Competitiveness Act

Commodity	Initiated	Completed	Decision/Result
Freon (5799C)[a]	9-26-88	2-23-89	Decontrol (2-28-89)
2,4-D (4707B)	10-31-88	2-23-89	Decontrol (2-28-89)
6,000-m SSS (1510A)	2-10-89	6-02-89	Negative finding (7-12-89)
Prepreg equipment (1357A)	4-18-89	8-18-89	National security override (3-15-90)
50-MB disk (1565A)	7-28-89	11-28-89	Decontrol (6-29-90)
Polysilicon[b] (1757A)	9-5-89	1-5-90	Licenses approved (6-19-90)
Polysilicon (1757A)	9-12-89	1-12-90	Decontrol (8-31-90)
Array processors I (1565A)	9-29-89	12-28-89	Negative finding (3-13-90)
Die bonders (1355A)	9-5-89	1-5-90	Negative finding (2-7-90)
Array processors II (1565A)	2-1-90	6-1-90	Decontrol (6-29-90)
Polyimides (1746A)	2-28-90	6-28-90	Positive finding; no action to date
D-RAMs (1564A)	3-5-90	7-5-90	Positive finding; no action to date
Diamond turning (1091A)	3-20-90	7-20-90	Negative finding (8-23-90)
Gallium arsenides (1757A)	5-15-90	9-15-90	Positive finding; no action to date

[a]The numbers in parentheses are export commodity control numbers (ECCNs).
[b]Denied license claim.

SOURCE: U.S. Department of Commerce, Bureau of Export Administration.

core list entries again could undermine the solidarity of CoCom if such proposals fall far short of European and Japanese expectations for decontrol.

Thus, in this key national security area, foreign nations and suppliers—not the U.S. interagency process—are driving the U.S. export control apparatus. Although the core list process has produced relatively

substantial results, it is doubtful that the institutionalized CoCom and U.S. list review processes could work effectively in less exigent circumstances.

Finally, in the proliferation area, the Zangger Committee meets regularly to update the nuclear trigger list. The Nuclear Suppliers Group, in contrast, has not met since its inception. Updates to the U.S. Nuclear Referral List are made on an ad hoc basis (a comprehensive update was completed in 1989). The annex of the Missile Technology Control Regime also is updated on an ad hoc basis. The annex itself is generic, which leaves the interpretation of actual items to be controlled up to national authorities. This type of national discretion leads to important discrepancies in national control systems, especially for dual use items. Conversely, chemicals that are considered sensitive precursors to chemical weapons are specifically identified by the Australia Group on a regular basis.

Ineffective Dispute Resolution

The process for dispute resolution is characterized by a lack of transparency resulting from unclear policy guidelines and complicated agency responsibilities. In considering whether to allow certain shipments, agencies disagree on levels of technology and the necessary conditions of sale. Agencies also disagree on the criteria for control or decontrol of list items and the interpretation of statutory guidelines for list review. For example, a foreign availability assessment for semiconductor wire bonders was begun in 1985, and decontrol was recommended, and approved by the President, in 1987. Despite the President's decision, negotiations with the foreign source to control the export of wire bonders were undertaken in 1988. The source country declined to cooperate based on the argument that the item was not strategically critical and was available in the Soviet Union and East Germany. Action was still blocked into 1990 by bitter interagency dissension. Similarly, in discussions in 1989 on whether to decontrol personal computer technology to the Soviet Union, the Commerce and Defense Departments sharply disputed almost every element of the congressionally stated criteria for determining foreign availability. The number of personal computers necessary to meet Warsaw Pact military needs and thereby satisfy the "available in sufficient quantity to render U.S. controls ineffective" criterion is a matter of subjective judgment, not established fact. **The other foreign availability criteria are also subject to interpretation and therefore ripe for interagency dispute. Yet, no working mechanism exists for resolving these disputes.**

The interagency procedure for resolving disputes on license decisions is confusing to industry and often takes too long for businesses to plan effectively. If an important dispute does reach as high as the under secretary level of review, the arguments for or against a case are frequently very technical in nature and the officials in charge often lack the technical expertise to address the matter adequately.

Although the Export Administration Review Board's process for resolving disputed licenses has worked fairly successfully for exports to proscribed destinations, as of late 1990 there was no parallel system for exports to nonproscribed countries or for proliferation cases. **The insufficient procedures for dispute resolution in licensing decisions cause further tension between agencies and disadvantage U.S. exporters. Clearer guidelines for case referral and more definitive standards for licensing decisions are needed.**

Exercise of Export Control Authority

Although a number of other countries maintain various types of export controls, the United States is alone in its historically frequent use of trade controls to respond to international events, beginning with the Stamp Act of 1765. Although U.S. law does not expressly state that trade is a privilege extended to citizens by the government, not a right of citizens, implementation of U.S. export control laws assumes that the universe of U.S. exports is controlled worldwide, unless otherwise stipulated. This assumption is inconsistent with foreign trade laws that operate on the basis of trade as a right, not a privilege. Thus, the willingness of foreign governments to use trade as a routine foreign policy tool is somewhat circumscribed.

Both the U.S. Congress and the executive branch routinely resort to trade controls or sanctions in response to human rights abuses or other politically distasteful activities. Other countries may also restrict trade with "pariah" countries, but it is rarely their first international response. **The proclivity of the United States to use trade sanctions as a ready tool of foreign policy has caused significant problems for U.S. exporters.**

An example of the disparity between U.S. and foreign practices is U.S. enforcement practices. A party convicted, or even suspected, of committing an export control violation may be placed on the Table of Denial Orders and embargoed from legal trade in any U.S. products or technical data. If a party is convicted of a criminal violation and serves prison time for the conviction, that party may not regain exporting or importing privileges for 10 years. In contrast, once a convicted party has served a sentence for export control violations in foreign countries, that party regains its original trading rights and may not be discriminated against on the basis of past records.

Nature and Extent of Unilateral Controls

One result of the bias toward trade as a privilege, rather than a right, is the unilateral nature of many aspects of U.S. control practices. Significant unilateral features of the U.S. control system include the following: reexport controls, foreign policy controls over U.S.-owned foreign entities, written assurance requirements and other importer certifications, more stringent controls on technical data (including visits and employment of non-U.S. citizens), controls over foreign products with U.S.-origin technology, parts, or components, control of many civil products and technologies under the munitions control regime, more burdensome and complex licensing regimes, and more stringent enforcement mechanisms. **In a world of diffuse economic and technological power, the widespread use of unilateral export controls is counterproductive.**

Although some CoCom countries practice limited or unofficial forms of reexport controls, the United States is the only country formally requiring that its permission be obtained by non-U.S. parties for the reexport of goods or technology that have come to rest in another country. In addition to items unchanged in form, non-U.S. technology may be controlled if it is commingled with U.S.-origin technology, and foreign-made goods may be controlled if they contain more than 25 percent U.S.-origin parts or components (10 percent if the destination is one of seven selected countries controlled for foreign policy reasons).

U.S. rules require that written assurances be obtained from recipients of controlled dual use technical data that neither the data nor their direct product will be reexported to a controlled country without U.S. permission. In addition, goods and technical data received under license from the Department of State cannot be reexported without U.S. permission, and State does not allow for a 25 percent *de minimus* on the foreign incorporation of U.S. parts and components.

These reexport rules are enforced through administrative, civil, and criminal penalties and by restricting or denying trade with the foreign violator. The U.S. rationale for reexport controls is that the absence of such controls allows third-party middlemen to make sales where U.S. firms are restricted and thus undercuts the purpose of the control program and disadvantages U.S. exporters. Other governments say that reexport controls cannot be effectively enforced, and most say they have no legal authority to require or enforce reexport controls. **The major adverse reaction to U.S. reexport controls arises when they are imposed in connection with U.S. unilateral foreign policy objectives and when their application is complex, such as the rules for parts, components, and technical data.**

Data collected in 1986 for the Allen panel showed that compliance with U.S. reexport controls is minimal among foreign parties who are independent of U.S. firms.[17] Although BXA licensing data show that more than 11,500 cases, at a value of close to $41 million, were approved for reexport in 1989, there is virtually no way to estimate the portion of total controlled reexports these figures represent (see Table 6-7).

The panel's European fact-finding delegation was told by a major German industrial association that member industries are advised to comply only with

TABLE 6-7   Department of Commerce Licensing Decisions, 1989

Destination	Exports		Reexports	
	Approved	Denied	Approved	Denied
By volume				
Free world[a]	59,995	154	6,450	35
CoCom	27,313	23	2,430	3
China	3,862	101	718	4
Eastern bloc	1,709	123	1,958	66
By value (in $ millions)				
Free world[a]	79,050	191	36,794	159
CoCom	33,895	106[b]	3,619	.088
China	3,170	.027	.225	.041
Eastern bloc	1,807	17	234	3

[a]Department of Commerce designation for all nonproscribed, non-CoCom countries.
[b]More than 99 percent of this figure represents computers.

SOURCE: U.S. Department of Commerce, Bureau of Export Administration.

the controls on reexports of goods with 25 percent U.S.-origin parts or components, thus ignoring U.S. foreign policy reexport controls on locally manufactured goods with lesser U.S. content. **In addition, there is an abundance of anecdotal evidence that, when possible, foreign manufacturers avoid U.S. sources in order to escape the encumbrance of U.S. reexport controls.**

Another contentious aspect of the licensing debate concerns whether the CoCom countries should practice "national discretion," that is, the export of certain controlled dual use items to proscribed destinations without first getting CoCom approval. (The licensing term for this kind of exception is an administration exception note.) The argument for national discretion is that it reduces the burden of license processing on CoCom and provides a paper trail for shipments that otherwise would not exist. Yet, because nations interpret quite differently the control threshold at which national discretion is employed, national discretion for dual use items undermines the principles of a multilateral regime.

Insufficient Judicial Review

The Export Administration Act generally exempts Commerce Department actions from the judicial review provisions of the Administrative Procedure Act. The Omnibus Trade and Competitiveness Act of 1988 provided limited judicial review only for Commerce Department civil enforcement actions. The question of whether to extend review to nonenforcement situations, such as licensing actions and the issuance of regulations, has been given new significance by the failure of the administration to implement various provisions of the EAA.* **Judicial review is no cure-all, however. Specifically, it is not the appropriate means for resolving interagency disputes on the very issues on which courts lack expertise and traditionally defer to the executive branch.** Unjustifiable burdens on the resources of the Commerce Department must be avoided, and the Commerce Department must retain unfettered discretion on fundamental questions of administration. **What courts can do, however, is correct agency errors in interpreting and applying statutory provisions, for example, a failure to dismantle unilateral controls when such action is mandated by Congress or the imposition of new foreign policy controls when statutory criteria have not been satisfied.**

Industry Participation

The Export Administration Act provides a formal mechanism for industry participation in the national security export control process. The secretary of commerce appoints a technical advisory committee for any goods or technology determined by the secretary to be difficult to evaluate because of technical matters or worldwide availability. The TACs also comment on the utilization of products and technology and licensing procedures. The TACs advise and assist the Commerce and Defense Departments and any other appropriate agency in establishing and administering national security controls. They consist of representatives of industry, the Departments of Commerce, State and Defense, and the intelligence community, and others at the discretion of the secretary of commerce. The State Department has established no comparable mechanism for obtaining industry input in matters related to the International Traffic in Arms Regulations.

The Commerce Department has established 10 technical advisory committees, which now include about 175 industry members, and it recently has begun to upgrade support for their participation and to integrate their input in list construction.† Industry members are chosen by the Commerce Department on the basis of individual company nominations. In addition to subject matter qualifications, appointments traditionally have been subject to the nominee's receipt of a security clearance and screening by the Office of the Secretary of Commerce and the White House Personnel Office. The latter has resulted in rejection of otherwise technically qualified applicants and has added months to the appointment process. Another avenue of industry input to the dual use control list is through the structure of technical working groups, whose members are not subject to White House screening.

---

*See Appendix H for further discussion of this issue.

†Appendix I discusses the technical advisory system for export controls and suggests a way to enhance the participation of the TACs.

Any truly effective export control system requires close cooperation between industry and government. Exporters must be involved in determining not only the goods to be controlled but also the rationale for controls. **Controls will be far more effective if industry fully understands and supports the rationale for controlling exports.** In practical terms, this involves comprehensive explanation from the government on the security concerns being addressed and detailed interaction between government and industry on how best to address them. In many cases, industry experts are more qualified to identify end uses and patterns of behavior that indicate sensitive or proscribed activity than government technicians.

Recently, there has been somewhat greater industry participation in list management. Technical advisory committees, for example, were given a role in the construction of the CoCom core list. **However, serious problems still remain with the extent of involvement by U.S. industry, which is a major reason why legitimate economic considerations are not taken into account at the start of the policy process. The traditional policy process does not lend itself to effective and fair presentation of industry views, particularly for small and medium-sized firms that are without Washington representation.**

The lack of sufficient business involvement in the system is partly self-inflicted. Too few companies make the effort or devote the resources necessary to placing qualified personnel on the advisory committees. Business must take a more active part in the process, particularly in the nomination of technically qualified personnel to work on the committees. Admittedly, much of the lack of response may be due to disillusionment with the current system and the conviction of industry that the government will not respond adequately to business advice even when it is given.

Unfortunately, the current system of export controls tends to cast government and industry as adversaries, rather than partners. **In the process of energizing and upgrading export control regimes, it is not enough to solicit the participation of other governments. The private sector must be brought in as a full and cooperative partner.**

NOTES

1. Sections 3.2(c), 3.2(a), and 3.2(b), respectively, Export Administration Act.
2. Section 5(d), Export Administration Act, as amended.
3. Part 120.3, International Traffic in Arms Regulations.
4. 15 C.F.R. 768-799.
5. Section 776.14, Export Administration Regulations.
6. Section 785.4, Export Administration Regulations.
7. Section 776.16, Export Administration Regulations.
8. Sections 785.1 and 785.7, Export Administration Regulations.
9. Section 785.4, Export Administration Regulations.

10. Section 776.19, Export Administration Regulations.
11. Section 778, Export Administration Regulations.
12. Section 776.18, Export Administration Regulations.
13. Section 776.19, Export Administration Regulations.
14. The stated purpose of the various statutes is as follows:

Export Administration Act, Public Law 96-72, Section 3(2): "It is the policy of the U.S. to use export controls only after full consideration of the impact on the economy of the U.S. and only to the extent necessary

(a) to restrict the export of goods and technology which would make a significant contribution to the military potential of any other country or combination of countries which would prove detrimental to the national security of the U.S.;

(b) to restrict the export of goods and technology where necessary to further significantly the foreign policy of the U.S. or to fulfill its declared international obligations; and

(c) to restrict the export of goods where necessary to protect the domestic economy from the excessive drain of scarce materials and to reduce the serious inflationary impact of foreign demand."

Arms Export Control Act, Public Law, 90-629, Senate 2778: "In furtherance of world peace and the security and foreign policy of the U.S., the President is authorized to control the import and the export of defense articles and defense services . . . Decisions on issuing export licenses under this section . . . shall take into account . . . whether the export will contribute to an arms race, support international terrorism, increase the possibility of outbreak or escalation of conflict or prejudice the development of bilateral or multilateral arms control arrangements."

Atomic Energy Act of 1954, as amended by the Nuclear Non-Proliferation Act of 1978, Public Law 95-467,

Section 3201: "The Congress finds and declares that the proliferation of nuclear explosive devices or of the direct capability to manufacture or otherwise acquire such devices poses a grave threat to the security interests of the U.S. and to continued international progress toward world peace and development."

Section 3202: "It is the purpose of this Section to promote the policies set forth (in Section 3201) by—

(a) establishing a more effective framework for international cooperation to . . . ensure that . . . the export by any nation of nuclear materials and technology intended for use in peaceful nuclear activities do not contribute to proliferation.

(b) authorizing the U.S. to take such actions as are required to ensure that it will act reliably in meeting its commitment to supply nuclear reactors and fuel to nations which adhere to effective non-proliferation policies;

(c) providing incentives to the other nations of the world to join in such international cooperative efforts and to ratify the Treaty; and

(d) ensuring effective controls by the U.S. over its exports of nuclear materials and equipment and of nuclear technology."

Trading with the Enemy Act of 1917, as amended by the International Emergency Economic Powers Act of 1977. H.R. 7738.

The purpose of the International Emergency Economic Powers Act is to redefine the power of the President to regulate international economic transactions in times of war or national emergency and to separate war and non-war authorities. Presidential powers are narrowed and made subject to congressional review in times of ''national emergency'' short of war. A national emergency is defined in Title II, Section 202 as an ''unusual and extraordinary threat which has its source in whole or substantial part outside the United

States, to the national security, foreign policy, or economy of the United States.''

Section 203 authorizes the President to regulate transactions in foreign exchange, banking transactions involving any interest of any foreign country or national thereof, and the importing and exporting of currency or securities, and to freeze any property in which any foreign country or national thereof has any interest.

Title III, Section 301, provides authority for control over exports of non-U.S. origin goods and technology by foreign subsidiaries of U.S. concerns. Section 302 provides authority to control U.S. exports.

15. *Federal Register* 50, October 11, 1985, pp. 41545–41546.
16. Institute for Defense Analyses, *Analysis of Militarily Critical Technologies List Implementation (Critical Technologies Implementation)* (Alexandria, Va., 1990), p. II-2.
17. National Academy of Sciences, National Academy of Engineering, and Institute of Medicine, *Balancing the National Interest: U.S. National Security Export Controls and Global Economic Competition* (Washington, D.C.: National Academy Press, 1987), p. 139.

7

Elements of a New Response: U.S. Policy

U.S. policy for national security export controls was established under the influence of three international conditions that molded its purpose, its feasibility, and its effectiveness. First, the central objective of denying or retarding access by the Soviet Union and other member countries of the Warsaw Treaty Organization (WTO) and the People's Republic of China to militarily relevant technology was a natural, politically accepted extension of the post-World War II Western security arrangement. Second, the feasibility of this policy depended substantially on the fact that the most advanced technologies were being developed almost exclusively by the Western allies (principally the United States) and were being produced largely at government initiative in direct support of weapons programs. Third, the effectiveness of export controls was considerably enhanced by the fact that the Soviet Union and its allies were dedicated to isolating their economies from the rest of the world.

Under these conditions, a strong consensus emerged among the Western allies to retard Soviet military development; a consensus that then translated operationally into U.S. and CoCom export controls. Controls were imposed on an extensive list of items, including many of only indirect military significance. The adverse consequences for East-West trade were minimized in the early years by prevailing market disjunctions—between military and commercial products and between "free market" and centrally planned economies.

For the United States in particular, its commanding economic and technological position in the post-World War II environment ensured that export controls would have only limited impact on the overall U.S. competitive position in international trade. By the beginning of the 1980s, however, those advantages had disappeared and the adverse consequences of export controls on commercial trade between the United States and other Western countries had become increasingly apparent. Moreover, by the end of the decade, radical political and economic changes in Eastern Europe and, to a lesser extent, in the Soviet Union had created a potentially new basis for East-West relations.

THE NEED FOR EXPORT CONTROLS IN THE NEW ERA

The conditions that determined the initial feasibility and effectiveness of national security export controls have now changed dramatically and the nature of the Western security alliance seems likely to change over the next decade as well. **The current challenge is to fashion a response that capitalizes on the enormous political and economic opportunities presented by the changes in Eastern Europe and the Soviet Union, while managing the risk associated with legitimate security concerns.**

The earlier review in Chapter 5 of the changing calculus of U.S. national security interests, which included an assessment of residual Soviet military capability and of new and growing dangers in other parts of the world, demonstrates the need to reexamine and reshape export control policy. In reality, although all of the CoCom countries are interested in eliminating restrictions on trade in dual use items with Eastern Europe and, to the extent that it is prudent, with the Soviet Union, no country in the Western alliance has expressed any willingness to see the capabilities of the Soviet *military*—particularly its strategic nuclear forces—enhanced through unrestricted exports. Thus, there continues to be a multilateral consensus within the traditional framework of CoCom, but with a narrower scope and focus.

Carefully tailored and/or refashioned, multilateral export controls can be appropriate and viable in support of the following policy objectives:

- **Constraining access by the *Soviet military* to technology and end products that contribute significantly and directly to the improvement of Soviet weapons systems capabilities.**
- **Constraining access to advanced technology and end products that contribute significantly and directly to the development of advanced conventional weapons systems by countries that pose a threat of aggression.**
- **Constraining access by countries of proliferation concern to nuclear, biological, chemical, and missile delivery technologies and know-how. (Export controls may not always be the optimal strategy for dealing with these problems, however.)**

• **Imposing multilaterally agreed sanctions for violations of international agreements or norms of behavior.**

These four objectives are very different from one another operationally. Constraining the improvement of Soviet weapons systems, for example, primarily involves a single target country and trade in high technology available from a relatively small group of nations. In contrast, constraining the proliferation of chemical weapons potentially involves many countries and many types of technology that are much less sophisticated and much more widely available. Consequently, forms of control that might be effective and sensible for constraining Soviet weapons systems improvement might be both ineffective and unreasonably burdensome in constraining chemical weapons proliferation.

With these differences in mind, the panel looked at various specific types of policy mechanisms. Table 7-1 lays out a typology along with the panel's judgment about the general circumstances in which each type of control is likely to be most appropriate. Only the first *five* mechanisms would fall within the traditional concept of "export controls," and different combinations of these mechanisms will be optimal in achieving the four policy objectives described above. Given the relative paucity of data concerning many of the issues surrounding the various proliferation problems, however, the panel has not formulated firm recommendations regarding which of these mechanisms of control is likely to be most effective in achieving nonproliferation objectives, although some general criteria are discussed in Chapter 8.

Given the importance of designing a system that does not *disproportionately* handicap U.S. trade, it is imperative that any of the legally binding forms of export management, whether embargo or any of the four other mechanisms of explicit control listed above, be imposed only on the basis of a careful analysis of the control-sensitive chokepoints and of whether the proposed solution is likely to be effective and equitable.

There is some potential that, in the future, circumstances in the Soviet Union and/or other currently proscribed countries will evolve to the point that it would be possible, and perhaps even desirable, to eliminate completely export controls on dual use technology to these destinations.

*   **To encourage this evolution and to ensure that institutional momentum does not maintain the use of export controls longer than prudence requires, the United States should work with the other CoCom countries to develop an explicit multilateral policy statement that outlines the circumstances under which dual use export controls can and should be terminated.**

TABLE 7-1   Mechanisms of Export Management

Type	Description	When Appropriate
Total embargo	All or substantially all exports to target country prohibited. Examples: embargoes of Vietnam, Libya, Iraq under the Trading with the Enemy Act or the International Emergency Economic Powers Act	Wartime or other acute national emergency or when imposed pursuant to United Nations or other broad international effort
Selective export prohibitions	Certain items barred for export to target country. Examples: no-license policies for the Soviet bloc under the International Traffic in Arms Regulations (ITAR)	When supplier countries agree on items for denial and cooperate on restrictions
Selective activity prohibitions	Exports for use in particular activities in target country prohibited. Examples: Department of Energy prohibition on nuclear activities in countries that are not signatories to Nuclear Non-Proliferation Treaty	When supplier countries identify proscribed operations and agree to cooperate on restrictions
Transactional licensing	Items require government agency licensing for export to particular country or country group. Example: Commerce Department individual validated license. Licensing actions may be conditioned on end-use verification, e.g., import certificate/delivery verification procedure, or postexport verification, e.g., for supercomputers	When items are inherently sensitive for export to any destination, e.g., munitions, or when items have both acceptable and undesired potential applications and are subject to an effective multilateral control regime
Bulk licensing	Exporter obtains government authority to export categories of items to particular consignees for a specified time period. Example: Commerce Department distribution license, ITAR foreign manufacturing license	Same as preceding circumstances, but when specific transaction facts are not critical to effective export control

(*continued*)

TABLE 7-1   (*Continued*)

Type	Description	When Appropriate
Preexport notification	Exporter must prenotify shipment; government agency may prohibit, impose conditions, or exercise persuasion. Example: requirement by Office of Foreign Assets Control for third-country subsidiary exports to Iran during the 1979–1980 hostage crisis	Generally regarded as an inappropriate export control measure because exporter cannot accept last-minute uncertainty
Conditions on general authority or right to export	Exporter not required to obtain government agency license but must meet regulatory conditions that preclude high-risk exports. Examples: Commerce Department general licenses; CoCom's general license free-world (GFW) and general license for intra-CoCom trade (GCT)	Appropriate when risk of diversion or undesired use is low
Postexport recordkeeping	Exporter must keep records of particulars of exports for specified period and submit or make available to government agency. Example: Export Administration Regulations §787.13	Appropriate means exist to monitor nonsensitive exports for possible diversion

Although the panel did not consider itself qualified to specify the circumstances in detail, some candidate criteria for determining when export controls should be terminated follow:

• Effective and verifiable conventional arms control agreements in Europe beyond those already agreed to in the Conventional Forces in Europe (CFE) treaty.

• Effective and verifiable nuclear arms control agreements among the United States, France, the United Kingdom, and the Soviet Union.

• Democratically elected government in the Soviet Union.

• Demonstration of a Soviet commitment to work cooperatively, both bilaterally and multilaterally (including within world organizations such as the United Nations), to achieve a stable and secure international environment.

A NEW APPROACH TO EAST-WEST EXPORT CONTROLS

The traditional definition of the Soviet Union, the other (former) member countries of the Warsaw Pact, and the People's Republic of China as the most immediately threatening adversaries of the Western alliance is, for reasons elaborated in Chapter 5, largely outdated. The circumstances, therefore, require a new approach. The political and economic changes in the Soviet Union and Eastern Europe have created new opportunities. Of greatest relevance to this study is the possibility that, for the first time since World War II, the United States and the Soviet Union can now work cooperatively in areas of *mutual* security concern, such as proliferation. Simultaneously, the disintegration of the WTO, combined with the internal economic and political problems in the Soviet Union, means that the West can accept somewhat larger risks without seriously endangering national security.

Taken together, these increased opportunities—and increased margin for error—suggest that the West can now safely move from a policy of general denial (with limited exceptions) of dual use controlled items to a policy of presumed *approval* to export, predicated on verifiable end-use conditions. The arguments for such a transition are clearly greatest for those nations of Eastern Europe that now pose a national security threat to the West *only* because of the possibility that goods and technologies sold to them might be reexported to the Soviet military or to countries of concern for other reasons. But the case also holds for the Soviet Union itself, which for the foreseeable future will need Western goods and technologies if its efforts at building a modern economy are to have any chance of success.

There undoubtedly are risks attendant to the improvement of long-term capabilities. The most obvious is the outright loss of control over the end use of sensitive dual use items, particularly in the event of an outbreak of hostilities (when it obviously would no longer be possible to verify end use). There also are dangers under this scheme of diversion (particularly diversion-in-place), reverse engineering, and dissemination of technical data and know-how. **But the fact remains that continued pursuit of a policy of general denial is neither administratively feasible in light of the multiple channels and sources for acquisition nor politically desirable in the context of the positive trend in U.S.-Soviet relations with the demise of the WTO and the signing of the CFE treaty.**

Under a new export control policy based in large part on verifiable end use, moreover, measures such as government assurances of civilian end use and restricted resale build confidence between trading parties and are useful tools in managing the security risk inherent in the export of advanced goods. Predicating the sale of advanced, and previously embargoed, end products on guarantees against military end use and unauthorized resale allows for economic progress while limiting military risk. Arrangements for continuing, periodic inspection of selected items could lend further confidence to the integrity of the sale. Certainly, the recent experience with on-site inspection in the execution of the Intermediate-Range Nuclear Forces treaty and the inclusion of comprehensive on-site inspection regimes in the CFE treaty enhance the possibilities for expanded monitoring of sensitive items across international borders.

NEW TARGETS FOR NATIONAL SECURITY EXPORT CONTROLS

The reduction of East-West tensions and increased trade opportunities are political and economic goals held not only by the United States and the Soviet Union, but also by the other members of NATO, Japan, Australia, and the East European countries. Moreover, these countries also share mutual security concerns that can be translated into mutually beneficial collective security measures. As noted in Chapter 5, the potential threat from state-supported acts of terrorism and escalating regional conflicts is on the rise. Defense against acts of terrorism is one of the most troubling challenges faced by governments.

In most, if not all cases, the regional enmity that threatens to escalate into armed conflict has existed for centuries. It is not the conflict that is new, but the ability of regional actors to wage war with increasingly dangerous military hardware, including weapons of mass destruction. The unconstrained spread of advanced conventional weapons also could have a dramatically destabilizing effect in many regions of the world. The prospect of a nuclear exchange or the widespread use of chemical weapons is a critical security issue of global proportion.

For the reasons identified in Chapter 8, traditional export controls, which focus on particular items and subject them to broad regulatory measures (e.g., transactional or bulk licensing), are not likely to be as effective in dealing with emerging proliferation concerns as they have been in addressing the Cold War threat, because they are not universally adhered to nor equally enforced, because they only partially constrain indigenous capacity, and because technical information and assistance cannot be contained completely. Moreover, many items that have proliferation significance in very selected circumstances are widely available and have predominantly innocent commercial applications. For example, as the concerns about the development of an alleged chemical weapons manufacturing facility at Rabta, Libya, demonstrate, the differences between a weapons facility and a pharmaceutical plant are often difficult to prove conclusively (particularly in the absence of on-site inspection).

On the other hand, traditional item-focused export controls, multilaterally applied and enforced, can help to constrain the spread of weapons and the technical capability to produce them. They also may be useful in isolating countries or parties that violate accepted standards of conduct. For export controls to be effective in this new environment, they must be fashioned so as to achieve a high level of international cooperation that will ensure even-handed application while avoiding unnecessary injury to world commerce.

The effectiveness of traditional export controls depends on a number of problematic conditions, including the following:

• Agreement by all countries that possess either the weapons or the capability to produce weapons to control trade in the component technologies and end products.

• Agreement by participating countries on the targets of export controls. This could be countries or regions that are considered dangerous or volatile, specific projects that raise concern, or specified, proscribed end uses.

• Agreement by participating countries on the items to be controlled.

• The actual controllability of the targeted items.

• Agreement by participating countries on appropriate licensing and enforcement measures.

• Agreement by participating countries on accountability to each other and on sanctions for violations.

*   **Despite the daunting problems inherent in the conditions listed above, multilateral consensus on the goals, targets, and mechanisms of export controls is essential and should be a critical foreign policy priority for the United States. This includes reviewing the organization and operation of control regimes aimed at East-West trade, as well as seeking the cooperation of the Soviet Union, China, and other countries in controlling the global proliferation of arms.**

In fact, superpower cooperation to prevent the proliferation of advanced conventional weapons and weapons of mass destruction could significantly improve the prospects for world stability. In more operational terms, it is critical to include the Soviet Union in any effort to control the spread of weapons and weapons production capabilities.

The inclusion of other supplier countries that have traditionally been the target of export controls is more problematic. Consider, for example, India and China. Neither country has signed the Nuclear Non-Proliferation Treaty (NNPT); China has already developed accurate, long-range missile launch capabilities and India reportedly has developed a similar but more limited missile delivery system. Thus, it is likely that such countries will remain the target of controls while, at the same time, their participation in nuclear and missile control regimes is being sought.

Perhaps the most pivotal factor in determining the success of export control regimes is the nature of members' responsibility to each other. It is the extent of this perceived responsibility that determines, in large part, whether a particular country becomes a member of a given regime or continues to be identified as a potential target of controls.

Beyond the effectiveness of export controls in terms of security objectives, multilateral cooperation is also important to minimize the economic costs of export controls. So long as controls are imposed multilaterally, in form and practice, the costs of controls are shared equally. The United States, however, has a history of unilateralism in its export control policies.

To be effective, proliferation controls must be focused only on narrowly proscribed military activities or items that are required *directly* **for weapons systems and must include, to the extent practicable, verifiable end-use assurances. Lacking such specificity, efforts to control exports of proliferation-related technologies create a risk similar to that encountered in the case of CoCom controls on dual use technology—namely, imposing significant economic costs that may be disproportionate to their effectiveness.**

LIMITATIONS ON CERTAIN TYPES AND USES OF EXPORT CONTROLS

Serious discontinuities exist between export controls on the commercial sale of munitions under the Arms Export Control Act and the implementing International Traffic in Arms Regulations on the one hand and the transfer of munitions on a government-to-government basis on the other. The problem of how to impose reasonable limitations on foreign military sales extends well beyond the United States, and it is being exacerbated by the overcapacity of arms production worldwide. **This is a significant and troubling problem; though not in the panel's mandate, it is urgently in need of study.**

A second conceptual problem—and one that lies more squarely within the panel's mandate—concerns the lack of clarity regarding the use of export controls to protect the national security interests of the United States versus their use to pursue broader U.S. foreign policy interests and commitments. In the Export Administration Act (EAA), a legal distinction is drawn between the application of *national security export controls,** which are imposed pursuant to Section 5, and *foreign policy export controls*,† which are imposed under Section 6. This distinction has not always been observed in practice. Indeed, proliferation controls, though directly relevant to U.S. national se-

---

National security export controls are procedures designed to regulate the transfer of items from one country to another in such a way as to protect militarily important technology from acquisition by potential adversaries.

†*Foreign policy export controls* are restrictions imposed on the export of general classes of items to one or more specified countries in order to further the foreign commitments and interests of the United States or to fulfill U.S. international obligations.

curity, currently are imposed under Section 6 of the EAA as "foreign policy" controls. The 1982 controls directed at the Soviet gas pipeline to Western Europe were justified as a foreign policy measure responsive to the Soviet suppression of the Solidarity movement in Poland. In contrast, the 1980 wheat embargo, which was designed to pressure the Soviet Union to change its policy toward Afghanistan, was justified as a national security measure.

Further confusion arises from the broad emergency power vested in the executive branch under the International Emergency Economic Powers Act (IEEPA). By declaring an "emergency," which may arise from either national security or foreign policy concerns, the President may invoke broad export control measures, free of the limitations that Congress has written into Section 5 of the EAA (e.g., prohibitions on unilateral national security controls) or Section 6 (e.g., determinations that controls will be effective in practice to achieve objectives).

National security is clearly the paramount goal of U.S. foreign policy.* But the blurring of the distinction between the uses of export controls permitted under the relevant U.S. laws detracts from the legitimate application of export controls for either purpose. It also creates confusion and doubts about U.S. intentions among those countries cooperating with the Western strategic technology control effort, as well as difficulties for U.S. exporters.

In contrast to national security controls, which have been applied relatively consistently over an extended period of time to a consistent group of countries, foreign policy controls may be applied in almost any situation in which another country is seen to be conducting its affairs in a manner not to the satisfaction of the United States. Moreover, because the need for the application of foreign policy controls cannot be anticipated by industry, they can affect virtually any transaction in international trade. Thus, the perceived threat of new foreign policy control measures probably is at least as responsible for causing foreign companies to design-out† U.S. products and suppliers as are national security export controls. Indeed, many of the current problems with the U.S. export control regime relate to *both* foreign policy and national security export controls. For example:

- The United States has imposed foreign policy and, to a lesser extent, national security controls unilaterally. U.S. implementation of multilateral national security controls generally has been more restrictive than that of other countries and therefore unilateral in practice.‡

---

*Foreign policy as used here, however, includes broader foreign interests of the United States than those related directly to national security.

†This is the phenomenon known as "de-Americanization" of product lines.

‡Both of these issues are addressed in greater detail in Chapter 6.

• Both sets of controls incorporate extraterritorial features that undermine their acceptance and effectiveness.

• Neither foreign policy controls nor national security controls state the conditions necessary for the restrictions to be relaxed or removed. Foreign policy export controls probably are more difficult to dismantle than national security controls as international conditions evolve. It is often argued, for example, that even though the imposition of new controls would not be justified by current conditions, ending old controls might send the wrong signal to the target country. The U.S. embargo on trade with Vietnam may have persisted largely for this reason.

• Both sets of controls are administered by more than one agency under statutes that have different criteria and under distinct regulatory regimes. These diverse approaches lead to inconsistent and disparate results that disadvantage U.S. industry.

In addition to the problems listed above, the distinction between some foreign policy controls and national security controls is artificial. For example, missile, nuclear, or chemical weapons proliferation could directly affect the national security of the United States and its allies. Despite this fact, missile- and chemical-related items are controlled primarily under foreign policy, rather than national security, legislative authority, and nuclear export controls are maintained as *both* a national security and a foreign policy concern as a result of the existence of another relevant statute. These threats should be recognized as legitimate national security concerns. **Serious consideration should be given to whether authority for export controls *other* than for reasons of national security or to implement the mandate of a responsible international organization or agreement can be justified, particularly given their relative ineffectiveness, and in light of today's highly competitive international economy.** Given the close relationship between national security export controls and controls based on foreign policy considerations, the panel makes the following recommendations:

* **Foreign policy controls maintained to prevent the proliferation of missile delivery systems or nuclear, chemical, or biological weapons should be reclassified under the rubric of "proliferation controls" to differentiate them appropriately as an element of U.S. national security policy.**

* **The United States should not impose foreign policy controls on a continuing basis, except in those circumstances in which sufficient multilateral agreement and cooperation exist to make them efficacious and to prevent discrimination against U.S. product and technology suppliers.**

* **If unilateral foreign policy controls are used, then the setting and enforcement of time limitations become imperative. The United**

States should, in all cases, seek to negotiate multilateral implementation and enforcement, or informal cooperation (whenever possible) from other countries in similarly restricting trade. However, the United States will find it difficult to lead if few other countries can be convinced to follow. Under these circumstances, the imposition of unilateral foreign policy controls may become counterproductive and damaging to U.S. economic interests and every effort should be made to remove them at an early time.

*   The criteria for the imposition and retention of national security and foreign policy controls set forth in Sections 5 and 6 of the Export Administration Act of 1979, as amended, should be reviewed and made more explicit.

*   To the extent that the President chooses to invoke export control measures through the use of the International Emergency Economic Powers Act, the criteria for its application should be reviewed and modified so that they are similar to the conditions that Congress has specified in Sections 5 and 6 of the EAA with respect to controls imposed for national security or foreign policy reasons. "Emergency powers" granted to the President under the IEEPA generally should not be imposed for more than six months before Section 6 of the EAA must be invoked.

*   The "sunset" provision for foreign policy controls should be enforced in order to ensure that, as in the case of more traditional national security controls, restrictions do not remain in force long after the political, military, or technological rationale for their enactment has ceased to exist.

8

Elements of a New Response: Multilateral Control Regimes

As noted in previous chapters, the effectiveness of multilateral export controls depends on a number of conditions, including the membership, the goals and targets, and the mechanisms of the regime. This chapter discusses (1) the objectives and operation of traditional, multilateral security export controls and (2) emerging multilateral security export control regimes. Because both problem areas involve considerable uncertainty, the emphasis in this chapter, and in Chapters 9 and 10, is on identifying flexible and adaptive control strategies whose specifics can be modified in response to changing international security realities.

COCOM: A NEW DIRECTION

Although support for denial of munitions items to the Soviet Union or East European countries is likely to continue, support for the control of dual use items is eroding. This is particularly true of controls on dual use items that are not highly sophisticated and have little military utility.

The traditional CoCom objective of retarding the qualitative progress of Soviet military capabilities could be preserved while allowing for expanded, legitimate trade by shifting the focus of CoCom from an embargo on the export of listed items to proscribed countries to approval of items on a sharply reduced CoCom Industrial List, contingent on acceptable, verifiable end-use conditions approved by CoCom. Rather than considering approved sales of controlled items to proscribed countries as ''general exceptions'' to an embargo, the denial of such sales would be the exception. Approval would be presumed for all transactions for which end-use conditions ensured an acceptable level of risk. The extensiveness of end-use conditions and the need for physical verification would depend on the nature of the item and the security risk inherent in the proposed transfer. Although assurances against military use or unauthorized retransfer would be uniform, physical verification of the end use would not be necessary for all transactions. Further, certain items would not be immediately amenable to end-use conditions at an acceptable level of risk, but the level of risk would be adjusted over time on the basis of demonstrated end-use reliability and political factors.

An administrative effect of this change in focus would be the requirement to monitor and ensure compliance with end-use conditions and deter diversions. License review would still be necessary, but once standard and uniform end-use conditions for the approval of the remaining Industrial List items were established, the focus of the control program would be to ascertain compliance with those conditions.

Although CoCom partners have always been opposed to extraterritorial application of export controls, the end-use verification practices envisioned in this proposal would not be universally applied to all transactions and need not be adversarial. Instead, end-use assurances against military use or unauthorized retransfer would be characterized as standard conditions of sale, and potential verification as a standard inspection or audit. Also, the inspections or audits of limited, selected transactions need not be performed by enforcement agents of the exporting country. There are a number of alternatives, including CoCom inspection teams; certified, private inspection companies; and a contractual arrangement between the trading parties. Although not directly applicable, lessons can be drawn from several existing audit or inspection arrangements, including the periodic governmental review of transaction records for U.S. distribution licenses,* the International Atomic Energy Agency (IAEA) inspection practices, the inspection regimes established under the Treaty on Conventional Forces in Europe, or the confidence-building measures of the Conference on Security and Cooperation in Europe. Whatever mechanism is employed, the end-use verification effort will undoubtedly be aided by the increasing openness of the Soviet Union and Eastern Europe.

In addition to the shift in focus from denial of Industrial List items to approval with end-use conditions, CoCom should review its traditional objective of controlling East-West arms transfers under the International Munitions List and International Atomic Energy List. Beyond maintaining these

---

*For a complete explanation of the U.S. distribution license audit requirements, see the "Internal Control Program" handbook prepared by the Department of Commerce, Office of Export Licensing.

control lists, there is currently no formal mechanism for coordinating national restrictions on the worldwide transfer of arms. Although a comprehensive discussion of munitions transfers is beyond the scope of this study, it is important to note that an upgraded role for CoCom in managing arms transfers is a viable future possibility.

The continued credibility of CoCom depends on the willingness of the members to recognize and respond to the new political, economic, and military realities. This requires that a new approach to control objectives be reflected in modified control practices and a higher threshold of military utility as a criterion for control.

To this end, CoCom should take the following steps:

* **Approve the sale of Industrial List items to the Soviet Union and Eastern Europe for civilian end uses when acceptable safeguards can be demonstrated to CoCom.**
* **To the extent feasible, publish standard end-use conditions necessary for favorable consideration of exports of controlled items.**
* **Provide for periodic, and in some cases unannounced, visits to the physical location to verify the end use of limited, selected items. The possibility of visitation would be a stated condition of sale. The visits might be performed by (1) members' individual enforcement agencies, (2) collective or joint member enforcement (i.e., the IAEA model), (3) the exporter (i.e., the distribution license model), or (4) by private inspection companies certified by CoCom.**

COCOM: A NEW ENVIRONMENT

The practical circumstances under which CoCom operates have been radically changed not only by the events in Eastern Europe and the Soviet Union, but also by changing world trade and finance patterns. **The continued viability of CoCom depends not only on a new approach to its traditional adversaries, but also a review of the total environment in which it operates and consideration of an expanded membership.**

"Borderless" Trade Within the European Community

The European Community (EC) is working to institute a single European market in 1992 with virtually "borderless" trade among its members. There has been much speculation about the effect this will have on CoCom controls. The current members of the European Community are also members of CoCom, with the exception of Ireland. Ireland, however, practices a system of export controls that is similar to the CoCom system. It is possible that the advent of "borderless" trade could exacerbate existing problems in those EC/CoCom countries with relatively fewer resources to devote to export control, since they could become targeted as relatively easier points of diversion for items originating elsewhere in the Community.

Article 223 of the Treaty of Rome states that EC national governments will retain authority over matters of national security and defense. The EC Commission has passed two resolutions related to collective export controls—one banning EC export of chemical weapons precursors and one restricting trade with South Africa. Neither of these resolutions signals EC intentions to displace individual EC member's roles in CoCom; in fact, they may presage increased EC attention to proliferation controls rather than East-West controls.

Despite discussion of CoCom in the European Community, there has been no formal request for an EC representative in CoCom, nor has there been any serious action to supersede the authority of national governments to implement CoCom controls. **Given the complicated business of organizing and administering monetary and economic unification, it is unlikely that the European Community will want to add to its responsibilities in the near future (i.e., prior to 1992).**

When the single market becomes operational in Europe, CoCom partners are likely to be practicing license-free trade among themselves, except for munitions and items controlled under other multilateral regimes, such as missile technology. From a governmental management perspective, the primary difference between current licensing practices and the license-free system will be the lack of an import certificate issued by the importing country. Most of the CoCom countries that operate what are perceived as inadequate control programs produce few controlled items indigenously and thus depend on the issuance of an import certificate as an alert that controlled goods are entering their jurisdiction. With very limited exceptions, however, U.S. Industrial List exports to *any* CoCom destination are shipped under either general or special licenses and therefore do not require an import certificate. In addition, CoCom members, including the United States, do not closely review individual licenses for the export of Industrial List items to other CoCom destinations and rarely, if ever, deny such exports. **Thus, because establishing a system of license-free trade in CoCom is an important step in eliminating burdens on West-West trade, the adoption of the common standard elements of licensing and enforcement by all CoCom members should be a continuing U.S. priority.**

Although there will be "borderless" trade within the European Community for most goods, that does not signal the elimination of all customs ports and authorities. The export of weapons will still be nationally controlled, and trade moving from an EC member to an outside destination will still be subject to appropriate national licensing and documentation requirements.

Perhaps the most fundamental effect of license-free CoCom trade or borderless trade in the EC will be the sharp reduction in government-created and -maintained paper trails of controlled transactions, which will reduce the availability of the most frequently used tools of enforcement. **The inclusion of a "control identifier" or control marking on the Single Administrative Document to be used by EC members, or a control marker on the standard Customs Cooperation Council trade documents (used internationally to identify the contents, origin, and destination of goods in trade), may have potential as a useful enforcement tool.** Since the information on standard trade documents is retained by importing and exporting governments for statistical purposes, incorporation of a control marker would allow for automated records on controlled transactions with relative ease.

In light of the changing operational environment for export controls, the U.S. should take the following steps:

* **Continue to press for the adoption of a license-free system of trade in CoCom, to be implemented consistently and in accord with "common standard" compliance in order to ensure effective controls and to avoid disadvantaging those countries that make the effort to comply.**
* **Promote the use of a generic control indicator in conjunction with internationally recognized import/export documents. The control indicator, or marker, could be used by all countries that maintain restrictions on the export of certain items.**

Third Country Cooperation

Recognizing that CoCom controls could not be effective if comparable goods were available from third countries, the United States urged its CoCom partners to undertake a "Third Country Initiative," now called Third Country Cooperation (TCC), with a number of European neutrals and newly industrializing countries (NICs). The trend of locating Western manufacturing plants in these third countries, or off-shoring, has added to their indigenous capabilities and increased the need for a cooperative program.

The "mutual security" motivation for cooperation among CoCom members has proved to be only marginally valid for gaining cooperation by third countries. The European neutrals have cooperated to some extent, based on the perception of a generalized threat to European security posed by the East. **The security interests of most Asian and Latin American NICs, however, derive principally from regional instability and are only indirectly related to East-West tensions.** Further, not only do third countries in Europe, Asia, and Latin America have varying national security interests, they also have divergent political and economic goals.

The Asian countries have generally perceived cooperation with CoCom as a means of improving their international political status and of pacifying the United States in one trade area while they continue contentious negotiations in other areas (e.g., intellectual property rights, import quotas, closed domestic markets). Thus, Singapore and South Korea have reached agreements with the United States on national security export controls, and Taiwan and Indonesia have expressed interest in cooperating with the United States and CoCom (see Table 8-1). But third countries in Asia have taken very few concrete steps to establish export control programs. The notable exception is Hong Kong, which, while it remains a Crown colony, administers an extensive export control program with the United Kingdom. Latin American countries, specifically Brazil and Argentina, tend to link any cooperation on East-West export controls to liberalization of U.S. nuclear export policies.

Since its initiation in 1984, the CoCom TCC initiative has enjoyed only limited success: Few CoCom members have actively pursued such agreements; the agreements negotiated* do not systematically cover all goods reexported from CoCom countries and indigenously controlled by CoCom; and the cooperating countries exhibit uneven will in implementation and enforcement.

The U.S. threat to restrict the export of certain high-technology items to countries that do not cooperate sufficiently with CoCom is hollow. U.S. export licensing statistics show that approval rates and average license processing times for exports to countries that do not cooperate with CoCom are not significantly different from those for cooperating countries (see Table 8-1). **More important, many U.S. industries would be economically disadvantaged without these markets, and third countries can easily turn to other foreign suppliers.**

Cooperating third countries are not direct participants in CoCom. They have no vote, cannot participate in the list review process, and must forward their general exception cases through a CoCom member for full CoCom review. They also have no vote on the cases of CoCom members. As the quality and sophistication of the goods third countries produce inevitably rise, their willingness to subject high-value exports to the decisions of a group in which they have no vote will decline rapidly.

Given the overall decline in the perception of the security risk posed by the Soviet Union and other WTO countries, combined with the increasing sophistication of goods produced in third countries, the prospects for improving third country cooperation are limited. To maintain current levels of cooperation, as well as to encourage expanded cooperation, it will be necessary to reduce the scope of CoCom-controlled goods and provide political and economic incentives for third country cooperation. To this end, CoCom should take the following actions:

---

*This conclusion is inferred from comments of both U.S. and foreign government officials. The panel was not able to analyze the actual agreements because access to the documents was denied by the State Department.

TABLE 8-1 Third-Country Licensing Comparisons (U.S. $ thousands)

Country	1987		1988		1989		Avg. Processing Time, 1989
	Number	Amount	Number	Amount	Number	Amount	
Switzerland[a]							
Approved	2,470	$ 696,044	2,125	$ 513,300	1,637	$ 575	9 business days
Rejected	5	343	0		1	4	
Finland[b]							
Approved	831	373,147	686	421,402	565	451,836	9
Rejected	2	787	3	782	1	143	
Austria[c]							
Approved	891	223,944	756	178,839	531	629,365	13
Rejected	5	2,608	3	859	4	897	
Singapore[d]							
Approved	1,560	3,108,254	1,391	3,876,306	1,294	2,712,754	10
Rejected	26	15,162	12	7,626	3	10,194	
South Korea[e]							
Approved	3,177	2,902,284	3,843	6,294,560	4,017	5,342,199	11
Rejected	5	680	0		0		

Taiwan[f]						
Approved	4,855	6,438,855	4,837	11,082,427	4,960	12,072,043
Rejected	5	171	3	21,981	12	12,703	17

[a] Switzerland has no formal agreement with the United States or other CoCom member, but it practices export controls on the basis of informal arrangements. Switzerland receives all available licensing benefits, except the general license for intra-CoCom trade (GCT).

[b] Finland does not have a formal agreement with the United States or other CoCom member, but it practices export controls on the basis of informal arrangements. Finland receives all available licensing benefits, except GCT.

[c] Austria does not have a formal agreement with the United States or other CoCom member, but it practices export controls on the basis of informal arrangements. Austria receives general license for CoCom and cooperating countries (G-Com), general license for cooperating governments (GCG), 15/15 day license processing, and PRC permissive reexport. The remaining licensing benefits, with the exception of GCT, were expected to be granted in late 1990.

[d] Singapore signed a Memorandum of Understanding with the United States in 1987 and was subsequently granted G-Com and GCG. The granting of further benefits is predicated on implementation of the agreement.

[e] South Korea signed a Memorandum of Understanding with the United States in 1987, but the agreement was not ratified by the Korean parliament until 1989. South Korea was scheduled to receive GCG and 15/15 day license processing benefits in late 1990. Further benefits are predicated on implementation of the agreement.

[f] Taiwan has not signed an agreement with the United States or other CoCom member. Taiwan does not have a formal system of export controls and does not receive any licensing benefits.

SOURCE: U.S. Department of Commerce, Bureau of Export Administration.

* Include on the CoCom core list only those items that are physically produced or sourced only in CoCom member nations or fully co-operating third countries.
* Initiate a plan whereby fully cooperating third countries can observe and contribute to CoCom list construction and case review. This may involve expanding the membership of CoCom or creating an "observer status."
* Eliminate reexport authorization requirements for goods being reexported *out of* fully cooperating third countries.
* Seek multilateral agreement to control the reexport of controlled goods out of noncooperating third countries.
* Offer extension of the license-free system of trade as a CoCom-wide benefit to cooperating countries that have operational export control systems. The Third Country Cooperation Working Group in CoCom should certify the cooperating countries that have adequate systems.

COCOM: ADMINISTRATION AND MANAGEMENT

The narrow focus of CoCom on an explicitly targeted group of countries and commodities has enabled it to function with relative effectiveness. CoCom's goals were clearly linked to the mutual security of all members and the guiding principle of consensus ensured that all members could exercise influence on the actions of the group. The combination of these factors enabled CoCom to operate on the basis of international consensus, without the need for a formal treaty.

Sharply differing views on the appropriate translation of CoCom objectives into actual export restrictions inevitably have created tensions among the member countries, however. Although these stresses pre-date 1989, the dramatic events in the Soviet Union and Eastern Europe exacerbate the problem. The continued viability of CoCom depends not only on its capability to respond to dramatic changes in the security, political, and economic environment, but also on its ability to agree on items requiring control and on control mechanisms.

The agreements reached at the June 1990 Executive Committee and High-Level meetings in Paris reconfirmed multilateral support—at least for the near term. **Thirty Industrial List entries were decontrolled, and the members agreed to develop an even more streamlined "core list" by early 1991.** In conjunction with a revised control list, CoCom partners are also discussing the conditions necessary for approved exports of controlled items. **The current secrecy surrounding the conditions that exist for the favorable consideration of exports subject to full CoCom review prohibits exporters from taking advantage of potential exceptions to a general**

embargo and discourages exporters from even attempting to establish trade with proscribed countries.

As stated in Chapter 6, the practice of allowing national discretion (administrative exception notes) on licensing decisions for controlled goods above the general exception level is inconsistent with the concept of uniform treatment among all members and the limitation of controls to critical items. **In short, national discretion translates into unilateral export controls.**

Another source of tension is the fact that national control systems vary widely, as does the methodology by which items are determined to warrant control or decontrol. **Despite the obvious connection to military utility of the CoCom strategic criteria, the role of the national defense agencies of member countries in the CoCom list review process is limited and inconsistent.** In the United States, the Defense Department has had major influence on both U.S. and CoCom policy for a number of years. The same has not been true, however, of the *defense and intelligence agencies* of most other CoCom countries. Moreover, the Strategic Technology Experts Meeting, which has been nominally affiliated with CoCom since 1985, has been ineffective as a forum for coordinating inputs from national military establishments. **Industry participation in list review, although seemingly more influential than defense input by the other CoCom countries, is also inconsistent.**

Perhaps the most potentially damaging discrepancies in CoCom are, however, members' practices in licensing West-West trade. In addition to the unilateral controls maintained by the United States, there are other differences in the approach of CoCom members to licensing and enforcement operations. The information required with license applications, the scrutiny with which such applications are reviewed, the investigation of potential violations, and the imposition of penalties on proven violators—all are critical to the effectiveness of members' control systems, as well as to the impact of controls on exporters. The resources and attention devoted to these factors vary starkly among CoCom members, however, particularly with respect to controlled exports to nonproscribed countries.

Despite disproportionate attention to licensing and enforcement, the U.S. practice of resisting decontrol in the CoCom forum while removing licensing requirements for nonproscribed trade (e.g., broad general and special licenses) promotes the belief that the United States is not concerned with the positions of its allies and uses CoCom as a tool to gain economic advantage. Moreover, the location of CoCom headquarters within the U.S. embassy annex in Paris furthers the perception of the United States as controlling the organization to its own national advantage.

Multilateral cooperation is an essential element in the effectiveness of any export control program. In addition, increased CoCom cooperation is necessary during this time of transition in Europe to ensure "equal

economic footing" among all members while managing the redefinition
of trade goals as they relate to mutual security. To this end, the United
States should press CoCom to undertake the following:

* Seek a common standard of licensing and enforcement practices
  for trade with nonproscribed countries. This should include controls on the reexport of controlled items (including those items
  eligible for approval with conditions) out of noncooperating countries.

* Eliminate the use of national discretion (administrative exception
  controls). The revised Industrial List ("core list") should be brief
  enough that all cases can be reviewed by CoCom.

* Improve the transparency of CoCom operations. This includes
  making the conditions necessary for favorable consideration of controlled exports standard and public, to the extent feasible.

* "Internationalize" the image of CoCom. For example, (1) move
  CoCom headquarters out of the U.S. embassy annex in Paris, (2)
  upgrade the involvement of other members in the administration
  of CoCom, and (3) share the costs of operation more evenly.

* Encourage increased input from members' national defense and
  intelligence agencies by upgrading and more fully integrating with
  CoCom the existing Strategic Technology Experts Meeting.

PROLIFERATION CONTROLS: THE NEED FOR COLLECTIVE SECURITY

The review of evolving U.S. national security interests in Chapter 5 made
clear the large and growing international security problems posed by the
militarization of a number of regions and the proliferation of advanced conventional weapons and weapons of mass destruction in those regions. By
their nature, these problems can only be addressed effectively through international measures. Effective export control regimes designed to address
these problems must also be collective and should include all the major
supplier countries. Without the cooperation of the major supplier countries,
weapons, weapons designs, and critical dual use technologies will continue
to be available to nations that are intent on acquiring advanced conventional
weapons or weapons of mass destruction.

The general issue of trade in weapons is in urgent need of international
attention, but the panel was unable to give adequate consideration to the
problem. **Future U.S. policy could be considerably informed by a study
of these issues undertaken by an appropriate group of experts.**

Exports of advanced dual use items often play a central enabling role in
the proliferation of advanced weapons. These problems can, in part, be

addressed through export controls outlined in the Export Administration Act. Chapter 6 reviewed the international regimes designed to deal with nuclear proliferation, the proliferation of missile technologies, and the proliferation of chemical weapons. That analysis leads to four general observations:

1. *There are at present insufficient linkages between the CoCom regime and the various other multilateral arrangements established to address nuclear, missile, or chemical exports and CoCom.* The reasons for this lack of coordination include the varying memberships, targets, and associations with broad treaties. The structure of the regimes and the accountability of each member to the regime itself also vary.

2. *There is insufficient high-level leadership and policy coordination for a collective approach to proliferation problems.* If the various potential supplier states are pursuing uncoordinated policies—at one moment supplying potential proliferators for reasons of short-term foreign policy or commercial interests, at others, imposing bans or staking out strong moral positions against proliferation—determined proliferators will generally be able to "play the field" and continue to achieve their goals.

3. *The three proliferation control regimes do not cover all the proliferation issues of greatest security concern.* For example, it is easy to imagine military situations in which smart targeting technology, advanced reconnaissance and intelligence-gathering capabilities, or sophisticated command and control systems could have military significance comparable to the availability of some weapons covered under the current proliferation regimes.

4. *The three proliferation regimes are not well coordinated at the operational level either internationally or within the U.S. government.* The same countries or groups are often involved in more than one type of proliferation control activity. The same intermediaries are often involved in obtaining needed goods for several destinations or several different kinds of proliferation projects. In limited cases, the same technologies can be useful in several different types of proliferation activity. Although there are a number of dissimilarities among the proliferation regimes as well, the facts still suggest a need for much closer national and international coordination at the operational level.

Coordination of Current Regimes

The 12 members of the Missile Technology Control Regime (MTCR) are also members of CoCom, the Zangger Committee,* and the Australia Group. Most of the projects targeted by the MTCR are in countries that have not signed the Nuclear Non-Proliferation Treaty. Both the Zangger Committee

---

*Except Spain.

and the Australia Group are corollary arrangements to broad treaties. Beyond these facts, there are few similarities among the actual control regimes. Each of the regimes in question addresses a unique issue with its own problems and distinguishing characteristics.

The objectives of the various proliferation control regimes are not as narrow or distilled as the objectives of traditional CoCom controls. **Perhaps the most important distinction between East-West and proliferation controls, however, is that the United States is not in a position to exercise the same level of influence over the suppliers of goods related to nuclear, chemical, and missile proliferation. Indeed, some of the potential suppliers of these weapons of mass destruction also are the targets of current control regimes.** Moreover, as discussed in Chapter 7, it is critical to include the Soviet Union in multilateral arrangements to control the sale of advanced weapons and weapons capabilities.

The appropriate membership in a control regime depends on more, however, than the potential suppliers. It also depends on the specific intent of the control regime and the context within which the regime operates (e.g., as an outgrowth of treaty commitments or as a result of political-military alliances). **The number of participants in a regime and the nature of their relationship to each other affect the collective ability to specify control targets and mechanisms. As the number of participants increases and objectives become broader, the specificity with which targets and mechanisms can be defined declines. On the other hand, the impact of possible sanctions increases with the number of participants. The challenge is to define the objectives and obligations of control regimes so as to optimize their participation and scope without diluting their effectiveness.**

High-Level Leadership and Policy Coordination

If proliferation is to be effectively managed, two conditions must be met. First, legitimate security concerns of potential proliferators must be recognized and addressed, most likely in a regional context. Without a reduction in the threat and subsequent demand and commercial incentives for arms exports, any strategy to manage proliferation will be severely limited. Second, there must be a well-coordinated approach to dealing with specific states or groups that have been identified as being intent on proliferating.

These conditions, coupled with political reality, suggest that the most effective approach involves close coordination among a relatively small number of countries, including at least the United States, the United Kingdom, the Soviet Union, France, Germany, Japan, and China. This should be combined with a broad plan to strengthen and coordinate

existing international regimes to which all interested states could be parties, with the long-term goal of eventual consolidation.

Coordination among the major players could be achieved on an informal basis through one or more existing international mechanisms or through some new organization. CoCom often is suggested as an appropriate forum for coordinating the nonproliferation efforts of the major players, although given the group's historic focus, it is difficult to envision the Soviet Union or China as participants in CoCom discussions. The United Nations, and particularly the revitalized Security Council, may be a viable forum for achieving broad political consensus on these issues. Since several types of coordination are required, ranging from the development of broad political consensus to the specific coordination of sensitive intelligence and enforcement activities, more than one organizational framework may be necessary, and frequent informal consultations will almost certainly be essential. It is equally important that each of the participants coordinates its internal management of these issues to remain informed and to avoid working at cross-purposes.

In principle, it is desirable to integrate the existing international export control regimes to manage nuclear proliferation, the proliferation of missile technologies, and the proliferation of chemical weapons. The resulting single, integrated framework also could address the proliferation of advanced conventional weapons and related systems.

In practice, however, because of the differences in the basis and operation of the existing regimes, and the obstacles to negotiating the necessary arrangements among large numbers of states, it seems unlikely that the integration of all the existing regimes will be possible in the near future. **Hence, the United States should give high priority to the following:**

- **The development of formal or informal mechanisms that allow close and effective coordination among existing international proliferation control regimes. This should include cross-referencing existing control lists, sharing intelligence on targets and acquisition efforts, and cooperating on enforcement activities.**
- **The expansion of one of the existing regimes, or development of a new regime, to cover proliferation of advanced conventional weapons and related systems.**
- **The expansion of an existing regime, or development of a new regime, to consolidate the existing proliferation controls and the control of advanced conventional weapons and related systems.**

Prospects for success in these tasks will be considerably increased if the major players are able to provide coordinated leadership.

In the United States, additional coordination is required within the Department of State, as well as other agencies. Further, in U.S. embassies abroad it would be desirable to have one office handle all pro-

liferation-related matters. According to information gathered on the panel's European fact-finding mission, nuclear and missile technology regimes are handled by science attaches, while chemical issues may be handled by different attaches within the same embassy.

The Applicability of Export Controls to the Control of Proliferation

Table 7-1 listed eight forms that export controls can assume, ranging from embargo on the one end to simple monitoring of export activity at the other. To the extent that export controls are used as a tool in managing proliferation, different kinds of controls are likely to be most effective for different parts of the problem. For example, embargo is probably the correct solution for certain specific items, such as plutonium or highly enriched uranium. The optimal strategy for technologies such as advanced computing may involve a combination of selective prohibition and discretionary licensing based on end-use control (but discretion that is internationally coordinated, not left to the varying judgments of individual countries). Notification may be sufficient for a large set of potentially sensitive technologies because tracking may be the best strategy for many items. Informal government persuasion may be the most effective way of dealing with others. **The choice of an appropriate mix of controls for managing proliferation risks is a complex and difficult problem that requires far more careful and extensive study than this panel or any other group has yet been able to conduct.** Such analysis should be an important factor in the implementation of proliferation controls.

Whatever mix of policy tools is adopted to manage proliferation risks, and whatever role export controls play within that mix, one lesson from the history of East-West controls is very clear. **When the United States (or any other country) is trying to exert international leadership, unilateral proliferation controls may be appropriate for short durations. To be effective in the long run, however, proliferation controls must be undertaken on a multilateral basis.**

Great care must be exercised in developing any multilateral system of dual use export controls imposed to manage proliferation given the large number of dual use technologies that could potentially be affected. In some situations, however, only a relatively small number of destinations are likely to be of serious concern at any given time. This is particularly true, for instance, in regard to chemical weapons—the chemicals necessary to produce weapons are widely available and the weapons production process is relatively unsophisticated, but relatively few countries are suspected of developing chemical weapons.

Across-the-board licensing and screening of a broad range of items to numerous destinations will not be an efficient or effective way of controlling exports related to proliferation. Export controls should focus on a limited set of items and on specific target countries. This is true for several reasons:

- Wide application of export controls to prevent proliferation is probably unachievable and, in any event, would reduce the vigilance exercised over any given transaction. If vigilance is to be maximized, the controls must be very focused.
- General searches for patterns of diversion in worldwide trade data are a far less efficient strategy for identifying diversion than more targeted efforts. This is because fraudulent exports will not be reported and diversions typically involve a small portion of the enormous amount of international commercial trade.
- Overly wide application of export controls to prevent proliferation is likely to impose high costs on U.S. and other developed world economies. Previous experience with East-West controls suggests that this can lead to a rapid breakdown in consensus, a decrease in effectiveness, and disadvantages for U.S. exporters.

The United States should learn from its experience with East-West controls and work to ensure that, in developing a strategy for the management of proliferation risks, a broad and burdensome export control regime is not unilaterally applied to U.S. exporters. In order to employ export controls effectively in managing proliferation risks, the United States should take the following steps:

* **Analyze the relative usefulness and advantages or disadvantages of alternative types of export controls for different proliferation or security concerns.**

* **Focus proliferation controls narrowly on the proliferation risks and activities of greatest concern, including technical assistance.**

* **Develop a new regime, or expand an existing regime, to cover proliferation of advanced conventional weapons and related systems.**

* **Seek active, specific, and operational coordination on proliferation controls among the major players, including at least the United States, the United Kingdom, the Soviet Union, France, Germany, Japan, and China.**

* **As part of a broader strategy of managing proliferation risks, seek to strengthen and coordinate existing proliferation control regimes with the long-term goal of eventual consolidation.**

Nuclear Export Controls

The panel was not able to devote sufficient attention to the detailed operation of this or the two other proliferation regimes to offer complete and specific recommendations. The panel has, however, made several observations concerning multilateral nuclear export controls. First, not all countries capable of producing specially designed nuclear equipment, technology, and material have agreed to control the export of such items. Second, not all countries that have committed to control the export of specially designed nuclear equipment, technology, and materials have corresponding controls on nuclear-related dual use items. Although a number of the countries that participate in the Zangger Committee and Nuclear Suppliers Group have recently begun to recognize the importance of certain critical, dual use items to the development of nuclear weapons systems, the United States is still the only country practicing formal export controls on such items.

The Nuclear Non-Proliferation Treaty will be up for renewal in 1995. In the period since the treaty was negotiated, several additional states have become nuclear states. **Thus, a strategy must be developed by which newly nuclear states are brought within the appropriate treaty structure and encouraged to cooperate in the export control arrangements corollary to the treaty. It is also important to step up discussions with other Zangger Committee members to control the export of critical dual use items.**

Missile Export Controls

Although the Missile Technology Control Regime has had some success, several major impediments to real effectiveness remain. One such impediment is the fact that several major sources of advanced missile technology, including the Soviet Union, India, and China, are not official participants. Perhaps the most limiting factor, however, is the secrecy that surrounds the projects of concern. It is difficult to engage the cooperation of other countries and industry when neither the rationale for controls nor the targets can be identified. Secrecy also severely strains cooperation on legitimate civilian projects in countries regarding which there may be concern about nuclear missile development.

Disagreements among the regime's participants on the targets of export controls and conditions for acceptable dual use sales further exacerbate strained relations with both the importing country and regime partners. Some partners maintain that only projects in countries with unsafeguarded nuclear facilities should be subject to controls; others maintain that the possibility of reexport or retransfer necessitates worldwide controls. Some countries argue that government assurances against nuclear-missile end use are adequate conditions for the sale of dual use items; others argue that the reliability of such government assurances is suspect. Moreover, investigations and prosecution of end-use violations are difficult to conduct when the top priority is to protect intelligence sources and methods.

The effectiveness of this regime would be improved if conditions for approved exports and sanctions against the importing parties for violations of the export conditions were made standard and public among regime members. It is also important to include other major suppliers in the regime, but this is unlikely to happen, or to lead to greater effectiveness, until existing internal disputes are resolved.

The structure of the MTCR is an impediment to its effectiveness as well. An ad hoc demarche process for export denials and an erratic meeting schedule contribute to licensing discrepancies and engender too many urgent bilateral meetings. If left unresolved, this problem would be complicated further as the number of participants increased.

The primary arguments against a more structured regime and an expanded membership have been the relative standing of existing missile capabilities as either appropriate or inappropriate depending on the military and political alliances to which the end-user countries belong and the sensitive nature of the intelligence that contributes to identifying the regime's targets. As long as the regime continues to focus on inappropriate end users, political-military alliance and shared intelligence will remain the most critical elements of cooperation. Nevertheless, regime partners often disagree on the translation of mutual security and intelligence analysis into trade decisions. **The future direction of this regime is clearly a trade-off between (a) attempting to identify and subsequently embargo specific nonpeaceful missile delivery systems in a very closed and limited environment or (b) more broadly and publicly defining regime goals and proscribed end uses in the global context. The nature of the regime will determine the attitude of non-regime countries toward cooperation.**

Chemical Export Controls

The Australia Group has been operating as an interim mechanism in anticipation of completion of the Chemical Weapons Convention (CWC). The final details of the convention are still being negotiated, but the broad outlines are clear. The production and possession of chemical weapons will be banned (use is already banned under the Geneva accords). The convention will likely hold signatory governments explicitly responsible for reporting to a secretariat on all international trade in specific chemical precursors. It is unclear what explicit responsibility signatory governments will have in reviewing or constraining trade in identified precursors with nonsignatories. To date, process equipment and technology specially designed for chemical weapons production have not been identified.

The secretariat will include an inspection function for signatories, but the specific form that inspections will take—routine, challenge, ad hoc—is still under discussion. The possibility of inspection for nonsignatories receiving chemical weapons precursors also is under discussion. A number of nations participating in these negotiations are working hard to avoid the awkward three-part grouping of official-haves, unofficial-haves, and have-nots that has characterized the Nuclear Non-Proliferation Treaty.

Several problems are associated with controlling the export of chemical weapons precursors. For example, the fungibility of chemicals and the ease with which civilian manufacturing plants can be converted to chemical weapons plants limit the effectiveness of export controls. In addition, there is no standard method of controlling the export of identified precursors, either under the Australia Group or CWC, which also reduces the effectiveness of the controls and creates serious commercial inequalities.

Further, it is unclear how export controls might be employed in the event that a country is determined to possess or to be developing chemical weapons. The matter of collective sanctions for violating the terms of the CWC, or U.S. sanctions for violating the terms of the U.S. export license, must be resolved. Given the demonstrated willingness of some countries to use chemical weapons and the potential impact of such use on the world community, collective sanctions for possessing or developing chemical weapons should be established in the immediate future.

There is reason to be concerned that export controls related to the CWC, as well as the reporting requirements of the treaty, could impose significant economic costs on the chemical industry. Thus, it is important to ensure that the resulting system strikes an appropriate balance between the objective of limiting proliferation and the imposition of costs on the world's process chemical industry and to ensure that the actual operation of the system is equitable.

Recommendations for Specific Changes in Proliferation Control Regimes

With respect to specific proliferation control regimes, the United States should undertake the following:

* **Prepare both a U.S. and multilateral approach to the problem of states that have become nuclear but that are currently treated as nonnuclear under the Nuclear Non-Proliferation Treaty.**

* Encourage other participants in the Zangger Committee and Nuclear Suppliers Group to control the export of critical, dual use items.
* Work to resolve the internal problems in the Missile Technology Control Regime concerning appropriate conditions for sale and to expand membership to include other important supplier states, including the Soviet Union, India, and China.
* Construct a positive list of civilian space launch or satellite projects that have committed to peaceful end use and are certified as acceptable recipients of missile-related items.
* To the extent feasible, state the retransfer restrictions and end-use conditions necessary for acceptable sales of dual use items subject to missile technology controls.
* In negotiating the Chemical Weapons Convention, explicitly consider collective export control responses (sanctions) to nonsignatories that develop or possess chemical weapons.
* Seek enforcement and inspection procedures that successfully focus on those few destinations that pose the greatest proliferation risks.

9

Elements of a New Response: The U.S. Control Regime

As described in Chapter 6, the U.S. domestic policy process for export controls is characterized by significant policymaking and structural deficiencies. Multiple and overlapping administrative agencies, statutes, and regulations confound those attempting to use the system. Inadequate definitions for munitions and dual use items further complicate application of statutes to controlled items. In addition, interagency conflicts have been exacerbated by weak procedures for prompt resolution of disputes.

Defects in the organizational and regulatory structure are compounded by a lack of consistent leadership in the formulation and execution of clear, overall policy direction. **The 1990 CoCom decontrol and core list exercise demonstrated the value of exerting strong presidential leadership on the U.S. export control regime.** Such skillful response to an immediate crisis must be transformed into lasting structural change, however. The administrative agencies will continue to interpret differently the rules for judging licensing cases so long as they lack clearly specified guidelines. Moreover, the already challenging task of constructing control lists is made more difficult by the lack of sufficient criteria to weigh different kinds of threat. Further, provisions for industry participation at meaningful stages of the policy formulation process are insufficient. **Thus, substantial reform will be necessary to achieve the goals of an effective U.S. export control process.**

POLICY PROCESS GOALS

The export control policy process should be reformed in order to achieve the following results:

- Policy issues are resolved in a timely manner and policy decisions are enforced by the executing agency.
- Views of relevant departments are heard and considered, and unresolved cases presenting significant policy issues are taken to a senior-level interagency group for prompt resolution.
- The system is made simpler, more open, and internally consistent so that policymakers, administrators, and U.S. and foreign business can more easily understand it and work with it.
- The development of export control policy is well balanced, and industry and other affected parties have appropriate opportunities for input into policy formulation, including regulatory changes and list development.

Achievement of these goals would be expedited by a process in which policy formulation is handled through a mechanism separate from that of policy administration. A clearer division of functions would help dispel the current confusion in the bureaucracy between policy formulation and its implementation. Further, both processes must be restructured and strengthened. Clear policy guidance should be established through firm presidential leadership, and a more rational administrative apparatus should be constructed for execution of policy established by the President.

POLICY FORMULATION

A workable regulatory scheme and efficient administrative structure require strong policy direction. The executive branch must formulate an efficient and coherent policy development framework and provide an appropriate administrative structure to ensure that policy is properly executed, particularly because the absence of such guidance in the past has led to deficiencies in the policy process.

Presidential Leadership

The National Security Act of 1947, as amended, and subsequent legislation provide ample authority for the President to formulate and execute national security policy through the National Security Council (NSC). This includes authority to establish policy on export controls. The act states that

> the function of the National Security Council shall be to advise the President with respect to the integration of domestic, foreign, and military policies relating to the national security so as to enable the military services and the other departments and agencies of the Government to cooperate more effectively in matters involving the national security.[1]

Further, the act states that it is the NSC's duty

> to consider policies on matters of common interest to the departments and agencies of the Government concerned with the national security, and to make recommendations to the President in connection therewith.[2]

The President has authority under the act over three main areas: economic security, foreign policy, and military affairs. **Export control policy, however, has not heretofore been considered a formal part of national security policy.** For example, it has not been addressed to a sufficient degree in formal national security directives (NSDs) as has been the case with other areas of national security policy.

* **Since the National Security Act of 1947 and subsequent legislation give the President authority to provide detailed instructions on key components of export control policy, an NSD should be the President's vehicle for the formulation and implementation of export control policy.** Such a directive would specify the interagency mechanisms for implementing the President's policy, particularly with regard to a streamlined licensing system and a fast, effective dispute resolution process.

* **Through the vehicle of an NSD, the President should provide guidance on the fundamental objectives for all national security export controls (including munitions, dual use, and nuclear, missile, and chemical/biological controls) and direction for achieving those aims.**

Policy Mechanisms

A framework for national security export control decision making must include appropriate mechanisms for carrying out the policy enunciated by the President. **The arrangement for export controls should be part of the same apparatus for policy implementation that an administration establishes for any important component of national security. The relevant executive branch agencies should retain a strong voice in policymaking. The basic function of the policy mechanism should be to integrate the existing policy roles of the various executive branch agencies.** The hierarchical structure of what would be the four main elements of the policy formulation system for export control is as follows:

1. A comprehensive national security directive
2. An Export Control Policy Coordinating Committee (EC/PCC)
3. National security export control interagency groups
4. Working groups and technical groups

* **The NSD should lay out formally the details of this executive struc-**

ture, which would correspond roughly to the current administrative structure. Lines of responsibility and accountability should be clearly established among all the participating groups. These groups are briefly discussed below.

EXPORT CONTROL POLICY COORDINATING COMMITTEE

* **An Export Control Policy Coordinating Committee should be established to formulate and review policy recommendations, resolve exceptional disputes among agencies, and monitor the work of the interagency groups.** The EC/PCC would be the locus for export control policy decision making within the framework of the NSD. It should comprise senior representatives of involved departments and agencies. To ensure objective evaluation of disputes reaching this level and the immediate attention of the National Security Council as necessary, the EC/PCC should be chaired by the national security advisor or the deputy advisor.

The EC/PCC and the interagency groups should function as "courts of last resort" for officials seeking resolution of matters under dispute. If necessary, important unresolved issues would be referred to the full NSC for final action, although such referrals should be extremely rare. **Ultimately, strong presidential leadership is required if the export control policy system outlined above is to work effectively.**

NATIONAL SECURITY EXPORT CONTROL INTERAGENCY GROUPS

Under National Security Decision Directive 10, authority is granted to establish interagency working groups deemed important to U.S. national security policy.

* **Interagency working groups should be established as necessary to consider the appropriateness of export controls as a means of addressing overall U.S. national security and foreign policy objectives. Serving as the principal operating policy groups, they should advise the President on the advantages and disadvantages of the various U.S. export control programs and on the need for modification of current programs or for new programs.**

The interagency groups would oversee working and technical groups, resolve agency differences, and refer unresolved matters to the Policy Coordinating Committee. They would also verify that policy is uniformly applied by each group. Further, the interagency groups would ensure that technical advice from U.S. industry is included through the various advisory groups working with the agencies on decisions about additions to or deletions from control lists.

*   **Because export control policymaking is an extremely complex field that demands a high degree of technical sophistication and in-depth command of the interagency apparatus, the interagency groups should be given adequate staff support.**

WORKING GROUPS AND TECHNICAL GROUPS

*   **Necessary working groups of the interagency groups, including technical groups, should be established. These groups should be charged with responsibility for all areas relating to export controls.**

The technical groups, which would include the technical working groups and the technical advisory committees, should build on the functions currently performed in list construction. They would have the responsibilities discharged in the past by the technical task groups and should have industry representatives assigned from the technical advisory committees. **The technical groups should be provided with special expertise, including substantial input from U.S. industry, to handle particularly complex technical matters.**

The NSD should establish a lead agency to chair each working group and provide the technical groups with the requisite authority to perform their responsibilities. The lead agencies must be encouraged to be responsive to the requirements and suggestions of the technical groups.

NSD Areas of Concern

The NSD should include, in particular, guidance on the following critical aspects of export control.

LIST CONSTRUCTION

The NSD should establish the general policy and specific procedures for constructing and reviewing the control lists. The guidance regarding process methodology should cover at least the following areas:

*   **Establish interagency methodology for list construction, including criteria or standards for determining military criticality, economic costs, and other factors.**
*   **Specify agencies responsible for assessing the national security importance of controlled items and clarify priorities (or burden of proof) for balancing diverse interests.**

- **Specify the process for resolving disputes over list construction.** (See Chapter 10 for a detailed discussion of list construction and review.)

REGULATORY PROCEDURES, LICENSING, AND DISPUTE RESOLUTION

The NSD should establish guidance for the development of regulatory control regimes, including establishing the targets of controls, such as destinations and end uses. **The NSD should also prescribe parameters for distinguishing between routine and exceptional licensing cases and detail the decision-making process for each.** The directive should identify responsibilities for review and resolution of exceptional cases. Time limits should be included to ensure expeditious decision making. **Designated authorities must define the criteria for referral of licenses to interagency resolution.**

*   **To eliminate the existing public confusion over the specific terms of U.S. export control policy, which is a major defect of the current system, presidential guidance should be made public to the extent feasible. Although elements of the NSD might require classification, broad policy concepts and the details of policy execution should be stated publicly.**

POLICY EXECUTION

More efficient case processing, better procedures for dispute resolution, and greater system transparency are among the potential gains from a revised administrative process.

Consolidated Administration

*   **In order to achieve a more rational and effective export control process, the U.S. domestic process should be reconfigured through consolidation of all day-to-day administrative functions in a single agency. Single agency authority for day-to-day functions will have the following advantages:**
  - **Establish a more rational and consistent regulatory structure.**
  - **Achieve efficiency in list administration and implementation of regulatory changes.**
  - **Attain further improvement in license processing.**
  - **Avoid jurisdictional disputes at the administrative level.**
  - **Facilitate industry's access to information on export control requirements.**

- **Increase efficiency by consolidating the electronic data processing functions of various administrative agencies.**

The reorganization and accompanying policy directives will give the single agency final authority to make decisions on routine licenses, to promulgate regulations, and to resolve interpretive disputes within the specific policy guidelines of the NSD. Many routine licensing decisions, for example, are of a level that can best be handled within the independent authority of a single administrative agency. Authority also should extend to administrative aspects of list management. The consolidation will entail combining regulatory regimes to achieve uniform administrative requirements with levels of control appropriate for attainment of policy objectives.

* **At the same time, the agency's decision making should be guided by the broad policy framework developed in the traditional interagency process. The goal of the reorganization is to consolidate *administration* of controls based on an internally consistent set of regulations while keeping broad *policymaking* and final dispute resolution in the hands of the President and responsible cabinet secretaries in the National Security Council and the Export Control Policy Coordinating Committee.**

* **Responsibility for the administration of restrictions on dual use items, munitions, items controlled for nonproliferation purposes, and trade-related items under "emergency" powers should be transferred to the single agency.**

* **The goal of a more transparent licensing process should be achieved through a "one-stop shopping" mechanism, that is, a single administrative window for exporters seeking to obtain licenses.**

Users of the proposed system should be able to submit license applications and obtain data on regulations and control criteria from the same office. A single-window approach should alleviate what is probably the single largest cause of processing delays: exporters' failure to provide sufficient licensing information. **A single-window approach will be considerably facilitated by setting up the single licensing agency.**

* **"One-stop shopping" should be established in harmony with other restructuring of the control apparatus lest it devolve into a well-intended but ineffective initiative.**

Administrative Alternatives

The panel evaluated two basic alternatives for consolidating agency functions. The first alternative is to put administrative functions in a newly created administrative structure. The second is to consolidate functions in an existing department or agency.

The first alternative has certain advantages. Creation of a separate agency could tie together the disparate threads of a complex policy based on multiple, sometimes contradictory, interests. A new agency would, in theory, put an end to bureaucratic battles over turf by placing previously established agencies under one roof. The importance of issues pertaining to export controls arguably justifies a separate agency devoted to such concerns. A new agency might be expected to give added status to export control issues.

A new agency would face several serious practical impediments, however. It would be dwarfed in size, budget, and influence by established organizations, particularly the Defense and State Departments. Its creation likely would encounter opposition from agencies and congressional committees defending current jurisdictional prerogatives. A new agency might simply lead to another layer of bureaucracy that would hobble instead of expedite the policy process. And it might have a self-interest in regulation that would lead to perpetuation of controls no longer justified by changing circumstances.

Given the progress that has been made so far in improving both policy and process, the panel concludes that it would be better to modify the current system rather than start anew. In consolidating administrative functions, it would be sensible to select as the chief administrative agency one of the three departments—State, Defense, or Commerce—primarily involved in export controls.

The State Department has an advantage in that its administrative agency has recently been reorganized, staff has been added, and facilities have been upgraded. **Yet, in several ways the State Department is not an optimal setting for an administrative agency. The State Department is oriented primarily to matters of high-level policy and foreign affairs, not the detailed work of a licensing bureau.** The emphasis on foreign policy also diverts attention from a focus on commercial matters that must be part of any trade administration system.

The Defense Department has been intensively involved with both license review and list construction, and it has substantial technical expertise on export control in its Office of the Under Secretary for Acquisition and its Defense Technology and Security Administration. It also has considerable experience in international commerce through the foreign military sales program. **Given its central mission, however, the Defense Department would not be sufficiently responsive to balancing military and commercial concerns, particularly in regard to exports of dual use items.**

Compared with the Departments of Defense and State, the Commerce Department does not possess the same amount of influence on, or participation in, national security affairs. In addition, the Commerce Department has the mission of promoting U.S. business, a condition that potentially could bias it toward relaxation of controls.

The Commerce Department's Bureau of Export Administration (BXA), however, already handles—in dollar value—the great majority of cases processed by the export control system, and it has undergone considerable administrative improvement of its own. *It has an established administrative apparatus*, which has achieved a reasonable degree of efficiency over the past few years. **Further, the agency has dealt with a broad spectrum of products and technologies, and it has a sophisticated and reasonably comprehensive regulatory scheme.** The Export Administration Act (EAA) already identifies the Commerce Department as the implementing agency for the act, which covers the broader portion of the export control spectrum.

The improved policy formulation process proposed here would alleviate some of the current inevitable mixing of policy formulation and execution in an agency charged with both export regulation and promotion. **In this regard, the panel has determined to its satisfaction that BXA's export administration functions are sufficiently separate from the export promotion activities of the Commerce Department.**

*   **Therefore, the Commerce Department's Bureau of Export Administration should be selected as the single administrative agency for export controls.**
*   **As part of the consolidation of functions, measures should be taken to lessen any remaining deficiencies at BXA, such as strengthening technical center staff at the Office of Technology and Policy Analysis and upgrading its professional grade levels.**

OTHER CHANGES RELATING TO PROPOSED REFORMS

The enhancement of policy decision making and the administrative reforms outlined above will not address all the issues and problems of the export control system. This is partly because no bureaucratic construct is perfect, and partly because the reforms will have to be accompanied by certain legislative and other administrative changes to become operative.

Changes in Agency and Legislative Authority

If the single agency scheme is to work, the U.S. government will have to make the necessary changes to existing legislation and governmental structure for export control administration. Some of the proposed changes can be implemented within existing legislative mandates, but certain reforms would require that Congress amend the relevant acts. For example, ending the overlap between the Export Administration Act and the Arms Export

Control Act would require amendments to legislation. **Harmonization of varying statutory authority will demand strong executive branch leadership and extensive cooperation on the part of Congress.**

Although the proposed changes would require some statutory revision and some transfer of functions among executive branch agencies, responsibilities for policy formulation would remain with the appropriate departments, subject to coordination with congressional bodies and the mechanism for interagency policy formulation. In addition, agencies with special expertise would be involved in the interagency and working groups and license reviews.

Standards for Munitions and Dual Use Items

The absence of clear policy direction is perhaps most evident in the definitional problems plaguing the current system. It is difficult to administer a set of dual use controls without firm guidance on the standards to be used in distinguishing dual use items from inherently military ones. Since separate laws and agencies regulate export controls, better criteria for defining the scope of the statutes are required to reduce the confusion over jurisdiction. A serious problem is the lack of an effective, balanced mechanism for resolving disputes among agencies over commodity jurisdiction, that is, the classification of an item as a dual use or munitions item.

* **If the control scheme is to involve separate lists for munitions and dual use items, the delineation between the two lists should be clear, especially if each list is separately administered, as at present.**

* **The terms *defense articles* and *dual use goods and technologies* should be clearly differentiated if the Munitions List is to remain distinct from the Commodity Control List. If a separate Munitions List is maintained, it should contain only (1) items specially designed for a significant and uniquely military application and (2) items that do not have essentially the same performance, capacity, or function as items used for commercial purposes.**

Integration and Review of Control Lists

Apart from improvements to the methodology for list construction and review (see Chapter 10), other enhancements to list management are recommended.

* **A set of integrated U.S. control lists should be fashioned so that the different lists are similarly structured and formatted.** Integrating the lists will lessen overlap and discrepancies among the control lists and conflicts among associated regulations. By keeping the system as simple as possible, the goal of greater transparency of the control system

will also be furthered. **The respective structures of the U.S. and international control lists should also be harmonized.**

* **Building on progress made so far in the policy process, the United States should continue to make the appropriate shift of administrative resources from traditional East-West export controls to controls directed at proliferation concerns and the end-use verification of more narrowly targeted East-West controls, as suggested by the panel.**

* **An interagency task group should regularly review the Munitions and Commodity Control Lists to eliminate duplication and ensure coordination with the CoCom Industrial List. The U.S. dual use list should be compatible with other multilateral control arrangements.**

Time Limits and Dispute Resolution

Deadlines for the resolution of differences among the export control agencies have been imposed in the past by Congress. For example, according to Section 10(e) of the Export Administration Act, an agency to which a Commerce Department export license application is referred must submit its recommendation within 20 days,[3] thereby preventing the equivalent of an agency pocket veto. **Deadlines have had some benefit in spurring decision making on case processing, jurisdictional determinations, and list review. Shorter, legislatively mandated deadlines in themselves could be ineffective, however, because if pressed for a decision, the "fast response" from the administering agency would likely be a recommendation of denial.**

* **Clear policy guidance, including guidance on timely procedures for resolving interagency disputes, should be provided to obviate most of the need for legislated deadlines.**

Administrative Due Process and Appropriate Judicial Review

* **The statutory exemption (Section 13(a) of the EAA) from the application of certain provisions of the Administrative Procedure Act (APA), including the appropriate level of administrative due process and judicial review of Commerce Department actions, should be removed.**

The application of the administrative due process and judicial review provisions of the APA is not inconsistent with the protection of national security or foreign policy interests. Classified information or other national-security-sensitive information can be safeguarded within the framework of the APA. When required, licenses may be revoked or new controls imposed without the otherwise-required opportunity for prior comment on or contest of the action. **The courts, which have traditionally deferred to the executive branch on matters of policy, would afford appropriate latitude for agency discretion.**

Congress has already afforded a significant measure of due process to parties that are the subject of civil enforcement proceedings under the EAA, including the opportunity to be heard before an administrative law judge and to seek judicial review under standards identical to Section 706 of the APA, that is, reversal for lack of substantial evidence or for abuse of agency discretion or error of law. **Removal of the Section 13(a) barrier would not significantly alter the current treatment of civil enforcement cases.**

Congress has expressed its "intent," in Section 13(b) of the EAA, that "to the extent practicable" regulations are to be "issued in proposed form with meaningful opportunity for public comment."

*   **This provision should be retained even if Section 13(a) is repealed, since under the APA any agency may exempt regulations from pre-issuance for public comment if security or foreign policy so require.**

The repeal of Section 13(a) would more effectively ensure public participation in the development of regulations. In addition, the repeal of Section 13(a) would more effectively ensure execution of congressional mandates. For example, a number of EAA amendments affected by the Omnibus Trade and Competitiveness Act of 1988 were not implemented within the time periods specified. The prospect of judicial intervention would ensure more timely agency responses.

The repeal of Section 13(a) also would afford access to the courts for unsuccessful license applicants. **The APA standard for judicial review, however, would deny relief except for absence of procedural due process and for arbitrary action.** The courts could not question policy decisions, including determination of what items should be subject to export control.

It is unlikely, in the panel's judgment, that these changes would unduly burden the Commerce Department in administering the EAA or lead to an excess of litigation. Such consequences have not been observed in similar programs under other statutes, including the Arms Export Control Act and the International Emergency Economic Powers Act, that are not exempt from the APA.

Enforcement Issues

In the area of sanctions, proposals have been made for certain agencies to take exclusive responsibility for enforcement of U.S. export controls. **Opposing views over which agency should have primacy in various enforcement areas are indicative of broader problems concerning admin-**

istrative responsibility for trade enforcement. Those problems extend well beyond the direct domain of export controls and involve a number of enforcement bodies, including the Customs Service, the Drug Enforcement Administration, and the Office of Export Enforcement. Examination by the panel indicated that more time and resources would be necessary to develop sound recommendations to resolve these issues.

* **Accordingly, the General Accounting Office should be requested to undertake a study of this important problem.** Questions the study should address include the following:
  - What are the requirements for enforcement in the various export control laws and how do they differ for the Export Administration Act, Arms Export Control Act, Atomic Energy Act, Nuclear Non-Proliferation Act, International Emergency Economic Powers Act, and the Trading with the Enemy Act?
  - To what extent are there problems with enforcement of the Export Administration Act? Specifically,
    — Are organizations effectively accomplishing their assigned enforcement missions?
    — Are enforcement resources allocated rationally?
    — Are there mechanisms to promote coordination and cooperation in enforcement efforts?
    — Do efficiencies result from linking administration to enforcement?
    — What is the degree of exporter cooperation with the Commerce Department and the Customs Service?
  - What enforcement improvements are required?
  - Is there a more effective basis for organizing enforcement responsibilities?

* **More specifically, an effort should be made to analyze and systemize the various criminal and civil sanctions in the U.S. export control statutes. In addition, given that a number of export control statutes lack civil enforcement provisions, consideration should be given to enactment of appropriate civil sanctions for export control violations, together with adoption of appropriate procedures for implementation of those sanctions.**

* **With regard to administration of enforcement, uniformity of administrative procedures should be part of the single administrative agency recommended by the panel. The existing Commerce Department enforcement procedures appear to be appropriate. In the absence of single agency administration, therefore, enforcement procedures similar to those of the Commerce Department should be instituted in the other affected agencies.**

U.S. Representation at CoCom

In addition to problems with the domestic process, the U.S. portion of the CoCom process is also flawed. Of particular note are the inadequacy of industry representation, insufficient dissemination of information on the control list and CoCom decisions, and the technical proficiency of the staff of the permanent U.S. mission.

* **Given the increasing relative importance of international economic concerns and the greater weight U.S. partners in CoCom attach to trade considerations, industry concerns should be more fully represented at CoCom discussions.**
* **As with the U.S. government domestic process, the CoCom process should be made more transparent. There is ample justification for publishing material such as the Industrial List, the CoCom schedule of list review, and, to the extent security considerations permit, commonly agreed criteria for CoCom decision making.**
* **The level of technical knowledge of the permanent U.S. mission to CoCom should be upgraded to the extent necessary.**

ENHANCING INDUSTRY PARTICIPATION

Greater balance and effectiveness in the export control system require a greater level of industry participation in the system. **A process in which defense, economic, and foreign policy concerns are all coordinated into a cohesive U.S. policy must be further encouraged.**

* **To improve the current level of industry input, the President should establish a permanent industry advisory committee on export administration.** To ensure continuity from administration to administration, the committee should be required by law. The committee should have the following features:
  * **Charter—Advise the government on all forms of export controls that may be authorized by law or executive order.** Responsibilities would include evaluation of and recommendation for the following:
    — the role and value of export controls in achieving national objectives;
    — the effectiveness and impact of current and proposed control policies, methodologies, and processes; and
    — improved approaches to achieving national objectives through controls or alternative means.

    The committee also would provide oversight and appropriate coordination of specialized advisory groups, such as the technical advisory committees.

- **Membership—Industry members (representing firms affected by export controls) would be appointed by the President from nominations made by the key agencies: Commerce, Defense, State, and Energy.** Policy-level officials of the four departments, the intelligence community, and the Treasury Department could be designated to serve by their agency heads. Delegates from the congressional committees responsible for export control oversight also would be desirable.

- **Terms—Industry members would be appointed for staggered, six-year terms to ensure continuity across changes of administration.**

- **Chairperson—The chairperson would be appointed by the President from the industry members.**

- **Secretariat—The Commerce Department would provide the necessary staff and resources to support the committee's work.**

*   In addition, the following changes should be made to the technical advisory committees to enhance the breadth of their charge, level of interagency participation, and amount of technical expertise:

- **The scope of the charge of the technical advisory committees should be broadened to include nonproliferation controls and munitions controls.**

- **The State and Defense Departments should appoint a portion of the industry members** to ensure their confidence in committee expertise in defense products and technologies.

- **The Defense Department should appoint at least one representative to each technical advisory committee to serve as a regular participant.** Other agencies should appoint participants to a committee when that committee's scope is relevant to the agency's charge or when agency participation is requested by a committee.

- **Representatives of the technical advisory committees should be assigned as regular participants in interagency or other established technical decision-making groups on export control lists and procedures.** Such participation should include substantial involvement in interagency meetings, from list construction and review all the way through to the end of the CoCom meetings.

- **Technical advisory committees should be supported with resources (provided equally by the Commerce, State, and Defense Departments) that are sufficient to provide technical staffing by the Institute for Defense Analyses and to pay the travel expenses of industry members.**

- **The activities of the technical advisory committees and working groups should be coordinated through the Institute for Defense**

Analyses to ensure the committees an adequate level of technical support.

In addition to implementation of a permanent advisory committee and the upgrading of the technical advisory committees, a third step should be taken to achieve greater balance among national security, foreign policy, and economic considerations: *economic security must be institutionalized in a national security framework*. It was for this reason that the previous Academies' study, the Allen report, recommended that the Commerce and Treasury Departments participate in National Security Council meetings on export controls.

The Department of Commerce is not a statutory member of the National Security Council. This privilege has been reserved for government officials most directly concerned with military security—the President, the vice president, and the secretaries of state and defense. The National Defense Act provides that the President may invite others to NSC deliberations, and statutes over the years have provided for specific individuals to serve as advisors at NSC meetings in particular areas of expertise. Thus, the chairman of the Joint Chiefs of Staff, the director of central intelligence, and the director of the Arms Control and Disarmament Agency have been designated by statute as advisors.

* **Because many important national security issues will involve serious economic concerns, those federal agencies responsible for economic matters should be formally brought into the policy process for meetings in which their expertise could serve the national interest. Specifically, the secretary of commerce should be included routinely as an advisor/participant in National Security Council discussions.**

NOTES

1. National Security Act of 1947, Section 101(a).
2. National Security Act of 1947, Section 101(b)(2).
3. Export Administration Regulations, October 1988, Section 10(e).

10

Improving Methods for List Construction and Review

Implementing U.S. export control policy involves balancing conflicting national interests. Achieving that balance requires trade-offs between the potential benefits that can accrue to national security from export controls and the potential costs that such controls can impose on U.S. foreign policy and economic objectives. Principal among U.S. foreign policy interests is encouraging economic liberalization and democratization in the Soviet Union and other countries that are the targets of controls. On the economic side, a principal interest involves building and sustaining U.S. economic strength and competitive position in world markets. If the control system was truly multilateral, the economic cost of controls would be modest, primarily forgone direct sales to the targeted destinations. If the United States continues to implement controls unilaterally, the costs to U.S. economic strength and competitive position in world markets could be substantial.

The process the United States has been using for list construction and review for East-West controls has not struck a balance among national interests in an efficient and satisfactory way. Although the list review undertaken by the Coordinating Committee for Multilateral Export Controls (CoCom) in mid-1990 has changed this situation somewhat, many fundamental problems remain. Historically, there have been five basic difficulties with the U.S. system for list construction and review:

1. The absence of significant constraints on the defense and intelligence communities with respect to the number of items that can be controlled. As

a result, there is an incentive to list everything that might conceivably have utility to the targeted destinations.

2. The absence of any mechanism that forces the defense and intelligence communities to reveal the strength of their preferences among the items they propose to control. The result is that it has often been impossible for high-level decision makers to determine the relative degree of criticality of the items proposed for control.

3. The absence of any mechanism that forces the foreign policy and commercial communities to reveal their views about the relative costs to short- and long-term U.S. foreign policy and trade interests that would result from controlling an item.

4. The absence of clear decision-making authority to "balance the national interest." This, combined with bureaucratic political maneuvering, has led to interagency gridlock, which has proved remarkably resilient to legislative "fixes."

5. The absence of a means by which the system can be easily tuned to respond to changing international political and military circumstances or to changing priorities and judgments of the national political leadership.

This chapter presents an improved method that addresses these five problems. An improved method can lead to more efficient and effective list construction and review, but it is not a magic solution. Consistent, high-level political will can make a variety of methods work; lacking such will, even very good methods may only marginally improve the system.

* **The process for choosing items for control within any particular control regime should involve the following:**
  * **Identification of items of potential concern.**
  * **A rank ordering and weighting of items in terms of the national security risks posed by an adversary's acquisition and use of each item, with careful consideration given to the controllability of items.**
  * **An approximate rank ordering and weighting of items in terms of the economic and foreign policy costs of restricting trade in each item of concern.**
  * **A policy judgment as to how the risks and benefits of control should be balanced.**
  * **A comparison of benefits and costs that allows a sorting into controlled and uncontrolled items.**

This chapter focuses on trade with the Soviet Union, beginning with how a control list should be constructed. A similar approach can also be applied, however, to other possible CoCom-controlled destinations, such as Eastern

Europe and China, and to the control of technologies important in the proliferation of advanced conventional weapons and weapons of mass destruction. The focus throughout is on developing a general philosophical approach.
Many detailed policy and administrative judgments would be required to
specify all the operational details of a new system. The ongoing construction
of the CoCom core list is methodologically ad hoc. Future list review, as
well as possible future reconstructions, would benefit from a more systematic
approach.

REDESIGNING LIST CONSTRUCTION AND REVIEW FOR EAST-WEST CONTROLS

Identify Items of Concern

Many dual use items might provide military benefits to the Soviet Union.
These can include systems, individual products, critical components, unique
or exotic materials, associated test and calibration equipment, software, and
technical data and know-how. For simplicity, these have been referred to
throughout this report as "items."

If the U.S. objective was to control, without constraints, all items that
might conceivably provide some military benefit to the Soviets, list construction would be simple. Listing any item would only require an argument about
how, if acquired, that item might contribute to Soviet military capabilities.
A balancing of benefits and costs, however, requires a more focused determination. For this, two refinements are required. First, the objective to be
served by control must be stated precisely. Second, items to be controlled
must be defined with precision so that judgments about relative preferences
for control can be made.

Broadly, trade in dual use items can provide military benefits to an adversary in four ways:

1. *Immediate* insertion of items into military systems. Examples include
substitution of a more reliable Western computer chip in a military system
and insertion of a modern telephone switch into an existing military command
and control system.*

2. Direct insertion of items into *future* military systems. Examples include
design of a high-performance Western computer chip into a new weapons
system and design of a high-performance array processor into a sonar target
acquisition and tracking system.

---

*Intelligence evidence suggests that the Soviet Union has rarely made such direct use of
Western hardware in fielded systems.

3. *Short-term enabling* of military systems. Examples include acquisition of high-performance machine tools that can make better tank fire-control systems or quieter submarine propellers.

4. *Long-term enabling* of military capabilities. Examples include almost any item that could accelerate or strengthen the development of the basic capabilities of Soviet high-technology industry, such as large numbers of medium-performance engineering work stations and joint ventures or technical exchanges that result in significant numbers of Soviet citizens learning how to manage manufacturing and research and development operations efficiently.

Any system that is designed to identify militarily critical items for potential control, however, will bog down in conflict and disagreement unless it receives clear presidential policy guidance through a national security directive (NSD) that specifies the objectives it is supposed to address and with what relative importance.

Once a class of items has been identified for potential control, it must be subdivided into smaller groups so that decisions can be made about the relative importance of controlling items with different characteristics. For example, suppose that under the general class of items called ''computers'' both high-performance engineering work stations and supercomputers are proposed as candidates for control. The security risks posed by trade in these two items are quite different. Both may be candidates for control, but the relative importance of controlling the two items is not simply a technical judgment; it also depends on the policy guidance that has been provided.

In order to determine the relative importance of controlling the two items, it must be possible to differentiate between them. The current system does not provide for such differentiation; rather, current regulations state only that ''computers with more than certain specified capabilities are controlled.'' The result is that if senior decision makers try to make balancing decisions among conflicting national interests, they are unable to determine how much more or less important military and intelligence authorities believe it is to control supercomputers versus advanced work stations. Under the current system, discussion of any such trade-off explodes into a mass of details, for which senior decision makers may not have the requisite expert knowledge or the time to analyze fully.

Given even the few classes of items that are proposed for control on the CoCom core list, the number of potential individual items is enormous. In order to make comparisons feasible, items must be grouped into sets. For convenience, these sets are called item-groups.*

---

*Defining item-groups poses some important technical problems. Details are discussed in Appendix J.

Identify the Relative National Security Benefits of Controls

Once a list of items proposed for control has been assembled and sorted into item-groups, military and intelligence authorities must assess the relative security risks that would be posed by trade with the Soviet Union in each item-group. To make these judgments, the following information is required:

• High-level policy guidance, in the form of an NSD, that spells out control objectives. Without such guidance, military and intelligence authorities may have difficulty making judgments about the relative importance of trade in different item-groups because they will not be able place their judgments in the context of U.S. policy objectives.

• An explicit assessment of the nature of current and likely future military threats posed by the Soviet Union and an understanding of how Western dual use items might contribute to the evolution of such threats. This is needed so that the relative importance of candidate item-groups can be assessed.

• An assessment of the controllability of each item-group. If the objective was simply to deny, without any limits, export of all items that might conceivably provide some military benefit to the Soviet Union, this factor would not matter. Even a very leaky export denial system would, to some limited extent, probably impede acquisition of Western technology. But export denial is not the objective. The objective is to limit the contributions of Western dual use items to the Soviet military while simultaneously balancing foreign policy and trade objectives. (The issue of controllability is discussed at the end of this chapter.)

In light of these three factors, defense authorities, with advice and assistance from the intelligence community, should take the following steps:

• Place the entire list of item-groups into a rank ordering, from those in most critical need of control to those that are least in need of control.

• Allocate a finite number of points (e.g., 1,000) across the item-groups in proportion to the intensity with which control is desired.

Such a process of ranking and weighting will pose some challenges to defense and intelligence authorities. Appendix J discusses how this might be done. Because it is likely to be sensitive, the weighted list should probably be classified.

Identify the Relative Economic and Foreign Policy Costs of Controls

If the control system was truly multilateral, so that every obstacle to trade that was faced by U.S. suppliers was faced by every other exporter, the economic costs of controlling exports to targeted nations would be fairly modest. As long as export control is not strictly multilateral, potentially much larger costs in terms of the impact on U.S. competitive advantages, such as early market position and relative reliability of suppliers, must also be considered.

Considerations of foreign policy costs must weigh the potential advantages to U.S. national security of promoting the current processes of restructuring, openness, and democratization that are under way in the Soviet Union. In theory, a full ordering and weighting of item-groups proposed for control could be undertaken to reflect considerations of U.S. national foreign policy and international competitiveness. Although such an exercise may be feasible for the hierarchically organized defense community, it may not be feasible for the heterogeneous groups that represent U.S. national foreign policy and trade interests.

Despite this, some approximate indication of the foreign policy and economic costs of controlling various item-groups would be helpful to decision makers faced with balancing national interests. Two possibilities exist. Costs could be factored in through a qualitative process, perhaps informed by advisory groups and by opportunities for public comment. Alternatively, an independent advisory group appointed by the secretaries of state and commerce could sort item-groups into a small number of very broad categories, such as the following:

Category 1:   trade with the Soviet Union in this item is of *great importance* to meeting U.S. foreign policy and/or trade objectives.

Category 2:   trade with the Soviet Union in this item is of *importance* to meeting U.S. foreign policy and/or trade objectives.

Category 3:   trade with the Soviet Union in this item is of *limited importance* to meeting U.S. foreign policy and/or trade objectives.

The NSD should provide guidance on the factors that should be considered in doing the sorting and weighting of items in the first two categories.* In contrast to the defense/intelligence weights, there is no reason to classify the results of this process. Indeed, making the results public should help to stimulate a full and balanced consideration of the relevant issues.

Compare and Balance Benefits and Costs

After the evaluation of the several national interests, the final step is to strike a balance among those interests and develop a list proposal that will guide the U.S. position in CoCom. Creating this balance requires that the NSD specify two things:

---

*In general, no weight would be assigned to the third category.

1. a decision-making process and a responsible decision maker, and
2. guidelines as to how the balance among interests is to be struck.

Balancing the several national interests involves more than simply looking at the rank ordering provided by the defense and intelligence communities and deciding where to draw a line. When the foreign policy and trade costs of controls are combined with the estimated national security benefits, the actual order of item-groups, in terms of "net benefits," may change.

If the process of enumerating foreign policy and trade costs is qualitative, the final estimation of net benefits and the resulting ordering of the list will similarly have to be qualitative. If foreign policy and trade costs have been sorted into several categories, as outlined above, a somewhat more quantitative sorting may be undertaken to guide and assist decision makers in regularizing the list construction process and enable them to focus their attention on those decisions that most require their powers of qualitative judgment.

In either case, the end result should be a proposed control list that can be presented for multilateral consideration in CoCom. In principle, the identification, prioritizing, ranking, and balancing tasks could be repeated on a multilateral basis within CoCom for final development of the CoCom list. It seems unlikely, however, that many of the CoCom allies would be prepared to adopt so systematic and labor intensive an approach to list construction. If the United States adopts a strategy based on this philosophical framework, however, the multilateral process should be able to share the benefits of the results.

List Review, Sunsetting, and Occasional Reconstruction

It is likely that the new control list would be shorter than previous lists. This should make it possible for CoCom to review the entire list annually. Indeed, review of the entire list as a single process is essential if the balancing of interests is to be achieved.

In order to develop the U.S. position for the annual process of CoCom list review, the internal U.S. evaluation and prioritization effort should be repeated annually. Although the first attempt will be time consuming, future annual cycles should be fairly simple.

In addition to annual review, a more automatic process that regularly removes older items from the CoCom list should be implemented. This might be done in a number of ways. The boxed insert "One Possible Procedure for Sunsetting CoCom List Items" provides a specific example. Another example is in the field of supercomputers. In the absence of periodic reviews, consideration should be given to other review mechanisms, such as indexing

One Possible Procedure for Sunsetting CoCom List Items

The West has, on average, been unable to sustain more than an eight-year technological lead over the Soviet Union. If, as expected, the Soviet Union grows increasingly open over the next few years, and if the perceived and actual threats continue to decline, export controls will probably be unable to maintain even this much of a lead.

These considerations suggest that technologies that are more than eight years old should be removed from the CoCom list. The removal process could be automated if, through its member governments, CoCom maintained a data base to which manufacturers could send information whenever they ship a new product that advances any performance parameter used in specifying a CoCom control. Eight years after the date of the first commercial shipment of that product, items with that level of performance would automatically come off the list. Submissions to the data base would be certified as authentic by participating member governments, subject to challenge through CoCom. The data base would be maintained as an open public record so that manufacturers in any CoCom country could have access.

A few special technologies may warrant control even after their performance specifications are more than eight years old. If CoCom wished to continue to control such a technology, before the end of the seventh year CoCom members could act unanimously to relist the item for up to an additional eight years.

Such a system could be started in either of two ways. Companies could submit shipping records over the past eight years in order to construct the necessary base lines, or the system could be applied only prospectively to new technologies.

(raising the threshold for controls as overall item-group performance capabilities increase).

Beyond annual list review, it may, from time to time, become appropriate to undertake additional reconstructions of the CoCom list. There are two reasons why such periodic reconstructions might be useful:

1. The direction of the CoCom unanimity rule is reversed so that unanimity becomes necessary to put something on the list rather than take it off. This could help to reduce the accumulation of low-end items, a problem that has plagued the CoCom list management process in the past.

2. The promise of list reconstruction, tied to accomplishment of certain specified milestones in arms control, might provide a useful additional incentive to the Soviet Union to be more forthcoming in strategic arms negotiations.

GENERALIZATION TO OTHER CONTROL REGIMES

The philosophy of list construction for controls on the Soviet Union can be generalized to other countries and other export control regimes. The same need to balance national interests applies in the context of other CoCom-controlled destinations, such as the People's Republic of China, and to destinations of proliferation concern. Because U.S. national security, foreign policy, and economic interests are significantly different in these contexts, however, separate prioritizations are likely to be necessary, although they should benefit greatly from the analysis that is done in support of controls on exports to the Soviet Union.

CONTROLLABILITY

In the long run, export controls are a defensible policy tool only if they are applied to items that are, in fact, controllable. Two kinds of controllability are important in East-West dual use export control: *export* controllability and *end-use* controllability. The first refers to the feasibility of denying or significantly limiting exports from the West to the targeted countries. The second refers to the extent to which, once exported to a targeted country, a dual use item can be prevented from being used to direct military advantage.

Effective East-West *export controls* require that the items to be controlled have the following properties:

- Manufactured and/or sold by only a modest number of suppliers whose actions can be controlled.
- Consumed or used by only a modest number of consumers whose export actions can be controlled.
- Individually traceable or not easily concealed or disguised.

Other, rather different properties may apply in the context of proliferation controls.

Modest numbers of suppliers and consumers are required to make policing possible. If the number of either becomes large, it becomes impossible to keep track of everyone, and the odds of undetected diversions increase rapidly. Similarly, if individual items cannot be accounted for, they can be easily concealed or disguised and/or can easily get ''lost'' and be diverted. The current system of foreign availability addresses only the first of these requirements. If items of concern are manufactured only in CoCom countries, or in countries subscribing to CoCom rules, the first requirement above can probably be met. If items are also manufactured in countries that are unwilling to abide by CoCom rules, however, this requirement cannot be met. It is for this reason that Congress implemented the foreign availability rules, which require the decontrol of items that are available in substantial quantities from countries that will not agree to abide by CoCom rules.

Foreign availability constitutes one dimension of controllability. Incorporating foreign availability considerations into the determination of controllability as an integral component of annual list review will obviate the need for a separate and independent foreign availability assessment process. Several other kinds of uncontrollable items can also be defined, three of which are listed below:

1. Items that, through economies of mass production and mass marketing, have evolved into the status of "commodities."
2. Many kinds of software (some but not all of which also have achieved commodity status).
3. Many kinds of technical know-how.

Personal computers and countless other once exotic, high-priced technologies like them have become commodities. Because they violate all three of the attributes for a controllable item listed above, technologies that have become commodities are not controllable.

Although many people "know a commodity when they see one," defining a commodity poses some challenges. One possible definition is provided in a boxed insert. Some computer software has achieved commodity status. Other software that is not yet a commodity is nevertheless uncontrollable because it is widely available and easily accessed or transferred over public and quasi-public computer networks.

Effective *end-use controls* require that items to be controlled have the following properties:

• Used or consumed by only a modest number of entities.
• Used or consumed in an environment in which access can be limited and/or in which users can be positively identified.
• Used or consumed by people and organizations that have the authority, means, and will to limit access.

Under the system proposed in Chapter 8, determination of end-use controllability would shift from national decision makers to a multilateral basis within CoCom.

In order to make such a system work, the United States will have to persuade CoCom to develop* collectively, and regularly promulgate, general

---

*Or revise in light of accumulating experience.

A Definition of Commodities

By nature, a workable definition of a commodity must be somewhat arbitrary. The following is one possible approach to identifying item-groups that are commodities.

The item-group must involve the following:
- Large* sales.
- Sufficiently low cost to be affordable by the general public.
- Breadth of civilian applications (e.g., a number of interchangeable uses for the items in the group).
- Widespread availability to the public at a large number of sales locations.

*The term *large* is sector specific. In the case of computers, the computer subpanel has recommended sales of at least 1 million units in cumulative worldwide production (for devices) or at least $100 million in cumulative worldwide sales (for materials). See the computer subpanel's report in Appendix C for further discussion of commodities in regard to computers and software.

---

policy guidelines on the attributes of an acceptable end-use control system. In addition, if end-use arrangements are approved for specific classes of items (e.g., software and data), CoCom will have to develop* descriptions of specific strategies that have proved to be acceptable. Although following a previously successful strategy in an application for approval of an end-use arrangement might speed CoCom approval, it should be explicitly stated that following such a strategy is not a requirement for approval. Exporters should always be free to innovate and to propose alternative strategies. To ensure that CoCom's criteria for judging the acceptability of proposed end-use controls do not become outdated by rapidly evolving political realities, the United States should urge CoCom to reconsider and revise its end-use control guidelines on a regular basis.

---

*Or revise in light of accumulating experience.

11

Key Findings and Conclusions of the Panel

THE NEED FOR EXPORT CONTROLS IN A CHANGED GLOBAL ENVIRONMENT

Growing Economic and Technological Challenges for the United States

The panel notes the following challenges to the United States:

- The changing structure of the global economy
- The increasingly rapid global diffusion of technology
- Declining U.S. technological and manufacturing preeminence
- Growing technological and manufacturing sophistication in Japan and the newly industrializing countries
- The changing distribution of global economic and financial power
- The weakening of the U.S. defense industrial base
- The growing importance of exports to U.S. economic vitality

A Redefinition of U.S. Export Control Policy

Export controls, sharply reduced in number and fully multilateral, are a necessary and appropriate policy instrument for responding to any remaining national security threat posed to the United States by the Soviet Union and the other former Warsaw Treaty Organization (WTO) countries, but a new

165

West-East policy approach must be developed if export controls are to remain an effective policy instrument under the changed national security conditions.

Given the new political realities, export controls will be viable only if they enable the United States and other nations that share common objectives to (a) remain vigilant and prepared during the period of economic and political transformation now under way within the Soviet Union and Eastern Europe; (b) facilitate (rather than obstruct) the pursuit of important political and economic objectives, such as further democratization and the development of market economies in the Soviet Union and Eastern Europe; and (c) address flexibly new types and sources of national security challenges, such as those derived from growing proliferation threats or the threat of terrorism, as they emerge.

Because of the enormous uncertainties inherent in the current situation, a new and clearly more sophisticated approach to export control policy is required, one that could be adapted and modified to a range of future conditions. Among its principal features would be the following interactive goals:

• Maintaining a qualitative edge in U.S. military systems as a deterrent against threats of aggression, including those posed by Soviet and Soviet-allied forces.

• Preventing or retarding the proliferation of items that could directly and immediately enhance the conventional or strategic capabilities of countries that may now or in the future pose a threat to the physical security or vital interests of the United States and other nations that share common objectives.

• Preventing or retarding the proliferation of items for use in acts of terrorism or other political violence against the interests of the United States and other nations that share common objectives.

• Preventing or retarding the proliferation of items that may be destabilizing to global or regional political structures and power alignments.

• Avoiding negative impacts on economic competitiveness and the overall viability of the free market economies that participate in global trade.

• Promoting further political democratization and economic development in the Soviet Union, Eastern Europe, and elsewhere.

• Encouraging conversion (or closure) of military industrial facilities in the Soviet Union and Eastern Europe to the manufacture of products for civilian consumption.

• Maintaining harmony with U.S. allies and cooperating countries in the administration of export control measures.

• Improving the structure and administration of export controls to increase efficiency and lessen adverse effects on the private sector.

THE IMPACT OF EXPORT CONTROLS ON U.S. INDUSTRY

The precise measurement of the quantitative effect of export controls on the U.S. economy is an elusive goal. Unlike other factors that contribute to

U.S. competitive difficulties, however, export controls are largely modifiable by changes in U.S. policy, and hence, their negative impact can be ameliorated, if not entirely eliminated.

U.S. industry's concern about the negative economic impact of export controls on U.S. industry has stemmed almost entirely from the unilateral aspects of U.S. policy, including restrictions and control practices not imposed by U.S. allies and partners in the Coordinating Committee for Multilateral Export Controls (CoCom).

Significant unilateral features of the U.S. control system include the following:

• controls on reexports of U.S. items to third countries and the requirement for written assurances regarding end use and reexport;
• controls on U.S.-owned foreign entities;
• controls on foreign products that use (or are made with) technologies of U.S. origin;
• controls on foreign products that have U.S.-origin components in them;
• control of some dual use items as munitions that other CoCom nations regulate less restrictively as dual use products;
• selective imposition of unilateral product and technology controls;
• more burdensome and complex licensing regimes; and
• more stringent enforcement mechanisms.

Unilateralism disadvantages the U.S. economy and can rarely be justified in a competitive world economy by security concerns. Unilateral features should be eliminated from U.S. national security export controls except in those rare instances in which such a unilateral action would be effective or holds the prospect of changing the position of other countries within a relatively short time.

EVIDENCE ON THE ACQUISITION OF SENSITIVE WESTERN TECHNOLOGY

Espionage

The panel finds that export controls cannot—and are not designed to— prevent espionage. Rather, they are designed to restrict the sale, either direct or indirect, of strategic technology and equipment.

Diversion and Legal Purchases

Evidence reviewed by the panel (both classified and unclassified), which was corroborated by information collected during the panel's fact-finding missions in Asia and Europe, indicates that the diversion practices of the Soviet Union and its Warsaw Pact allies continued through 1990.

Similarly, the panel was unable to identify any overall change *during the late 1980s* in the efforts by the Soviet Union and its WTO allies to acquire through legal purchases technology in the West for incorporation into military systems.

The Role of the Intelligence Community in the Export Control Policy Process

The panel recognizes that one of the most valuable contributions of the intelligence community has been to develop "red side" methodological approaches that have made it possible to examine Soviet technology acquisition efforts from the standpoint of *Soviet*, rather than Western, military needs and capabilities. "Red side" thinking, however, is not yet sufficiently institutionalized in the intelligence community's support for U.S. export control policy. As a result, policy analyses for export controls have tended to continue to use "mirror image" assumptions regarding Soviet requirements for Western technology, based on *Western*, instead of Soviet, military systems and capabilities.

The panel takes note of the continuing paucity of reliable data on changes in the nature and pattern of Soviet technology acquisition efforts since 1989. It also finds an even more serious lack of reliable data on the scope and extent of technology acquisition in the West by countries that are the focus of proliferation concern.

THE CHANGING CALCULUS OF U.S. NATIONAL SECURITY INTERESTS

The Growing Importance of Exports to U.S. Economic Vitality

The panel notes that, taken together, problems with the U.S. defense industrial base, the shift from defense- to commercially driven innovation, the emergence of Asian and European industrial competitors, and the increased importance of exports to the U.S. economy have led to a growing realization that economic factors must be given increased weight in the formulation of U.S. national security policy.

Changes in the Soviet Union and Eastern Europe

The panel deems it reasonable to assume that the Warsaw Pact has lost its fundamental meaning and for all practical purposes no longer makes possible a forward-based, Soviet strategic offensive capability in Central Europe. Indeed, trends in Europe will soon foreclose the very possibility of stationing Soviet forces outside the borders of the Soviet Union.

The panel recognizes that German reunification may give the Soviet Union access to some technologies that it would otherwise have been denied, as refurbished former East German firms honor outstanding contracts, but the panel also believes that the larger processes at work are sure to erode the Soviet ability to acquire technology throughout eastern Europe.

The Soviet Union is becoming a far more transparent and penetrable society, which has important implications for the West's estimation of its security concerns. It now appears possible to establish and maintain a distinction between commercial and military applications in considering technology trade with the Soviet Union. Cooperation in regulating general weapons exports also appears feasible in this new context, as do mutually supportive policies on regional conflict. This relief from traditional concerns and the expansion of constructive opportunities enable a shift in Western export control policy from one emphasizing general denial to one focusing on positive behavioral change, along with verifiable end use. In other words, the panel believes that the West can move from an export control regime characterized by negative sanction to one characterized by positive inducement.

On the basis of the announced reductions in Soviet and East European military forces (assuming that they are completed in good faith), the apparent dissolution of the Warsaw Pact as a military alliance, and the emerging, defensive Soviet military posture in Asia, the panel accepts the conclusion drawn by the Department of Defense that there is *no* credible scenario in which the Soviet Union could mount a theater-wide conventional attack against the West in either the European or Asian theaters with less than 18 to 24 months preparation. There is a continuing concern, however, about Soviet capabilities to launch local attacks within regions near the Soviet border with as little as 90 days mobilization.

Growing Economic Exchanges with the East

The panel believes that the likely result of large-scale Western economic assistance is that Eastern Europe and, to a lesser extent, the Soviet Union will become more dependent on the West, while the West will have a greater stake in the success of the economic and political reforms now under way. At the same time, debate will continue over where to draw the line in imposing East-West export controls. It is now in the West's security interest to permit the flow to Eastern Europe and the Soviet Union of dual use technology, apart from a few highly critical items. Indeed, the liberalization of controls could be part of a broad strategy to encourage further the process of political and economic reform in Eastern Europe and the Soviet Union, thereby strengthening that region's stability and security.

The People's Republic of China as a National Security Threat

The panel concludes that a cautious policy toward China is warranted by the impending generational change in Chinese political leadership, with its associated potential for further political upheaval. At the same time, it is in the interest of the United States to nurture a deeper and more cooperative relationship with the current Chinese leadership, which would include further efforts to convince China to participate more fully in the major nonproliferation regimes.

Ultimately, establishing a certain degree of symmetry between the export control regime for China and the new rules that are under development for the democratizing East European countries and the Soviet Union may be desirable. As in the case of the former Warsaw Pact countries, however, the rate of further change in U.S. and CoCom export controls for China is likely to be governed by the stated foreign and domestic policies and actual practice of the Chinese government.

The Changed Traditional Threats to U.S. National Security

It is the judgment of the panel that the threat presented by Soviet military capabilities has fundamentally changed. Together with the United States, the Soviet Union is now attempting to move beyond the traditional paradigm of alliance confrontation to establish a new security relationship.

In Western Europe in particular, the calculation of the need for export controls has changed as a result of the dramatic political events that have taken place since late 1989. The result is that support in Europe for the continuation of dual use export controls beyond the short term is disappearing rapidly. The continuation of viable controls even for the next few years will require a major reduction in the scope of the control list and a shift in the policy governing dual use export controls to allow controlled items to be exported to the Soviet Union if they are verifiably for civilian (i.e., commercial) end use.

The Proliferation Threat

Tensions in areas outside Central and Eastern Europe, the region traditionally of greatest Western concern, are being exacerbated by the spread of weapons of mass destruction and high-performance weapons. This trend adds to the need for a close reexamination and restructuring of existing nonproliferation regimes.

The panel believes that, in all likelihood, the policy responses to the growing proliferation threat will require the creation of new multilateral regimes, or strengthening of existing regimes, involving both the Soviet Union and China. There will be little chance for long-term success if these two key players are not officially included in all proliferation control regimes at the earliest opportunity. Without comprehensive multilateral regimes, the chances for effective control of proliferation threats are critically weakened.

THE U.S. AND MULTILATERAL EXPORT CONTROL REGIMES

Third Country Cooperation

The panel takes note of the fact that no other CoCom partner requires the type of authorization for reexport out of a CoCom or cooperating country required by the United States. The end result is a serious disadvantage for U.S. economic interests.

Nine distinct licensing benefits are available to cooperating third countries. Given the current licensing guidelines and processing times for most third countries, however, the only benefits of any significant value are the enhanced distribution license, permissive reexport exceptions, the broad general license for CoCom (G-CoCom), and the new general license for intra-CoCom trade (GCT).

Basic Problems of the U.S. Export Control Regimes

MULTIPLICITY OF STATUTES, AGENCIES, AND REGIMES

Export controls are issued under a multiplicity of statutes with differing objectives and criteria. The statutes themselves were not coordinated at the time they were written and come under the supervision of different congressional committees. Over a dozen agencies, plus the military services, are engaged in administering controls and apply distinct regulatory provisions that often overlap and conflict. Acting at the request of the panel, the Congressional Research Service was unable to find any area analogous to export controls that had a comparable number of differing bureaucracies and regulatory categories.

The lead agencies in constructing export control policy hold strongly diverse positions corresponding to their separate interests. As a result, these disparate agencies are often unable to integrate the various national security, economic, and foreign policy issues and give executive authorities a balanced, coherent view of the key issues.

Jurisdictional Disputes

The panel believes that, in many instances, it is unclear which administrative agency has jurisdiction over a particular category of items. Neither the trade laws nor the implementing regulations of the various agencies provide clear standards for determining the correct authority covering the export. A disproportionate amount of bureaucratic resources are thus expended in resolving disputes, rather than administering and enforcing the export control system. The confusion over which law and which set of agency regulations pertain to particular items has caused delay and expense for U.S. exporters.

Overlapping Enforcement

Domestically, overlapping jurisdiction and lack of communication between the U.S. Customs Service and the Commerce Department's Office of Export Enforcement have sometimes resulted in their working on the same case without each other's knowledge. The levels of sanctions for violations and the circumstances that must be established for their imposition vary from statute to statute. The sanctions that have developed over the years are the result of ad hoc legislation, and no effort has been made to assess and systemize these penalties. Moreover, unilateral U.S. adoption of extraterritorial sanctions may seriously undermine U.S. efforts to achieve effective export control cooperation.

Outdated and Confusing U.S. Control Lists

The system of U.S. list management suffers from a lack of clear definitions and criteria for control and decontrol, as well as the widely varying formats and structures that exist for domestic and international lists. The fact that an item is taken off the Militarily Critical Technologies List, for example, does not necessarily lead to U.S. action to delete it from the CoCom or U.S. control lists.

The foreign availability assessment process that was established to determine the controllability of items on the Commodity Control List has proven largely ineffective. Although data from foreign availability assessments are sometimes used in list review, the assessment process is costly and contentious and has rarely resulted in timely decontrol.

The President was able to present a coherent decontrol plan to CoCom in June 1990 only by short-circuiting the existing process. Continuing White House pressure on the participating agencies was necessary to bring about significant loosening of restrictions. Under ordinary circumstances, in this key national security area, foreign nations and suppliers—not the U.S. interagency process—are driving the U.S. export control apparatus. Although the June 1990 process has produced relatively substantial results, it is doubtful that the institutionalized CoCom and U.S. list review processes could work effectively in less exigent circumstances.

INEFFECTIVE DISPUTE RESOLUTION

The process for dispute resolution is characterized by a lack of transparency resulting from unclear policy guidelines and complicated agency responsibilities. The insufficient procedures for dispute resolution in licensing decisions cause further tension between agencies and disadvantage U.S. exporters. Clearer guidelines for case referral and more definitive standards for licensing decisions are needed.

NATURE AND EXTENT OF UNILATERAL CONTROLS

The panel believes that in a world of diffuse economic and technological power, the widespread use of unilateral export controls is counterproductive. Although some CoCom countries practice limited or unofficial forms of reexport controls, the United States is the only country formally requiring that its permission be obtained by non-U.S. parties for the reexport of goods or technology that have come to rest in another country.

The major adverse reaction to U.S. reexport controls arises when they are imposed in connection with U.S. unilateral foreign policy objectives and when their application is complex, such as the rules for parts, components, and technical data. In addition, there is an abundance of anecdotal evidence that, when possible, foreign manufacturers avoid U.S. sources in order to escape the encumbrance of U.S. reexport controls.

INSUFFICIENT JUDICIAL REVIEW

The panel has concluded that, while judicial review is no cure-all, it can be a useful and effective instrument of policy. Specifically, judicial review is not the appropriate means for resolving interagency disputes on the very issues on which courts lack expertise and traditionally defer to the executive branch. What courts can do, however, is correct agency abuses in interpreting and applying statutory provisions, for example, a failure to dismantle unilateral controls when such action is mandated by Congress or the imposition of new foreign policy controls when statutory criteria have not been satisfied.

INDUSTRY PARTICIPATION

The panel believes that if U.S. industry fully understands and supports the rationale for controlling exports, the controls will be far more effective.

Serious problems remain, however, with the extent of involvement by U.S. industry, which is a major reason why legitimate economic considerations are not taken into account at the start of the policy process. The traditional policy process does not lend itself to effective and fair presentation of industry views. The lack of sufficient business involvement in the system is partly self-inflicted, however. Too few companies make the effort or devote the resources necessary to placing qualified personnel on export-related advisory committees. The panel concludes that U.S. business must take a more active part in the process, particularly in the nomination of technically qualified personnel to work on the committees.

In the process of energizing and upgrading export control regimes, it is not enough to solicit the participation of other governments. The private sector must be brought in as a full and cooperative partner.

THE NEED FOR EXPORT CONTROLS IN THE NEW ERA

The panel believes that the current challenge presented by the changes in Eastern Europe and the Soviet Union is to fashion a response that capitalizes on the enormous political and economic opportunities while managing the risk associated with legitimate security concerns. Carefully tailored and/or refashioned, multilateral export controls can be appropriate and viable in support of the following policy objectives:

1. Constraining access by the *Soviet military* to technology and end products that contribute significantly and directly to the improvement of Soviet weapons systems capabilities.

2. Constraining access to advanced technology and end products that contribute significantly and directly to the development of advanced conventional weapons systems by countries that pose a threat of aggression.

3. Constraining access by countries of proliferation concern to nuclear, biological, chemical, and missile delivery technologies and know-how. (Export controls may not always be the optimal strategy for dealing with these problems, however.)

4. Imposing multilaterally agreed sanctions for violations of international agreements or norms of behavior.

NEW TARGETS FOR NATIONAL SECURITY EXPORT CONTROLS

The panel believes that to be effective, nonproliferation controls must be focused only on narrowly proscribed military activities or items that are required *directly* for weapons systems and must include, to the extent practicable, verifiable end-use assurances. Lacking such specificity, efforts to control exports of proliferation-related technologies create a risk similar to that encountered in the case of CoCom controls on dual use technology—namely, imposing significant economic costs that may be disproportionate to their effectiveness.

LIMITATIONS ON CERTAIN TYPES AND USES OF EXPORT CONTROLS

The panel finds that the problem of how to impose reasonable limitations on foreign military sales, which is being exacerbated by the overcapacity of arms production worldwide, is a significant and troubling problem that is urgently in need of study.

The panel concludes that the distinction between some foreign policy controls and national security controls is artificial. Serious consideration should be given to whether authority for export controls *other* than for reasons of national security or to implement the mandate of a responsible international organization or agreement can be justified in light of today's highly competitive international economy.

COCOM: A NEW DIRECTION

It is the judgment of the panel that the traditional CoCom objective of retarding the qualitative progress of Soviet military capabilities could be preserved while allowing for expanded, legitimate trade by shifting the focus of CoCom from an embargo on the export of listed items to proscribed countries to approval of items on a sharply reduced CoCom Industrial List, contingent on acceptable, verifiable end-use conditions approved by CoCom.

The continued credibility of CoCom depends on the willingness of the members to recognize and respond to the new political, economic, and military realities. This requires that a new approach to control objectives be reflected in modified control practices and a higher threshold of military utility as a criterion for control.

COCOM: A NEW ENVIRONMENT

"Borderless" Trade Within the European Community

Given the complicated business of organizing and administering monetary and economic unification, it is unlikely that the European Community will want to add export controls to its responsibilities in the near future. Because establishing a system of license-free trade in CoCom is an important step in eliminating burdens on West-West trade, the adoption of the common standard elements of licensing and enforcement by all CoCom members should be a continuing U.S. priority.

Third Country Cooperation

Since its initiation in 1984, the CoCom Third Country Cooperation initiative has enjoyed only limited success: Few CoCom members have actively pursued such agreements; the agreements negotiated do not systematically cover all goods controlled by CoCom; and the cooperating countries exhibit uneven will in implementation and enforcement.

The U.S. threat to restrict the export of certain high-technology items to countries that do not cooperate sufficiently with CoCom is hollow. U.S. export licensing statistics show that approval rates and average license processing times for exports to countries that do not cooperate with CoCom are not significantly different from those for cooperating countries.

The panel believes that given the overall decline in the perception of the security risk posed by the Soviet Union and other WTO countries, combined with the increasing sophistication of goods produced in third countries, the prospects for improving third country cooperation are limited. To maintain current levels of cooperation, as well as to encourage expanded cooperation, it will be necessary to reduce the scope of CoCom-controlled goods and provide political and economic incentives for third country cooperation.

COCOM: ADMINISTRATION AND MANAGEMENT

The narrow focus of CoCom on an explicitly targeted group of countries and commodities has enabled it to function with relative effectiveness. However, the current secrecy surrounding the conditions that exist for the favorable consideration of exports subject to full CoCom review prohibits exporters from taking advantage of potential exceptions to a general embargo and discourages exporters from even attempting to establish trade with proscribed countries.

Despite the obvious connection to military utility of the CoCom strategic criteria, the role of the national defense agencies of member countries in the CoCom list review process is limited and inconsistent. Moreover, industry participation in list review, although seemingly more influential than defense input by the other CoCom countries, is also inconsistent.

Despite disproportionate attention to licensing and enforcement, the U.S. practice of resisting decontrol in the CoCom forum while removing licensing requirements for nonproscribed trade (e.g., broad general and special licenses) promotes the belief that the United States is not concerned with the positions of its allies and uses CoCom as a tool to gain economic advantage.

Multilateral cooperation is an essential element in the effectiveness of any export control program. In addition, increased CoCom cooperation is necessary during this time of transition in Europe to ensure "equal economic footing" among all members while managing the redefinition of trade goals as they relate to mutual security.

COORDINATION OF CURRENT NONPROLIFERATION REGIMES

Perhaps the most important distinction between East-West and proliferation controls is that the United States is not in a position to exercise the same level of influence over the suppliers of items related to nuclear, chemical, and missile proliferation. Indeed, some of the potential suppliers of these weapons of mass destruction also are the targets of current control regimes.

The number of participants in a nonproliferation regime and the nature of their relationship to each other affect the collective ability to specify control targets and mechanisms. As the number of participants increases and objectives become broader, the specificity with which targets and mechanisms can be defined declines. On the other hand, the impact of possible sanctions increases with the number of participants. The challenge is to define the objectives and obligations of control regimes so as to optimize their participation and scope without diluting their effectiveness.

The choice of an appropriate mix of controls for managing proliferation risks is a complex and difficult problem that requires far more careful and extensive study than this panel or any other group has yet been able to conduct.

When the United States (or any other country) is trying to exert international leadership, unilateral proliferation controls may be appropriate for short durations. To be effective in the long run, however, proliferation controls must be undertaken on a multilateral basis. Across-the-board licensing and screening of a broad range of items to numerous destinations will not be an efficient or effective way of controlling exports related to proliferation. Export controls should focus on a very limited set of items and on specific target countries.

The United States should learn from its experience with East-West controls and work to ensure that, in developing a strategy for the management of proliferation risks, a broad and burdensome export control regime is not unilaterally applied to U.S. exporters.

Nuclear Export Controls

A strategy must be developed by which newly nuclear states are brought within the appropriate treaty structure and encouraged to cooperate in the export control arrangements corollary to the treaty. It is also important to step up discussions with other Zangger Committee members to control the export of critical dual use items.

Missile Export Controls

The effectiveness of the Missile Technology Control Regime would be improved if conditions for approved exports and sanctions against the importing parties for violations of the export conditions were made standard among regime members and public. It is also important to include other major suppliers in the regime, but this is unlikely to happen, or to lead to greater effectiveness, until existing internal disputes are resolved.

The future direction of this regime is clearly a trade-off between (a) attempting to identify and subsequently embargo specific nonpeaceful missile delivery systems in a very closed and limited environment or (b) more broadly and publicly defining regime goals and proscribed end uses in the global context. The nature of the regime will determine the attitude of nonregime countries toward cooperation.

Chemical Export Controls

The Australia Group has been operating as an interim mechanism in anticipation of completion of the Chemical Weapons Convention (CWC). The final details of the convention are still being negotiated, but the broad outlines are clear. The production and possession of chemical weapons will be banned (use is already banned under the Geneva accords). The convention will also likely hold signatory governments explicitly responsible for reporting to a secretariat on all international trade in specific chemical precursors.

There is reason to be concerned that export controls related to the CWC, as well as the reporting requirements of the treaty, could impose significant costs on the chemical industry. Thus, it is important to ensure that the resulting system strikes an appropriate balance between the objective of limiting proliferation and the imposition of costs on the world's process chemical industry. It is especially important to ensure that the actual operation of the system is equitable.

CHANGES TO THE U.S. CONTROL REGIME

The panel has concluded that substantial reform will be necessary to achieve the goals of an effective U.S. export control process. The export control policy process should be reformed in order to achieve the following results:

• Policy issues are resolved in a timely manner and policy decisions are enforced by the executing agency.

• Views of relevant departments are heard and considered, and unresolved cases presenting significant policy issues are taken to a senior-level interagency group for prompt resolution.

• The system is made simpler, more open, and internally consistent so that policymakers, administrators, and U.S. and foreign business can more easily understand it and work with it.

• The development of export control policy is well balanced, and industry and other affected parties have appropriate opportunities for input into policy formulation, including regulatory changes and list development.

Policy Formulation

Achievement of the above goals would be expedited by a process in which policy formulation is handled through a mechanism separate from that of policy administration. A clearer division of functions would help dispel the current confusion in the bureaucracy between policy formulation and its implementation.

The arrangement for export controls should be part of the same apparatus for policy implementation that an administration establishes for any important component of national security. The relevant executive branch agencies should retain a strong voice in policymaking. The basic function of the policy mechanism should be to integrate the existing policy roles of the various agencies. Clear policy guidance should be established through firm presidential leadership, and a more rational administrative apparatus should be constructed for execution of policy established by the President.

Administrative Alternatives

The panel evaluated two basic alternatives for consolidating agency functions. The first alternative is to put administrative functions in a newly created administrative structure. The second is to consolidate functions in an existing department or agency.

Given the progress that has been made so far in improving both policy and process, the panel concluded that it would be better to modify the current system rather than start anew.

In several ways the State Department is not an optimal setting for an administrative agency. The State Department is oriented primarily to matters of high-level policy and foreign affairs, not the detailed work of a licensing bureau.

Given its central mission, the Defense Department would not be sufficiently responsive to balancing military and commercial concerns, particularly in regard to exports of dual use items.

The Commerce Department's Bureau of Export Administration, however, already handles—in dollar value—the great majority of cases processed by the export control system, and it has undergone considerable administrative improvement. Further, the agency has dealt with a broad spectrum of products and technologies, and it has a sophisticated and reasonably comprehensive regulatory scheme.

Enforcement Issues

In the area of sanctions, proposals have been made for certain agencies to take exclusive responsibility for enforcement of U.S. export controls. Opposing views over which agency should have primacy in various enforcement areas are indicative of broader problems concerning administrative responsibility for trade enforcement. Those problems extend well beyond the domain of export controls, however, and involve a number of enforcement bodies, including the Customs Service, the Drug Enforcement Administration, and the Office of Export Enforcement.

Enhancing Industry Participation

Greater balance and effectiveness in the export control system require a greater level of industry participation in the system. A process in which defense, economic, and foreign policy concerns are all coordinated into a cohesive U.S. policy must be further encouraged.

12

Summary of Recommendations of the Panel

RESHAPE U.S. NATIONAL SECURITY POLICY IN RESPONSE TO THE CHANGING CALCULUS OF U.S. NATIONAL SECURITY INTERESTS

Changed Traditional Threat

In response to the changed nature of the traditional threat to U.S. national security, U.S. export control policy toward the Soviet Union and Eastern Europe should reflect a mixed strategy of encouraging political and economic reform and making further relaxation of controls contingent on evidence of additional change. To this end, U.S. national security policy should keep in mind the following elements:

* Continue to constrain access by the *Soviet military* to technology and end products that contribute significantly and directly to the improvement of weapons capabilities.
* Ensure that export controls do not impede the permanent conversion (or closure) of Soviet military industrial facilities to the manufacture of products for civilian consumption.
* Encourage further positive changes in the security policy of the Soviet Union, including additional force demobilizations and redeployments.
* Encourage stable political and economic transition in the Soviet Union through a broadened process of democratization and economic reform.

* Maintain consensus with U.S. allies on the coordination of further liberalization of export controls on trade with the Soviet Union.
* Move progressively toward the removal of export controls on dual use items to the Soviet Union and the East European countries for commercial end uses that can be verified.

Increased Proliferation Threat

The growing capacity of many nations to develop and employ weapons of mass destruction poses new threats to U.S. and international security and requires new and innovative policy responses. Those policy responses should be predicated on the following considerations:

* Proliferation of weapons of mass destruction, their delivery systems, and advanced conventional weapons is a U.S. national security concern, and it should be treated as such in U.S. law and policy.
* The principal focus should be on those proliferation problems—nuclear weapons, chemical and biological weapons, and missile delivery systems—that, in combination, have the potential to create expanded negative impacts.
* Control regimes must be tailored to the particular circumstances of specific proliferation threats and, to be effective, must be as fully multilateral (i.e., involve the maximum number of suppliers) as possible. Some of these regimes are likely to rely, at least in part, on properly fashioned export controls. Such controls should be targeted only on those technologies or products directly essential to the development and/or manufacture of weapons of mass destruction.

Role of the Intelligence Community in the Export Control Process

In this period of rapid change and uncertainty within the Soviet Union and Eastern Europe, and new threats from countries of proliferation concern, the quality, accuracy, and timeliness of intelligence information are ever more critical. For this reason, the panel recommends the following:

* The intelligence community should expand its efforts to develop reliable assessments of changes in the nature and pattern of *current* Soviet technology acquisition efforts—and current patterns of Soviet utilization of the technology it acquires—and should make this information available to the relevant agencies of the U.S. government and to the countries participating in the Coordinating Committee for Multilateral Export Controls (CoCom).
* The intelligence community should continue and expand its recent efforts to develop an analytic capability to examine Soviet technology acquisition and utilization *from the standpoint of the actual state of*

Soviet technological progress, both civilian and military, and the internal dynamics of technology diffusion within the Soviet Union and East European countries.

* The executive branch should give serious consideration to reallocating resources—and/or identifying additional resources—to develop better information about the acquisition and utilization of sensitive Western technology by countries of proliferation concern.

DEVELOP NEW U.S. AND MULTILATERAL EXPORT CONTROL REGIMES

U.S. Policy

Circumstances in the Soviet Union and/or other currently proscribed countries may evolve to the point that export controls on dual use technology to those destinations can be completely eliminated.

* To encourage this evolution and to ensure that institutional momentum does not maintain the use of export controls longer than prudence requires, the United States should work with the other CoCom countries to develop an explicit multilateral policy statement that outlines the circumstances under which dual use export controls can and should be terminated.

* Multilateral consensus on the goals, targets, and mechanisms of export controls is essential and should be a critical foreign policy priority for the United States. This includes reviewing the organization and operation of control regimes aimed at East-West trade, as well as seeking the cooperation of the Soviet Union, China, and other countries in controlling the global proliferation of arms.

Foreign Policy Controls

Given the close relationship between national security controls and controls based on foreign policy considerations, the panel makes the following recommendations:

* Foreign policy controls maintained to prevent the proliferation of missile delivery systems or nuclear, chemical, or biological weapons should be reclassified under the rubric of ''proliferation controls'' to differentiate them appropriately as an element of U.S. national security policy.

* The United States should not impose foreign policy controls on a continuing basis, except in those circumstances in which sufficient multilateral agreement and cooperation exist to make them efficacious and

to prevent discrimination against U.S. product and technology suppliers.

* If unilateral foreign policy controls are used, then the setting and enforcement of time limitations become imperative. The United States should, in all cases, seek to negotiate multilateral implementation and enforcement, or informal cooperation (whenever possible) from other countries in similarly restricting trade. However, the United States will find it difficult to lead if few other countries can be convinced to follow. Under these circumstances, the imposition of unilateral foreign policy controls may become counterproductive and damaging to U.S. economic interests, and every effort should be made to remove them at an early time.

* The criteria for the imposition and retention of national security and foreign policy controls set forth in Sections 5 and 6 of the Export Administration Act (EAA) of 1979, as amended, should be reviewed and made more explicit.

* To the extent that the President chooses to invoke export control measures through the use of the International Emergency Economic Powers Act (IEEPA), the criteria for its application should be reviewed and modified so that they are similar to the conditions that Congress has specified in Sections 5 and 6 of the EAA with respect to controls imposed for national security or foreign policy reasons. "Emergency powers" granted to the President under the IEEPA generally should not be imposed for more than six months before Section 6 of the EAA must be invoked.

* The "sunset" provision for foreign policy controls should be enforced in order to ensure that, as in the case of more traditional national security controls, restrictions do not remain in force long after the political, military, or technological rationale for their enactment has ceased to exist.

Proliferation Controls: The Need for Collective Security

Export controls are not universally effective in slowing proliferation, but if multilaterally applied and enforced, they can help to constrain the proliferation of weapons and the technical capability to produce them. To employ export controls effectively in managing proliferation risks, the United States should take the following steps:

* Analyze the relative usefulness and advantages or disadvantages of alternative types of export controls for different proliferation or security concerns.

* Focus proliferation controls narrowly on the proliferation risks and activities of greatest concern.
* Develop a new regime, or expand an existing regime, to cover proliferation of advanced conventional weapons and related systems.
* Seek active, specific, and operational coordination on proliferation controls among the major players, including at least the United States, the United Kingdom, the Soviet Union, France, Germany, Japan, and China.
* As part of a broader strategy of managing proliferation risks, seek to strengthen and coordinate existing proliferation control regimes with the long-term goal of eventual consolidation.
* Prepare both a U.S. and multilateral approach to the problem of states that have become nuclear but that are currently treated as nonnuclear under the Nuclear Non-Proliferation Treaty.
* Encourage other participants in the Zangger Committee to control the export of critical, dual use items.
* Work to resolve the internal problems in the Missile Technology Control Regime and to expand membership to include other important supplier states, including the Soviet Union, India, and China.
* Construct a positive list of civilian space launch or satellite projects that have committed to peaceful end use and are certified as acceptable recipients of missile-related goods and technology.
* To the extent feasible, state the retransfer restrictions and end-use conditions necessary for acceptable sales of dual use items subject to missile technology controls.
* In negotiating the Chemical Weapons Convention, explicitly consider collective export control responses to nonsignatories that develop or possess chemical weapons.
* Seek enforcement and inspection procedures that successfully focus on those few destinations that pose the greatest proliferation risks.

Multilateral Control Regimes

CoCom: A New Direction

In response to new political, economic, and military realities, CoCom should develop a flexible control strategy. To this end, CoCom should take the following steps:

* Approve the sale of Industrial List items to the Soviet Union and Eastern Europe for civilian end uses when acceptable safeguards can be demonstrated to CoCom.

* To the extent feasible, publish standard end-use conditions necessary for favorable consideration of exports of controlled items.
* Provide for periodic, and in some cases unannounced, visits to the end-use site to verify the end use of limited, selected items. The possibility of visitation would be a stated condition of sale. The visits might be performed by (1) members' individual enforcement agencies, (2) collective or joint member enforcement, (3) the exporter, or (4) by private inspection companies certified by CoCom.

Borderless Trade Within the European Community

In light of the changing operational environment for export controls within the European Community, the United States should press CoCom to take the following steps:

* Adopt a license-free system of trade in CoCom, to be implemented consistently and in accord with "common standard" compliance in order to ensure effective controls and to avoid disadvantaging those countries that make the effort to comply.
* Promote the use of a generic control indicator in conjunction with internationally recognized import/export documents. The control indicator, or marker, could be used by all countries that maintain restrictions on the export of certain items.

Third Country Cooperation

To encourage expanded third country cooperation, CoCom should take the following actions:

* Include on the CoCom core list of controlled items only those items that are physically produced or sourced only in CoCom member nations or fully cooperating third countries.
* Initiate a plan whereby fully cooperating third countries can observe and contribute to CoCom list construction and case review. This may involve expanding the membership of CoCom or creating an "observer status."
* Eliminate reexport authorization requirements for goods being reexported *out of* fully cooperating third countries.
* Seek multilateral agreement to control the reexport of controlled goods out of noncooperating third countries.
* Offer extension of the license-free system of trade as a CoCom-wide benefit to cooperating countries that have operational export control systems. The Third Country Cooperation Working Group in CoCom should certify the cooperating countries that have adequate systems.

CoCom Administration and Management

Increased cooperation is necessary during this time of transition in Europe to ensure "equal footing" among all members while managing the redefinition of trade goals as they relate to mutual security. To this end, the United States should also press CoCom to undertake the following:

* Seek a common standard of licensing and enforcement practices for trade with nonproscribed countries. This should include controls on the reexport of controlled items (including those items eligible for approval with conditions) out of noncooperating countries.
* Eliminate the use of national discretion (administrative exception controls). The revised Industrial List ("core list") should be brief enough that all cases can be reviewed by CoCom.
* Improve the transparency of CoCom operations. This includes making the conditions necessary for favorable consideration of controlled exports standard and public, to the extent feasible.
* "Internationalize" the image of CoCom. For example, (1) move CoCom headquarters out of the U.S. embassy annex in Paris, (2) upgrade the involvement of the other members in the administration of CoCom, and (3) share the costs of operation more evenly.
* Encourage increased input from members' national defense and intelligence agencies by upgrading and more fully integrating with CoCom the existing Strategic Technology Experts Meeting.

The U.S. Control Regime

Policy Formulation

A workable regulatory scheme and efficient administrative structure require strong policy direction. The executive branch must formulate an efficient and coherent policy development framework and provide an appropriate administrative structure to ensure that policy is properly executed, particularly because the absence of such guidance in the past has led to deficiencies in the policy process. To accomplish this, the executive branch should undertake the following:

Provide Explicit Presidential Leadership

* Since the National Security Act of 1947 and subsequent legislation give the President authority to provide detailed instructions on key components of export control policy, a national security directive (NSD) should be the President's vehicle for the formulation and implemen-

tation of export control policy. Such a directive would specify the interagency mechanisms for implementing the President's policy, particularly with regard to a streamlined licensing system and a fast, effective dispute resolution process.

* Through the vehicle of an NSD, the President should provide guidance on the fundamental objectives for all national security export controls (including munitions, dual use, nuclear, missile, and chemical/biological controls) and direction for achieving those aims.

The directive should include, in particular, guidance on the following critical aspects of export control:

List construction
* The NSD should establish the general policy and specific procedures for constructing and reviewing the control lists. The guidance regarding process methodology should cover at least the following areas:
  * Establish interagency methodology for list construction, including criteria or standards for determining military criticality, economic costs, and other factors.
  * Specify agencies responsible for assessing the national security importance of controlled items and clarify priorities (or burden of proof) for balancing diverse interests.
  * Specify the process for resolving disputes over list construction.

Regulatory procedures, licensing, and dispute resolution
* The NSD should establish guidance for the development of regulatory control regimes, including establishing the targets of controls, such as destinations and end uses. The NSD should also prescribe parameters for distinguishing between routine and exceptional licensing cases and detail the decision-making process for each. The directive also should identify responsibilities for review and resolution of exceptional cases. Time limits should be included to ensure expeditious decision making.
* To eliminate the existing public confusion over the specific terms of U.S. export control policy, which is a major defect of the current system, presidential guidance should be made public to the extent possible. Although elements of the NSD might require classification, broad policy concepts and the details of policy execution should be stated publicly.

Develop Formal Policy Mechanisms
* The NSD should lay out formally the details of this executive structure, which would correspond roughly to the current administrative structure.

Lines of responsibility and accountability should be clearly established among all the participating groups. These groups are briefly discussed below.

Export Control Policy Coordinating Committee

* An Export Control Policy Coordinating Committee (EC/PCC) should be established to formulate and review policy recommendations, resolve exceptional disputes among agencies, and monitor the work of the interagency groups. The EC/PCC would be the locus for export control policy decision making within the framework of the NSD. It should comprise senior representatives of involved departments and agencies. To ensure objective evaluation of disputes reaching this level and the immediate attention of the National Security Council as necessary, the EC/PCC should be chaired by the national security advisor or the deputy advisor.

National security export control interagency groups

* Interagency working groups should be established as necessary to consider the appropriateness of export controls as a means of addressing overall U.S. national security and foreign policy objectives. Serving as the principal operating policy groups, they should advise the President on the advantages and disadvantages of the various U.S. export control programs and on the need for modification of current programs or for new programs.

* Because export control policymaking is an extremely complex field that demands a high degree of technical sophistication and in-depth command of the interagency apparatus, the interagency groups should be given adequate staff support.

Working groups and technical groups

* Necessary working groups of the interagency groups, including technical groups, should be established. These groups should be charged with responsibility for all areas relating to export controls.

Institutionalize Economic Security in a National Security Framework

* Because many important national security issues will involve serious economic concerns, those federal agencies responsible for economic matters should be formally brought into the policy process for meetings in which their expertise could serve the national interest. Specifically, the secretary of commerce should be included routinely as an advisor/participant in National Security Council discussions.

Develop Standards for Munitions and Dual Use Items

* If the control scheme is to involve separate lists for munitions and dual use items, the delineation between the two lists should be clear, especially if each list is separately administered, as at present.

* The terms *defense articles* and *dual use goods and technologies* should be clearly differentiated if the Munitions List is to remain distinct from the Commodity Control List. If a separate Munitions List is maintained, it should only contain (1) items specially designed for a significant and uniquely military application and (2) items that do not have essentially the same performance, capacity, or function as items used for commercial purposes.

Set Time Limits and Dispute Resolution Procedures

* Clear policy guidance, including guidance on timely procedures for resolving interagency disputes, should be provided to obviate most of the need for legislated deadlines.

POLICY EXECUTION

More efficient case processing, better procedures for dispute resolution, and greater system transparency are among the potential gains from a revised administrative process. To this end, the U.S. government should take the following steps:

Consolidate Administration in a Single Agency

* In order to achieve a more rational and effective export control process, the U.S. domestic process should be reconfigured through consolidation of all day-to-day administrative functions in a single agency. Single agency authority for day-to-day functions will have the following advantages:

- Establish a more rational and consistent regulatory structure.
- Achieve efficiency in list administration and implementation of regulatory changes.
- Attain further improvement in license processing.
- Avoid jurisdictional disputes at the administrative level.
- Facilitate industry's access to information on export control requirements.
- Increase efficiency by consolidating the electronic data processing functions of various administrative agencies.

The reorganization and accompanying policy directives will give the single agency final authority to make decisions on routine licenses, to promulgate regulations, and to resolve interpretive disputes within the specific policy guidelines of the NSD. Many routine licensing decisions, for example, are of a level that can best be handled within the independent authority of a single administrative agency. Authority also should extend to administrative aspects of list management. The consolidation will entail combining regulatory regimes to achieve uniform administrative requirements with levels of control appropriate for attainment of policy objectives.

* At the same time, the agency's decision making should be guided by the broad policy framework developed in the traditional interagency process. The goal of the reorganization is to consolidate *administration* of controls based on an internally consistent set of regulations while keeping broad *policymaking* and final dispute resolution in the hands of the President and the responsible cabinet secretaries in the National Security Council and the Export Control Policy Coordinating Committee.

* Responsibility for the administration of restrictions on dual use items, munitions, items controlled for nonproliferation purposes, and trade-related items under "emergency" powers should be transferred to the single agency.

* The goal of a more transparent licensing process should be achieved through a "one-stop shopping" mechanism, that is, a single administrative window for exporters seeking to obtain licenses.

* "One-stop shopping" should be established in harmony with other restructuring of the control apparatus lest it devolve into a well-intentioned but ineffective initiative.

Designate the Commerce Department's Bureau of Export Administration as the Single Administrative Agency for Export Controls

Careful consideration of the alternatives for consolidating agency functions led the panel to make the following recommendations:

* The Commerce Department's Bureau of Export Administration (BXA) should be selected as the single administrative agency for export controls.

* As part of the consolidation of functions, measures should be taken to lessen any remaining deficiencies at BXA, such as strengthening the technical center staff at the Office of Technology and Policy Analysis and upgrading its professional grade levels.

OTHER CHANGES RELATED TO PROPOSED REFORMS

The reforms proposed above will have to be accompanied by certain legislative and other administrative changes to become operative. Although the proposed changes would require some statutory revision and some transfer of functions among executive agencies, responsibilities for policy formulation would remain with the appropriate departments, subject to coordination with congressional bodies and the mechanism for interagency policy formulation. In addition, agencies with special expertise will be involved in the interagency and working groups and in license reviews.

Harmonize the Structure of Control Lists

* A set of integrated U.S. control lists should be fashioned so that the different lists are similarly structured and formatted. Integrating the lists will lessen overlap and discrepancies among the control lists and conflicts among associated regulations. By keeping the system as simple as possible, the goal of greater transparency of the control system will also be furthered. The respective structures of the U.S. and international control lists should also be harmonized.
* The process for choosing items for control within any particular control regime should involve the following:
  • Identification of items of potential concern.
  • A rank ordering and weighting of items in terms of the national security risks posed by an adversary's acquisition and use of each item, with careful consideration given to the controllability of items.
  • An approximate rank ordering and weighting of items in terms of the economic and foreign policy costs of restricting trade in each item of concern.
  • A policy judgment as to how the risks and benefits of control should be balanced.
  • A comparison of benefits and costs that allows a sorting into controlled and uncontrolled items.
* Building on progress made so far in the policy process, the United States should continue to make the appropriate shift of administrative resources from traditional East-West export controls to controls directed at proliferation concerns and the end-use verification of more narrowly targeted East-West controls, as suggested by the panel.
* An interagency task group should regularly review the Munitions and Commodity Control Lists to eliminate duplication and ensure coordination with the CoCom Industrial List. The U.S. dual use list should be compatible with other multilateral control arrangements.

Provide for Administrative Due Process and Appropriate Judicial Review

* The statutory exemption in Section 13(a) of the EAA from the application of certain provisions of the Administrative Procedure Act (APA), including the appropriate level of administrative due process and judicial review of Commerce Department actions, should be removed.

* The provision in Section 13(b) of the EAA for "meaningful opportunity for public comment" should be retained even if Section 13(a) is repealed, since under the APA any agency may exempt regulations from pre-issuance for public comment if security or foreign policy so require.

Resolve Enforcement Issues

* The General Accounting Office (GAO) should be requested to undertake a study of the appropriate mechanism(s) for enforcement of export controls.

   Questions the GAO study should address include the following:

   • What are the requirements for enforcement in the various export control laws and how do they differ for the Export Administration Act, Arms Export Control Act, Atomic Energy Act, Nuclear Non-Proliferation Act, International Emergency Economic Powers Act, and the Trading with the Enemy Act?

   • To what extent are there problems with enforcement of the Export Administration Act? Specifically,

     — Are organizations effectively accomplishing their assigned enforcement missions?

     — Are enforcement resources allocated rationally?

     — Are there mechanisms to promote coordination and cooperation in enforcement efforts?

     — Do efficiencies result from linking administration to enforcement?

     — What is the degree of exporter cooperation with the Commerce Department and the Customs Service?

   • What enforcement improvements are required?

   • Is there a more effective basis for organizing enforcement responsibilities?

* More specifically, an effort should be made to analyze and systemize the various criminal and civil sanctions in the U.S. export control statutes. In addition, given that a number of export control statutes lack civil enforcement provisions, consideration should be given to enactment of appropriate civil sanctions for export control violations, to-

gether with adoption of appropriate procedures for implementation of those sanctions.

* With regard to administration of enforcement, uniformity of administrative procedures should be part of the single administrative agency recommended by the panel. The existing Commerce Department enforcement procedures appear to be appropriate. In the absence of single agency administration, therefore, enforcement procedures similar to those of the Commerce Department should be instituted in the other affected agencies.

Enhance U.S. Representation at CoCom

* Given the increasing relative importance of international economic concerns and the greater weight U.S. partners in CoCom attach to trade considerations, industry concerns should be more fully represented at CoCom discussions.

* As with the U.S. government domestic process, the CoCom process should be made more transparent. There is ample justification for publishing material such as the Industrial List, the CoCom schedule of list review, and, to the extent security considerations permit, commonly agreed criteria for CoCom decision making.

* The level of technical knowledge of the permanent U.S. mission to CoCom should be upgraded to the extent necessary.

Increase Industry Participation

Greater balance and effectiveness in the export control system require increased industry participation in the system. A process in which defense, foreign policy, and economic concerns are all coordinated into a cohesive U.S. policy would be further encouraged by the following steps:

* To improve the current level of industry input, the President should establish a permanent industry advisory committee on export administration.

  To ensure continuity from administration to administration, the committee should be required by law. The committee should have the following features:

  • Charter—Advise the government on all forms of export controls that may be authorized by law or executive order.

  • Membership—Industry members (representing firms affected by export controls) would be appointed by the President from nominations made by the key agencies: Commerce, Defense, State, and Energy.

  • Terms—Industry members would be appointed for staggered, six-year terms to ensure continuity across changes in administration.

- Chairperson—The chairperson would be appointed by the President from industry members.
- Secretariat—The Commerce Department would provide the necessary staff and resources to support the committee's work.

* In addition, the following changes should be made to the technical advisory committees to enhance the breadth of their charge, level of interagency participation, and amount of technical expertise:

- The scope of the charge of the technical advisory committees should be broadened to include nonproliferation controls and munitions controls.
- The State and Defense Departments should appoint a portion of the industry members to ensure their confidence in committee expertise in defense products and technologies.
- The Defense Department should appoint at least one representative to each technical committee to serve as a regular participant. Other agencies should appoint participants to a committee when that committee's scope is relevant to the agency's charge or when agency participation is requested by a committee.
- Representatives of the technical advisory committees should be assigned as regular participants in interagency or other established technical decision-making groups on export control lists and procedures. Such participation should include substantial involvement in interagency meetings, from list construction and review all the way through to the end of the CoCom meetings.
- Technical advisory committees should be supported with resources (provided equally by the Commerce, State, and Defense Departments) that are sufficient to provide technical staffing by the Institute for Defense Analyses and to pay the travel expenses of industry members.
- The activities of the technical advisory committees and working groups should be coordinated through the Institute for Defense Analyses to ensure the committees an adequate level of technical support.

APPENDIXES

Report of the Subpanel on Advanced Industrial Materials*

EXECUTIVE SUMMARY

Nature of the Problem

• Although U.S. national security export controls apply only to a limited portion of worldwide trade in advanced materials, their estimated impact on U.S. competitiveness is significant.

• In general, it is not the advanced materials that are militarily critical, but rather the application of design and fabrication technology for weapons systems.

• The basic contents of advanced materials are generally made public in U.S. patents. The application technology and processing know-how, however, are closely guarded as trade secrets.

---

*The Subpanel on Advanced Industrial Materials was appointed by the Committee on Science, Engineering, and Public Policy to work in conjunction with the main panel to examine the impact of both current policy and alternative future policies on its specific industrial sector. The subpanel was not asked to consider the full range of issues addressed by the main panel; rather, it was given a specific set of tasks to undertake. The subpanel met less frequently than—and independently of—the main panel, and it had considerable latitude in conducting its discussions.

Thus, it should be noted that the conclusions and recommendations of this subpanel report, while providing valuable input to the deliberations of the main panel, do not necessarily reflect the main panel's views and, therefore, should not be considered to be a part of its findings.

• Although military funding has driven research and development (R&D) in advanced materials in the past, the majority of applications for advanced materials today are commercial, not military.

• A significant part of U.S. industrial know-how in advanced materials is being "exported" through the sale of small U.S. companies to larger, multinational firms.

• A Department of Commerce study indicates that the United States no longer leads Japan in advanced materials or component technologies that are highly dependent on advanced materials. Consequently, the ability of the United States to control global diffusion of these technologies is limited. Further, there is a growing shortage of domestic suppliers of specialty materials for defense-related purposes.

Findings and Conclusions

• Advanced materials should be grouped and defined differently than they currently are for control purposes. The physical or chemical properties of materials do not necessarily indicate criticality. Design code and fabrication technology generally lead to military use.

• A number of materials currently controlled were developed under Department of Defense (DoD) contract, but they have not yet been incorporated into weapons prototypes or systems.

• Advanced materials should be controlled on the basis of their demonstrated ability to enhance significantly the performance of weapons systems.

• Based on a selective review of the U.S. Commodity Control List, a number of advanced materials currently controlled for national security purposes should be decontrolled (see Annex A3).

THE U.S. ADVANCED MATERIALS INDUSTRY AND U.S. EXPORT CONTROLS

Defense-critical materials technologies figure prominently in those emerging technologies identified by a Department of Commerce study as potentially having a multitude of civilian applications and substantially advancing production and quality levels.[1] The same study also concluded that the United States is currently behind Japan, and likely to continue to lose ground, in advanced materials and technologies that are highly dependent on advanced materials, such as semiconductor devices, optical electronics, and high-density data storage media.

The ability of the United States to compete in the advanced materials market is being further weakened by the sale to large, multinational firms of small U.S. companies that specialize in fabricating advanced materials. Foreign ownership of U.S. materials suppliers also is increasing. Foreign multinational firms active in acquiring U.S. firms include, among others, Badische Anilin Soda Fabrik (BASF), Hoechst Celanese, Imperial Chemical Industries, CIBA-Geigy, Rhone-Poulenc, Morgan Crucible, Bayer, and Kyocera Corporation. The most active buyer has been Courtalds (Great Britain), which acquired 27 U.S.-based materials suppliers and fabricators in the late 1980s.[2]

Foreign materials suppliers gain further competitive advantage because the U.S. materials industry is stratified. There is limited integration between suppliers and fabricators, which allows for more flexibility in the purchase of raw materials from foreign sources. Many of the foreign raw materials suppliers are increasingly moving up the value-added chain by investing capital in processing and fabrication industries, thus displacing similar U.S. industries (e.g., ferro compounds, smelter and mill products, and tool and die blanks). For example, Malaysia has recently emerged as a leading contender in the supply of aircraft subsystems for such customers as Airbus Industrie, Fokker, Boeing, Donnjer, Mitsubishi, Fuji, and Kawasaki Heavy Industries.[3]

The result of these factors is a significant diffusion of processing technology in the industry and, in some specialty materials (e.g., specialty steel, functional ceramics, high-purity compounds), a shortage of domestic suppliers for U.S. defense-related purposes. **Thus, the ability of the United States to control access to these technologies unilaterally is limited and eroding. In fact, continued controls may have a negative impact on U.S. defense capabilities.**

Although there are a number of critical military applications of advanced materials, and military funding typically drives R&D in advanced materials, the majority of potential applications for advanced materials are commercial, not military. One result of defense-driven R&D is that much of the technical data related to the capabilities and performance of advanced materials is classified. The lack of publicly available data on the operational performance of advanced materials reduces interest in potential applications and forces firms that may wish to use certain advanced materials in commercial applications to duplicate work that has already been done. In addition, advanced materials can involve a relatively long lead time between development and application, which discourages commercial materials R&D in the United States, where the cost of capital is relatively high. In foreign countries in which the cost of capital is lower, private investment in the commercial development of advanced materials outpaces that in the United States.[4]

Despite the fact that defense funding is responsible for many developments in advanced materials, advanced materials themselves are not inherently critical. **The physical and chemical parameters used to identify materials for control do not necessarily reflect critical use, and military perfor-**

mance characteristics do not necessarily differentiate militarily critical use from commercial use. It would be more useful to control the design of special, military-application materials rather than basic, commodity materials. In some instances, however, controls on the basic material have been maintained while the manufacturing process and end product that use the material have been decontrolled (e.g., polysilicon is controlled but personal computers have been decontrolled).

Controlling the export of the material itself does not necessarily control the militarily critical application. For example, canopies for jet aircraft, which can be made from polycarbonate sheet, are controlled as a munitions item. The polycarbonate sheet is controlled for export by the Commerce Department. Although only a certain quality sheet is used, it is the process for forming it into the canopy, not the material itself, that is complicated and protected, even in the United States, for proprietary reasons. In fact, such factors as fabrication and processing techniques and ingredient percentages are closely guarded as trade secrets, but the basic physical properties and contents of advanced materials are revealed in U.S. patents. Given the market implications, materials firms are more likely to reveal specific contents and processing techniques in patents for materials that may be reverse engineered than in patents for materials for which there is little chance of reverse engineering. **Thus, export controls on advanced materials may be somewhat redundant in that the most critical aspects of advanced materials fabrication are either closely guarded as trade secrets or published in patent applications.**

RELATIONSHIP OF ADVANCED MATERIALS AND ASSOCIATED TECHNOLOGY TO MILITARILY CRITICAL WEAPONS SYSTEMS

Military funding has been a principal driver in advanced materials R&D since World War II. Significant advances in structural and electronic materials can be traced to DoD funding. **Given cuts in military spending, however, defense-related incentives for continued development of an advanced materials technology base are likely to decline.** This is particularly important to the U.S. materials industry, because much of the foreign investment in U.S. materials firms in the 1980s reflected an effort to participate in the development of new materials technologies funded by U.S. defense spending. For example, Imperial Chemical Industries purchased the Fiberite and LNP Engineering Plastics divisions from Beatrice in 1985 to gain access to both military and commercial aerospace developments involving advanced composite systems and to gain an avenue through which to introduce its polyetheretherketone (PEEK) thermoplastic resins into U.S. defense programs.

The combination of uncertain investment prospects for the U.S. materials industry and the technological lead of the Japanese and some European materials firms is highly significant to the U.S. defense posture because advanced materials figure prominently in DoD's science and technology strategy for the long-term qualitative superiority of U.S. weapons systems. The problem is further compounded by the unspecified lifetimes of military-platform equipment and technologies. Advanced materials that have some application to current military equipment may be controlled, even though they represent relatively old technology and are produced in a number of foreign countries. In fact, many of the avionics suites incorporated in the Boeing 757 and 767, the McDonnell Douglas MD-80 and MD-90, and the Airbus 330 and 340 series aircraft are more advanced and easier to use than those found in the current U.S. inventory of fighters and bombers.

On the other hand, advanced materials for which there is no specific advanced development program or weapons procurement plan may be classified or controlled due to their potential applications, and consequently, they languish in the DoD technology base. Examples include superconducting magnets, which are likely to be used in Maglev (magnetic levitation) and people-mover applications before being used in weapons systems, and the National Aerospace Plane (NASP) project, in which the benefits of research in new metal, ceramic, and polymer matrix materials are likely to be applied to high-speed civil transport before they are applied to an aerospace plane to replace the current shuttle fleet. **Clearly, technological progress occurs at a pace that outstrips the U.S. ability to incorporate such developments in weapons systems.**

The subpanel agreed that only materials marked for procurement for a prototype or existing system should be subject to commercial restrictions or export controls. If advanced materials that have high commercial potential continue to be subject to export restrictions, the U.S. technology base will not be able to "breathe," and there will be little foundation for investment risks in research and development. The natural counterpart to allowing freer circulation of U.S. advanced materials would be to source foreign materials technologies for integration in U.S. defense systems if long-term access can be assured.

Based on these considerations, the subpanel identified the following as examples of materials that are militarily critical:

- chemical weapons precursors
- high-temperature, nonablating structural materials for hypersonic aircraft and missiles
- silicon carbide, fiber-reinforced titanium aluminides for high-performance military jet engines

- certain optically switched coatings and laminates for spacecraft threat resistance
- ultraclean, nickel-based alloys, powders, processes, and products for high-performance jet engine parts
- initiators for ultrahigh energy materials
- high-performance armor and penetrator materials

REVIEW OF THE CONTROL/DECONTROL OF ADVANCED MATERIALS*

Current Methodology

The subpanel reviewed advanced materials controlled under various export commodity control numbers (ECCNs) and made the following observations concerning the methodology by which the materials are determined to warrant control. A specific analysis of several entries on the Commodity Control List is attached as Annex A1.

- The ECCN entries are defined too broadly and the rationale for control is not clearly stated in either the Commerce Department's Commodity Control List or in the Defense Department's Militarily Critical Technologies List.
- Although the Commerce Department's technical advisory committees (TACs) are sometimes consulted on the foreign availability of materials, they are not consulted in determining the critical nature of materials. Moreover, the TACs do not adequately interact with the State Department's technical working groups.
- The list construction/management process does not take into account the dynamic nature of technology transfer from military to commercial applications, or vice versa. No attempt is made to assess the market opportunity or economic impact of restricting trade in the materials.
- Some of the advanced materials on the Commodity Control List have no direct relation to a current DoD mission area (e.g., superconductor magnets, NASP technology).
- Foreign countries often have superior capabilities in producing some of the controlled materials (e.g., Soviet Union in energetic materials, Japan in silicon chips).

---

*This review was undertaken prior to the development of a core list of CoCom-controlled items that was begun in the latter half of 1990. Although the analysis of the subpanel remains valid, the categorization and control status of many materials will change when the core list exercise is completed.

New Methodology*

The subpanel recommends a new methodology based on a series of filters, or stages of review. For example, the first filter might be R/O, where R represents the risk associated with decontrol and O represents the economic opportunity of decontrol.

The subpanel identified five categories of risk:

V.   supercritical and unilaterally controllable
IV. supercritical and multilaterally controllable
III. supercritical, not multilaterally controllable, or critical and multi-
     laterally controllable
II. critical, not multilaterally controllable
I.   not critical

A chart separating certain selected ECCN materials entries into these five categories is attached as Annex A2. Definitions of supercritical and critical (see Annex A2) address whether the material is directly related to a primary mission capability and the effect that an adversary's acquisition and exploitation of the material would have on the balance of power.

Opportunity is defined for the purpose of this example as the product of the unit price (dollars/pound) of a material and world market volume. Five categories are then established using appropriate bounds. For example,

V.   > 200 million
IV. 50–200 million
III. 20–50 million
II. 5–20 million
I.   < 5 million

Numerical values are assigned to the categories of risk and opportunity by using the well-known mathematical relationship 2^n, where n is the number of the category. Category V $= 32$. Category IV $= 16$. Category III $= 8$. Category II $= 4$ and category I $= 2$. The ratio of risk (R) to opportunity (O) can then be calculated.

Bounds are placed on the resulting numbers to indicate items for continued control, items for further consideration, and items for decontrol. For example, $R/O \geq .5$, and $R > 8$, continue control.
$.5 \leq R/O \leq 1$ and $R \leq 8$, consider further ("middle ground").
$R/O < .5$, decontrol.
Note that this formula favors the risk factor. A chart of this formula applied to certain selected ECCN materials entries is attached as Annex A3.

---

*The methodology described herein was tested on advanced materials only. A more generic methodology applicable to all items is described in Chapter 10.

Illustrations

An item in risk category V is 3604A, zirconium. Because this material has a nuclear proliferation possibility, it is assigned an R of 32 ($n = 5$) and an O of 8 ($n = 3$). R/O then calculates to 4, which indicates continued control.

An item in risk category III is 1702A, hydraulic fluid. Because of foreign availability, it is assigned an R of 8 ($n = 3$) and an O of 8 ($n = 3$). R/O then calculates to 1, which indicates middle ground, or consider further.

An item in risk category I is 1631A, magnets. Because of extensive foreign availability, the item is assigned an R of 4 ($n = 2$) and an O of 32 ($n = 5$). R/O calculates to .0625, which indicates decontrol.

The second filter or stage of review would then apply to those items in the category that calls for further consideration. Factors for consideration in this stage include the following:

• the learning curve and technology diffusion rate associated with the item,
• the cost of efficiently controlling the item,
• a productivity index of sales per employee multiplied by a skill index,
• the ratio of value added to labor costs (capital intensity), and
• economic incentives for trade.

This stage favors the opportunity factor since most, if not all, supercritical items would be recommended for continued control in the first stage.

The third stage of review should include an analysis of the foreign policy objective in controlling the item and foreign commitments to continue control. The results of the third stage of review should be compared with the results of the second-stage analysis to determine the eventual control or decontrol of middle-ground items.

A further elaboration on the possible series of filters or stages for list construction is contained in Annex A4.

RECOMMENDATIONS

Based on its review and analysis, the subpanel makes the following recommendations:

*   **The U.S. government should adopt a multistage control methodology, similar to that outlined above, that takes into account both military and commercial aspects of trade in advanced materials.**

*   **Commercial restrictions or controls should be applied only to those advanced materials marked for procurement for a prototype or existing weapons system.**

* Controls should focus on the design code and fabrication technology necessary for military application, rather than the basic material.
* A number of advanced materials should be decontrolled, including those listed under export commodity control numbers (Eccns) 1648A, 1587A, 1760A, 1749A, 1675A, 1746A and 1631A, 1110A, 1129A, 1145A, 1203A, 1301A, 1561A, and 1635A.

NOTES

1. U.S. Department of Commerce, Technology Administration, *Emerging Technologies: A Survey of Technology and Economic Opportunities* (Washington, D.C.: U.S. Government Printing Office, 1990).
2. Personal Communication, Robert D. Wilson, November 2, 1990.
3. Personal Communication, Robert D. Wilson, November 2, 1990.
4. U.S. Department of Defense, Defense Logistics Agency, *Strategic and Critical Materials* (Report to Congress) (Washington, D.C., 1990).

Annex A1

ANALYSIS OF U.S. COMMODITY CONTROL LIST ENTRIES

BASE MATERIALS*

This is the control entry for the most advanced ceramic and ceramic composite materials. The entry covers high-purity fine powders that are crucial to making high-tech fine ceramics and whose control is of strategic concern. However, the entry also covers many compounds, precursors, and composites and is in effect a "catchall." Some of these materials, particularly the composites, are becoming significant for military (especially aircraft) applications.

For these materials, the technology of synthesis and fabrication is more important than the materials themselves. Many new organic precursors have recently been developed, but others have been known for about 10 years. The best are still being made by the Japanese, despite the investment of many U.S. research dollars in this area. U.S. work on composites, however, is as good as any. Reverse engineering is very difficult.

The problem with this control entry is that it contains too many materials, a number of which are not critical. For example, the reason for controlling either silicon carbide or boron carbide powders, as described in the entry,

---

*ECCN 1733A. Contributed by Neil Ault.

is not apparent. Some of the precursors should be controlled, but controlling the fibers, the methods for making them, and the composites from them is far more important. Many of the materials in 1733A belong in category II, critical but not controllable.

QUARTZ CRYSTALS*

I do not know the capabilities of the Soviet Union or East European countries in regard to these crystals, which are used in military equipment. These controls are not a hardship in terms of lost business for U.S. companies, however, and the controls seem to be justified.

I am not familiar with the capabilities that exist within the Coordinating Committee for Multilateral Export Controls (CoCom). I would place 1587A in either category III, critical and multilaterally controllable, or II, critical but not controllable.

POLYMERIC SUBSTANCES AND
MANUFACTURE THEREOF†

Nature of Criticality

The 12 classes (a through l) of polymers indicated in this entry can be categorized as follows:

1. Have been commercially available for >15 years—a, c, h, j, k, l.
2. Have been commercially available for 7 to 10 years—b.
3. Are not commercially available—d, e, f, i.
4. Uncertain—g.

None of these materials qualifies as being supercritical or critical. On the other hand, specific formulations, fabricated forms, and recipes for end-use applications may very well be supercritical.

Examples of use: Large manufacturing facilities ranging up to 20×10^6 lbs/yr exist for items listed under category 1 above. Hence, the number of applications is very large. Nomex (c) is used in flame-resistant textiles and honeycomb structures; Kevlar (c) is used in bulletproof vests and as reinforcement for secondary structures in aircraft. Item (b) is proposed for use in fabric filter systems.

In terms of product life cycle, materials such as those in (a) and (c) have been available for 20 to 30 years, and there does not appear to be any diminution of interest in these systems.

---

*ECCN 1587A. Contributed by Neil Ault.
†ECCN 1746A. Contributed by James Economy.

Foreign Availability

Polyimide materials are manufactured in Japan and in Germany. Generally speaking, the preparation of polyimides is well known throughout the world. Surprisingly, the polyimide film is excluded from control, even though that system, to my knowledge, is manufactured only in the United States (by Du Pont).

Item (b) is also manufactured solely in the United States (by Hoechst Celanese), but I know of little commercial utility for it. Items (d), (e), (f) and (i) are not, to my knowledge, manufactured anywhere.

Item (c) is manufactured in the United States, the Netherlands, and Japan. Pilot quantities of Kevlar fibers were prepared in the People's Republic of China in the late 1980s.

Item (h) is manufactured in the United States, Japan, England, and Italy. The knowledge for making these polymers is readily available throughout the world.

Item (j) is primarily available from England, and the knowledge for fabricating composites from polyetheretherketone (PEEK) (j) remains proprietary with Imperial Chemicals Industries in England.

Many of the systems listed under butadiene polymers are manufactured throughout the world, and the specific knowledge to prepare any of these systems is readily available.

Rather than enumerate specific items available from foreign countries that are comparable or identical to those manufactured in the United States, it is safer to state that the sophistication of polymer synthesis and scaleup is at a level that almost any country could set up a capability to produce such items.

Relative Importance of Design Technology vs. Materials

There is little question that polymeric substances afford considerable opportunity for control. Polyimide film is still manufactured only in the United States, primarily because of the large capital investment required. Fibroids of Nomex that are used in paper manufacture remain proprietary knowledge to Du Pont. Typically, the following factors have resulted in one company being the sole manufacturer of a polymer:

1. High cost of capital investment
2. Limited market
3. Strong patents

The following factors promote entry into manufacturing a polymer developed by another company:

1. The tradition that the second company makes far more money than the first because of its much smaller R&D cost and its ability to exploit developed markets.

2. The ability to skirt existing patents and still produce a competitive material.

3. The availability of patent literature that provides the details of the invention.

Substitutability

The field of specialty polymers has reached a level of sophistication that one skilled in synthesis and processing can generally design alternative systems to achieve a given end. Further, many of the major manufacturers of polymers in the United States look on themselves as global companies without any particular allegiance to the country of origin. Hence, the site for manufacture of key materials is often determined primarily by economic considerations.

Conclusions

I would assign all the materials listed under 1746A to category II, critical but not controllable. I would also eliminate controls on those items that are not manufactured today, such as items (d), (e), (f) and (g), although I am not sure about item (g). In fact, the only areas I would consider appropriate for control are those concerned with processing of polymers into finished articles. Even here, only a very few items might warrant control.

FIBROUS AND FILAMENTARY MATERIALS THAT MAY BE USED IN ORGANIC "MATRIX," METALLIC "MATRIX" OR CARBON MATRIX*

Nature of Criticality

• The parameter of 1×10^8 in. restricts the export of all carbon fiber, Kevlar, boron, and silicon carbide composites.

• These fibers are used in commercial and military aircraft in many parts of the world. U.S. military aircraft would include the F-16, F-15, F-14, F-18, F-111, B2, AV8-B, and others.

• Estimated length of product life cycle for commercial applications is 30,000 flight hours; for military applications, approximately 8,000 flight hours.

---

*ECCN 1763A. Contributed by William Yee.

Foreign Availability

The fibers in this entry are available from Taiwan, Japan, South Kórea, Israel, Germany, England, France, the Netherlands, the Soviet Union, and China. T300/epoxy and H46/epoxy are available from Japan; G30/epoxy is available from Germany. Graft carbon composites are available from Great Britain.

Relative Importance of Design Technology vs. Materials

The design technology is distinct from the material. It is not likely that design technology could be understood or reverse engineered from the composite material.

Substitutability

In most cases, other products could not be used to accomplish the same military or critical objective because of the structural tailoring and dielectric properties involved in structural applications.

Conclusions

These fibers belong in category II, critical but not multilaterally controllable.

Perhaps a fiber that has the stiffness of pitch carbon fiber, which has a specific modulus of 1×10^9 in., should be restricted. Another consideration is to restrict the fibrous material by some measure of the dielectric properties as well.

POLYCARBONATE SHEET*

Nature of Criticality

The polycarbonate sheet with the optical property and strength described in the entry is not militarily critical because many of the new military aircraft do not use it exclusively. However, commercial applications, such as window material for office buildings, are gaining rapidly. In any event, this item is not considered critical and is not multilaterally controllable. It belongs in category I, not critical.

Foreign Availability

The polycarbonate sheet described within this control list entry is considered to be a standard polycarbonate sheet of optical quality and defined

---

*ECCN 1749A. Contributed by William Yee.

thickness. This material is manufactured by numerous companies both within and outside the United States.

The technology to process this material is therefore not specific to the United States. The number of U.S. manufacturers is too large to even begin to list in this review. However, the following is an abbreviated list of companies in foreign countries that possess the technology and capability to process this type of polycarbonate sheet:

Imperial Chemicals Industries	England
Shell	The Netherlands
Mobay-Bayer	Germany
Rhone-Poulenc	France
Mitsui	Japan

The manufacturing of this polycarbonate sheet is by no means limited to the countries listed, however. The technology necessary to produce the sheet is old, well distributed, and readily available.

Export control of this material would simply limit the U.S. ability to compete in the worldwide polycarbonate market and would not be safe-guarding sensitive technology. In addition, limiting the use of this material to Defense Department projects would negatively affect the automotive industry and its conversion to plastics technology.

TANTALATES AND NIOBATES*

Nature of Criticality

- No criticality. These salts have little or no military or nuclear applications, and purities cited are low in the industry.
- Lithium niobate is used in the military and in civilian applications as a piezoelectric.
- Salts are used primarily as a precursor to making the elements of tantalum and niobium. Salts have a zero product life cycle. Elements are alloy additions and have a product life cycle of the alloys from which they are made.

Foreign Availability/Design Technology/Substitutability

These salts are available worldwide as commodity chemicals.

Design technology is not applicable to this item, and there is no substitutability because these salts are the precursors to the metals.

---

*ECCN 1760A. Contributed by Edward Van Reuth, subpanel consultant.

Conclusion

These salts are not critical and are not controllable. They belong in category I, not critical.

TITANIUM-BASED ALLOYS WITH 12 PERCENT ALUMINUM AS TiAl*

Nature of Criticality

- Critical as primary structure for the NASP (leading edges) and other hypersonic aircraft.
- Domestic funding has been entirely by the Department of Defense.
- Key parameters are specific strength and low strain rate above 1000°F.
- Length of product life cycle is difficult to extrapolate because titanium alloys are 35 years old and show little sign of degradation.

Foreign Availability

The following countries have supersonic transport designs: France (Hermes), Germany (Sanger), United Kingdom (Hotel), Japan, and the Soviet Union.

Relative Importance of Design Technology vs. Materials

Design technology is not distinct from the material. Reverse engineering could be determined from the material.

Substitutability

There are no substitutes for this material. The nearest substitutes would be nickel-based alloys (which are too heavy), ceramics (which are too brittle), or carbon-carbons (which are too prone to oxidation).

Conclusion

This entry should be assigned to category III, critical and multilaterally controllable.

---

*ECCN 1672A. Contributed by Edward Van Reuth, subpanel consultant.

Annex A2
SELECTED ECCN MATERIALS ENTRIES CLASSIFIED BY CATEGORY OF RISK

V: Uni- Controllable, Super- Critical	IV: Multi- Controllable, Super- Critical	III: Not Multi- Controllable, Super- Critical	III: Multi- Controllable, Critical	II: Not Controllable, Critical	I: Not Controllable, Not Critical
3604A	1733A		1673A	3605A	1110A
3608A	2603A		1702A	3609A	1129A
1675A	2616A		1734A	1661A	1145A
2708A	1701A		1767A	1763A	1203A
3709A	1781A		1573A	1587A	1301A
1757A	1755A		1574A	3711A	1561A
1759A	1588A		1601A	1715A	1631A
			1672A	1754A	1635A
				1675A	1648A
				1746A	1760A
					1749A

NOTES: A *supercritical* technology is one whose acquisition and exploitation by a potential adversary would negate or impair a primary U.S. mission capability to such an extent that a major commitment of national resources would be needed to offset the loss. Such technologies typically enable primary mission capabilities or provide a qualitative superiority essential to maintaining the balance of power. Primary missions are those having high mission value and leverage, such as strategic deterrence, power projection, air superiority, or sea control.

An item is *multilaterally controllable* if it is *not* produced outside the United States, United Kingdom, Canada, Germany, France, Japan, Norway, Denmark, Netherlands, Belgium, Luxembourg, Australia, Italy, Spain, Portugal, Greece, Turkey, Austria, Finland, Switzerland, or Sweden.

Annex A3
ILLUSTRATIVE APPLICATION OF RISK/OPPORTUNITY FORMULA TO SELECTED ITEMS ON COMMODITY CONTROL LIST

ECCN	Risk Category	Risk Value	Opportunity Category ($)	Opportunity Value	Risk ÷ Opportunity	Decontrol?
1733A	IV	16	>200	32	0.5	No
1672A	III	8	<5	2	4	No
1588A	IV	16	5–20	4	4	No
1763A	III	8	>200	32	0.25	Yes
1573A	III	8	20–50	8	1	Maybe
1574A	III	8	20–50	8	1	Maybe
1648A	I	2	<5	2	1	Yes
1587A	II	4	>200	32	0.125	Yes
1760A	II	4	<5	2	2	Yes
1749A	I	2	50–200	16	0.125	Yes
1675A	II	4	5–20	4	1	Yes
1746A	II	4	>200	32	0.125	Yes

NOTE: ECCN = export commodity control number.

Annex A4

TOWARD A NEW MECHANISM OF TECHNOLOGY EXPORT CONTROL

Peter Cannon
Conductus Inc.

RATIONALE FOR A NEW MECHANISM

One of the principal difficulties with the export control process is the severity of export restrictions, which are, in themselves, unexpected in a free market society. They have become more onerous because the U.S. economy has, once again, become mercantile. The nation has evolved from a "Fortress of Freedoms" to a "Purveyor of Values"; it exports concepts of government and law, along with increasing quantities of goods. Increasingly, the United States should promote truly progressive trade practices, rather than enforcing restrictions. The United States has accumulated a number of contradictory and inhibiting bilateral agreements, which have not kept pace with rapid political changes. In addition, the General Agreement on Tariffs and Trade (GATT) talks are not moving fast enough to provide conditions for the expansion of U.S. trade. The champions of the current export control regime are the "Whigs" of the twentieth century. The appropriate premise for export control has changed from the goal of disadvantaging an adversary to one of global consent that there should not be traffic in arms.

In addition to the outdated premise, export controls, which involve case-by-case review by experts, have become cumbersome, nonuniform, and unpredictable in their application. Moreover, engineers who graduated in the 1980s might not recognize some of the obsolete terms used to describe restricted items. It would be desirable to see an end to case-by-case restriction and use of a broad self-administered rule.

In such a scheme, export control becomes a system of voluntary questioning by a producer of propriety and a process of exception rather than one of rule. Fixed requirements for analysis are replaced by the conscience of the individual and the language of self-inquiry, which leads to voluntary submission for further examination.

A process of self-assessment by those engaged in exports and world trade must be based in the language of trade, that is, in manufacturing, value, time, and usage terms. Since this process would be subjective and imperfect, its utility would be improved by the simple artifice of multiple filters—a cascade of decisions, each perhaps only 80 to 90 percent relevant or accurate, but multiplied through four or five steps to improve performance to a 99.9

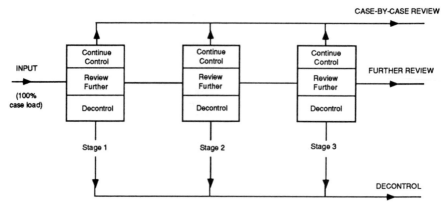

CASE-BY-CASE REVIEW

FIGURE A 4-1   The cascaded filter for export control decision making

or 99.99 percent (see Figure A4-1). Such a process, voluntarily certified (within a statute of sanctions for violation) could enable an enormous simplification in the bureaucratic implementation of the policy of export control.

At the risk of overemphasis, note that this paper presumes that some control is necessary. The purpose of the paper is to provide notional limits to the requirement of sufficiency. What are the guiding values, the purposes of control? The broad policy principle of U.S. export control is to deny to a potential adversary those articles, and means of manufacture, that could be used in the near term to damage or destroy the property or lives of U.S. citizens (private, public, or corporate), wherever they might be.

The general environment for application of export controls is currently one in which invasion or other use of major military force between superpowers is thought to be highly unlikely. The United States should also recognize, from the standpoint of human interdependence, a need for some systematic exclusions from trade controls. Immediately, the export of articles and knowledge intended for the long-term benefit of broad populations everywhere, including U.S. adversaries, should be excluded from control. Thus, the United States should not seek to control the export of the following:

- Food
- Medical supplies, including pharmaceuticals
- Humanitarian aid
- Telecommunications and computer apparatus (at a consumer or user level)
- The means of education, even at risk to the current generation of new technology

The last category raises the issue of timing in controlling the export of the technical-base infrastructure (''6.1 and 6.2,'' in Defense Department parlance).

A great deal of such information is generated in academic institutions, which pride themselves on being noncontrollable and which depend on the enrollment of foreign nationals to sustain low-cost operations. Moreover, the real issue is the time frame within which such information becomes operational. Much of the information is, at best, existence proof of principle and does not achieve operability, for at least a decade. The possibility of control at any point in the development process reduces the incentive for private development of such information into dual use technology. When the political uncertainties of the federal budget process are added, it becomes totally likely that export-controlled, technical-base information will molder in classification. Depending on its intrinsic merit, such information may in fact be rediscovered or arrived at independently in a more aggressive economy.

The exclusions listed above still clearly contemplate the control of weapons exports. But even such a list is equivocal given that there are technologies of transportation and communication that permit delivery or projection of belligerent or military intentions, as well as provide useful social functions. Among these key areas are telecommunications encryption, heavy-lift space vehicles, and even fuel-efficient jet transports if built in quantities in excess of prompt civil demand and stockpiled. It is these "dual use" uncertainties that have created a complex bureaucratic conflict among cabinet departments and that have rendered the purpose of export control, except in the case of obvious weapons, moot. What is needed is a real simplification of purpose and process.

This paper advances the idea that goods have clear characteristics that can be described in the language of business and that could enable a voluntary screening of prospective exports in the interest of national security. Those characteristics can be expressed in quantitative microeconomic terms that relate to military sensitivity. An important condition for application of this concept is that the economic interest of producers must frequently coincide with the broad policy interests of the United States, as exemplified by the proposed liberalization of trade with specific members of the former Soviet bloc.

The natural wish to protect profitable trade today mimics the wish to maintain military advantage. This is because unlike the situation as recently as 40 years ago, today's U.S. military advantage depends on technology and value-laden means of force multiplication and projection. So it is the value, value density (some quotient of price over unit volume or mass), and value rate of change that should form the basis of the criteria for self-inquiry.

In the particular case of advanced materials, the primary means of insertion into trade is through substitution of improved parts during system upgrading. Examples include substituting a gallium arsenide processor or high-density mass storage subsystem for older, less capable components and retrofitting a composite wing for aircraft. Here, the justification and motive are clearly known in economic terms, and thus, the argument for the use of economic criteria, as opposed to implication of military value, is highly relevant. The system use is known, and the cost numbers are available. It should be possible to state clearly which part of the dual use item relates to unacceptably sensitive military technologies without breaching security.

THE CASCADE OF FILTERS

The first decision filter is specific value density. Here, the selling price (market value) is divided by a dimension, usually weight. This quantity for a number of familiar industrial products is shown plotted against annual production, on a log-log scale, in Figure A4-2. This kind of aggregate treatment has a number of flaws, but the value of such a broad treatment is that it clearly shows regimes of value—commodity products (at the bottom); items that should be in museums, military arsenals, or other noncommercial protected environments (at the top left); and items of dual use, high commercial value as well as military potential (in the middle).

It is highly instructive to reflect that the two internal bounds between inexpensive goods and those priced by their technical labor or scarcity on the one hand, and between obviously scarce or costly components and nuclear materials essential for weapons making on the other, can also be identified with the value of bullion silver and the value of bullion gold. It could be concluded from Figure A4-2 that anything worth less than the value density of silver should not be controlled at all; anything over the value density of gold requires case-by-case clearance; and items in the middle ground should be subject to further examination.

The second filter could be technical value density. This might be expressed as the professional labor content of the product divided by its market value. In general, high-tech products have high professional labor content, and custom systems exhibit the highest such quotient. The highest values would lead to probable control, the lowest would probably lead to decontrol, and the middle ground would require yet a further look (Figure A4-3).

The third filter might involve the rate of change of the technology, as exemplified by the change in the value of the product as experience with the product accumulates (the slope of the so-called price-experience curve). In this well-known business analysis, price (or more rigorously cost) per unit of experience is plotted on a log scale against the log of the cumulative number of units of experience (Figure A4-4). The slope is naturally negative, given competition, and typically is between $-.1$ and $-.2$. These values are usually quoted in percentages, 10 percent or 20 percent, and the minus sign is dropped. The larger the value, the more rapid the evolution (downward) of competitive market value, which implies a more vigorous competition and which can imply a more rapidly improving product technology. It is in these

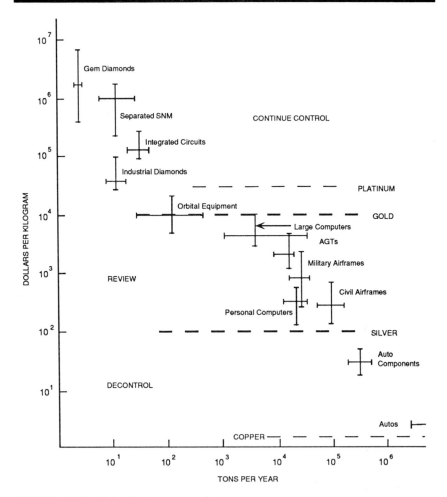

FIGURE A 4-2   Value density versus volume

latter, fast-moving areas that dual use technologies can usually be found. A zero slope, that is, stable prices regardless of volume, usually implies complete control of the commercial marketplace under protection or monopolistic control—the same consequence that is sought under rigorous export control. So, while the mapping of the evolution of market value onto the evolution of technology is inevitably imprecise, the broad correlative truth appears valid.

Finally, one has to think about the broad social consequences of excessive export control. After reviewing the above criteria, it is easy to conclude that an overly rigorous control program cuts a nation off from exporting the

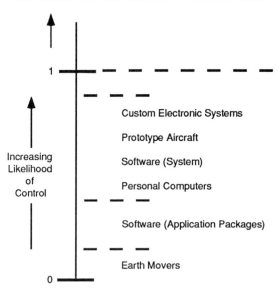

FIGURE A 4-3   Screening on professional labor content

highest value-added products it is capable of building, that is, export control damages the national capacity for wealth generation. It is important to recognize that this affects more than the high-tech professional. Most manufacturing businesses depend on a ratio of contribution of value to pay and benefits for their profitability. In mass production, the pay and benefits are traceable to planned rates and numbers of direct labor employees. The ratio is usually known and is frequently used as a management control variable.

In high-tech or custom engineering businesses, it is essential to include professional labor in this measurement, and the apparent ratios are less than for regular, repetitive production. In the latter case, the notion of the percentage gross prime margin (GPM)—the complement of the direct manufacturing cost proportion of the selling price—is sometimes also used as a general indication of the health of the enterprise or product line. This latter measurement should be 80 percent or higher to ensure the continued ability to employ a professional work force in direct support of production, and it is fairly typical of young instrument or electronics activities. These are also typical areas of sensitivity to military use or purpose. Therefore, the fourth filter would be the percentage GPM. A product family that has higher than 80 percent GPM should be considered for control; between 80 and 55 percent, a "maybe" for control; and anything less than 55 percent GPM (i.e., a

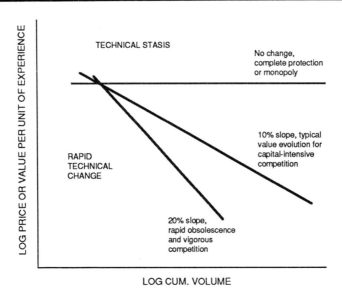

FIGURE A 4-4   Rate of technical change screen (identified with price-volume experience curve)

benefit of less than about twice), decontrolled. For final filtering, total business volume should be considered.

Given the administrative advantages of sequential, quantitative filters using the producer's own statistics, it seems an attractive possibility to reduce the current complexity and uncertainty (almost arbitrariness) of the existing export control process.

Report of the Subpanel on Commercial Aircraft and Jet Engines*

This report provides an overview of the U.S. and world civil aircraft industry, describes the increased globalization of and competition within the industry, and briefly assesses critical Western and Soviet aircraft technology. The report then examines export controls and the civil aircraft industry—in particular, the impact of export controls on U.S. firms, industry characteristics that inhibit or enhance the effectiveness of export controls, and specific problems with the export control system—and offers recommendations for change.

SYNTHESIS OF MAJOR FINDINGS

The major findings of the subpanel are as follows:

1. U.S. export controls imposed for foreign policy reasons have had a far greater impact on the export of commercial aircraft and jet engines than have national security export controls.

---

*The Subpanel on Commercial Aircraft and Jet Engines was appointed by the Committee on Science, Engineering, and Public Policy to work in conjunction with the main panel to examine the impact of both current policy and alternative future policies on its specific industrial sector. The subpanel was not asked to consider the full range of issues addressed by the main panel; rather, it was given a specific set of tasks to undertake. The subpanel met less frequently than—and independently of—the main panel, and it had considerable latitude in conducting its discussions.

Thus, it should be noted that the conclusions and recommendations of this subpanel report, while providing valuable input to the deliberations of the main panel, do not necessarily reflect the main panel's views and, therefore, should not be considered to be a part of its findings.

2. The dynamism, innovative nature, and increasing internationalization of the aircraft and jet engine industry render export controls difficult to administer and maintain.

3. The critical technology related to commercial aircraft and jet engines lies in the design, materials, and manufacturing processes, not in the end products.

4. The competitive and technological position of the United States relative to West European and Japanese commercial competitors may be of greater future importance than its military standing vis-à-vis the Soviet Union.

5. Unilaterally imposed foreign policy and national security export controls on commercial aircraft and jet engines should be sharply limited. If controls are to be imposed, they should be imposed on a multilateral basis.

6. U.S. management of export control lists has been characterized by inconsistent administration, discrepancies between U.S. and CoCom (Coordinating Committee for Multilateral Export Controls) lists, and use of overly broad export controls.

U.S. AND WORLD CIVIL AIRCRAFT INDUSTRY

Major Companies

The West's commercial aircraft industry is a global enterprise comprising a few large, integrated airframe and engine producers that draw from a large and varied U.S. and international base.

The industry has five prime airframe contractors: Airbus Industrie, a consortium composed of Aerospatiale (France), British Aerospace, Construcciones Aeronauticas (Spain), and Daimler-Benz (Germany); Boeing (U.S.); British Aerospace; Fokker (the Netherlands); and McDonnell Douglas (U.S.).* The historic rise in market share of the largest commercial transport companies, in terms of aircraft orders, is shown in Figure B-1.

In addition to the prime airframe contractors, there are major subcontractors in the United States, Japan, Germany, France, the United Kingdom, Italy, Spain, and Canada. Suppliers in the People's Republic of China, Sweden, and Indonesia are playing increasingly larger roles.

Three principal manufacturers in the West design and build engines for large commercial aircraft: General Electric Aircraft Engines, Pratt & Whitney Group, and Rolls-Royce.

---

*There is one other major player in the industry, namely, the huge Soviet civilian aircraft industry. It may eventually become a major factor on the international commercial market.

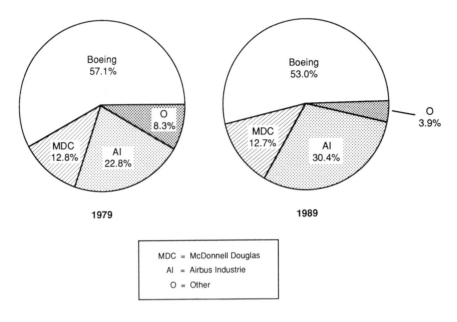

FIGURE B-1   Increase in market share of largest commercial air transport companies

Features of the Civil Aircraft Industry

Among the characteristics peculiar to the civil aircraft industry are the complexity, high unit costs, and low-volume production of commercial transports. Market supply and demand are such that relatively few aircraft are manufactured. From 1952 to 1989, for example, the largest number of jet transports produced in the non-Communist world in any single year—1968—was only 742.

Another reason for the relatively low production rates is the long product life of most civil aircraft. A new computer may become relatively obsolete in two or three years, but a commercial aircraft may be 10 years in development and then stay in service for 20 to 35 years. While in operation, aircraft systems undergo continual improvements to the technology embodied in them. These improvements occur in far shorter cycles than the product life itself. New navigation and communications equipment and changes to the composition of high-strength metal alloys are among the ongoing enhancements.

The aircraft industry is a volatile, highly competitive business that involves extraordinary risks in bringing new products to market. As an example, it takes about 12 to 14 years to reach a break-even point, and relatively few commercial airplane programs have become profitable. As with civil transports, engine development is fraught with large front-end investments; long lead times and a production run of at least 2,000 units over a 10-year period are required for a successful program. In both the aircraft and engine segments of the industry, it typically takes 3 1/2 to 4 1/2 years from design go-ahead to first delivery. And significant product improvements may still be introduced 3 to 10 years after first delivery.

The industry's innovative dynamism makes it all but impossible for any one firm to hold a lead indefinitely in a particular technological area. Aircraft technology is a perishable commodity; efforts to stand still or to control change are likely to prove futile. Much know-how diffuses rapidly throughout the industry by way of product sales, patents, licensing, publications, and competitive research and development (R&D).

Effect on U.S. Economy and National Security

In 1989, the U.S. commercial jet aircraft industry employed 304,000 people, including 35,000 engineers and scientists, and it had a positive trade balance of $10 billion. Exports of civil transports in 1989 reached $12.8 billion; turbine engines, $1.9 billion; and aircraft and engine parts, $9.9 billion. By the end of 1990, the transport industry was expected to have reached nearly $31.9 billion in sales, and new orders were expected to have added significantly to its backlog of $76.6 billion in orders.*[1]

In 1989, the major U.S. airframe and engine manufacturers let subcontracts valued at nearly $20 billion to U.S. firms and over $3 billion to foreign suppliers.† Approximately 10,000 supplier firms, both domestic and foreign, contribute 60 to 70 percent of the value of the airframe. Suppliers provide subassemblies, components, parts, and other goods and services for civil aircraft and engine manufacturers.

The U.S. civil aircraft industry serves as a production and transportation base in the event of national emergency and provides military derivatives of commercial airplanes and engines. In addition, Boeing, General Electric, McDonnell Douglas, and Pratt & Whitney together spend well over $2 billion a year in commercial R&D. Much of the industry's research efforts are concentrated on leading-edge technology, such as electronics, aerodynamics, propulsion, advanced materials, and manufacturing design.

CONTINUING TREND TOWARD GLOBALIZATION AND FOREIGN COMPETITION

For much of the post-World War II period, U.S.-based firms dominated the manufacture of civil aircraft. **Today, far from being a one-nation**

---

*Over the next 15 years, the commercial aircraft industry is expected to try to meet an estimated $626 billion in additional orders.

†Annexes B1 and B2 list domestic and foreign purchase orders, respectively, for 1989.

industry, the aircraft business is becoming increasingly globalized, which
has attendant negative implications for control by any single nation of
the export of production technology. The customer base is spread across
nearly every country in the world and is made up of about 600 airlines,
leasing companies, and foreign governments. At the same time, the global
aircraft industry is being transformed by a wave of consolidation among
companies within and among various nations— 68 percent of all civil aircraft
is purchased by about 5 percent of the non-Communist world's airlines.

**The trend toward a truly worldwide industry is illustrated by the
growing number of recent major international joint ventures.*** In April
1990, for example, Japan's Mitsubishi Heavy Industries and Germany's
Daimler-Benz (which controls the aircraft firm Messerschmitt-Bolkow-Blohm)
signed an agreement on joint aerospace research.† Also in 1990, West Germany's Bayerische Motor Werke (BMW) and the United Kingdom's Rolls-
Royce, the major European manufacturer of jet airplane engines, agreed to
collaborate on the development and construction of new jet engines. These
and other transnational activities are in addition to the well-established joint
ventures in the engine field between General Electric and SNECMA (Société
Nationale d'Etude et de Construction de Moteurs de Aviation) and the International Aero Engines venture involving Pratt & Whitney, Rolls-Royce,
MTU (Motoren-und Turbinen-Union GmbH), Fiat Aviazione, and a Japanese
consortium.‡

A useful indicator of dispersion of technical expertise throughout the world
is the number of domestic and foreign facilities able to perform extensive
aircraft maintenance. According to figures compiled by the major U.S. aircraft and engine manufacturers, there are 52 maintenance facilities in the
United States, 15 of which are capable of heavy maintenance.§ There are
220 maintenance facilities overseas, about 40 of which can do heavy maintenance.‖

Another indicator of how internationalized the aircraft industry has become
is the geographical breadth of the companies that supply parts and components
to major manufacturers. The industry's five prime contractors obtain a large

---

*A customer base for Western aircraft has already been established in the Soviet Union and
Eastern Europe. General Electric, for example, has conducted negotiations to sell engines in
the Soviet Union, Poland, and Czechoslovakia. Airbus Industrie has taken orders for aircraft
from the Soviet Union and Romania. And Boeing aircraft are operated by Polish, Hungarian,
and Romanian airlines.

†Officials at Japan's Ministry of Trade and Industry (MITI) have suggested that the two
companies cooperate to build a new midsize commercial airliner, the initial research for which
is being sponsored by the Japanese government.

‡Annex B3 lists recent foreign partnerships involving Boeing, General Electric, McDonnell
Douglas, and Pratt & Whitney.

§*Heavy maintenance* refers to the capability to tear down a system and completely rebuild
it.

‖Annex B4 lists nations with a heavy maintenance capability.

percentage of their aircraft content from thousands of different suppliers, some of whom sell to multiple prime contractors. More than 5,000 firms, both foreign and domestic, are suppliers to just one firm—U.S. engine maker Pratt & Whitney; 3,800 suppliers from 33 countries provide parts for Boeing commercial aircraft.

With the increasing globalization of the civil aircraft industry, foreign aircraft manufacturers are mounting an increasingly effective competitive challenge to the United States. The share of the global aircraft market held by U.S. firms steadily dropped during the 1980s from about 85 percent to about 65 percent. The stated goal of Airbus Industrie is to achieve a 43 percent global market share by the mid-1990s, leaving the rest to be split among the remaining four competitors.

U.S. civil aircraft and engine manufacturers are private companies competing without special government assistance or subsidies, but some foreign competitors receive large-scale financial and marketing support from their governments. From the time of its inception in 1970, for example, it is estimated that Airbus Industrie has received $25.9 billion in subsidies.[2] In contrast, U.S. firms must recover the immense cost of development and production themselves, while returning a profit to shareholders and retaining sufficient earnings to fund research and the development of successive generations of new aircraft.

The products of Airbus Industrie, moreover, are being steadily "Europeanized." The company's earliest aircraft, the A300, had a U.S. content of 30 to 35 percent of total manufacturing cost in the 1970s. But a 1989 report of the French Senate tracked a decline in U.S. content for various Airbus Industrie aircraft.[3] Apart from engines, the newer A330 and A340 series will depend almost entirely on non-U.S. suppliers.

An assessment of the technological standing of U.S. versus foreign commercial rivals reveals a narrowing U.S. lead in many technological areas. According to the Defense Department's 1990 *Critical Technologies Plan*, for example, Japan has comparable technology in composite materials and a lead in semiconductor materials and microelectronic circuits, areas of relevance to commercial aircraft.[4]

An overview of foreign aerospace technology by Operations Research, Inc. (ORI) lends support to the widely held view that European firms now hold a lead in some aspects of aerospace technology application and manufacturing, and that the once commanding U.S. lead in technology has been significantly reduced.[5] It is widely believed the United States has a small but shrinking edge in technology over the West European countries and now lags the Europeans and, to a lesser extent, Japan, in areas of aerospace manufacturing and technology application.

In subsonic transports, Airbus Industrie is now considered competitive in high-lift systems and equal or ahead in transonic wing design. In the advanced materials area of advanced carbon-epoxy composites, the U.S. position is roughly comparable to that of its trading partners and competitors in analysis and design, fiber/resin system qualification, and automated manufacturing processes. In flight systems, the United States is at least even in overall technology, but it is behind in certain applications and has become dependent on foreign companies for some components.

The United States leads in overall propulsion technology, but foreign competitors are growing stronger in applications and in components. Engine controls is one particular area in which the Europeans are gaining ground. According to ORI, European and U.S. capabilities in computational methods and turbine engine digital controls are even. (In the former category, the Soviets have compensated for a relative lack of computational power with innovative mathematics.) In aerodynamics, the construction of planned research centers in Europe could add to the lead the British and French hold in some applications.*

In short, it would be a mistake to maintain the long-held assumptions of easy and continued U.S. dominance in aerospace technology. **The most significant trend in U.S. aerospace technology may not be the U.S. position vis-à-vis the Soviet Union but the narrowing margin of superiority the United States has over its Western commercial competitors.**

CRITICAL WESTERN AND SOVIET AIRCRAFT TECHNOLOGY

Aircraft and Jet Engine Technology

The technology of commercial jet aircraft and jet engines can be examined in a number of ways. One approach is to break down the aircraft into its major components. Figure B-2 shows the systems, subsystems, and components of a typical commercial jet aircraft. The figure highlights the critical design and production technologies inherent in a commercial jet aircraft, which is made up of millions of pieces.

The first level shown in the figure is the end product—the commercial transport. The end product is a combination of processes constituting the know-how of the manufacturer making the end product. This know-how consists of various techniques for design integration, materials selection and processing, and manufacturing and assembly procedures critical for production. The product that results is not in itself critical technology but the result of a combination of processes constituting the know-how of the end product's manufacturer.

---

*The British also are competitive with the United States in several areas of supercritical wing design, and they have undertaken a joint effort with the Germans to overtake the United States in research for laminar-flow wing design.

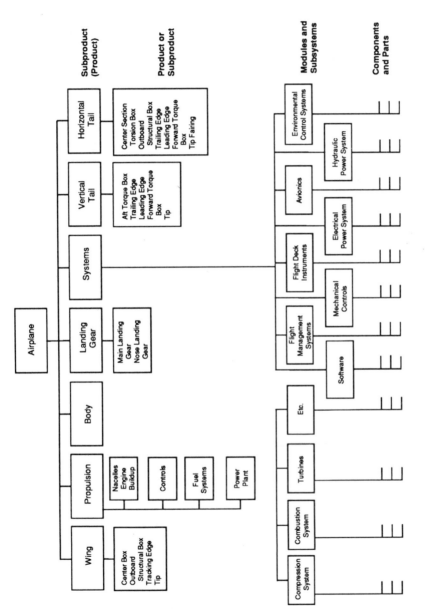

FIGURE B-2   Aircraft breakdown, by systems

The second level consists of the aircraft's subproducts—propulsion engines and major components and systems—which are, in most cases, end products in their own right. As with the aircraft as a whole, subproducts should not be considered technology but the end product of technology. Thus, they typically have little in themselves that would add significantly to the military capabilities of a controlled country.*

Given that commercial aircraft and their subproducts are not technology, but the end products of technology, the subpanel makes the following recommendation:

* **The products of commercial aircraft and associated jet engines should no longer be subject to national security export controls.**

Another way to view aircraft "technology" is to examine its major process technologies—design, materials, and manufacturing. Examples of design technologies are performance and structural analyses and structural and aerodynamic testing. Examples of materials processing technologies are turbine blade castings of single crystals and design of metal matrix composites. Examples of aircraft manufacturing technologies are detailed parts fabrication and flexible automated assembly. Figure B-3 depicts the dynamic interaction of the three processes. The most important technology is found where these three processes overlap. The "know-how" is much more important than the end product, and this know-how is not transferred with the export of the end product. "Aircraft and engine technology" is made up of all three processes. Each element is often not critical in itself; its success typically is highly dependent on the success of the others. For example, a manufacturing process may only be as good as the design process that determines the required quality of composite material used in production. **The key to product superiority is not the acquisition of any single technique or associated product but the integration of all relevant systems.†**

Technologies Critical to Western Military Lead

To help explain the know-how illustrated in Figure B-3 and to assist in identifying technologies critical to maintaining the military lead of the West, the subpanel constructed separate tables identifying representative critical technologies for commercial jet transports (Table B-1) and engines (Table

---

*The principal military benefit of the end product is additional airlift capacity. However, purchase of large transports in excess of purely commercial requirements would be readily apparent due to the documentation and tracking that accompany commercial sales. If the quantity of the purchase seems to fit true commercial needs, prohibitions on sales would be difficult to justify.

†From the standpoint of the manufacturer, these highly proprietary processes often make up the most important part of a firm's competitive advantage.

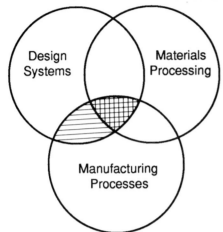

FIGURE B-3   Dynamic interaction of major aircraft process technologies

B-2). The technologies in each table represent know-how; none is simply an "end item."

Commercial aircraft and jet engines are designed and manufactured against demanding standards of safety, reliability, and cost. Many of the technologies involved can contribute to the needs of both commercial and military aircraft. For example, process technologies that produce cooled turbine hardware for improved fuel consumption in commercial aircraft also result in better thrust-to-weight ratios in military aircraft.

The process technologies listed in Tables B-1 and B-2 are available to some degree in controlled countries. Few are unilaterally controllable. The great majority of "end items" in commercial aircraft and jet engines are not "enabling" technologies,* and thus, they are inappropriate targets of controls.

In determining whether to control the export of a product, an assessment of the criticality of the product and associated technology should be made and should answer the following questions:

1. What is the level of criticality or importance to national security of the product itself, its separable subproducts, subsystems, subcomponents, or piece parts?

2. Does the product or its components provide an enabling technology for the advancement of critical products?

3. What is the level of criticality or importance of any associated enabling technology?

---

*For the purpose of this report, an *enabling technology* is the know-how required to design and produce a product or its separable subproducts, subsystems, subcomponents, or piece parts. This includes know-how regarding design systems, materials processes, manufacturing processes, or components thereof.

TABLE B-1   Representative Critical Technologies for Commercial Aircraft

Technology	Relative Rank		Criticality
	Non-U.S./ Non-Communist World	Controlled Countries	
Process (design) systems			
Software technology	–	–	IV
Higher order language			
Artificial intelligence			
Neural networks			
System architecture	=	–	IV
Common models			
Multiprocessing architecture	–	–	III
Data fusion/processing	=	–	IV
Computer-aided design/	=	–	III
manufacturing (CAD/CAM)			
Carbon/carbon composites	=	–	IV
Design and analysis techniques			
Control technologies	–	–	IV
Touch, voice, programmable switches			
Advanced computational fluid	=	=	III
dynamics (CFD) methods			
Advanced test facilities/	=	–	III
CFD verification			
Materials and materials processing			
Aluminum-lithium alloy applications	=	+	IV
Machining, forming			
Carbon/carbon composite applications	=	–	IV
Fiber/resin system qualification			
Resin transfer molding			
Metal matrix composite applications	–	–	IV
Properties, machining, forming			
Superplastic forming	=	=	IV
Aluminum, titanium			
Fiberall-aluminum/carbon composite	+	–	IV
sandwich			
Advanced manufacturing processes			
Electronic chip manufacture	+	–	III
Superconductivity, LSI/VLSI			
Automated carbon-carbon composite	=	–	IV
Automated layup			
Automated aircraft assembly	+	–	IV

NOTES: Each technology within a group has been assigned a relative order of "criticality"; I is the most critical and IV is the least critical. An equals sign means countries have capability in that technology that is essentially equal to that of the United States. A minus sign signifies less advanced capability relative to the United States, and a plus sign denotes more advanced capability than the United States.

These technology rankings are approximations based on the best available estimates of technological capability. They should be considered as somewhat subjective evaluations of relative capabilities.

TABLE **B-2**   Representative Critical Technologies for Jet Engines

Technology	Relative Rank		Criticality
	Non-U.S./ Non-Communist World	Controlled Countries	
Process (design) systems			
High-temperature turbine design	−	−	I
methodologies			
High cooling effectiveness			
Definition of flow passages			
Configurations			
Combustion design methodologies	−	−	III
Control of discharge profiles			
High cooling effectiveness			
Aerodynamic design codes	=	−	IV
High stage loading			
Swept aerodynamics			
Advanced aeromechanics			
Advanced computational fluid	−	−	IV
dynamics (CFD)			
3-D codes and Naiver-Stakes			
Digital electronic controls	=	−	II
Logic, software, and codes			
Advanced structural design	=	−	IV
Methodology			
Statics and dynamics			
Advanced system design	−	−	III
Methodologies			
Life, operability			
Test instrumentation	−	−	III
Materials and materials processing			
Nickel-based superalloys	=	−	III
Melting and casting			
Powder metal			
Extrusion			
Isothermal forging			
Single crystal castings	=	−	III
Large structural castings	=	=	IV
Thermal barrier coatings	−	−	III
Composites	=	−	IV
Metal matrix composites	−	−	III
Ceramics	+	−	III
Advanced manufacturing processes			
Metal joining	=	−	III
Laser drilling	−	−	II
Plasma spray deposition	=	−	III
Composites	=	−	III
Hollow fan blades	+	−	III
Nondestructive inspection techniques	−	−	III

(NOTES continued)

TABLE B-2 (*Continued*)

NOTES: Each technology within a group has been assigned a relative order of "criticality"; I is the most critical and IV is the least critical. An equals sign means countries have capability in that technology that is essentially equal to that of the United States. A minus sign signifies less advanced capability relative to the United States, and a plus sign denotes more advanced capability than the United States.

These technology rankings are approximations based on the best available estimates of technological capability. They should be considered as somewhat subjective evaluations of relative capabilities.

An export control approach focused on process technologies, which would harken back to the 1976 Bucy report of the Defense Science Board,[6] could make controls conform to the language of the Export Administration Act, as follows:

> The establishment of adequate export controls for militarily critical technology . . . shall be accompanied by suitable reductions in the controls on the products of that technology and equipment.[7]

With respect to the civil aircraft industry, however, the U.S. export control system fails to recognize adequately the relative importance of processes over product.

Status of Soviet Aircraft Industry

In examining civil aircraft technologies useful to the armed forces of controlled countries, the subpanel limited its examination—because of resource constraints—to the Soviet Union. The subpanel made the basic assumption that commercial technology obtained from the West could indeed be "critical," that is, helpful in the significant enhancement of an adversary's military capability.

In evaluating Soviet aircraft technology, the subpanel drew on unclassified publications and information gathered during recent trips panel members and associates made to Soviet design bureaus and production facilities in order to make a limited assessment of Soviet design and manufacturing practices.

Some of the important weaknesses and strengths of the Soviet civil aircraft and jet engine industry are as follows:

Weaknesses

- Outdated design and manufacturing know-how
- Inadequate engine maintenance, noise reduction, repair, and reliability
- Avionics
- High operating costs, including excessive fuel consumption
- Poor machine fabrication
- Heavily labor-intensive production

- Inadequate worker training
- Shortages of spare parts

Strengths

- Composites (e.g., carbon-carbon brakes and aluminum lithium alloys)
- Long-range, heavy-lift transports
- Engine test facilities
- Supercritical wings
- Certain areas of basic research

The Soviet military has influenced the design philosophy of the Soviet civil aircraft industry, whose outlook has differed significantly from that of Western aircraft industries. The Soviets exhibit a preference for the use of proven components and systems even if they represent a comparatively low level of technological sophistication. In addition, sizable production runs are made to ensure large quantities of end products.

The primary goals of the Soviet aircraft industry appear to be the following:

- Improve production efficiency and technological level.
- Integrate industry with Western industries and obtain badly needed Western technology.
- Shift focus from the military to the commercial sector.

The Soviets are undertaking extensive internal reforms in an effort to reduce the widespread inefficiencies of their aircraft industry. They are cutting back the resources devoted to production of military aircraft, but they are attempting to replicate in the civilian sector the relatively successful management approach of their defense sector. Thus, the Ministry of Aviation Industry, which performs much military work, has become the institutional model for the Ministry of Civil Aviation. In addition, the Soviets have been attempting to establish links with Western commercial aircraft and jet engine firms.

The Soviets recently made their first significant purchases of Western transports and engines. In 1989, Aeroflot ordered five Airbus Industrie A310s and signed a $150 million contract with General Electric for jet engines. In addition to direct purchases, the number of research agreements with the West, especially in Western Europe, has been increasing, as has the number of joint ventures. The Soviet's Sukhoi Design Bureau, for example, has formed a partnership with Western firms to build a supersonic business jet.[8] The growing relationship between the aircraft industries of the West and the Soviet Union should render more difficult continued restrictions on the transfer of civil aircraft technology.* However, most joint ventures so far have

---

*Greater Soviet involvement with Western aerospace firms is being extended to the area of commercial space flight. In July 1990, for example, the Bush administration approved Soviet launch of U.S. commercial satellites.

been small and primarily service oriented. More important, the uncertain political and economic situation in the Soviet Union (and Eastern Europe) makes predictions about the extent of future cooperation and the size of future markets very speculative.

Reduced Soviet restrictions on doing business with the West have important implications for the aircraft industry, including making the maintenance of export controls more difficult.* At least in theory, Western companies can now contract directly with Soviet enterprises without having to deal with so many intervening layers of Soviet bureaucracy. Many Soviet aircraft firms are being restructured to operate under a pricing system by which they must pay their own way. Although extremely secretive in the past, the Soviets have surprised recent Western trade show attendees by providing demonstrations of and extensive information on their aircraft products.

Although deep-seated economic and political problems inhibit, at least in the short term, the attempt of Eastern Europe and the Soviet Union to shift from command to market economies, the Soviet Union constitutes an important potential market. Today's limited sales and joint ventures might best be viewed as forerunners of expanded interchange between East and West.

Comparison of U.S. and Soviet Aircraft Technologies

In determining which items in the civil aircraft industry are important to maintaining the Western military lead, two key assumptions are usually made. The first is that the technology associated with civil aircraft plays a role in military systems. The second is that the West does indeed have a significant lead in that technology.

Both assumptions are generally true, although there are important nuances. **In various areas, the Soviet Union has roughly comparable technology, although much Soviet technology lags as much as 8 to 10 years behind that of the West.**

To aid in a broad comparison of commercial jet aircraft and engine technology in the United States and the Soviet Union, the subpanel assessed basic product performance resulting from the application of airframe and propulsion technology. The comparison involves the recently developed but not yet operational Soviet TU-204 and the U.S. Boeing 757-200. These aircraft are medium-range civil transports alike in configuration.

A large number of advanced features are common to both aircraft. Similar to current Western capabilities are such advanced TU-204 features as su-

---

*However, it should be noted that during the Cold War period, the small amount of commercial aircraft and jet engine exports to the Warsaw Pact countries was the result more of the Soviets' self-imposed import restrictions than of U.S. and CoCom restrictions.

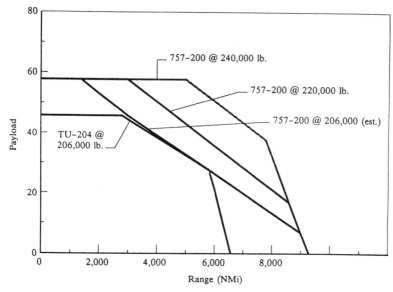

FIGURE B-4   Payload-range comparison at given take-off gross weight (TOGW): B-757-200 and TU-204

percritical wing design with winglets, full-span leading edge slats, double-slotted trailing edge flaps, carbon composite structure, carbon brakes, triplex fly-by-wire control systems, and high bypass ratio turbofan engines.

One measure of capability—payload-range performance for a given take-off gross weight (TOGW)—permits a rough comparison of the two aircraft. Figure B-4 shows the payload-range capability of the TU-204 and the 757-200, the latter at three TOGW values.

As shown in Figure B-4, the 757-200 has greater range capability than the TU-204 at their respective maximum TOGW. However, comparing the aircraft at the same TOGW provides a rough idea of the aerodynamic, structural, and propulsion system technology inherent in the two aircraft. This stems from the fundamental relationship for payload-range performance, which says that for a given TOGW, the range is defined by the product of aerodynamic efficiency, the structural efficiency (weight empty + payload/ TOGW), and propulsion efficiency. If published data on the TU-204 reflect true capabilities, the result of equal range with equal payload at equal TOGW would suggest that the aerodynamic efficiency, structural efficiency, and propulsion efficiency are similar or offsetting in the two aircraft. This admittedly restricted analysis does not extend to all technologies and other factors related to reliability and operating costs, in which Western transports have traditionally had the advantage over Soviet models. For example, the

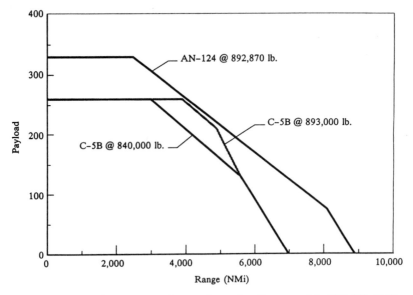

FIGURE B-5   Payload-range comparison at given take-off gross weight (TOGW): C-5B and AN-124

direct operating costs related to either Soviet fuel consumption or maintenance are not thought to be comparable to those for Western aircraft.

The subpanel performed the same analysis on two military transport aircraft: the Soviet AN-124 and the U.S. C-5B. Advanced features of the AN-124 include fly-by-wire controls, advanced airframe composites, and 24-wheel undercarriage.[9] The product availability of the AN-124 trails that of the C-5B by about five years. Figure B-5 compares the two aircraft.

Given that the payload-range performance for the two sets of aircraft is approximately equal at the same TOGW, it may be inferred that the aerodynamic and structural technologies are reasonably close. In engine technology, and particularly in thrust efficiency, however, the U.S. aircraft have the advantage.

In sum, it appears the Soviets have aircraft technologically comparable in many aspects of basic performance to their advanced U.S. counterparts, although they lag in general efficiency.

Based on this analysis, the subpanel recommends the following:

*   **When the technologies of the Soviet Union and other controlled countries are comparable to those available in the West, the U.S. government as a general rule should seriously reconsider controls over such items.**

IMPACT OF EXPORT CONTROLS ON U.S. FIRMS

The subpanel found that U.S. export controls, and in particular foreign policy controls, can have a generally deleterious effect on the export sales of the U.S. civil aircraft industry. Export controls affect the industry in the following ways:

- Loss of sales
- Loss of follow-on sales
- Loss of U.S. jobs
- Labeling of U.S. firms as unreliable suppliers
- De-Americanization of products
- Encouragement of foreign competitors' products
- Imposition of direct and indirect costs of implementing export control safeguards
- Lost or reduced investment in R&D

Conservative estimates are that for every $50 million of lost sales, the United States suffers a $30 million trade loss and a decrease of 3,500 person-years in employment. Once an airline has chosen an aircraft model, it may continue to buy airplanes from the producer of that model over several decades. Thus, the loss of one sale can bring about the loss for an extended time of all or most of the market for a given customer.

The decision whether to purchase U.S. or foreign aircraft is often a narrow one in which export controls can tip the balance. The long-term ability of U.S. firms to provide product support in the face of unpredictable U.S. government export control policies can become a determining factor. Further, unilateral embargoes not only make sales impossible but can encourage foreign competitors to establish relationships with the airlines of the embargoed countries.

Controls on technical data increase business uncertainty and make it more difficult for foreign suppliers to obtain technical data. As joint ventures and co-development arrangements become more common, U.S. regulations inhibiting the exchange of detailed data and functional information required for cooperative ventures will increasingly drive foreign suppliers to avoid using U.S.-made components or parts.

The direct and indirect costs associated with complying with export controls are also significant. Large companies must establish dedicated staffs to deal with the bureaucratic procedures involved in obtaining export licenses and to keep track of changing laws and regulations. Moreover, in the event of delayed deliveries of aircraft or engines due to suspended and/or pending licenses, the manufacturer can incur significant inventory costs and interest expense from deferred deliveries. The seller also may be subject to legal action for nonperformance of contract.

INFLUENCE OF INDUSTRY STRUCTURE ON EFFECTIVENESS OF CONTROLS

The international aspects of the commercial aircraft industry inhibit the effectiveness of export controls. The industry has a worldwide customer base and a cross-national network of suppliers. Competitive concerns and considerations of cost and market access lead to a sharing of technology through subcontracts, licenses, joint ventures, and other cooperative arrangements. The growing number of joint ventures between U.S. and non-U.S.-based companies is leading to increased technology transfer.*

Extensive information sharing among manufacturers and airlines is indispensable to safety and efficiency. To this end, there is open communication across national boundaries among engineers, manufacturers, and suppliers. A variety of technical publications, conferences, and symposiums are also available to the public.

Offsets—the mandatory placement of subcontracts with a foreign country's industry—also contribute to the transfer of technology overseas. As a condition of making a sale, some foreign governments impose offset demands to gain access to higher technology or to increase the business base of their industry. Nearly all offsets involve lower level technology, however, and thus they do not constitute a significant technology transfer concern.

Several characteristics heighten industry's ability to protect critical technology without the imposition of export controls. Most important, the high costs and risks associated with new product development help drive the major competitors into protecting critical technologies from their business rivals. Provisions for the protection of proprietary data are routinely included in contracts, supplier subcontracts, and joint venture and offset arrangements. And because all the major aircraft and engine manufacturers and most of their first- and second-tier subcontractors have considerable experience with military contracts, carefully developed security controls are routine.

Technology protection and transfer have also been influenced by the changing competitive nature of the industry. In earlier decades, many airlines making equipment purchases emphasized acquisition of the latest technology. Today, technology must "buy its way" onto an aircraft by offering more than just a technical edge. It must have a demonstrated operational, safety, or reliability advantage to overcome its acquisition and maintenance costs.

Another important consideration in determining the effectiveness of export controls is the recognition that the complexity of aircraft technology makes

---

*Corporations enter into joint venture agreements for such diverse reasons as risk sharing, obtaining new technology, and gaining or retaining access to markets that might otherwise be closed.

it difficult to reverse-engineer aircraft and engine products. Although individual parts can be measured and analyzed for mechanical reproduction and materials content, such scrutiny is unlikely to reveal the design, manufacturing, or materials know-how necessary to produce an acceptable duplicate or substitute product.

Finally, the relatively low volume of aircraft and engine sales improves the ability of U.S. companies to protect technology. Unlike the situation prevailing in low-cost, high-volume industries, it is practical to do after-sale tracking on aircraft and engines sold to controlled countries and to perform extensive maintenance on controlled-country sales at facilities in Western countries.*

SPECIFIC PROBLEMS WITH THE EXPORT CONTROL SYSTEM

Broadly speaking, the subpanel concluded that CoCom controls played a positive role in protecting the West's military lead during the Cold War. More specifically, however, in examining pertinent areas of the U.S. Commodity Control List (CCL) and Munitions List (ML), **the subpanel found that similar items are placed on different lists or are administered by different agencies in often unpredictable fashion.** The failure to update the lists regularly and consistently has resulted in control of items that have been superseded by newer technologies or that have diffused into the public domain.

The subpanel examined export commodity control numbers (ECCNs) of the CCL pertaining to commercial aircraft and engines and found controls that were overly broad or inappropriate in each category examined.† For example, in comparing ECCN 1460A (aircraft and helicopters, aero-engines, and aircraft and helicopter equipment) against the equivalent category in the CoCom Industrial List (dual use items), the subpanel determined that the United States has various, tighter restrictions relating to foreign policy controls and treatment of technical data than its CoCom partners. In category 1485A (inertial navigation systems), controls are imposed on various flight instruments, automatic pilots, accelerometers, and gyroscopes that can be classified as commodities, not critical know-how. The basis of controls for inertial navigation systems should lie in performance criteria that focus on militarily significant as opposed to civil applications.

---

*Such maintenance agreements are currently typical of leases or sales to East European operators, although the political changes in the region may lead to a loosening of these requirements.

†It should be noted that the subpanel's examination took place before the end of the effort within CoCom to reduce the Industrial List ("core list exercise").

A comparison of the U.S. Munitions List with CoCom's International Munitions List (IML) reveals an array of categories considered dual use by CoCom allies but controlled by the United States under the International Traffic in Arms Regulations (ITAR) for military-related items. In the following aerospace categories, the United States controls items that are not on the IML:

- Aircraft modified or equipped, but not specially designed, for military equipment.
- Aircraft engines not specially designed or adapted for military aircraft.
- Airborne equipment not specially designed for military aircraft.
- Components not specially designed for military aircraft or equipment.
- Inertial navigation systems.
- Spacecraft and satellites, including all related equipment.

The more difficult licensing of these items required by ITAR constitutes a disadvantage to U.S. firms because their CoCom competitors administer these items through CoCom's less exacting Industrial List. Consequently, the subpanel recommends the following:

*   **Items on the U.S. Munitions List that are on the CoCom Industrial List should be transferred to the U.S. dual use Commodity Control List.**

Administrative steps consistent with the ones outlined above would help to alleviate the confusion among the different control lists. However, such actions are unlikely to prevent similar confusion from recurring in the future. Therefore, the subpanel concludes that, for the sake of clarity, the United States should endeavor to integrate the U.S. control lists into a single list.

In the increasingly important area of foreign policy restrictions, the subpanel believes that unilateral U.S. controls are too frequently used to ''punish'' or signal U.S. disaffection with both controlled and noncontrolled countries. **It is the subpanel's strong sense that foreign policy restrictions affect U.S. trade significantly more than national security controls.** In some cases, foreign countries have refused to comply with such restrictions or have not maintained sufficient controls to prevent unauthorized transfers. **Unilateral controls are ineffective unless they are soon accompanied by timely, full, and effective multilateral controls.** In general, unilateral U.S. controls are ineffective, particularly in the growing number of areas in which competitor nations have attained technological parity or superiority. This is partly because many U.S. foreign policy controls engender little support from other countries.

The subpanel supports efforts to treat generally available technical data with a general license (Part 779.3 of the Export Administration Regulations) and recommends similar treatment for sales and operational data.

*   Controls properly placed on technical data related to manufacturing processes—a truly important component of an effective control regime—should not include essentially descriptive information necessary to the efficient and safe operation of aircraft systems.

Finally, any policy on export controls must include, along with the objective of denying militarily useful items to controlled countries, the objectives of avoiding undue constraints on U.S. trade and permitting a free flow of technology and technical information. To this end, the subpanel recommends the following:

*   **The importance of the economic benefits of trade should be given greater weight in designing an effective export control system.**

NOTES

1. Aerospace Industries Association, *1989 Year-End Review and Forecast: An Analysis* (Washington, D.C., 1989), p. 5.
2. U.S. Department of Commerce, *An Economic and Financial Review of Airbus Industrie* (Washington, D.C.: U.S. Government Printing Office, 1990), p. 2–2.
3. *Rapport Général*, French Senate, November 21, 1989, p. 44.
4. U.S. Department of Defense, *Critical Technologies Plan* (for the Committees on Armed Services, U.S. Congress) (Washington, D.C., March 15, 1990), pp. A-16 and A-209.
5. National Aeronautics and Space Administration, *Foreign Technology Assessment* (Operations Research Inc., NASA A138) (Washington, D.C., 1988).
6. U.S. Department of Defense, Office of the Director of Defense Research and Engineering, *An Analysis of Export Control of U.S. Technology—A DoD Perspective* (Report of the Defense Science Board Task Force on Export of U.S. Technology) (Washington, D.C.: U.S. Government Printing Office, 1976).
7. Export Administration Act, Section 5(d)(6).
8. *Aviation Week & Space Technology*, July 2, 1990, p. 30.
9. Michael J.H. Taylor, *Commercial Transport Aircraft* (London: Tri-Service Press, 1990), p. 121.

Annex B1

DOMESTIC AIRCRAFT-RELATED PURCHASE ORDERS, BY STATE, 1989

Listed below, by state, are 1989 aircraft-related purchase orders for Boeing, General Electric, McDonnell Douglas, and Pratt & Whitney. The amounts listed are in thousands of dollars.

Alabama	$ 3,963	Missouri	$ 38,471
Arizona	779,745	Montana	276
Arkansas	1,236	Nebraska	976
California	4,157,992	Nevada	7,549
Colorado	23,281	New Hampshire	38,908
Connecticut	3,827,347	New Jersey	169,393
Delaware	28,912	New Mexico	22,813
District of Columbia	1,518	New York	788,733
Florida	169,183	North Carolina	97,237
Georgia	93,638	North Dakota	76,087
Hawaii	20	Ohio	5,153,423
Idaho	4,205	Oklahoma	47,361
Illinois	390,403	Oregon	117,664
Indiana	212,775	Pennsylvania	234,105
Iowa	144,849	Rhode Island	15,769
Kansas	104,863	South Carolina	11,477
Kentucky	32,868	South Dakota	1,235
Louisiana	18,156	Tennessee	11,132
Maine	7,421	Texas	634,123
Maryland	47,826	Utah	73,385
Massachusetts	457,142	Vermont	37,413
Michigan	413,152	Virginia	59,865
Minnesota	54,480	Washington	990,920
Mississippi	25,353	West Virginia	3,024
		Wisconsin	89,686
		TOTAL	$19,721,353

Annex B2

FOREIGN AIRCRAFT-RELATED PURCHASE ORDERS, BY COUNTRY, 1989

Listed below, by country, are 1989 aircraft-related purchase orders for Boeing, General Electric, McDonnell Douglas, and Pratt & Whitney. The amounts listed are in thousands of U.S. dollars.

Argentina	$ 2		Italy	$ 688,610
Austria	4,178		Japan	157,854
Australia	83,894		Mexico	2,156
Belgium	26,395		The Netherlands	10,417
Brazil	62		New Zealand	395
Canada	173,481		Norway	15,321
China	20,114		Pakistan	437
Denmark	367		Scotland	2,710
England	1,400,885		Singapore	925
Finland	269		South Korea	54,180
France	44,242		Spain	177,676
Germany	59,801		Sweden	25,774
Hong Kong	22		Switzerland	32,859
Hungary	4		Turkey	1,234
India	1		Venezuela	14
Indonesia	15,188		Wales	2,448
Ireland	11,619		Yugoslavia	4,398
Israel	141,565			
			TOTAL	$3,159,497

Annex B3

FOREIGN PARTNERSHIPS

Boeing, General Electric, McDonnell Douglas, and Pratt & Whitney have recently entered into or strengthened partnerships with the following foreign companies:

Aeritalia—*Italy*
Eldim—*The Netherlands*
Fabrique National—*Belgium*
Fiat Aviazione—*Italy*
Japanese Aircraft Development Corporation—*Japan*
Kawasaki Heavy Industries—*Japan*
Mitsubishi Heavy Industries—*Japan*
MTU (Motoren-und Turbinen-Union GmbH)—*Germany*
Norsk Jetmotor—*Norway*
Rolls-Royce—*The United Kingdom*
Samsung—*South Korea*
Singapore Aircraft Industries—*Singapore*
SNECMA (Société Nationale d'Etude et de Construction de Moteurs d'Aviation)—*France*
Volvo Flygmotor—*Sweden*

Annex B4

NON-COMMUNIST NATIONS WITH HEAVY MAINTENANCE CAPABILITY

Listed below are non-Communist nations that have the capability to perform aircraft-related heavy maintenance.

Argentina	Indonesia	South Africa
Australia	Italy	South Korea
Austria	Japan	Spain
Brazil	Jordan	Sweden
Canada	Kenya	Switzerland
Denmark	Malaysia	Taiwan
Egypt	Mexico	Thailand
Ethiopia	The Netherlands	Turkey
Finland	New Zealand	The United Kingdom
France	Norway	United States
Germany	Pakistan	Tunisia
Greece	Philippines	Venezuela
Hong Kong	Portugal	Yugoslavia
India	Singapore	

Report of the Subpanel on Computer Technology*

EXECUTIVE SUMMARY

• A number of trends in global computer technology have lessened the feasibility and desirability of controlling exports of many dual use computer hardware and software products.

• Controllability of computer technologies is a central issue. Trying to control exports of inherently uncontrollable products damages U.S. competitiveness abroad, undermines the credibility of export controls, and wastes government resources.

• The risks of misuse may be reduced for some classes of products through forms of end-use control. "Sunset" provisions, also, would allow for automatic decontrol of certain classes of hardware and software products after a number of years, subject to appeal by relevant government agencies.

• The foreign availability assessment (FAA) procedure is seriously flawed and has not functioned well as a mechanism for removing products from

---

*The Subpanel on Computer Technology was appointed by the Committee on Science, Engineering, and Public Policy to work in conjunction with the main panel to examine the impact of both current policy and alternative future policies on its specific industrial sector. The subpanel was not asked to consider the full range of issues addressed by the main panel; rather, it was given a specific set of tasks to undertake. The subpanel met less frequently than—and independently of—the main panel, and it had considerable latitude in conducting its discussions.

Thus, it should be noted that the conclusions and recommendations of this subpanel report, while providing valuable input to the deliberations of the main panel, do not necessarily reflect the main panel's views and, therefore, should not be considered to be a part of its findings.

control lists. A revised procedure could serve as a proactive mechanism for decontrolling some product classes.

• High-performance computers have been subjected to rigorous and cumbersome export controls for years. The advancing capability of both high-performance and mainstream computing has made established static thresholds for supercomputers obsolete. A more reasonable approach for indexing levels of performance would track ongoing advances in computing technology. The subpanel does not recommend the removal of all controls on supercomputers, however.

• Interconnected computer networks now extend worldwide. Transborder data flow and network access are commonplace, and demand for network security products has increased significantly for a range of commercial end-use applications. U.S. industry has lost its competitive lead in the design, manufacture, and testing of protocols and network products. Global competition will be directed toward increases in data transfer performance and lower costs. It is not practical to expect legislative or regulative solutions to control unauthorized flows of technical data over networks. The first line of defense must lie in protection of data against unauthorized access.

• Software sold over the counter should be decontrolled worldwide; the sale and distribution of other object code should be decontrolled within the member countries of the Coordinating Committee for Multilateral Export Controls (CoCom), but subjected to licensing controls for other nations. Source code to such object code should be tightly controlled.

• The traditional computing industry in the Soviet Union has undergone considerable changes. The potential for technology transfers has increased greatly, which makes it even harder to restrict the flow of Western technology. Soviet attempts to acquire Western technology can be expected to continue.

• Monitoring of technological developments with military applications of concern to national security should continue and be extended. More comprehensive attention should be paid to commercial as well as military applications in a much larger number of countries, including both developed and newly industrializing nations.

INTRODUCTION

The computer industry (including the manufacture of computer hardware, software, microelectronics, and telecommunications equipment) is, in a number of ways, quite different from the other industrial sectors examined by the study's subpanels. Manufacture does not require scarce raw materials, and given the necessary capital and expertise, can take place almost anywhere. Product assembly from components requires moderate technical knowledge and can make use of a relatively unspecialized work force. Moreover, the pace of innovation is very rapid, and new technological generations may succeed one another in less than two years. Finally, the pervasive applicability of computer-related products distinguishes the computer technologies sector from other industrial sectors.

Although the U.S. computer industry still leads the world in systems engineering, systems integration, and computer-aided design and engineering (CAD/CAE) technologies, it faces increasingly stiff competition in many areas from Europe, Japan, and a number of newly industrializing countries.

In its deliberations, the subpanel drew heavily on the 1988 National Research Council report, *Global Trends in Computer Technology and Their Impact on Export Control* (hereafter *Global Trends*).*[1]

The subpanel reaffirms the four major trends identified in that report:

1. Rapid technological progress, leading to the extension and "filling in" of the technological spectrum.

2. Globalization of the technologies, along with increased international competition.

3. Commoditization of many products, a trend typified by low and steadily decreasing prices, high production volumes, a multiplicity of producers, and high degrees of substitutability of increasingly more powerful computer equipment.

4. Changes in the Soviet Union and Eastern Europe that, together with the three trends above, have lessened the feasibility and desirability of controlling many dual use computer hardware and software products.

Detailed descriptions and analyses of these trends may be found in *Global Trends* and in the work of Goodman and colleagues.[2] All of the trends have continued and, in some cases, accelerated since *Global Trends* was published in 1988. This subpanel report focuses on a number of new issues and includes a more comprehensive set of recommendations than did the earlier report.

Given the characteristics of the industry, controllability of the technology is a central issue. The subpanel's discussion begins with an examination of controllability, followed by an analysis of various means of control and decontrol (as applied to computer technologies), and an evaluation of the foreign availability assessment procedure. The discussion next focuses on the control of a number of specific technologies and products, and then closes with an examination of some international issues in the context of computer-related export control policy.

---

*Seven members of the subpanel were also members of the Committee to Study International Developments in Computer Science and Technology, which wrote the *Global Trends* report. Seymour E. Goodman chaired both committees.

CONTROLLABILITY

Today, technological innovation and product engineering and manufacturing are taking place all over the world. As a result, a major constraint on the effective use of export controls lies in the uncontrollability of access to given products. **Trying to control classes of products that are inherently uncontrollable is counterproductive: It damages U.S. competitiveness abroad, undermines the credibility of export controls, and wastes government resources.**

The subpanel determined that computer products may be divided into four classes of controllability: militarily critical products, "high-walls" products, commodities, and "middle-ground" products. Each of these classes is discussed briefly below.

Militarily Critical Products

These are products exclusively or predominantly used by the military and clearly linked to essential military goals or capabilities. Such products are covered by munitions controls, the International Traffic in Arms Regulations (ITAR), and similar control lists and were excluded from further consideration by the subpanel.

"High-Walls" Products

These are products that can be located, verified, traced, observed, or otherwise tracked in a protective environment. The concept of "high walls" involves the existence of product characteristics that enhance the ability to manage the protection of products on an individual basis. High-walls products are generally produced in unit fashion by the tens or hundreds, can be identified by serial or manufacturing sequence numbers, and are often large enough to inhibit undetected transport. High-walls products are amenable to the inclusion of internal tracking mechanisms, which can be used to create an audit trail of users. They are distributed by few suppliers, and vendor participation in training, service, maintenance, and product upgrading remains vital, often over the lifetime of the product. Disposal of such large and expensive items may be problematic as well.

An example of a high-walls product is the high-performance system, or "supercomputer." Supercomputers are usually heavy and large, are produced in small quantities, maintain internal audit trails of users, and require prolonged vendor support. The Supercomputer Safeguard Plan is a current "high-walled" protection mechanism applied to the shipment of supercomputers to countries other than the United States, Canada, and Japan.

Commodities

Commodities are products that are widely available, inexpensive, and in many cases, substitutable. Indeed, they are so widely available that they cannot effectively be controlled, and generally should not be controlled. The following definition for computer hardware is suggested as a guide to the determination of commodity status. In the view of the subpanel, a computer hardware product becomes a commodity when six of the following eight characteristics are satisfied:

1. *Production volume*: at least 1 million units in cumulative worldwide production. If a sequence of increasingly advanced versions of the candidate product exists, the candidate for commodity status would be the least sophisticated version necessary to add up to the 1 million unit level.

2. *Unit cost*: less than $25,000.

3. *Number of source countries*: at least two countries that are not participants in CoCom.

4. *Distribution methods*: at least two of the following: a minimum of three distinct purchasing channels, value-adding intermediaries, multiple outlets (e.g., chain stores), lot purchases of 100 or more units.

5. *Substitutability*: product performs tasks that could be similarly performed by another product.

6. *Size*: less than 1 cubic meter in volume.

7. *Purchasability*: no special qualifications are required to purchase the product.

8. *Service and maintenance*: no service or maintenance required, or multiple service alternatives to the manufacturers exist.

(Software has different characteristics and is discussed separately below.)

A good example of a hardware product that is a commodity is the personal computer (PC) based on the Intel 80286 chip. Well over 1 million IBM PC/AT-compatible machines have been produced, and supply and service of the machines are widely available through many channels and from many sources worldwide. Costs are well below $25,000 for all common configurations and rapidly approaching $1,000 in some cases. Unit size is less than 1 cubic meter.

"Middle-Ground" Products

All products not included in any of the three categories above fall into this category. Products in the "middle ground" are not sold in sufficiently large numbers to be considered commodities. They are sold in small numbers because they are new, are specialized for niche markets, or are expensive. Because of availability, size, portability, low maintenance demands, or easy disposability, they may not be protectable by high walls, and yet they may have important military applications. Examples of middle-ground products include on-board signal processors, graphics work stations, advanced software development systems, math coprocessor chips, and high-end personal computers (e.g., those based on the 80486 chip).

SOME MEANS OF CONTROL AND DECONTROL

The following risks of product misuse should be considered if a product is to be physically located on foreign territory:

- Inspection and analysis with the intent to duplicate the product.
- Diversion-in-place, for example, the use of a supercomputer located in a weather research facility to run military-related applications.
- Relocation and diversion, for example, the movement of array processors to a different facility for use in military applications.
- Diversion of manufacturing capability, for example, the use of Western-made microelectronics manufacturing equipment to produce components used in weapons systems.

End-Use Controls

The risks of product misuse may be reduced through end-use controls. These can take several forms, including on-site inspections, technical controls and inspections, and restrictions that place the product "under U.S. eyes," for example, at a facility under the management or supervision of U.S. citizens. The most effective on-site inspections are those that can be made without advance notice. Technical end-use controls might include software configured to run on a limited number of hardware hosts and remote monitoring of machine performance. Remote monitoring might be limited to observation for signs of inappropriate application (e.g., running large floating-point applications on a mainframe that is intended for administrative and data processing applications at a hospital). Another form of technical control might be a "shut off" mechanism to enforce sanctions against misuse. Very high level foreign government guarantees that would result in severe political repercussions if diversions were exposed might also serve as a form of end-use control in conjunction with other methods.

The subpanel makes the following recommendation concerning end-use controls.

*   **End-use controls should be considered as one way to permit the sale of a number of high-walls or middle-ground products under acceptable risks. These controls would be most effective against relocation and diversion. The effectiveness of end-use controls against** other forms of misuse is strongly dependent on specific local conditions, and end-use controls should not be used in circumstances in which violations would be difficult to detect or strong deterrence is required.

A "Sunset" Provision

Computer products frequently have a useful life of five to eight years. However, commodity products, such as personal computers, may be superseded by newer models in only 18 months. To compensate for this performance upgrade, industry adjusts prices to maintain a competitive price/performance growth curve. For example, at release in 1985, a Sun 3 work station cost about $10,000 per million instructions per second (MIPS), whereas in 1990 the latest model Sun SPARCstation cost less than $750 per MIPS. Supercomputers and computer networks have followed a similar pattern. Parallel processing is leading to considerable price/performance improvements in supercomputers. Again, published figures suggest a rapid upgrading process, in these cases on about a three-year cycle.

The useful life of software is much longer. Software evolves incrementally; successive updates are released about a year apart for most unclassified software, three to five years apart for classified software.

Given these facts, the subpanel proposes the establishment of a "sunset" provision for both hardware and software, which would cause computer products to be automatically decontrolled after a certain number of years, subject to appeal by relevant government agencies.

A distinct advantage of a sunset provision is that it provides an easy, semiautomatic method for decontrolling items as they become readily available to proscribed countries, but still provides concerned government agencies with the opportunity to challenge the removal of any item whose decontrol is considered a threat to national security. Mechanisms to prevent abuse of such challenges must, however, be included.

To this end, the subpanel recommends the following:

*   **Controlled hardware and software should be subject to an overridable decontrol, or "sunset," provision. The length of time of this provision for a given technology might be based on cost, which usually reflects technological level and availability.** For example, a product costing $1 million or more might have a sunset period of 10 years; $4,000 or less, 2 years, with a nonlinear scale for products in between these extremes.

Unclassified software, because of its longer life cycle, should be decontrolled less frequently than low-end hardware. A five-year sunset provision is suggested in this case. For classified software, a sunset provision should be developed along the lines of the automatic reclassification provisions on most classified documents, which provides for downgrading every 10 years.

FOREIGN AVAILABILITY ASSESSMENTS

The subpanel conducted an evaluation of the current procedure for determining the foreign availability of export-controlled products.* The evaluation included examination of the U.S. decision to decontrol PC/AT-compatible microcomputers and of the export control implications of reduced instruction-set computer (RISC) technology. On the basis of its discussions, the subpanel reached the following conclusions:

• **The foreign availability assessment (FAA) procedure is seriously flawed and has not functioned well as a mechanism for removing products from control lists.**

• **A revised procedure may function well to remove middle-ground products from control lists and could provide a proactive mechanism for decontrolling products that have attained "commodity" status in advance of the automatic sunset provisions discussed earlier.**

The central focus of the FAA process is the control of dual use products of importance to foreign military forces. The process does not recognize, however, the rapid rate at which technology is advancing in the global computing industry. The operational aspects of the process, moreover, are subject to interpretation by various agencies, which leads to contentious debates regarding the determination of foreign-available status for products. For example, there are no satisfactory operational definitions for terms that are key to the assessments, such as "availability-in-fact," "evidence of use," or "sufficient quantity." This allows agencies to interpret the terms in ways that favor their individual concerns. Lack of timely options for conflict resolution and/or arbitration exacerbates the contention and places the U.S. computer industry at a significant disadvantage with respect to global competition.

On the basis of its conclusions, the subpanel makes the following recommendations:

* **The focus of the FAA process should be shifted toward a proactive mission of removing from control lists those middle-ground products that either have reached, or are about to reach, commodity status or that satisfy reasonable foreign availability conditions, rather than a passive mission that requires "after-the-fact" evidence of use in proscribed countries.**

---

*The determination of foreign availability can be used as an argument for removing export controls on an item.

* The revised process should also be used to remove from control lists dual use, middle-ground niche products that may never reach commodity status due to their inherent low-production volumes. However, satisfactory, noncontentious operational definitions focused on non-U.S. availability, rather than on evidence of use, must be developed to make this process effective.

* The participation of industry and the decision-making capability of expert committees involved in reviewing hardware and software products for removal from control lists should be increased to ensure timely arbitration of disagreements and conflict resolution.

EXPORT CONTROL OF SPECIFIC TECHNOLOGIES AND PRODUCTS

Commodities

In June 1990, CoCom removed many commodity products from the list of controlled items. The subpanel concurs with this decision and believes that once a computer product enters the commodity classification, it is inherently uncontrollable. Therefore, the subpanel recommends the following:

* Computer products that meet defined criteria for commodity status should not be controlled.

* A mechanism should be developed to ensure that products that are nearing commodity status are removed from the list in a timely fashion. This mechanism might be a modified version of the foreign availability assessment outlined earlier.

Technologies

MANUFACTURING EQUIPMENT

In contrast to many computer end products, computer technology manufacturing equipment tends to have a much longer lifetime because components no longer considered state of the art still must be produced for use in high-volume commodity products or the upgrading of existing machines. Moreover, the denial of manufacturing equipment to a proscribed country limits that country's ability to develop its own production facilities. For these reasons, the subpanel recommends the following:

* There should be no semiautomatic decontrol or "sunset" provision for computer manufacturing equipment. Export of each piece of equipment should be individually licensed for the life of that equipment.

HIGH-PERFORMANCE COMPUTING

As a class, supercomputers have been subjected to rigorous and cumbersome export controls for years. This class of product is ideal for high-walls classification and has been controlled as such for use within all countries except the United States, Canada, and Japan by the Supercomputer Safeguard Plan. The safeguard plan, however, has become obsolete and cumbersome for two main reasons: (1) indiscriminate use of controls without regard to a nation's trustworthy practice or status and (2) adherence to outmoded, static performance levels.

The subpanel favors consideration of a hierarchical implementation of controls, in which countries that are considered low risk are treated more favorably than those considered less trustworthy. The subpanel questions the concept of high-walls controls within CoCom countries, and perhaps within 5(k) countries.* The threat of diversion-in-place within CoCom countries to benefit other countries is overstated. The subpanel questions the value of cumbersome reexport controls within CoCom at all.

The Departments of Commerce and State and other involved agencies have continued to invoke supercomputer controls at the level of 100 Mflops (millions of floating-point operations per second) calculative speed. However, the capability of mainstream computing has already made that threshold obsolete, and experts project that desktop computers will exceed 100 Mflops in 1991. Thus, the static threshold fails to recognize the realities of technological progress to the point that some desktop personal computers will be considered, by U.S. government standards, to be supercomputers. This means that the number of potential sites for policing will rapidly rise from a few hundred to tens of thousands, a situation with which no agency can adequately cope.

A more reasonable approach for indexing the levels of performance at which special export controls go into effect would track ongoing advances in computing technologies. Performance levels requiring controls would increase with advances in computational speed. The approach proposed in *Global Trends*—establishing a relative performance threshold (e.g., the *n* percent most powerful, as measured by generally accepted benchmark tests)— should be seriously considered.

The subpanel makes the following recommendations regarding export controls on supercomputers:

* **Diversion-in-place protection (i.e., the Supercomputer Safeguard Plan) should be discontinued for all CoCom, and possibly also 5(k), nations.**

---

*Non-CoCom countries that have signed export control agreements with the United States.

*   The technological level at which high-performance computing export controls would go into effect should be higher for countries of moderate concern than for those of significant concern. Hence, the subpanel supports the concept of tiered control management for this technology.

*   A more flexible and timely indexing method must be developed to replace the obsolete static control-level scheme, which does not recognize the rapid rate at which computing technology is progressing. As technology advances, the supercomputer protection rules must keep pace in order to focus enforcement effectively on state-of-the-art, high-performance systems.

The subpanel does not recommend the removal of all controls on supercomputers. This technology has significant military value to any receiving country, as well as enormous value as a scientific and industrial tool. The technology, however, has great potential for high-walls protection and it fits well within the scope of end-use controls. The subpanel does not advocate the decontrolled shipment of supercomputers to the Soviet Union or certain other countries, but it believes that the export of advanced systems could be considered for specific applications, given appropriate end-use controls to prevent diversion for military uses.

Industry's concern that continued use of export controls at low performance levels will lead to a significant competitive disadvantage for mainstream U.S.-produced products is valid. Thus, the subpanel believes that export controls should be (1) focused on those products that are truly state of the art, (2) significantly liberalized within CoCom and 5(k) countries, and (3) dynamic enough to accommodate rapidly changing technological capabilities.

COMPUTER NETWORKS

Computer networks are leading to the homogenization of computer systems. With the strong trend toward "open systems" (i.e., those that employ common standards), universal interoperability of commodity products of different manufacturers is possible over interconnected networks, which constitute a worldwide "internet." The networks themselves are part of the homogeneity. They are built from standard products, such as common operating systems, common file standards, common user interfaces, and standardized interface devices to connect host computers to networks and the networks to one another.

The subpanel supports the original conclusions and recommendations in *Global Trends* regarding computer networks, and it notes that little progress has been made in modifying existing policies governing transborder network access and in establishing more reasonable ITAR restrictions on network security products. The trends cited in the 1988 *Global Trends* report have accelerated rapidly since then, however. For example,

• Transborder data flow and network access are now commonplace and are primary corporate resources for sustaining competitive advantage among global competitors.

• Commercial demand for network security products, including encryption devices and trustworthy systems, has increased significantly for a range of commercial end-use applications. Current ITAR restrictions, however, retard the U.S. ability to compete with foreign producers, who have developed network products that support the International Standards Organization's (ISO) protocol standards.

• U.S. industry has lost its lead in the design, manufacture, and testing of protocols and network products to European and Pacific Rim competitors. This is due to the rapid emergence of products for 100 megabit/second local area networks (LANs) that follow the ISO's Fiber Distributed Data Interface (FDDI) standards.

Given these trends, global competition will be directed toward increased performance of data transfer and lower costs for network interconnections. Today, FDDI 100 megabit/second LANs represent the state of the art. Products incorporating the FDDI international standard are beginning to sell in numbers that will lead to commodity status within the next few years. These products have clear dual use potential: for commercial transaction systems and in new distributed command/control/communications systems.

* **The export control level for high-speed network products should be a moving threshold measured in ''cost/termination'' units comparable to processing data rates (PDRs).**

Transborder data flow is now the rule for the homogenized worldwide network. It is not practical to expect legislative and/or regulatory solutions, such as tariffs, export controls, and restrictions on network interconnections or communications traffic, to restrict potential unauthorized flows of technical data. The first line of defense must be protection of data against unauthorized access, whether while in storage or during transmission.

* **Control of network proliferation, restriction of U.S.-international network interconnection, and regulation of traffic (including transborder data flow) should not be the means by which export control of software and technical data is achieved.**

Data security must increase in the worldwide network to ensure the integrity of traditional business practices conducted through this new medium. Measures employed to prevent fraud should include authentication of the transaction, authentication of the parties in the transaction, authorized transactions, notarized transactions, valid receipting, transaction secrecy, protection of "soft" assets transferred in the transaction from corruption or unauthorized replication, and validation of the asset and its ownership.

* **Control of exports of restricted software products through trans-border network data flows should be carried out by "authorized transaction" technical means. Encryption technology is the best way to achieve transaction protection.**

If foreign encryption technology is imported into the United States to meet ISO standards but is prohibited from use by ITAR regulations, U.S. industry, the U.S. government, and other users will be isolated from the worldwide network for much of the future commerce that increasingly will use such technology. Further, U.S. industry will be unable to manufacture and export compatible equipment to compete in the world market.

* **Existing ITAR regulations should be revised to enable the use of high-quality encryption protocols for the worldwide network. Otherwise, U.S. interests will be sidestepped by ISO encryption schemes and standards currently progressing internationally.**

SOFTWARE

Effective, enforceable controls are very difficult to define for software because of its particular characteristics. Software is easy to conceal and easy to duplicate. Hence, once a single copy of a piece of software is obtained in the United States on behalf of a proscribed country, it is a trivial matter to smuggle it to that country or transmit it by a computer or telephone network. Under such conditions, the only reasonable choices are total decontrol of readily available software and tight controls on software requiring protection, especially on the source code. Consequently, the subpanel makes the following recommendations:

* **Software should be divided into the following three classes for control purposes:**
  1. **Military-use software. Software built or customized for direct military applications, and the customized tools used to build such software, should be tightly controlled. In most cases, classification procedures should be used for such controls, especially for source code.**
  2. **Publicly available software. Over-the-counter software, that is, software available for purchase from multiple sources and without qualification, as well as software in the public domain, should be decontrolled worldwide. Over-the-counter software embodied in other forms (as hardware or "firmware") should similarly**

be decontrolled. The widespread availability of such software, coupled with its difficulty of detection and ease of reproduction, makes any attempt at control impossible.

3. Other object code. The sale and distribution of all other object code should be decontrolled within CoCom countries, but subject to licensing controls on exports to other countries. Source code to software in this class should be tightly controlled, and export licenses should be granted on a case-by-case basis for all foreign organizations.

* Given the ease of acquisition and use of most software, any complete control system should include controls that promote respect for intellectual property rights. In particular:

• Companies, especially startups, should be warned that the release of source code can easily compromise their ability to control the use of their software.

• The U.S. government should spearhead an effort to bring about worldwide enforcement of copyright protection of software. Countries that do not enforce such regulations should be subject to sanctions.

INTERNATIONAL ISSUES

The Soviet Union

Since the publication of *Global Trends* in 1988, computing in the Soviet Union has undergone considerable changes. The potential for technology transfers has increased greatly, and political and economic changes have gone far beyond what was anticipated.

THE TRADITIONAL COMPUTER INDUSTRY

The changes in the Soviet industrial structure described in *Global Trends* have continued, but they have failed to make a significant difference in the performance of the computer industry. Mainframe and minicomputer producers continue to produce enhanced versions of earlier functional duplicates of Western machines, such as the IBM 370 and the PDP-11 and VAX series of the Digital Equipment Corporation (DEC).

A number of trends and conditions illustrate the current state of the industry. First, the use of hard currency for intra-CMEA (Council for Mutual Economic Assistance) sales, and the sale of East European assets to Western companies, will open new channels for the purchase of higher quality computers by Soviet consumers who have access to hard currency, but it will eliminate the availability of some of the better machines for other consumers.

In addition, the Soviet computer industry will be deprived of the technical assistance it received from some East European partners, which may hinder Soviet duplication of Western machines.

Second, the Soviets admit that their microelectronics industry is no longer able to produce the components necessary to continue with the functional-duplication policy. Laboratory samples of more powerful components may exist, but evidence of the availability of industrial quantities of VLSI chips, high-density storage chips, application specific integrated circuits (ASICs), and so on, is still lacking.

Third, indigenous Soviet efforts to build high-performance computers will continue. However, despite some progress since 1988, the lack of suitable components and production facilities continues to constrain the production of such machines.

Fourth, also since 1988, many software cooperatives have been created in the Soviet Union. As many as one-fifth of all Soviet programmers may work primarily for cooperatives or moonlight for them. The pervasive use of copied Western software, the absence of copyright protection, and the continued existence of various forms of state controls have hindered the development of the industry. Nevertheless, Soviet software cooperatives are experiencing rapid growth and finding many customers.

Fifth, the area of networks continues to be one of the weakest for the Soviet computer industry. The Soviets are only now on the verge of having sufficient numbers of installed computers to make interconnection via a network worthwhile. Electronic mail in the Soviet Union remains a rarity, and access to foreign computer networks is limited. The indigenously con-structed network Akademset' remains underdeveloped and underexploited.

Finally, many parts of the Soviet computer industry remain clouded in secrecy. This casts suspicion on the industry's activities and inhibits more extensive approaches to the relaxation of export controls.

TECHNOLOGY TRANSFER

As predicted in *Global Trends*, East-West technology transfer has contin-ued and accelerated. Several new methods of technology transfer have be-come available, which has made it even harder to restrict the flow of Western computer technology to the Soviet Union.[3]

As Western personal computers have become available and Soviet con-sumers have gained more control over their finances, demand for indige-nously produced machines has dropped precipitously. Joint-venture contracts have been signed for importing components, production technologies, and complete machines. Some agreements may be stalled by hard currency pay-ment problems, but a large number of agreements have been signed and it is unlikely that all will fail. Some factories have already opened. According to Soviet sources, factories in Shuya and Kishinev will have a combined production capacity of over 1 million machines annually. Such output in the near future is highly unlikely, however. Joint-venture agreements that include shipments of personal computers to the Soviet Union have been signed with countries all over the world, including the United States, the United Kingdom, France, Finland, Germany, Norway, Poland, Luxembourg, Austria, India, Malaysia, Singapore, and South Korea.

Recent changes in CoCom regulations will make possible agreements involving larger machines. Data General has already signed an agreement that will allow a well-established software supplier for process control systems to bundle its software with Data General minicomputers. Few Western or Far Eastern computer concerns can be unaware of the ready market waiting for them to replace their existing minicomputer and mainframe base with much more reliable and powerful machines. DEC has already started a joint venture in Hungary and will be moving ''aggressively'' into the rest of Eastern Europe.

It seems likely that Soviet industry will become considerably more dependent on the West and Far East, buying components and assembling machines for the internal market. The scope of indigenous development areas will be scaled back to high-performance computers and other areas directly related to military needs, perhaps at an even greater cost to maintain because the bulk of the industry will be involved in the purchase and assembly of components.

Several other technology transfer mechanisms have become available, including the following:

- publication in the Soviet Union of translations of Western computer journals;
- increased foreign travel by Soviet computing professionals;
- the employment of Soviet programmers by Western companies to develop software in the Soviet Union;
- increased availability of network connections to the West; and
- removal of restrictions on the number of Soviets who can be present in the United States to do business.

The removal of some internal Soviet restrictions, increased interest in the Soviet market by Western businesses, and relaxed CoCom controls mean that the impact of the conditions that have helped to restrict technology transfer has diminished. The number of channels by which the Soviets can acquire foreign computers continues to increase, especially through Eastern Europe. The flow of technology to the Soviets is less stoppable than ever, and poor internal Soviet protection mechanisms for intellectual property contribute to the spread of the technology once it crosses the border. These changes confirm a trend toward commoditization noted in *Global Trends*.

The shift in demand away from indigenous machines to machines made in the West or made with Western components could have one of two effects on the Soviet industry. The industry may become, on the one hand, more desperate to produce bigger and better mainframes and minicomputers, which could force it into more illegal acquisitions of technology or more licensing agreements. On the other hand, the industry may crumble to a large extent, and Western machines may come to dominate the Soviet market. For the time being, Soviet attempts to acquire Western technology can be expected to continue.

Based on the trends and conditions discussed above, the subpanel recommends the following:

* **The relaxation of controls should continue to be gradual given the instability of the current situation.**
* **Given U.S. interest in strengthening Soviet private business and promoting the free flow of information in the Soviet Union, most middle-ground and commodity hardware should be gradually decontrolled as long as the process of Soviet reform continues. In particular, the shipment of commodities to the Soviet Union should now be considered desirable.**
* **For larger computers and networks, end-use controls are likely to be necessary. Because of the absence of an indigenous infrastructure to perform maintenance, end-use controls are less risky because withdrawal of support would constitute a substantial threat. In addition, as the hegemony of the military in the Soviet economy declines, the risk of diversion-in-place is likely to diminish.**

International Coverage

Although the U.S. intelligence community monitors technological developments with military applications of concern to national security in a small number of countries, including the Soviet Union, it should give more comprehensive attention to commercial as well as military applications in a much larger number of countries. These should include both developed and newly industrializing countries. The government should undertake periodic reviews of technological and market trends along the lines of the *Global Trends* study of 1988. Rapid change in these technologies makes trend assessments perishable, and thus this type of review should be conducted at least once every three years.

* **The U.S. government should more comprehensively track rapidly changing developments in computing technologies (microelectronics, telecommunications, computer hardware and software), as well as associated worldwide market trends. This coverage is necessary**

if sound decisions are to be made on issues of importance to traditional national security, export controls, the proliferation of high-performance conventional weapons, and trade negotiations and other matters related to the economic competitiveness of the United States.

NOTES

1. National Research Council, *Global Trends in Computer Technology and Their Impact on Export Control* (Washington, D.C.: National Academy Press, 1988).
2. Seymour E. Goodman, Marjory S. Blumenthal, and Gary L. Geipel, "Export Control Reconsidered," *Issues in Science and Technology* (NAS), vol. VI, no. 2 (Winter 1989–90), pp. 58–62; Seymour E. Goodman, "Trends in East-West Technology Transfer," *IEEE Computer* (July 1990), pp. 94–95.
3. See National Research Council, *Global Trends*; Goodman, "Trends in East-West Technology Transfer."

Panel Foreign Fact-Finding Mission Reports

During the first half of 1990, delegations of panel members and staff traveled on fact-finding missions to five West European countries (Belgium, the Federal Republic of Germany, France, Switzerland, and the United Kingdom), to five Asian countries (Hong Kong, Japan, Korea, Macao, and Taiwan), and to Canada. The objectives of these missions were to seek the views of government officials, industrial leaders, academics, and others regarding (1) the U.S. national security export control regime, (2) the indigenous export control policies and procedures of each country, and (3) changes required in the multilateral control effort in view of the altered political-military circumstances in Europe and the growing threat of proliferation.

At each stop on a particular delegation's itinerary, the group received a briefing from the appropriate country team at the U.S. embassy. At the request of the panel, embassy control officers, who accompanied each delegation to meetings with government officials, generally were not present for meetings with private industry. All meetings were considered unofficial.

The three major sections of this report, one concerning each of the three missions, are based on the detailed trip notes prepared by the members of the particular delegation. Each section is divided into, first, a summary of the most significant generic policy issues that emerged from discussions during the mission and, second, a brief summary of the discussion with each group with which the delegation met.

I.
EUROPEAN MISSION*

The delegation arrived in Europe on April 29, 1990, and on May 1 the United States announced its proposed changes for the administration of the Coordinating Committee for Multilateral Export Controls (CoCom) and its control lists. This timing provided the delegation with a unique opportunity to gauge the reaction of the Europeans to the U.S. proposal.

GENERAL ISSUES

The Need for Export Controls

Almost no one with whom the European delegation met advocated the complete abolishment of export controls. Although there was general consensus that the Soviet and Warsaw Pact threat had diminished, most interlocutors thought that some controls should be retained. But it was abundantly clear that the West Europeans now viewed the Soviet Union in a different light and no longer viewed as credible the scenario that assumed a Warsaw Pact invasion of Western Europe. Moreover, much of Europe, especially Germany, was looking to the East as a potential marketplace. Thus, many expressed the view that some controls on very advanced technology should remain, but that the West and CoCom should decrease the number of items that are controlled to the proscribed nations.

U.S. Proposal to CoCom

The May 1990 U.S. proposal to modify the current CoCom control lists and its agreement to move toward a "core list" of controlled items was universally applauded in Europe. There was, however, concern about how far the United States actually was willing to go to decontrol the export of advanced technology to the former members of the Warsaw Pact. A recurring theme was the need to assist Soviet President Gorbachev in his attempts to restructure the Soviet economy. The Soviet effort will require a dramatic infusion of Western technology, especially in the field of telecommunications, and many of the Europeans were eager to provide such assistance and technology.

---

*The delegation was chaired by panel member Kenneth Dam and included panel members Boyd McKelvain and Granger Morgan, project director Mitchel Wallerstein, and staff member Thomas Snitch. (Mr. Dam did not participate in the meetings in Belgium, and Mr. McKelvain did not participate in the meetings in Great Britain.)

Concerns over U.S. Policy

Throughout Europe there was strong adverse reaction to U.S. export control policy, in particular its extraterritorial aspects. The Europeans have major problems with U.S. controls on the reexport by any country of U.S.-origin items. Nearly all the Europeans with whom the delegation met thought their country was doing an adequate job of maintaining a domestic export control regime. They argued, therefore, that U.S. reexport controls on CoCom items were both unnecessary and an unneeded intrusion. In a sense, such controls were seen as a threat to national sovereignty and as driving a wedge between the United States and Europe. As U.S. allies, the Europeans found it hard to understand why the United States placed such controls on intra-CoCom trade. Although some believed that the nations of Europe would not give up their right to control exports, the overall feeling was that European integration in 1992 would increase pressure for the removal of intra-CoCom trade controls, except for munitions items.

MEETINGS IN GREAT BRITAIN*

Government Officials

The delegation met with a group from the British government, including representatives of the Foreign and Commonwealth Office (FCO), the Ministry of Defense (MoD), and the Department of Trade and Industry (DTI).

CoCom

The FCO representative opened the meeting by discussing the current situation in CoCom. In his view, although it was difficult to measure the extent of the change in the threat from the Soviet bloc, it was clear that if CoCom was to remain credible in the eyes of the British business community, it would have to identify those technologies that should and could be controlled. CoCom had had 40 years of complicated lists that were difficult to understand and even harder to implement.

The FCO representative also stated that a top-down approach to accelerating the streamlining of the CoCom lists was too cumbersome and no longer appropriate. Rather, a new, core list should be created from "the bottom up" and should not contain more than 12 categories of technologies to be controlled.

The United Kingdom is a participant in the CoCom initiative for a common standard level of effective protection. The British have argued for the "de-

---

*The May 1990 U.S. proposal to CoCom had not been announced at the time of the meetings in Great Britain.

mystification'' of what individual countries control within CoCom. This is clearly under way in regard to chemical weapons. The basic British policy is to "guard against the erosion of national confidence."

The British also believe that some type of third country initiative* is better than no effort at all. However, they also believe other CoCom countries do not completely share their view and are allowing controlled technology to be reexported.

DIFFERENTIATION

The British stated that a core list should apply to all destinations, a view that is consistent with the British opposition to differentiation.† They acknowledged that the nations of Eastern Europe could still prove to be a vehicle for diversions of Western technology to the Soviet Union, but they countered that differentiation would only encourage the Soviets to increase their efforts to divert technology.

The FCO representative said that guarantees from East Europeans against diversion must be considered suspect at best, and more likely worthless. As a result, verification schemes would be of little use. In practice, they could only be effective if they ensured that controlled items went to the proper end users, and such checks would have to remain in place for the lifetime of the equipment. The British government does not believe that such schemes would be cost effective, or that there would be sufficient financial resources for maintaining long-term verification measures. Moreover, the British argue that any type of end-use verification regime ultimately would result in an expansion of the United States' extraterritorial reach, which they already find unacceptable.

It was noted that the United Kingdom, in effect, maintains a policy of differentiation between the Warsaw Pact countries and the People's Republic of China. The British acknowledged this, but they maintained that at the completion of a core list, British policies toward China would have to be reviewed, in consultation with the allies. However, if a "Green Line"‡ to Eastern Europe and the Soviet Union was established, it would presumably affect controls to China as well.

---

*Efforts to convince countries that are not part of CoCom and not proscribed by CoCom to cooperate with CoCom export control policies by preventing reexports of CoCom-controlled items.

†*Differentiation* is the concept under which the level of export controls imposed on importing countries is based on a given country's determination of the national security threat posed by the importing country.

‡Refers to substantial relaxation within CoCom of the restriction on strategic technology exports to the People's Republic of China in order to assist China's modernization efforts.

LIST CONSTRUCTION

The MoD representative suggested that the United Kingdom was taking a pragmatic approach toward construction of a core list. This entailed sitting down with technical experts and asking three basic questions:

1. Is the technology static?
2. Can it be controlled?
3. Is it available in other countries and not under control?

Based on these criteria, for example, some computer software should not be on a core list because it is so widely available in non-CoCom countries.

The MoD representative also noted that, over the years, the CoCom lists had become more technically defined, which had led to an expansion of the lists. At the same time, the United Kingdom believes that sunset provisions, which provide for automatic decontrol at a specified time, are dangerous and that, in fact, items should be reviewed on a case-by-case basis. Thus, the current, reduced lists must remain in place until a core list is agreed upon. The CoCom unanimity rule must also remain in place because only consensus can keep the playing field level for all.

PROLIFERATION CONTROLS

The United Kingdom is a member of the Australia Group* (AG) on chemical weapons. The British vigorously watch trade in the precursor chemicals on the AG's control list and have added six more to that list; they have also established a warning list in an effort to work with the British business community. There are no chemical weapons related controls on process technology, but such technology may be controlled for other reasons. Because it would be impossible to create an all-encompassing chemical weapons control list, the British found it preferable to work with the business community to create a corporate watch process for chemical weapons control. The British said that they had begun a similar effort for biological weapons, and they will soon be circulating information to British industry to make companies aware of potentially risky sales.

Finally, the British see the Missile Technology Control Regime (MTCR) as an adjunct to the Nuclear Non-Proliferation Treaty. At present, however, they consider the MTCR a weak instrument of control because of the lack of a permanent secretariat, among other reasons. Additionally, the fundamental issues surrounding missile technology control overlap with civilian outer space issues, and therefore, the British believe that it will be difficult

---

*A group of nations, under the leadership of Australia, that have agreed to restrict, if not ban, the sale of chemical weapons precursors.

to separate peaceful from nonpeaceful intentions in determining whether to impose controls.

ENFORCEMENT

The British Customs Department is the major export control enforcement unit. It is responsible for general enforcement, criminal investigations, and the routine administrative functions of customs work. The United Kingdom maintains, but does not publish, a "gray list" of suspected violators. Penalties are divided into two types: Part I involves less serious violations, which carry a penalty on conviction of 2,000 pounds or three times the value of the seized export, plus up to six months in jail. Part II crimes are more serious; there is no limit on the cash penalty that can be levied and prison sentences can be up to seven years. These crimes come under a 20-year statute of limitations. The British representatives emphasized that the government does not maintain a denial list that would cause a convicted individual or firm to lose export privileges. The government believes that after the penalty has been paid, there is no need for additional, long-term recriminations.

The British stated that, after the 1992 European market integration, the government will still maintain some form of national administration of export controls. The British see Article 223 of the Treaty of Rome as a warrant for the protection of national interests. The British are concerned that, although a liberal control regime may exist within the European Community (EC), it will be difficult to create a common external enforcement arrangement. They believe that the end result will be a control system that gravitates toward the least common denominator and not necessarily toward the most effective system.

Parliament Member

The delegation met with a senior member of the House of Commons, who is the chairman of a parliamentary group that had recently held hearings and released a report on the possibility of trade between Great Britain and Eastern Europe. He favored increased business cooperation with the Soviet Union and East European countries, and he urged that serious attempts be made to assist the Soviet Union to upgrade its domestic telecommunications systems.

Industry Representatives

The delegation met with a group of British industrialists who had recently formed a corporate organization that is a cooperative venture between two trade associations, the Electronic Equipment Association and the Telecommunications, Engineering and Manufacturing Association. The purpose of the group is to provide a forum for the development of ideas on export controls within the British business community. The Department of Trade and Industry sees the organization as a body that represents the general views of the British electronics and communications industries.

The industrialists stated that strategic technology controls remain an essential element in the defense of the West, but such controls should cover only those items that may be relevant to the Soviet military effort. Moreover, items cannot be controlled by CoCom if they are readily available from other, non-CoCom sources. At the same time, the industrialists argued that export controls should not be used as a form of punishment against the West's adversaries, such as was the case with the Soviet Union after its invasion of Afghanistan. In fact, U.S. unilateral controls, and especially the U.S. insistence on reexport controls, amounted to little more than "damned interference" with international trade. The trade organization also criticized the extraterritorial reach of U.S. controls, saying that it had caused many firms to avoid working with U.S. firms for fear of changes in U.S. policy. The group thought that export controls should stop at the water's edge.

The trade group believes that, in the future, Eastern Europe cannot be considered any more threatening than China. Yet, because China has received more favorable treatment from CoCom than Eastern Europe, the trade group has asked the British government to give the Soviet Union and the other Warsaw Treaty Organization (WTO) countries the same treatment as China. The organization also believes that a policy of differentiation is unnecessary because, in essence, the Warsaw Pact no longer exists. Further, the group believes that it is important to bring chemical weapons, missile technology, and nuclear trade into a CoCom-like framework. Finally, in the group's view, the act of European integration should create a unified market that is bound around its external border by an export control regime that is a "ring of steel."

The industrialists saw telecommunications as a very high priority for the economic development of Eastern Europe. They saw trade in the telecommunications field as the carrot that could get the Soviet Union and Eastern Europe to move more rapidly on the political front toward greater democratization. Telecommunications technology, in which the trade group believes the West leads by 10 to 15 years, is precisely what spread the notion of democracy throughout Eastern Europe. And, while they acknowledge that the availability of foreign currency is a problem, the industrialists nevertheless believe that creation of a trans-Soviet communications link is a necessity.

In regard to the interaction between the trade group and the British government, the industrialists reported that the organization's members serve on British delegations to CoCom and that the organization meets every six weeks with DTI for technical discussions. The purpose of these meetings is to analyze matters that are currently under discussion in CoCom. The organization also prepares consensus position papers on export control issues for DTI. The members of the organization's CoCom and DTI advisory groups hold security clearances so that they can fully participate in all CoCom-related discussions.

MEETINGS IN FRANCE

Government Officials

The delegation had a lengthy meeting with a senior official of the Ministry of Foreign Affairs (MFA) the day after the new U.S. proposal to CoCom was announced. The MFA official reported that a recent French strategic assessment had shown the following:

• Soviet military capabilities have not decreased, but Soviet intentions have become less threatening.
• The Warsaw Pact has, in effect, lost its cohesion.

He then provided an overview of the French assessment of the key issues at hand:

• A strict control system must be maintained based on strategic realities.
• CoCom must be completely revamped if it is to remain in existence.
• The focus of CoCom must be on what should and can be controlled.

In discussing Soviet technology acquisition efforts, the MFA official reported that the French have seen no change in the level of activity. He did note, however, that the Soviet intelligence networks in Poland, Hungary, and Czechoslovakia had not been disbanded, and therefore, it must be assumed that some former operatives were still at work.

For the French the main question was still how to manage politically a policy of differentiation without making it appear that the West was trying to foster the collapse of the Warsaw Pact. And, although the theoretical concept of differentiation is viable in the French view, the basic objective of revamping the entire CoCom system must be paramount. In this regard, the French do not have any difficulty with the idea of a core list, but they do support the need to continue applying the rule of consensus in creating it. The French do not see how any real changes could take place in CoCom if 1 nation could effectively block the wishes of 16 others.

The French do not understand the concern over exporting machine tools to the Soviet bloc, because such tools are so widely available. The officials also noted that telecommunication equipment is essential to infrastructure development in Eastern Europe. In this regard, the French do understand the objections of the U.S. intelligence community to the installation of fiber optic systems in the Soviet Union. Nevertheless, because CoCom was not created to enhance the collection of intelligence against the Soviet Union, the loss of signal intelligence is a separate issue.

The MFA official also addressed the question of greater transparency within CoCom. He stated bluntly that confidentiality within the organization was dead and that he saw no reason why final documents could not be given to the media. Indeed, the French government's inclusion of industry representatives in technical advisory meetings was designed to increase the transparency of the process.

On the matter of alternative proliferation control regimes, the French government already maintains control lists for the export of munitions, nuclear items, and missile technology. The government would work to harmonize its efforts with those of the international community, but only on an informal basis. The French government was not willing to codify such arrangements at the time, and it saw no need to expand the responsibilities of CoCom into these areas.

Industry Representatives

The delegation had an informal discussion with a diverse group of French industrialists. They stated that the industrial sector can accept the notion of differentiation toward the Soviet Union as long as a strategic threat remains. Nonetheless, a movement was needed within CoCom toward shortening the control list. A troubling point that remained for the French was the U.S. reexport regulations and the entire issue of extraterritoriality. For example, U.S. regulations force a French firm to comply with both French and U.S. laws, which imposes a serious administrative burden on the firms. The industrialists pointed out that although the United States had moved to expand trade with the Soviet Union, it was imposing conditions on foreign companies that constrained their ability to do the same. They also pointed out that U.S. regulations are too complicated, are only provided in English, have been used to enable U.S. firms to maintain technological leads over foreign firms, and have forced foreign firms to "design-out" U.S. components.

There was general discussion about the philosophy of export controls. The French emphasized the delineation between tangible and intangible controls: the United States enforced the latter, but the French government controlled only physical goods. As an example, it is difficult, if not impossible, to control visits or telephone calls about technical topics.* They also mentioned the differences between export of goods and the export of production technology. They were not prepared to control the export of all production

---

*The French, in any case, do not control technical data exports.

technology, but they thought certain restrictions should be applied to some technologies destined for the Soviet Union and Eastern Europe.

The point was made that France must export to remain an economically viable nation. Over 50 percent of all manufactured goods produced within France are ultimately exported, because the domestic market is too small to be economically viable. This need to export is complicated by CoCom rules, by U.S. export control regulations, and by a general worry over U.S. foreign policy actions.

The industry representatives noted that the French government maintains strict controls on the sale of military goods to Iran, Libya, and South Africa. In addition to the CoCom list, the government maintains and publishes a separate military list, with the result that every export of French military equipment to every destination is controlled by the Ministry of Defense.

In discussing their interaction with the government, the industrialists said that industry representatives attend technical meetings of CoCom and that they are present to provide technical advice. During a CoCom meeting, industry representatives sit with the official delegation, but they do not speak for the government. They only converse with other members of the French delegation.

Finally, the industrialists remarked that it has always appeared to them that the United States simply did not trust the French export control regime. As industrialists, they were willing to accept multilateral controls, even those imposed as a result of the European market integration. But they could never accept unilateral policy dictates, especially from the United States. They were willing to assist in reformulating the mission of CoCom, but they believed its future activities should be dedicated to the creation of a core list of controlled items.

U.S. Representatives at CoCom Headquarters

The delegation met with the U.S. representatives to CoCom at CoCom headquarters in the U.S. embassy annex in Paris. The United States currently contributes 25 percent of the annual CoCom budget. The U.S. delegation consists of 3 officers (2 from the State Department, 1 from the Department of Defense), 3 secretaries, and 2 embassy assistants (who log in license applications). The entire CoCom secretariat consists of 32 individuals.

It was estimated that the United States may account for 99 percent of all new additions to the CoCom control lists. In general, over the years, the lists have become much more detailed in terms of performance characteristics. This, in turn, requires more technical participation by U.S. agencies in export control matters. About 1,500 exception cases were submitted to CoCom in 1988 and in 1989, nearly half of which were submitted by the United States, and many of those were related to the People's Republic of China.

Center for Study of Relation Between
Technologies and Strategies

The Center for Study of Relation between Technologies and Strategies (CREST) is a university-based research center created in 1982 as part of the Ecole Polytechnique. The center is primarily involved with the evaluation of strategic technology for the French Ministry of Defense. For example, CREST has examined such issues as the nuclear hardening of microelectronics and hypersonic flight.

A large portion of the discussion with CREST staff centered on the definition of the term "dual use." In particular, the members of CREST thought that it is becoming increasingly difficult to define almost any product as purely civilian. This lack of a precise definition is a crucial issue in the creation of a CoCom core list of controlled technologies.

French Institute of International Relations

A discussion with a staff member of the French Institute of International Relations covered a wide range of proliferation issues. It was noted that time is the key factor in slowing the pace of technology proliferation. In a sense, additional time would enable developing proliferation control regimes, primarily those concerned with chemical weapons and ballistic missile production, to develop and become codified.

Organization for Economic Cooperation and Development

A brief session was held at the Organization for Economic Cooperation and Development to discuss the activities of the recently established Center for Cooperation with Economies in Transition in Eastern Europe. The center planned to hold three international conferences in 1990–1991 focusing, respectively, on economic statistics, transitional issues, and taxation. These conferences are to be supplemented by seminars and workshops aimed at easing the transition from controlled to market economies for the nations of Eastern Europe.

MEETINGS IN FEDERAL REPUBLIC OF GERMANY (FRG)

Government Officials

The delegation had an extensive meeting with representatives of the Economics Ministry, the Foreign Ministry, and the Ministry of Defense. The discussion covered a broad range of topics, which are summarized below.

CoCom

The session began with a lengthy review of the U.S. CoCom proposal. Overall, the officials were very positive about the changes in U.S. policy on CoCom. They believed that the proposal was a strong effort, although it did not address all of Germany's concerns. In particular, they were pleased with the action on machine tools. In the area of telecommunications, Germany wanted the United States to go further with decontrol for Eastern Europe, but not necessarily for the Soviet Union. The Germans understand the differentiation issue, especially in regard to fiber optics, but not with regard to microwave restrictions. Germany does not believe that the Soviets need state-of-the-art telecommunications equipment. Rather, the West should supply basic systems that can adequately serve current Soviet needs and that can be readily updated in the future.

In terms of the future of CoCom, the FRG government does not question the basic principles of control, but it believes the lists and procedures must be fundamentally changed and that the process must be made more transparent. The Germans believe a good place to start would be a basic rethinking of the question of "what is a strategic item?" Next, the question of "burden of proof" should be revisited. In the past, before an item could be decontrolled, one had to demonstrate either that it was available from non-CoCom sources or that it had become obsolete. In contrast, the new core list being constructed should include only those technologies that have been definitively proven to be strategic.

Export Controls After German Unification

With unification of the two Germanies, a German-wide export control system was planned for the former German Democratic Republic (GDR). Key aspects of this plan included the following:

• The territorial border of export controls would be moved to the eastern border of what was the GDR.

• A short list of very sensitive items would not be sold in the former GDR (the so-called bikini list).

• Former GDR companies would not be permitted to engage in intra-CoCom trade in munitions and nuclear and missile technologies.

• Former GDR customs officials would be trained in CoCom rules and procedures. The training was expected to take time because those to be trained lacked the requisite technical expertise.

• Indigenous production of technical goods within the former GDR under existing contracts would not be subject to export controls even if the item was on a control list.

• Former GDR companies wishing to export non-FRG, Western goods would be expected to request direct permission for reexport from the originating country. In the meantime, the FRG was requiring an import certification/destination verification (IC/DV) document, and this paper trail would help to introduce the former GDR companies to the CoCom control system.

The Germans noted that the Soviet Union was in the process of moving its sensitive military technology out of the former GDR so that the West would not have access to it. At the same time, because the Soviets will not have all of their troops out of German territory in the immediate future, there is the possibility of increased Soviet industrial espionage.

PROLIFERATION ISSUES

The FRG government sees alternative proliferation regimes as important elements in any future control policy. Currently, there is no official government policy toward these alternative regimes, but the FRG officials thought it would be helpful if the various policies were harmonized, if only for commercial reasons. This would mean, in reality, one all-encompassing list for all types of proliferation controls. The FRG would crosscheck applications for licenses to export these technologies by way of a computerized ''gray list.'' And, although there should be multilateral cooperation in controlling trade in nuclear and missile technology, the officials did not believe that CoCom—in its present form—was the proper institution to carry it out.

The FRG government treats the proliferation of chemical weapons as a separate issue because it has already sought to expand control substantially through domestic legislation. The impetus for this came from the embarrassment generated by the public disclosure that German manufacturers had participated in the development of the alleged Libyan chemical weapons facility at Rabta. Trade in all chemical weapons precursors on the Australia Group's control list, along with 50 specific chemicals, now require an FRG export license. In addition, new legislation has been passed that forbids the participation of German nationals working abroad in nuclear, chemical, or biological weapons activities. Violation of this new law could bring up to 10 years in prison.

EUROPEAN COMMUNITY

The FRG government believes that, in a post-1992 environment, the European Community will be reluctant to get involved in export control issues. This is primarily because the European Community has few resources of strategic value and little experience in the export control arena. Germany has suggested, however, that the European Community adopt a common standard of training for all customs officials.

DIFFERENTIATION

Differentiation has always been a problem within Germany. The government would not object to differentiation below the China Green Line, but it believes the problem could basically be solved by streamlining the CoCom control lists in general. The FRG officials acknowledged the difference between the threat posed by the Soviet Union and that posed by the nations of Eastern Europe, but they also pointed out that the Soviet Union is a major market for Eastern Europe. To that end, Germany believes care must be taken that the East European countries do not suffer further economic dislocation and that they continue to have access to energy supplies from the Soviet Union.

INDUSTRY PARTICIPATION

The FRG officials said that the government relied heavily on German industry when deciding on technical export control issues and in official delegations to CoCom, because it does not maintain the necessary expertise within its bureaucracy and intentionally excludes its Ministry of Defense from involvement in CoCom matters. In fact, the government is encouraging greater industry and trade association participation in the CoCom process.

Industry Representatives

BONN

The delegation met with a senior member of the Association of German Chambers of Commerce (DIHT). The DIHT in Bonn represents 69 individual chambers throughout the FRG. By law, all companies in the FRG (over 2 million firms), regardless of product, must belong to the DIHT. The organization is totally independent of the government. Although DIHT does lobby, the government, in turn, seeks DIHT's opinion on export issues.

After the European market integration in 1992, individual licenses for intra-CoCom trade will be eliminated, but written, non-retransfer notices will be sent to CoCom after the shipments have been made. In effect, these new regulations will place greater reliance on industry to provide "assurances" as to end use and final product destinations. German firms have been setting up internal compliance procedures, many of which have been suggested by the government.

The matter of former GDR firms joining the DIHT is a delicate issue because the Soviets are concerned that many firms within the former Soviet bloc may go into bankruptcy during their efforts to move toward a more capitalistic system and not make good on existing contracts. The DIHT is aware of these concerns and is helping to form 15 new, but separate, chambers of commerce within the former GDR.

The delegation also met with the director of another key German industrial association, the Federation of German Industries (BDI). The BDI director said that his group was anxious to begin work on the creation of a core list. In his view, although most dual use items no longer needed to be controlled, some restrictions should remain on some very specific technologies that may be critical to Western military systems.

The BDI director also reported that former GDR companies want the same machine tools that are available in the West. He asked rhetorically, "Why would General Motors want to produce cars in two locations with radically different equipment?" It only makes sense, he continued, for former GDR companies to bring themselves into line with commonly available technologies that are prevalent in the West.

The BDI director said that the Western alliance was in dire need of the "creation of confidence." To do this, CoCom must become more transparent, more reliable, and simpler for business to work with. However, most of Europe sees the current U.S. proposals as favoring U.S. business interests.

The BDI director also pointed out that Germany is often blamed for proliferation problems simply because it has been used as a transshipment point. In practice, however, Germany has been at the forefront of many proliferation controls, and the U.S. Chemical Manufacturers Association has used Germany as a model for controlling chemical precursors. The BDI director's personal opinion was that it would be useful to formalize the Australia Group, perhaps at the Conference on Disarmament in Geneva.

Although few German firms have deliberately avoided U.S. components in order to escape U.S. reexport controls (i.e., "de-Americanization"), U.S. firms are not viewed as reliable suppliers because of the capricious nature of U.S. foreign policy controls. Moreover, these controls do not fit into the way the world exists. Rather, they are applied purely to make the U.S. media and the public believe the U.S. government is doing something.

The DIHT and BDI representatives expressed dismay over the U.S. decision to allow differentiation in the telecommunications area. They postulated that this was probably due to the influence of the U.S. intelligence community, but they said Germany had no desire to assist the United States in eavesdropping on the Soviets. Thus, if the United States is serious about helping to build an effective telecommunications infrastructure in Eastern Europe, it should base its policy on what the countries actually need.

FRANKFURT

The delegation met in Frankfurt with two industrial associations—the German Electrical and Electronics Manufacturers Association (ZVEI) and the U.S. Chamber of Commerce. The meeting with the ZVEI began with another review of the U.S. CoCom proposals. In general, the ZVEI was pleased with the U.S. decision to decontrol personal computers and to give favorable consideration to the China Green Line.

The ZVEI group particularly stressed the need to assist the economic development of the former GDR and the East European countries by providing greater access to Western technology. In this regard Soviet President Gorbachev had to be able to demonstrate to his critics that such economic development was actually being realized. The ZVEI group appreciated the U.S. proposals for greater streamlining of CoCom, but they were concerned that the process could become bogged down in technical details. Indeed, ZVEI questioned the continuing need for controls on dual use technology, arguing that the West should move toward a system of controls only on items that are *directly* relevant to military systems.

The ZVEI group stressed the importance of industry to FRG participation in CoCom meetings. They said that industry provided all the technical expertise to the German delegation, a role that was fulfilled in the United States by the Department of Defense. Industry nominates individuals to serve with the German delegation, either in Bonn or at CoCom headquarters in Paris. At the time of the fact-finding mission, seven computer specialists were serving as official members of the German delegation. The Germans noted that the Canadians, Italians, British, Japanese, Dutch, and Belgians also brought industry representatives to CoCom meetings.

The Germans stated that the U.S. Export Administration Regulations were far too difficult to understand. The regulations were also said to place an especially heavy burden on small and medium-sized German firms that could not afford to maintain an internal compliance staff. (At the same time, German firms were said to have problems in complying with FRG rules and regulations.) The *de minimus* rule regarding U.S. content (25 percent for continued U.S. control) has reduced the problem of the extraterritoriality of U.S. export controls, but it has not eliminated it. German firms also continue to be concerned about the impact of U.S. foreign policy controls. It was suggested that certain German firms may want to design-out U.S. components in order to minimize these restrictions.

The U.S. Chamber of Commerce group represents a wide range of U.S. industrial firms. A number of the issues discussed with this group applied to the spectrum of specific industries. Among the assertions made by this group were the following:

• The CoCom regulations are difficult to understand and implement.
• In many instances, original equipment is not controlled by CoCom but spare parts and service contracts are.
• The processing time for obtaining U.S. export licenses is too long, which puts U.S. companies at a disadvantage.
• U.S. firms have problems obtaining licenses to demonstrate equipment at trade fairs in the Soviet Union and Eastern Europe.

- There is a general feeling in Germany that the People's Republic of China is being treated more favorably than Eastern Europe.
- Increased amounts of CoCom-controlled equipment from non-CoCom countries are showing up throughout Eastern Europe.
- East European economic problems will continue to slow the potential for trade. In fact, a number of U.S. firms are doing business on a deferred-payment basis.

MEETINGS IN BELGIUM

During its stay in Brussels, the delegation held meetings with representatives of the Belgian government, the Commission of the European Community, the European Parliament, and the U.S. Mission to the North Atlantic Treaty Organization (NATO). It also met with two Dutch academic experts on strategic technology trade who traveled to Brussels specifically to meet with the delegation.

Government Officials

The Belgian approach to export controls can be explained by the following points:

- 60 percent of the Belgian economy depends on exports, but less than 1 percent of those goods are CoCom controlled.
- Twice this century the United States has come to the rescue of Belgium. This has left a favorable view of the United States, NATO, and a united Europe.
- The Soviet threat is seen in Belgium as diminishing.

Belgian officials stated that the government viewed the new U.S. proposals for CoCom with great interest. In particular, they noted that Belgium had called for greater streamlining of the control lists at an earlier meeting of CoCom. The government believes that CoCom has been a positive force over the past four decades, but that it can only remain effective if it has the support of the international business community. That is why streamlining the control lists is so important. The Belgians noted that the country has export controls of many types, which are carried out by Royal Decree and under the authority of the Export Act of 1964. The regulations control both tangible products and written materials, but a Belgian citizen can transfer technical data verbally without violating the law.

The government representatives noted that Belgium was a signatory to the Nuclear Non-Proliferation Treaty and that it would soon join the Missile Technology Control Regime. Moreover, due to its geographic location, Belgium is very sensitive to the need to control chemical and biological weapons and believes that there should be a universal ban on such weapons. The problem, as Belgium sees it, is how to develop a practical, international control regime. The Belgian government believes that the establishment of a new secretariat for the coordination of proliferation control regimes within CoCom would probably not be practical. Such a secretariat would provide bureaucratic problems for the Belgian government, because CoCom affairs and proliferation issues are handled by different ministries.

The Belgian government does not allow members of industry to be accredited members of Belgian delegations to CoCom. However, it does hold wide-ranging, informal consultations with industry. Some industrial representatives do assist the Ministry of Economic Affairs, but only as technical advisors.

The government believes that it is very difficult to justify imposing domestic Belgian export controls on third countries when it is obvious that many other members of CoCom do not. However, Belgium does maintain the IC/DV system for exports to third countries.

Commission of the European Community

The delegation met with the head of the Directorate General for International Affairs of the Commission of the European Community. The representative stated that there were two reasons for the European Community to become involved in CoCom matters: (1) anything that affects the welfare of Europe affects the European Community and (2) after the elimination of internal trade borders in 1992, anything that would make trade more difficult, including CoCom trade restrictions, is opposed by the European Community.

According to the commission representative, the commission has kept a low profile on the CoCom issue because of its sensitive nature and because military matters are involved. Additionally, Ireland, a member of the European Community, does not belong to CoCom. However, the changes occurring within CoCom are a positive accomplishment in the view of the European Community. The European Community will have to become involved in setting up some type of system for external trade control, and that system must be compatible with a "common external frontier."

As for proliferation controls, the commission had no specific, ongoing work regarding chemical and biological weapons. Although the European Atomic Energy Community (Euratom) exists to coordinate the development of nuclear resources, the issue of EC trade in dangerous substances has only recently been brought up. The important thing according to the commission representative is to get an agreement in principle on chemical and biological weapons that involves specific responsibilities among the members and then work out the details.

The commission does not have a position on the possibility of conflict among the Single European Act, the Treaty of Rome, and the positions of the EC member governments. The governments involved have different positions on whether this issue should be dealt with on a national or multilateral basis.

The delegation also held a roundtable discussion with 12 staff members and senior managers of the commission. In general, the point was made that, at a broad level, the European Community is striving toward greater industrial integration among its members. The 1992 market integration does not mean that all export controls will disappear, however. Rather, the emphasis will shift to creating strengthened external trade borders.

To achieve these objectives, the commission staff noted, the first step will have to be the adoption of a uniform list of controlled exports. Some nations have suggested, however, that they may control exports for other reasons. Next is the issue of who will process applications for export licenses. Currently, national governments maintain individual systems of licensing. Thus, it may become necessary for each member state to trust the receiving nation not to reexport that good. Moreover, within the European Community, there will be no paper trail on traded goods. The trail will begin only *after* goods leave the European Community. If this approach is to be accepted, it would appear that all the member states must have the same policies, that is, a common standard level of effective protection.

The commission has begun to examine certain proliferation issues, primarily in the chemical weapons area. However, eventual agreements in these areas will have to remain flexible to allow national governments to maintain their own regulatory systems.

The European Parliament

A session was held with members of the European Parliament, including a member who had recently introduced a resolution calling for the removal of *all* CoCom controls. The resolution was premised on the following assertions:

• More and more Europeans understand the nature of the declining Soviet threat and that security must now be viewed in economic rather than military terms.

• There is a great need to invest in Eastern Europe because those nations cannot achieve economic stability without modern technology.

• Proliferation controls should be kept on a national level.

• Exports of arms should remain under national discretion.

• The future security of Europe is tied to economic cooperation, not in continuing existing military partnerships.

• The real threat is environmental pollution.

• U.S. troops should be withdrawn from Europe and there should be an overall reduction in U.S. defense spending in Europe.

U.S. Mission to NATO

In a meeting with staff of the U.S. Mission to NATO, the delegation was told that worldwide proliferation issues are being watched closely by NATO countries. Many would like to see every member of NATO join the MTCR, but the French, in particular, might not want NATO involved in this area.

The U.S. ambassador to NATO recently proposed that NATO establish a formal body to look at defense-related trade issues. For example, a "defense GATT" could work toward eliminating international barriers to defense-related trade among the NATO countries, Japan, Australia, New Zealand, and South Korea. This forum could seek to coordinate restrictions on technology transfer and to deal with common proliferation concerns. Such cooperation might be justified by smaller defense budgets, the increasing costs of weapons systems, and the need for more efficient production within defense-related industries. It might also reduce concerns about the United States as an unreliable supplier in the area of military assistance.

Dutch Academics in Brussels

Two university researchers from the Netherlands who study export control issues met with the delegation in Brussels to discuss Dutch views on export controls. They believed the Netherlands had taken a considerable amount of initiative within CoCom, given the size of its international trade. In 1989, the Dutch made 10 percent of the proposals for revisions to the control lists and requested only 2 percent of the exceptions.

The Dutch believe that the criteria used to determine strategic importance in a control system should be interpreted as strictly as possible and should be coordinated through multilateral channels. The government supports a core list approach and believes that controls should be maintained at least at the China Green Line level.

MEETINGS IN SWITZERLAND

A member of the delegation met with a number of officials of the government of Switzerland, the deputy director of the Swiss Machine Tools Association, and staff of the U.S. embassy in Bern. Topics of discussion included the May 1990 U.S. proposals to CoCom, Swiss export control procedures, and chemical weapons and missile technology issues.

The discussion with government officials was chaired by the Ministry of Economics and began with a discussion of the recent U.S. proposals to

CoCom. The Swiss talked at length about their neutral status and, while acknowledging they could not join CoCom, pointed out that they nevertheless maintained strict export controls. For example, the Swiss government processed 20,000 license requests in 1989, fewer than 2,000 of which involved trade with either the Soviet Union or East European countries. The 2,000 cases involved legitimate end users, and "Swiss blues"* were provided to any government that requested them. The United States is the single largest requester of "Swiss blues," but Germany, Great Britain, and France also routinely make such requests.

The Swiss acknowledged that in the past some diversions through Switzerland had occurred. Since then, however, controls had been tightened and enforcement activities had been strengthened. The government was convinced that the chance for diversion of Swiss technology was fairly remote.

In regard to proliferation controls, the Swiss government is an active participant in the Australia Group and would support any multilateral effort to control chemical weapons. Although Switzerland is not a major producer of chemical processing equipment, the government examines all license applications for exports to Iran, Iraq, Libya, and Syria to check for possible diversions of dual use equipment.

A general discussion was also held on the dangers presented by the proliferation of ballistic missile technology. When informed that the Benelux countries were about to join the MTCR, the Swiss appeared to be quite surprised and said that perhaps Switzerland should now consider joining the MTCR.

II.
ASIAN MISSION†

GENERAL ISSUES

Economic Growth

It is clear that Japan will remain a key economic rival of the United States. The rapid and sustained economic growth of the Pacific Rim countries suggests that those nations are on a path similar to that of Japan. In particular, Korea and Taiwan are exhibiting economic characteristics similar to those

---

*"Swiss blues" are copies of Swiss licenses, which are provided to other governments when an export involves the retransfer of goods or goods that contain non-Swiss components.

†The Asian delegation visited Taiwan, Hong Kong, Macao, the Republic of Korea, and Japan in February 1990. The delegation was headed by panel chairman Roland Schmitt and included panel members Seymour Goodman and Ruth Greenstein, project director Mitchel Wallerstein, and staff member Thomas Snitch. Panel member Benjamin Huberman joined the delegation for the visit in Japan. (Dr. Schmitt did not participate in the meetings in Taiwan and Hong Kong.)

that were, in large part, responsible for the meteoric rise of Japan's economy. In all of the countries the delegation visited, however, a marked movement toward the production of more technologically advanced products was evident. In fact, there has been a concerted movement away from cheap, basic consumer goods to the production of computer and electronic goods. At the same time, all of the countries visited are faced with high land costs, a shortage of skilled labor, and increased domestic demand for high-technology goods.

Perception of the Threat

THE SOVIET UNION

All of the countries visited recognized the declining nature of the Soviet military threat. Indeed, the extraordinary changes that were sweeping both the Soviet Union and its former allies in the Warsaw Pact were viewed as positive trends that were likely to continue. And although there was concern in Asia, primarily in Japan, that the changes in Europe would result in the transfer of Soviet military equipment to the Far East, there was an overall belief that the threat from the Soviet Union had diminished dramatically.

THE PEOPLE'S REPUBLIC OF CHINA

All the countries visited, including especially Hong Kong, remain concerned about the political situation in China. The 1989 uprising in Tiananmen Square, coupled with the uncertainty over the future direction of Chinese domestic policies, still causes concern. Moreover, there was a general feeling that even though a thaw in East-West relations was occurring throughout Europe, tensions remained high in Asia, in terms of China and especially with regard to North Korea. The failure of North Korea to sign a nuclear safeguards agreement with the International Atomic Energy Agency has spawned concern about the future direction of that nation's nuclear program.

Despite lingering worries about the future of China, considerable trade, much of it indirect, was still being conducted. Indirect trade is primarily unofficial, that is, it is unlicensed. The delegation heard assertions that large amounts of goods were being sent into China through the northern land borders with Hong Kong and, especially, through Macao. In a sense, Macao is an open and unregulated door into China.

Export Control Issues

The delegation was impressed by the sophisticated levels of technology embodied in goods and products that were available throughout Asia. CoCom-controlled 386 personal computers were available for purchase nearly everywhere. For example, controlled technology, such as 386 memory chips, was available in street-corner shops in Hong Kong.

The delegation was given the opportunity to tour research and development centers and production facilities throughout the region. It was abundantly clear that dynamic economic growth is taking place. The firms, and their employees, are driven by a sense of purpose to produce high-quality, technically sophisticated goods.

At the same time, the delegation was frequently told that the goods they saw being produced were "not that sophisticated" and that there was little need for any type of local export control. In Korea and Taiwan the delegation was given extensive briefings about the evolving domestic export control regime, while simultaneously being told that there was little to control. Although the plans for domestic control regimes were thoroughly developed on paper, there was often little demonstrable evidence that steps were being taken to implement those plans.

The issue of diversion was raised frequently. In each country, it was asserted that every *other* country in Asia was responsible for vast amounts of diversions to the Soviet bloc and China, but that the host country maintained strict adherence to "CoCom-like" rules.

The delegation took note of the efforts being made by Japan and Hong Kong to stem the illegal flow of controlled goods from within their borders. It was obvious that, in the wake of the 1983–1984 Toshiba-Kongsberg incident,* the Japanese government had taken a series of concrete steps to upgrade Japan's export control efforts. Similarly, the delegation was impressed with the efforts in Hong Kong to execute a vigorous plan of export control.

MEETINGS IN TAIWAN

Ministry of Economic Affairs—Industrial Development Bureau

The delegation met with members of the Industrial Development Bureau (IDB) of the Ministry of Economic Affairs. Bureau staff highlighted development's in the three industries (computers, advanced materials, and machine tools) the Ministry of Economic Affairs has identified as most likely to lead Taiwan's export efforts. That discussion was preceded by an analysis of the current state of the Taiwanese economy. Key points included the following:

- Land costs are rising rapidly.
- There is a small labor pool and almost no unemployment.

---

*A highly publicized illegal sale of high-precision machines to the Soviet Union. The two firms involved were Japan's Toshiba Machine Company and Norway's Kongsberg Vaapenfabrikk.

- The Taiwanese dollar has appreciated almost 60 percent since 1988.
- Taiwan must export because of its very small domestic market.
- Rising land and labor costs, coupled with currency appreciation, have forced Taiwan to move toward more technologically sophisticated industrial manufacturing.

THE COMPUTER INDUSTRY

Taiwan has 700 computer firms, which employ 80,000 workers and produce U.S. $5.5 billion of computers a year, of which U.S. $5.2 billion is exported. In 1989, North America was the leading importer, with a 42 percent share of Taiwan's exports; Western Europe followed at 38 percent and Asia, primarily Hong Kong and Singapore, at 15 percent. Because of the changes in Eastern Europe, Taiwan plans to increase its exports to those nations over the next five years.

The types of computer exports shifted dramatically throughout the 1980s. Beginning in the early 1980s with simple monitors and terminals, Taiwan exported unsophisticated personal computers from 1985 to 1988. Since then, there has been a shift toward the export of more sophisticated items, such as PC 386s and 486s. It is expected that Taiwan will be exporting complete work stations as early as 1991.

MACHINE TOOL INDUSTRY

Like Taiwan's computer industry, the machine tool industry has grown at a dramatic rate. Three hundred manufacturers produced over U.S. $1 billion of machine tools in 1989, 65 percent of which were exported. Taiwan expects these numbers to double by the year 2000.

The IDB staff noted that 95 percent of all the machine tools manufactured were of low precision but highly durable. The industry is now shifting toward the production of more sophisticated machine tools. All of Taiwan's exports of machine tools are regulated under CoCom-like rules, and the IDB staff said that the policy will continue even though Taiwan is not a member of CoCom.

ADVANCED MATERIALS INDUSTRY

The government, industry, and universities have cooperated to build Taiwan's advanced materials industry. Recent economic trends indicate that Taiwan has chosen to focus on a few materials, such as fine ceramics, polymer composites, and alloy steel, as areas of major emphasis. For each of these advanced materials, Taiwan was experiencing annual growth rates of from 20 percent (polymer composites) to over 100 percent (alloy steels).

Other Government Officials

The delegation also had a roundtable meeting with all the relevant major Taiwanese government agencies. The meeting was hosted by the Ministry of Economic Affairs; attending were mid-level officials from the Ministries of Foreign Affairs, Defense, Justice, and Finance (Customs). All were part of a working group that is putting together Taiwan's export control regime. The officials asserted that they were prepared to participate in a bilateral agreement with the United States on national security export controls.

The officials repeatedly declared that, because Taiwan did not produce any high-technology products, there would be little to control. Although Taiwan had not yet prepared a control list, the officials thought they would be controlling items that came from CoCom countries in the near future.

As of early 1990, Taiwan had had little actual experience with customs enforcement. A number of legislative initiatives were under way, and if fully implemented, they will eventually provide the basis for an official export control and enforcement regime. Nevertheless, it will take considerable time for such legislation to be put into force.

Taiwan National Science Park

The delegation was taken to Taiwan's National Science Park for a tour of some of the park's computer plants and for talks with the senior administrators and managers of the park. The National Science Park was built in 1980 and patterned after California's Silicon Valley. The park was created to attract overseas Chinese and other foreign investment to the developing high-technology industries of Taiwan. The government provided U.S. $200 million for the land and built most of the primary infrastructure. There were 105 companies in the park, and Japanese, U.S., and a number of European firms were involved. The park's director noted that between 70 and 80 percent of the goods manufactured within the park were being exported.

The delegation visited the ACER computer facility in the park. ACER is the largest manufacturer of personal computers in Taiwan. Its sales grew from U.S. $25 million in 1986 to U.S. $500 million in 1988 and U.S. $700 million in 1989. ACER exports personal computers to 76 countries, and in early 1990 was producing three types of personal computers: 8086/8088-based XT clones, 286 AT clones, and 386 machines. The XT clones were being phased out, however. ACER expected to start producing 486 machines by the end of 1990.

ACER claims to be among the top five manufacturers in sales of 386 personal computers in the United States. It has about 4.4 percent of the U.S. market.

U.S. Chamber of Commerce

The delegation met with 20 U.S. business representatives in Taiwan. The feeling among the business group was that, although Taiwan was experiencing widespread economic growth, the United States was deliberately being denied access to the growing Taiwanese market. Two factors were cited. First, it was difficult, if not impossible, to integrate U.S. components into finished Taiwanese products because of a bias to use Taiwanese components, even if they are more costly than U.S. equivalents. Second, the Taiwanese were more likely to turn to Japanese rather than U.S. firms for components. The U.S. business group also noted that there was a large volume of "indirect trade" with the People's Republic of China, which was undertaken through trading companies and transshipment of manufactured Taiwanese goods by way of Hong Kong.

MEETINGS IN THE U.K. CROWN COLONY OF HONG KONG

Hong Kong Department of Trade

The delegation had a lengthy session with the deputy director and the senior unit heads of the Department of Trade. The Hong Kong system of export control is an extension of the British system. Although Hong Kong has no direct links to CoCom, it adheres to all CoCom rules. Hong Kong's import/export laws are clear, and the regulations applying to strategic commodities are quite simple. The Hong Kong Control Schedule is actually a published transposition of the CoCom embargo list.

An import or export license for trade with a nonproscribed destination can be obtained from the Hong Kong Department of Trade within three working days. Licenses for any destinations that have been proscribed by the United Kingdom take longer. In these specific cases, the U.K. Department of Trade and Industry (DTI) will issue a license only on the basis of an existing CoCom license. These cases must be referred to DTI in London.

The Department of Trade maintains a "watch list" of companies that are suspected of engaging in illegal exports. However, license requests are considered on a case-by-case basis. If a company or firm is placed on the Hong Kong watch list, it does not mean that its license applications are automatically denied, only that they are subject to greater scrutiny. Even if convicted of an illegal export, a firm does not lose its privileges to export in the future. In a recent change to Hong Kong's licensing system, either an original or a "true copy of the original license" is required for the reexport of a good. In this way, an inspector in Hong Kong can verify that a license is genuine.

The number of licenses being processed every year is said to be causing strains on the system. In 1988, 160,000 import and 290,000 export licenses were issued. Nine thousand of the export licenses were for shipments to the People's Republic of China, and no licenses were issued for any controlled destination other than China. The Department of Trade does not believe that China is using Hong Kong as a point of diversion, and it has found that nearly 70 percent of the licenses issued for China have been backed by CoCom member-country licenses.

According to the director of the Department of Trade's enforcement unit, 300 control officers conduct strategic commodity checks, both preshipment and "disposal" checks (i.e., when a good is moved). An additional 200 officers are involved in prosecutions. From 1985 through 1989, the enforcement unit conducted 103 prosecutions, 2 of which resulted in prison sentences. A high percentage of the prosecutions were related to computer shipments to Macao, which suggests that Macao is a major point of diversion of computers into China.

U.S. Chamber of Commerce

The delegation held two lengthy meetings with some 30 representatives of U.S. firms. In both discussions, the central topic was China—both the situation in Hong Kong after the 1997 reversion to China and U.S. reactions to the government's actions against Chinese students in Tiananmen Square in June 1989. Virtually every chamber member expressed unhappiness with U.S. sanctions against China. They believed that the sanctions were having little, if any, effect on Chinese policies and that they were badly hurting U.S. business interests in China and Hong Kong.

There was considerable speculation about the future of Hong Kong and about what will happen in China when the country's aged leaders begin to die. Most thought that it was in China's long-term interests to ensure that an economically prosperous Hong Kong survives beyond 1997. However, the prospects that this will happen were being jeopardized by an exodus of highly trained technical workers and managers from Hong Kong.

Many of the representatives stated that Hong Kong was not an export sieve for goods destined for China. In general, they praised the efforts of the Hong Kong Department of Trade to carry out British/CoCom export policies.

A common complaint was that many nations allow their firms to trade with Vietnam, but the United States does not. Because Hong Kong is a center for pan-Asian trade, it is a logical outpost from which U.S. firms could move into the Vietnamese market. Some of the group suggested that Japanese and French companies were already doing business with Vietnam, and they expressed the fear that, if the United States did not move soon, U.S. firms could be permanently shut out of Vietnam.

Finally, the issue of "trading companies" was brought up. Trading companies are in many cases simply covers, often just post office boxes, through which exports are laundered. Ultimate end users are falsified, goods are surreptitiously moved from one location to another, and there is little accountability or overall control. While citing the existence of the trading companies, most agreed there was little, if anything, that could be done to control them.

VISIT TO MACAO

The delegation made a one-day trip to the Portuguese territory of Macao. Macao's current status is that of a Portuguese-administered enclave of the People's Republic of China. Portugal will withdraw entirely in 1999. Even though Portugal is a member of NATO, export controls do not exist in Macao. The territory borders on one of China's special economic zones, and traffic flows freely from Macao to China. In addition, there is almost constant waterborne traffic between Hong Kong and Macao, and few, if any, customs inspections. Unlike Hong Kong, Macao appeared to the delegation to have little indigenous high-technology industry.

MEETINGS IN THE REPUBLIC OF KOREA

Government Officials

MINISTRY OF FOREIGN AFFAIRS

At a meeting at the Ministry of Foreign Affairs (MFA), officials confirmed Korea's willingness to adopt some form of bilateral export control relation with the United States. However, it appeared that negotiations toward a ''5(k) agreement''* had not progressed quite as far as previously had been claimed.

Much of the meeting was spent talking about the Soviet Union, Eastern Europe, and North Korea. The MFA vice minister discussed the Korean perspective on the Soviet Union and Eastern Europe, which is very different from that of the United States. The United States has a global concern about Soviet strategic capabilities and the diversion of technology from Eastern Europe to the Soviet Union. South Korea is most concerned about North Korea and about the Soviets as the major arms supplier to the north. In light of the recent political developments in the Soviet bloc, South Korea views Eastern Europe as no direct threat and as a potential new market for cheap consumer and middle-technology items. Korea would like to improve relations with the Soviet Union and the Eastern bloc as an important way to get those countries to moderate their support for North Korea. Given the state of the North Korean economy, a cutoff of Soviet and East European aid,

---

*A bilateral export control agreement between the United States and a non-CoCom, non-proscribed country.

especially the supply of weapons, would seriously hurt North Korea's ability to wage war.

MINISTRY OF TRADE AND INDUSTRY

The delegation also had two meetings at the Ministry of Trade and Industry. One was with the managers of the department that will handle export controls, and the second was with a large group of middle-managers who would be involved with policy implementation. Like the Taiwanese, the South Koreans think their manufactured products are "low tech" and therefore not subject to controls. It is not clear, however, whether they have seriously considered how their exports would be affected if the 5(k) agreement with the United States is implemented.

The most interesting part of the second meeting was an expression of Korean interest in joining CoCom instead of simply having a memorandum of understanding with the United States. The Koreans believed that there were at least three potential advantages to such a step: (1) the government could lobby to make North Korea a proscribed country for all of CoCom, (2) the government could directly argue for the decontrol of what it wishes to sell, and (3) membership in a body of advanced countries would provide South Korea with an important form of international political recognition.

The delegation found no evidence of Korean companies trying to downgrade the U.S.-manufactured content of their products in order to avoid the need to comply with U.S. export controls. However, there did seem to be an effort to increase the percentage of Korean-made components going into locally produced products, while decreasing the percentage of U.S.-made components. It appeared that this was being done for commercial and nationalistic reasons rather than to circumvent the U.S. control regime.

CUSTOMS SERVICE

The delegation met with a senior South Korean customs official, who said that his department would enforce whatever regulations were agreed to with the United States. He indicated that the Customs Service was still learning about checking shipments and enforcing export controls, but that progress was being made. The official gave examples of punishing exporters of illegally copied products that were shipped to the United States.

U.S. Business Community

Representatives of the U.S. business community raised a number of issues about South Korean business practices. They deplore (1) the lack of respect for intellectual property rights, (2) the government's "collusion" to help

Korean businesses gain advantages over foreign companies, (3) a nationally perceived need to export, and (4) an "umbilical cord" attitude toward Koreans living abroad. They also criticized the U.S. willingness to tolerate these practices.

The South Korean government has long insisted on the heavy participation of Korean companies as the price U.S. companies must pay to do business there. Much of this participation has been in the form of joint production facilities in Korea or "set aside" agreements. Some U.S. companies are reluctant to issue licenses to Korean companies because they fear that there is no way they could enforce the conditions of the license and protect intellectual property rights.

Korean Institute for International Economic Policy

The delegation met with officials of the Korean Institute for International Economic Policy to discuss a broad range of economic issues, primarily the reporting of its results to the Korean government. The institute provided a review of a number of problems currently facing the Korean economy, including the following:

- A U.S. $14 billion current account surplus, which has generated excessive financial liquidity.
- Virtually no unemployment, which is forcing wage rates to rise and causing inflationary pressures.
- Growing internal market liberalization.
- A minimal appreciation of the Korean currency.

To back up these assertions, the institute provided the delegation with a large amount of statistical data, much of it from the Korean Customs Department, which focused primarily on the consumer electronics and textiles industries.

Visit to a Samsung Manufacturing Plant

One member of the delegation visited the Samsung plant at Suwon, which manufactures computers, medical systems, consumer electronics, and miscellaneous electronics. It employs 35,000 people and covers 1.6 million square meters of manufacturing space. In addition to personal computers, Samsung expects to manufacture the Videotext system, an improved definition television (IDTV), and a picture-in-picture (PIP) system for supporting two or more pictures on a monitor screen.

MEETINGS IN JAPAN

The delegation held a number of meetings in Tokyo. These included discussions with the Ministry of International Trade and Industry (MITI), the Ministry of Foreign Affairs, the Customs Service, the Center for Information on Strategic Technology, and the American business community.

The insular features of Japanese society (including loyalty to major companies by lifetime employees) reduce the likelihood that there will be diversions of goods to proscribed countries. This applies less to the smaller manufacturers or trading companies, but it is still a factor. Because the system is based on culture and trust, Japan had, until recently, placed little emphasis on inspection and review for export licenses. The tradition has been to believe the word of the major companies and therefore licenses are quickly approved.

The shock of the Toshiba-Kongsberg affair caused great embarrassment to the Japanese government. Since then, customs checks by the Japanese government have become more extensive, paper oriented, and bureaucratic. The government has noted that these efforts have had the effect of lengthening the export licensing process for all Japanese firms.

Government Officials

MINISTRY OF INTERNATIONAL TRADE AND INDUSTRY

As a result of the Toshiba-Kongsberg affair, the Ministry of International Trade and Industry, the lead agency in Japan's export control regime, increased its staff devoted to export controls from 43 to 106 people, and has become more attentive to end-user and end-use statements. Approvals for MITI licenses (similar to U.S. distribution licenses) are now dependent on a company's past record of compliance.

One message that was repeated several times during the delegation's meeting with MITI officials was that Japan does not approve of reexport controls. The officials stated that this was a major impediment to U.S. exports to Japan and a great inconvenience to Japanese companies. They were especially critical of reexport controls applied to intra-CoCom trade. The officials urged that the United States should place more trust in CoCom members.

Japan issues 30,000 export licenses per year to South Korea, Taiwan, Hong Kong, and Singapore. This is roughly 40 percent of all licenses issued. Japan hopes that there will be no diversions through those countries, and it would prefer not to have bilateral, 5(k)-like agreements with them.

The MITI officials commented on the recent CoCom-mandated intensive streamlining of the computer, telecommunications, and machine tools lists, noting that they handle Japanese list reviews. They believe that there should be a nearly continuous, ongoing review, in addition to such special reviews.

The officials also said that they have a "system" for deciding on the control or decontrol of dual use items. When questioned further, they said that their guiding principles were strategic criticality and foreign availability and that they review performance parameters on an item-by-item basis. They also restated the "high-walls" principle (i.e., use of product characteristics to enhance the protectability of the product). Finally, they believe that priority should be given to the decontrol of finished products, and they seemed to be particularly concerned with machine tools.

MINISTRY OF FOREIGN AFFAIRS

The delegation met at the Ministry of Foreign Affairs (MOFA) with the chief of the Japanese delegation to the CoCom Executive Committee and with a member of that delegation. The delegation had wide-ranging discussions about the U.S. and Japanese positions on export controls. The MOFA officials believe that it is critical to streamline the control lists as soon as possible, with respect to both their length and their complexity.

The MOFA officials noted that the Japanese government holds interagency meetings on export control matters on a frequent, but irregular basis, and usually at the director or deputy director level. Official national approval of CoCom list changes takes place at the MOFA vice minister level. Japan would like to see intra-CoCom trade simplified, but it is concerned about how to avoid the "weakest link" problem in CoCom after European market integration in 1992.

JAPANESE CUSTOMS SERVICE

The Toshiba-Kongsberg case improved the atmosphere in Japan for customs enforcement. In particular, Japanese customs officials have become more energetic. However, "sting operations" are illegal and are regarded very negatively. The Japanese also are not likely to give their export control policies any extraterritorial reach, although Japan was considering participating in the CoCom Third Country Cooperation initiative.

The Japanese Customs Service has greatly expanded its staff and inspections since 1984. It also has improved its training methods, for example, sending customs officers to MITI so that they can learn to identify controlled equipment.

In 1989, the Customs Service made special checks on 7 percent (450,000 instances) of export licenses. Twenty-five percent of those shipments were physically inspected. Customs also maintains a watch list of suspicious companies, and exports from those companies are more likely to be physically inspected. About 100 companies are on the national watch list; the companies are graded "A," "B," or "C," reflecting the degree of suspicion. Also, each regional customs office maintains an additional local list.

All reshipments of goods with high U.S. content require a MITI license, but the Japanese government does not attempt to control items once they leave Japan. When the Customs Service has a question about shipments for export, it checks with MITI for a definitive answer. This happens with some frequency because customs officers sometimes have trouble recognizing whether an inspected item is what it is claimed to be.

Center for Information on Strategic Technology

The Center for Information on Strategic Technology (CISTEC) was created in 1989 as a nongovernmental organization concerned with research and data collection on export controls. It provides information and analytic reports to Japanese industry and government. The center has 25 full-time employees, and it maintains a large number of technology-specific advisory committees composed of some 700 members of industry and the Japanese government (mainly MITI). Fifty percent of the center's funding comes from MITI. The center was not involved in the intensive CoCom list review for computers, telecommunications, and machine tools.

The directors of export control affairs for three major Japanese companies attended the CISTEC meeting. They discussed how Japanese companies are very careful to observe both Japanese and U.S. export controls. However, all the industry representatives reiterated their displeasure about having to observe U.S. reexport controls.

U.S. Business Community

According to U.S. business representatives in Japan, the Japanese export control inspection system has changed dramatically since the Toshiba-Kongsberg affair. Pre-Toshiba, the license review was primarily to see that the application papers were in order. Post-Toshiba, much more attention is being paid to substantive issues, such as product content, final destination, and ultimate end user.

At this time, Japan may be the best CoCom partner the United States has. This is the case for several reasons. First, Japan does not want any further trade friction with the United States and export controls are an issue on which friction can be relatively easily avoided. Second, there is a great deal of embarrassment in Japan over the Toshiba-Kongsberg affair. Third, the Toshiba-Kongsberg affair has generated some genuine concerns about national security related technology transfer.

In addition, Japanese foreign policy controls on technology exports are similar to those of the United States, and the trend is moving even more in that direction. The Japanese are strongly against nuclear proliferation and against selling technology with direct military application to countries that have or could potentially come into conflict (e.g., Iran and Iraq). The Japanese are also increasingly concerned about technology going to countries that support terrorists.

The U.S. business representatives also said the Japanese are better at protecting their technology (from CoCom-proscribed countries or allies) than U.S. companies. In fact, they asserted that several U.S. companies have a long and unfortunate history of giving up their technology too readily and too cheaply.

With the possible exception of some civilian nuclear power technologies, the group offered no examples of the Japanese developing any technologies or products primarily to avoid U.S. export and reexport controls. Some thought this might have been a secondary factor in a few cases, but that it would be hard to distinguish that motivation from others that are more basic.

Finally, the U.S. business representatives thought that U.S. export controls were a secondary or tertiary factor with respect to the lack of U.S. competitiveness in Japan in particular and in the Far East more generally. Once again, basic structural and cultural asymmetries were cited as far more important.

III.
CANADIAN MISSION*

On May 30 and 31, 1990, the delegation met with officials of the Canadian government, members of the Canadian exporting community, and staff of the U.S. embassy. The discussions covered a variety of topics, in particular the following:

• The effect of CoCom and U.S. foreign policy export controls on U.S.-Canadian relations.
• The Canadian government's administration of CoCom export controls.
• The future of East-West trade controls.
• The future of non-East-West trade controls.
• The input of Canadian industries into the export control process.

The Canadian participants were well informed and clearly had an in-depth understanding of security-related trade restrictions. The Canadian officials explained the Canadian export licensing and enforcement processes and commented on U.S.-Canadian bilateral relations, as well as the state of CoCom.

---

*The delegation was headed by panel vice chairman General William Burns and included panel member John Ellicott and staff consultant Karin Berry.

The delegation was left with the impression that the Canadian government was willing to "go the extra mile" to achieve multilateral consensus, as long as the domestic imperative of demonstrating independence from U.S. policy was met. The Canadian government is also serious about proliferation controls and would continue to control Canadian exports conscientiously, even in the event of Quebec's secession.

GENERAL ISSUES

Two issues bearing on U.S.-Canadian relations were repeatedly brought up. First, the Canadians believe that the application to Canadian firms of U.S. foreign policy restrictions on trade with Cuba is not only irritating but an obstruction of what they perceive as legitimate trade. Second, the Canadians are also irritated by the U.S. requirement for an import document on Canadian munitions exports transiting the United States, particularly because the Canadians do not require import documents for U.S. munitions exports transiting Canada. Other matters of concern are U.S. controls on the reexport of Canadian goods with U.S. content; U.S. "unilateralism" in CoCom and in other control groups; and U.S. inflexibility in CoCom negotiations (e.g., large U.S. delegations with no authority to change the initial U.S. position).

Although Canadian officials thought that the CoCom High-Level Meeting scheduled for June 1990 would resolve immediate problems in CoCom, they were concerned that the CoCom process is still too slow and inflexible. Moreover, they believe the process does not adequately address such issues as the unification of Germany, the increasing threat from missile proliferation, and the surplus of arms in Europe.

MEETING WITH GOVERNMENT OFFICIALS

The meeting with government officials was hosted by the Ministry of External Affairs. Economic and commercial policy staff members of the Export Control Division made presentations on the administration of Canadian export controls as background for the discussion. Officials from the Ministry of National Defense, the Royal Canadian Mounted Police, and Canada Customs also attended the meeting.

Canadian export controls are administered under the authority of the Export/Import Permits Act. This act prohibits unilateral controls and requires that the control list be linked to CoCom. The government is working to update its legislation to take into account export controls based on such issues as human rights violations and missile/chemical proliferation. Given Canada's large aerospace and telecommunications industries, the government is particularly concerned with missile-related controls.

All export licensing is handled by the Ministry of External Affairs, although cases may be referred to the Atomic Energy Control Board or the Ministry of National Defense for review and recommendations. The Ministry of External Affairs may overrule recommendations, on notice, or forward disputes to the Canadian cabinet. Most, if not all, disagreements are resolved below the cabinet level. In addition, the ministry may determine whether a Canadian export with U.S. content requires U.S. authorization. Although U.S. regulations state a *de minimus* of 25 percent U.S. content for continued U.S. control, Canada considers 51 percent U.S. content to be the control *de minimus*.

The Atomic Energy Control Board reviews applications for permits to export goods on the Nuclear Exporters Committee (Zangger) control list or the CoCom Atomic Energy List. The Ministry of National Defense reviews both missile-related and CoCom general exception cases. The National Defense official stated, however, that the ministry typically interacts more with other countries' defense ministries on missile controls than on CoCom controls.

The Ministry of External Affairs also consults the Ministry of Defense in preparing the Canadian positions for CoCom list review. Neither the External Affairs nor the Defense ministry use any set criteria in determining what should be controlled or decontrolled.

In the area of enforcement, the Royal Canadian Mounted Police (RCMP) is the federal enforcement authority and maintains all international contacts. Canada Customs polices the borders. Customs also maintains a command and control center with an elaborate computer network for tracking export and import information. The center is used to generate information for joint investigations with the United States and other CoCom countries and for domestic investigations.

Both RCMP and customs officials stated that the new CoCom liberalization and decontrol will make enforcement more difficult because much of the paper trail that facilitates enforcement will be eliminated and they will have to re-train their personnel on the updated control list. Closer cooperation with industry, better understanding of foreign enforcement practices, and a possible control indicator on shipping documents were cited as means of improving enforcement.

On a more conceptual level, Canadian officials anticipated that the upcoming CoCom High-Level Meeting would resolve immediate problems, but would not address other major issues looming on the horizon, for example, German unification and increasing chemical, nuclear, and missile proliferation. They expressed the view that, while it might be useful for CoCom to address proliferation issues administratively, it would be impossible for CoCom to change its political or diplomatic focus. They also believe that linking trade sanctions to compliance with export controls was counterproductive.

MEETING WITH INDUSTRY REPRESENTATIVES

The representatives of Canadian industry were primarily senior officials within their respective companies, and they demonstrated a much greater understanding of export controls than that typically found among their U.S. counterparts. This was due, in part, to an industry-government employee exchange program that both industry and government believe is very beneficial.

Canadian Export Association

Approximately 20 Canadian firms were represented by senior executives in a meeting organized by the Canadian Export Association. In general, the group viewed export controls as a restriction on legitimate business, and they questioned whether export controls really address security concerns or are a mechanism for protecting markets. They believe that the primary determining factor in licensing a sale should be the end use, not the technical capabilities, of a product. They pointed out that the loss of profit and name recognition from forgone sales eventually precludes technological lead.

Specific complaints voiced by the group included the time delays inherent in license review and the fact that differing interpretations of the CoCom Industrial List by member countries create an "unlevel playing field." The telecommunications representatives said that controls on computers were much more liberal than those on telecommunications due to pressure from U.S. computer exporters.

The group also noted that U.S. *and* Canadian reexport restrictions were an irritant. The United States actually requires licenses for some reexports, but the Canadian government expects exports to be "significantly consumed" at the original export destination. The participants did not think that exporters should be responsible for the activities of the importers after completion of the initial sales transaction.

On the positive side, the industry representatives thought that there had been significant improvement in both Canadian and CoCom licensing procedures in the past three years. They attributed much of the improvement in Canadian administration to the government-industry employee exchange program. As part of this program, an exporting firm may detail an employee to a government agency for up to three years. Government employees may similarly be placed in private firms. (The salary differential between the government and private sectors is minimal.) The exchange program allows the government to draw on specific, up-to-date expertise in a particular product category and enables industry to learn government procedures.

Canadian Aerospace Industries Association

The delegation met with the president and two vice-presidents of the Canadian Aerospace Industries Association (CAIS). The Canadian aerospace industry is primarily a supplier industry for U.S. companies.

The CAIS executives believe that U.S. export controls are more liberal than Canadian controls. They noted, however, that the United States has major problems in the areas of commodity jurisdiction and distinguishing between technical facts and policy factors. They also believe that more attention should be focused on the loss of technologies through joint manufacturing ventures and foreign ownership of local companies.

Congressional Request for the Study

Omnibus Trade and Competitiveness Act, Section 2433

STUDY ON NATIONAL SECURITY EXPORT CONTROLS

(a) ARRANGEMENTS FOR AND CONTENTS OF STUDY.—

(1) ARRANGEMENTS FOR CONDUCTING STUDY.—The Secretary of Commerce and the Secretary of Defense, not later than 60 days after the date of the enactment of this Act, shall enter into appropriate arrangements with the National Academy of Sciences and the National Academy of Engineering (hereafter in this section referred to as the "Academies") to conduct a comprehensive study of the adequacy of the current export administration system in safeguarding United States national security while maintaining United States international competitiveness and Western technological preeminence.

(2) REQUIREMENTS OF STUDY.—Recognizing the need to minimize the disruption of United States trading interests while preventing Western technology from enhancing the development of the military capabilities of controlled countries, the study shall—

(A) identify those goods and technologies which are likely to make crucial differences in the military capabilities of controlled countries, and identify which of those goods and technologies controlled countries already possess or are available to controlled countries from other sources;

(B) develop implementable criteria by which to define those goods and technologies;

(C) demonstrate how such criteria would be applied to the control list by the relevant agencies to revise the list, eliminate ineffective controls, and strengthen controls;

(D) develop proposals to improve United States and multilateral assessments of foreign availability of goods and technology subject to export controls; and

(E) develop proposals to improve the administration of the export control program, including procedures to ensure timely, predictable, and effective decision-making.

(b) ADVISORY PANEL.—In conducting the study under subsection (a), the Academies shall appoint an Advisory Panel of not more than 24 members who shall be selected from among individuals in private life who, by virtue of their experience and expertise, are knowledgeable in relevant scientific, business, legal, or administrative matters. No individual may be selected as a member who, at the time of his or her appointment, is an elected or appointed official or employee in the executive, legislative, or judicial branch of the Government. In selecting members of the Advisory Panel, the Academies shall seek suggestions from the President, the Congress, and representatives of industry and the academic community.

(c) EXECUTIVE BRANCH COOPERATION.—The Secretary of Commerce, the Secretary of Defense, the Secretary of State, the Director of the Central Intelligence Agency, and the head of any department or agency that exercises authority in export administration—

(1) shall furnish to the Academies, upon request and under appropriate safeguards, any classified or unclassified information which the Academies determine to be necessary for the purposes of conducting the study required by this section; and

(2) shall work with the Academies on such problems related to the study as the Academies consider necessary—

(d) REPORT.—Under the direction of the Advisory Panel, the Academies shall prepare and submit to the President and the Congress, not later than 18 months after entering into the arrangements referred to in subsection (a), a report which contains a detailed statement of the findings and conclusions of the Academies pursuant to the study conducted under subsection (a), together with their recommendations for such legislative or regulatory reforms as they consider appropriate.

(e) AUTHORIZATION OF APPROPRIATIONS.—There are authorized to be appropriated $900,000 to carry out this section.

COSEPUP Charge to the Panel

Having carefully studied the terms of the legislation, and consulted with the relevant federal agencies, COSEPUP has developed a five-point plan of action, outlined below, that incorporates all of the major issues raised in the legislative request. The charge, as stated below, reflects the changes made at the August 24, 1989, organizational and planning meeting of the panel. Changes are denoted by brackets.

(1) The Academy panel will consider various existing and alternative conceptual approaches to the design of national security export controls, including methodologies for determining which end products and technologies are likely to make a significant difference in the military [capabilities] of controlled countries. The panel will reach an independent judgment regarding which, if any, of the alternative approaches is most viable, given (a) the changing nature of the threat posed by the Soviet Union and its Warsaw Pact allies, (b) the current estimate of Warsaw Pact military capabilities and its requirements for technology, (c) the need to harmonize U.S. control policies to the greatest possible extent with those of the other CoCom allies, and (d) the realities of the global diffusion of some technologies to countries that are beyond the effective reach of CoCom controls and, [(e) **the need to maintain a balance between the protection of U.S. (and Western) advantage in key military systems and the promotion of economic vitality and trade**]. The panel will not restrict itself to evaluate incremental changes to the current system.

(2) Based on its consideration of point one, the Academy panel will seek to develop a set of dynamic and implementable principles for determining which technologies should be subject to control and at what point technological diffusion and/or obsolescence dictates that a particular technology should be decontrolled. In making its prescriptions, the panel will take account of both "process" problems in administering controls within the U.S. government and the CoCom framework, and the [changing] global political, economic, and technological [trends].

(3) The Academy panel will attempt to demonstrate how its principles would be applied to a few selected technologies corresponding to sections of the Control List (CL), maintained by the Department of Commerce, and the Militarily Critical Technologies List (MCTL), maintained by the Department of Defense. However, because the technology subject to control is in most cases highly dynamic, such an exercise can at best represent only a "snapshot" example of what must be a continuously evolving process of list revision.

(4) In addition to the problem of technological obsolescence, the effectiveness and currency of both the CL and the MCTL are constrained by the availability of identical or functionally similar technology beyond the effective reach of the CoCom allies. The Academy panel will first seek to clarify in operational terms the meaning of "foreign availability." It will examine the process used within both the U.S. Government and CoCom for certifying the existence of "foreign availability," making recommendations as appropriate for improvements in the methodology. Finally, it will develop proposals to rationalize and harmonize the U.S. and CoCom procedures for dealing with identified cases of foreign availability.

(5) The Academy panel will continue the examination of the administration of the export control program begun in its earlier study, *Balancing the National Interest*. To the extent warranted, the Academy panel will develop proposals for new procedures and organizational arrangements to ensure more timely, predictable, and effective decisionmaking. As instructed in the report of the congressional conferees, the committee will pay particular attention to the questions of (a) how the extensive knowledge and expertise of private industry can be better integrated into all aspects of the export control policy process, and (b) how fundamental policy disputes involving questions of economic competitiveness vs. military security can be resolved in a fair, expeditious, and regularized fashion.

Approved by COSEPUP, October 30, 1989

The Evolution of U.S.
Export Control Policy: 1949–1989

Mitchel B. Wallerstein
with William W. Snyder, Jr.

INTRODUCTION

The policy of the United States with respect to the control of exports of strategic technology has reached a critical watershed. If the policy is to remain effective beyond the short term, it will have to adapt to dramatically changed political, economic, and technological circumstances. Indeed, this analysis takes the imperative for change as a given and examines the historical evolution of U.S. export control policy since the end of the Second World War in an effort to inform the conceptualization of a new policy framework.

For the purposes of this analysis, restrictions on the export of dual use technologies and munitions are treated together, except where noted. Moreover, the three major dimensions of the policy—national security, foreign policy, and (the much less important) short supply controls—are distinguished only in those cases in which their purposes or implementation has diverged, or in some cases conflicted. The interest here is not so much to establish a detailed chronology of the evolution of each type of control, but rather to identify major changes in the rationale for and objectives of overall U.S. export control policy.

THE EARLY HISTORY OF U.S. CONTROLS

The earliest use of export controls by the United States was an outgrowth of perceived wartime necessity. In 1917, the Congress passed the Trading with the Enemy Act, which empowered the President to limit economic activities severely, including exports, imports, financial transactions, investment, and so on, with designated enemy countries or nationals of those countries.[1] Although the act fell into virtual disuse between the world wars, further restrictions were added that empowered the President to impose restrictions on trade with *all* nations, not just designated enemies.*

The U.S. government did not establish an arms export control regime until 1935. In August 1935, the Congress, fearing that the nation could be dragged into war by other belligerent nations, passed the Neutrality Act of 1935, which gave the President a legal basis for controlling the export of arms. Specifically, it established the National Munitions Control Board under the chairmanship of the secretary of state. That board was the forerunner of today's export licensing system.

By 1940, the war had begun in Europe, and Congress moved to give the President authority to control the export of militarily significant goods and technology. Section 6 of Public Law 703, "An Act to Expedite the Strengthening of the National Defense," gave the President authority to prohibit or curtail the export of "military equipment or munitions or components thereof, or machinery, tools, or material, or supplies necessary for the manufacture, servicing, or operation thereof. . . ." The President was required only to determine that his actions were necessary and in the interest of national defense and to issue a proclamation describing the articles or materials included in the prohibition or curtailment.

Following the Second World War, U.S. export control policy began for the first time to assume significant peacetime dimensions. The war had created major worldwide shortages of many critical materials, including chemicals, raw materials, and food. Further, the United States was engaged in the Marshall Plan recovery in Western Europe, which increased the demands for these items. This resulted in the continuation of the wartime restrictions during the period from 1945–1947, albeit largely for reasons of "short supply." It is significant that, in contrast to the current policy rationale, national security during this period was being defined largely in terms of the sanctity of critical materials supplies, rather than in strategic, ideological, or other terms. This situation was soon to change.

---

*In the years preceding and during World War II, Congress passed several amendments to the Neutrality Act of 1935 and to "An Act to Expedite the Strengthening of the National Defense" (Ch. 508, 54 Stat. 712), which expanded the President's authority to impose controls on exports, first, to nations where civil strife existed and then, finally, to *any* nation as long as sufficient justification could be made. Though originally temporary, these acts and their amendments were extended several times until the Export Control Act was passed in 1949. For further detail, see Harold J. Berman and John R. Garson, "United States Export Controls—Past, Present, and Future," *Columbia Law Review*, vol. 67, no. 5 (1967), pp. 791–805.

THE COLD WAR AND THE POLICY OF CONTAINMENT

As late as June 1947, with the "Cold War" still only in its infancy, the United States continued to offer to include the Soviet Union in the Marshall Plan for the reconstruction of Europe.* In July 1947, George Kennan published his now-famous *Foreign Affairs* article, "The Sources of Soviet Conduct," under the "X" pseudonym, in which he argued for an active and coordinated policy of "containment" of Soviet imperialistic ambition. And, by late the following year, the United States had begun to impose export licensing requirements on the Soviet bloc countries.

The Congress formally recognized the need for continuing peacetime controls in the Export Control Act of 1949. Although controls were still seen as a "temporary" measure, the act's stated objectives were (1) to reduce continuing shortages in critical materials, (2) to aid the President in implementing foreign policy, and (3) to control items deemed critical to U.S. national security.[2] The act did not specify the particular national security concerns it was intended to address, but the accompanying Senate report stated that:

> Equally important is the close scrutiny which is thus made possible over shipments of industrial materials which may have direct or indirect military significance. In the light of growing concern of democratic nations over the policies of the Eastern European nations, it is quite clear that our national security requires the exercise of such controls to complement export controls over arms, ammunition, and implements of war.[3]

Two important principles were embodied in the 1949 legislation and have survived virtually intact through multiple revisions. First, the executive branch was to enjoy broad authority to determine what products or technical data should be subject to export licensing, to administer the licensing system, and to impose penalties for violations. Second, the rule-making process, including the composition of the control list, was (and continues to be) largely exempt from the usual process of public comment and virtually immune from judicial review.

Paralleling the U.S. recognition of a monolithic national security threat from the Soviet bloc was the establishment of the North Atlantic Treaty Organization (NATO) in August 1949. To ensure the effectiveness of NATO and the other regional alliances, the United States transferred military technology, mostly in the form of hardware, directly to its allies. And because the recovering West European countries (and later Japan) also were becoming potential sources of advanced militarily relevant technology, President Tru-

---

*However, the Soviets formally rejected the U.S. offer that same month. For more detail, see Charles L. Mee, *The Marshall Plan—The Launching of the Pax Americana* (New York: Simon & Schuster, 1984).

man sent Secretary of Commerce Averell Harriman to Europe to enlist allied cooperation in denying the Soviet Union and its allies access to such strategic technology. This led to the establishment of the Coordinating Committee for Multilateral Export Controls (CoCom) in Paris in 1949 to coordinate for the first time an explicit strategy of "technology denial" to the Soviet bloc countries. From the start, however, the items on which the United States imposed controls differed from those controlled by CoCom. That is, the United States controlled many items unilaterally, particularly those technologies in which it held a virtual monopoly.

Although Congress continued to hope that export restrictions could be removed eventually, increasing tensions within Europe—including, for example, the Berlin blockade—and the outbreak of the Korean War on June 25, 1950, left little doubt as to the need to renew the Export Control Act in 1951.[4] At about the same time, the Congress enacted the Mutual Defense Assistance Control Act, also known as the Battle Act.[5] The Battle Act allowed the United States to embargo shipments of arms, ammunition, implements of war, nuclear materials, and other strategic items to nations that posed a potential threat to U.S. national security, and it provided statutory authority for U.S. participation in CoCom.* The act also threatened to cut off U.S. economic assistance to any country that would not cooperate in controlling the export of strategic goods or technology to the Soviet Union.

By the early 1950s, U.S. and NATO strategy was firmly based on the need to contain Soviet (and Chinese) expansionist ambitions and to maintain the political and territorial integrity of the West (which, by this time, included Japan). And soon after, the NATO alliance became opposed formally by the Warsaw Pact,† which was signed on May 14, 1955.

Having financed the successful reconstruction of the European and Japanese economies through a combination of credit, intentional trade deficits, and direct aid and investment, the United States was determined to protect its political and economic investment. Moreover, because its economy and technological base were so much more robust than those of its allies, the United States was prepared and able to absorb the economic costs associated with functioning as the paragon of the Western technology denial effort. At the same time, the European countries were more focused on the need to

---

*The Battle Act was designed to increase multilateral cooperation in controlling strategic exports by enabling the United States to prohibit military, economic, and financial assistance to any country not in compliance with the act, and it provided the first codification of U.S. participation in CoCom. For more detail, see William J. Long, *U.S. Export Control Policy— Executive Autonomy vs. Congressional Reform* (New York: Columbia University Press, 1989), p. 18.

†The original members of the Warsaw Pace were Albania, Bulgaria, Czechoslovakia, the German Democratic Republic, Hungary, Poland, Romania, and the Soviet Union. Albania has not participated since 1962 and formally denounced the treaty in September 1968.

complete their economic recovery than on the potential for trade with the East European countries.

It also had become apparent by this time that, for political and economic reasons, it was neither possible nor even desirable for the West to attempt to maintain numerical equality with the mobilized troop strength or fielded conventional weaponry of the Warsaw Pact countries. This reality led the NATO countries in evolutionary fashion to the so-called "force multiplier" strategy, which sought to capitalize on Western technological superiority in order to maintain strategic parity through the development of more advanced and effective weapons than those possessed by the Warsaw Pact countries. The decision to rely on technology lead was confirmed indirectly by former NATO Secretary General, Lord Ismay, who recalled that

> the following December (1952) the [NATO] Council directed that, while the build-up should continue, primary emphasis should be placed for the future on improving the quality rather than the quantity of the NATO forces.[6]

Two inevitable implications of a strategy that depends on the maintenance of technology lead are, however, (1) a continuing need to prevent the potential adversary from gaining access to the technology, which would neutralize the strategic advantage, and (2) a continuing need to produce new "generational" technological advances in order to maintain lead times. Thus, the NATO decision in the early 1950s to rely on a strategy emphasizing technology lead also inevitably locked the alliance into a parallel policy of technology denial, a situation that has continued to the present day.

The Export Control Act subsequently was extended several times, in most cases without amendment, through 1965.* The 1962 renewal, however, did contain an important amendment that restricted the export of materials that could "contribute to the military or economic potential of . . . nations which would prove detrimental to the national security" of the United States.[7] This provision appeared to enable the President to engage in a more direct economic warfare strategy in the denial of trade to a particular country, if he deemed it to be in the U.S. national security interest.

PROMOTING TRADE AND NATIONAL SECURITY IN THE ERA OF DÉTENTE

With the advent of the era of détente and the emphasis on "linkage" between trade and other foreign policy issues, U.S. export control policy underwent its first serious congressional reexamination and revision in 20 years. In the Export Administration Act (EAA) of 1969, Congress sought

---

*The Export Control Act was renewed in 1951, 1953, 1956, 1958, 1960, 1962, and 1965.

for the first time to establish a balance between the need to protect technology essential to U.S. national security and the desire to promote U.S. trade. This change was designed, in part, to engage the Soviets in an expanded set of trade relationships and, in part, to acknowledge the growing importance of U.S. export trade to overall national economic well-being. The change in emphasis was reflected in the very name of the act itself, in which the word, "administration," was substituted for the word, "control." The EAA of 1969 was the first of many subsequent legislative attempts to limit the number of items subject to control, and it also marked the first time that Congress recommended that foreign availability of controlled items be taken into account explicitly in the licensing process.

The Nixon administration, however, did not support unilateral liberalization of national security export controls. It preferred instead to use partial relaxation of controls as part of an explicit linkage strategy whereby nonstrategic trade could be used as leverage to promote other positive changes in Soviet behavior. One of the principal concerns at this time was the growing international outcry over Soviet mistreatment of political dissidents and its refusal to permit expanded emigration of Jews and other minorities. The Congress subsequently formalized its commitment to human rights by passing the Jackson-Vanik amendment to the 1974 Trade Reform Act, which linked the granting of most favored nation (MFN) trade status to the Soviet Union and other countries to human rights improvements and liberalized emigration policies.* Passage of the act largely ended for the moment any possibility of further liberalization of the U.S.-Soviet trade relationship.

Congress also renewed and amended the EAA again in 1974, reiterating its interest in balancing the protection of national security and the promotion of trade and introducing a 90-day time limit in the review of license applications under some circumstances. The intent of Congress was further underscored in the EAA renewal of 1977, wherein it attempted (still without much success) to shorten the license processing time by setting stricter time limits for the Department of Commerce's review of license applications. Also during this period, in 1976, Congress revised the Arms Export Control Act, which regulates the import and export of defense articles (i.e., arms, ammunition, and implements of war), defense services, and directly related technical data.

THINGS FALL APART

By 1978, East-West relations had begun to deteriorate seriously, due in part to Soviet mistreatment of dissidents and foreign journalists. The United

---

*Reportedly, this amendment was largely drafted by Richard N. Perle, who was then a staff aide to Senator Henry (Scoop) Jackson.

States also had stated publicly its misgivings about the economic and security implications of Western participation in and dependence on the Soviet-European gas pipeline. These tensions were, in turn, reflected in the 1979 revision of the EAA, which authorized the control of exports of commercial goods and technologies that would make a significant contribution to U.S. military adversaries. The act also authorized the continuation of controls to achieve U.S. foreign policy objectives and reaffirmed continuing concerns about the short supply of certain strategic materials. In the act Congress also explicitly endorsed and incorporated the recommendations of the 1976 Bucy task force report to the Defense Science Board,[8] which called for a shift in the focus of controls away from end products to arrays of know-how, keystone equipment, and turnkey manufacturing facilities. Also in 1979, the Battle Act was repealed and the authority for multilateral export controls was shifted to the EAA.

From the standpoint of export controls, the period of détente clearly ended in 1979 with the Soviet invasion of Afghanistan and the mounting evidence that the Soviets had used Western dual use technology, obtained both legally and illegally as a result of relaxed trade controls, to modernize its conventional and strategic forces.* As a result, President Carter acted under the provisions of the EAA to restrict the sale of U.S. grain and to deny all pending and future validated export licenses for technology exports to the Soviet Union. These unilateral U.S. actions subsequently were reinforced by the adoption of a "no exceptions" policy within CoCom, wherein the allied nations agreed not to propose individual export case exceptions for the Soviet Union while it continued its occupation of Afghanistan.

A CHANGE IN POLICY APPROACH: THE REAGAN ADMINISTRATION

The Reagan administration entered office at a time of rising U.S.-Soviet tension and with a distinctly different view of the Soviet Union and its potential threat to U.S. and Western se urity interests. In congressional hearings and in other public statements, administration officials† and members of Congress made repeated assertions that the Soviets had moved systematically, through both legal and illegal means, during the period of détente to gain expanded access both to the results of basic research and to embodied

---

*Evidence was brought to light at this time that the Soviets had used trucks manufactured at the Kama River truck factory, a turnkey facility built by Western companies, to support the invasion of Afghanistan.

†The principal administration spokesman on the need to modify and tighten U.S. export control policy was Richard N. Perle, who by this time had been appointed assistant secretary of defense for international security policy.

technology and end products. Among the more notable examples of such statements were the following:

• "There is no longer doubt that our technology has materially aided Soviet expansion. It has improved Soviet weapons, intelligence devices, and economic leverage . . . The need for a clear and comprehensive technology transfer policy is compelling and urgent." (Statement by Sen. Henry M. Jackson before the Permanent Subcommittee on Investigations of the Committee on Governmental Affairs, U.S. Senate, May 4, 1982)

• "The concentration by the Soviets has been on illegal trade diversions and collection directly against defense contractors and high technology firms working in advanced technology, both classified and unclassified, foreign firms and subsidiaries of U.S. firms abroad, and international organizations with access to advanced and or proprietary technology . . . They are also stepping up their efforts to acquire new and emerging technologies such as very high-speed integrated circuits and VLSI technology from Western universities and commercial laboratories for both military and commercial applications." (Statement by Rear Adm. B.R. R. Inman, deputy director, Central Intelligence Agency, before the Subcommittee on Science, Research, and Technology, and the Subcommittee on Investigations and Oversight of the Committee on Science and Technology, U.S. House of Representatives, March 29, 1982)

• "We are now in a situation, Mr. Chairman, in which every new Soviet weapons system that we see is produced at least in part, and some cases in significant part, with the aid of modern technology, equipment, know-how, expertise, acquired in the West. Indeed, the Soviets have become almost arrogant in the ease with which they assert both their access to and the utility they make of Western technical solutions to their military problems . . . We in the West are facing a well-organized, orchestrated and dedicated effort by the Soviets to acquire our technology with the specific purpose of altering the balance of power in their favor." (Statement by Richard N. Perle, assistant secretary of defense for international security policy, before the Technology Transfer Panel of the Committee on Armed Services, U.S. House of Representatives, June 9, 1983)

Evidence supporting these claims was provided in April 1982 by the U.S. intelligence community in the form of an unclassified white paper, *Soviet Acquisition of Western Technology*, which was later updated in 1985.[9] And the evidence was quite compelling at that time, particularly in terms of the leakage of dual use technologies controlled under CoCom. In fact, it was subsequently revealed that much of the information contained in the white papers was based on the so-called "Farewell affair," which was the code name for a Soviet double agent who provided the French intelligence service with the actual Soviet shopping list for Western technology from 1979–1981, including targets and ruble allocations for each targeted item. On this basis, the administration contended that the West had indeed been "selling the Russians the rope" and that, until such time as there were definite and dramatic changes in Soviet military doctrine, force posture, and industrial policies (i.e., heavy emphasis on military over civilian manufacturing requirements), it would be necessary to undertake a major tightening of U.S. and multilateral technology denial policies and to maintain such controls in place.

Political pressure forced an early removal of the grain embargo that had been imposed by President Carter, but the new administration soon demonstrated that, in conjunction with its announced intention to promote a major buildup in U.S. defense forces, it was prepared to get serious about restricting Soviet access to anything, including especially advanced technology, that would help it achieve its allegedly imperial ambitions (i.e., the Reagan notion of an "evil empire"). Accordingly, a variety of actions were taken, mostly by executive order,[10] to expand the range of technologies and end products subject to control, to bolster the role of the Department of Defense in export licensing decisions* and to restrict the flow of technical information and, in some cases, people. In addition to its tightening and increased use of foreign policy and national security controls, the administration also moved to shore up and reinvigorate CoCom, which had become semi-moribund during the détente era, by pouring substantial human and financial resources into modernizing CoCom headquarters in Paris and by using its political resources to pressure the other CoCom countries into abiding more closely by the Industrial List of controlled items.

The success achieved in the implementation of this policy was due to an unusual confluence of factors, including (a) the conservative shift in the country as evidenced by the outcome of the 1980 elections, (b) the extraordinary political adroitness of Richard N. Perle and others in pressing the responsible line agencies to adopt a unified—and more restrictive—policy direction, and (c) the unusually close ideological alignment of the key players within the Department of Defense and the National Security Council staff and, of course, the President himself. Rarely, if ever, in the postwar era had a policy direction been reversed so quickly and with such thoroughgoing and far-reaching effect.

The opportunity for additional action soon arose with the imposition of martial law in Poland. The administration responded by invoking the foreign policy control provisions of the EAA and restricting the export of oil and gas drilling and gas pipeline laying equipment to the Soviet Union. The restrictions were opposed both by domestic industry, because of its inability

---

*The Defense Technology Security Administration (DTSA) was established at this time, largely at the initiative of Richard N. Perle, to bring together the various elements of the Department of Defense with responsibility for reviewing license applications to export strategic dual use technology.

to fulfill previous contractual arrangements, and by U.S foreign subsidiaries and foreign companies using U.S. parts and components.

The concept of "contract sanctity" for U.S. exporters subsequently became a major issue of debate in, and a new provision of, the Export Administration Amendments Act (EAAA) of 1985. But the extraterritorial extension of U.S. law and regulatory authority, as epitomized by the imposition of the oil and gas controls, had even more profound and far-reaching consequences. First, it led a number of CoCom countries, most notably the United Kingdom and France, to legislate "blocking statutes"[11] that explicitly prevented companies operating within the territory and under the authority of their respective governments from complying with the extraterritorial reach of another country's law, particularly when the activity in question was not illegal under the laws of the host country. Second, it reinforced and amplified the long-standing opposition in most other CoCom countries to extraterritoriality in general, with the effect that no other country has subsequently agreed to undertake intrusive end-use checks on dual use technology exports or to impose reexport authorization requirements. Finally, it "poisoned the well" (so to speak) for many years to come with the leading non-U.S. members of CoCom, who became deeply suspicious of U.S. motives, often failing (or refusing) to distinguish between unilateral U.S. foreign policy objectives and legitimate multilateral CoCom objectives.

NEW CONCERNS ABOUT "BALANCING THE NATIONAL INTEREST"

By the start of the second Reagan term, there was a growing perception, manifest both in the Congress and private industry, that the administration had perhaps been too successful in reversing the policy course of the détente period. This emerging new mood was first reflected in the debate over and final language of the EAAA of 1985. For the first time, there was undeniable evidence that U.S. industry *was* losing market share to its rivals because U.S. controls were more rigorous and far reaching than those of the other CoCom countries.* When combined with other evidence that a substantial number of controlled items were becoming increasingly available through third countries (i.e., non-CoCom, non-Communist countries), and that the other CoCom countries were not enforcing controls on "low end" controlled items that they believed (but were unable to convince the United States) no longer were really strategic, the pressure for change began to mount. As a

---

*This evidence, largely anecdotal in nature, often has been referred to collectively as "de-Americanization" of product lines, wherein foreign buyers look for alternative sources of supply for parts and components—and often for complete systems—to avoid becoming entangled in the extraterritorial reach of U.S. laws.

result, the EAAA of 1985 attempted to micromanage the policy approach to be pursued by the executive branch by calling for the elimination of licensing requirements for the export of "low end" items to other CoCom countries and attempting to place specific limits on the ability of the executive branch to deny licenses in situations in which there was demonstrated foreign availability.*

Little more than a year later, the report of the National Academies' Panel on the Impact of National Security Controls on International Technology Transfer, otherwise known as the Allen report (after its chairman, Dr. Lew Allen, Jr.), was released. For the first time, the actual scope and extent of the impact of licensing on U.S.-manufactured exports was documented. According to the Allen report, the United States exported about $62 billion worth of dual use manufactured goods under validated licenses in 1985, which constituted approximately 40 percent of total U.S. exports of manufactures in that year.[12] Moreover, a consultant working under the supervision of the panel estimated that the overall economic impact of export controls on the U.S. economy in 1985, as measured in terms of lost West-West export sales, lost East-West export sales, and other factors, was approximately $9.3 billion. These data, together with the report's blunt conclusions about the new global economic and technologic circumstances that confronted the country—and the growing importance of economic vitality to the overall security of the nation—appeared to provide the impetus for a thoroughgoing reappraisal of U.S. export control policy at both ends of Pennsylvania Avenue.

Then, not coincidentally, revelations about a major illegal sale of controlled technology made headlines just two months after the release of the Allen report. The Toshiba-Kongsberg affair, so named as a result of the illegal sale of a nine-axis, numerically controlled machine tool to the Soviet Union by the Toshiba Heavy Machine Corporation of Japan and the Kongsberg Vaapenfabrikk Corporation of Norway, neutralized the political pressure for meaningful change in the policy, while playing directly to the rising anti-Japanese sentiment in the Congress and among the general public. At its nadir, the drama was played out on the television nightly news, with members

---

*Export Administration Amendments Act of 1985, Public Law 99-64, 99th Congress, Stat. 120, 1985. The major aspects of the EAAA were that it:

— Required the President to make certain determinations and to consult with Congress in a more meaningful way before imposing foreign policy controls.

— Included a "grandfather clause" to provide immunity for existing contracts from foreign policy controls.

— Placed limitations on the Department of Commerce's power to deny applications for export of technology or goods that are available in comparable forms from foreign sources.

— Eliminated the need for licenses on certain low-technology items that were to be transferred within CoCom countries and required the Department of Commerce to expedite further the review of applications for exports to CoCom countries.

of Congress wielding sledgehammers on the front lawn of the Capitol to smash Toshiba consumer products, a scene shown over and over again in subsequent months on Japanese television.

The Toshiba-Kongsberg affair marked the end of any serious consideration of liberalizing export control policy during the Reagan administration. This fact was recognized and lamented by the other leading CoCom countries, who continued to pressure the United States for fundamental changes in both the extraterritorial dimensions of its unilateral policy and for a more accommodating position within CoCom. For its part, the Congress also continued to press ahead with yet another attempt to micromanage change in the executive branch policy under the terms of the Omnibus Trade and Competitiveness Act (OTCA) of 1988.* But it had become increasingly apparent that Congress was poorly equipped to *force* fundamental changes in U.S. export control policy in the absence of political will by the executive branch. Indeed, as an element of U.S. foreign policy, such a change could come about *only* as the result of a shift in the calculus of domestic and international political interest on the part of the executive branch of government.

BACKING INTO THE FUTURE

Whether or not one accepts currently fashionable arguments of the United States as a declining hegemonic power,[13] it is undeniable that, as the dawn of a new century approaches, the political, economic, and technologic "balance of power" in the world *has* changed. But the United States has continued to drive the vehicle of export control policy while "looking in the rearview mirror." That is to say, the U.S. approach—namely, agreeing to incremental change in national and multilateral export control policy only under severe pressure from its allies—is based on a set of assumptions about American economic, technological, and political influence that, while certainly true for the first two decades or so following the Second World War—and perhaps even as late as the mid-1970s—simply no longer reflects prevailing global circumstances. At the same time, the United States is "trapped" by its perceived continuing obligation to exercise political and moral leadership as the paragon of the industrialized democracies.

---

*Omnibus Trade and Competitiveness Act of 1988, Public Law 100-418, August 3, 1988. The export control provisions of the OCTA of 1988 focused mainly on national security controls and were divided into two main categories: (1) reduction of export disincentives (e.g., elimination of certain licenses to export within CoCom, reduction of Commodity Control List items, more foreign availability consideration, and expansion of trade with the People's Republic of China) and (2) strengthening of multilateral export control enforcement (e.g., more power given to the Department of Commerce to enforce U.S. controls and provisions for sanctions to penalize those involved in the Toshiba-Kongsberg affair and any future violators of CoCom regulations). For more information, see Glennon J. Harrison and George Holliday, "Export Controls," *CRS Issue Brief* IB87122, updated May 11, 1989.

With the advent of the Bush administration and the dramatic political changes that occurred in 1989–1990 in both Eastern Europe and the Soviet Union itself, it now appears that U.S. policy has indeed reached a point of decision. The choice for the United States has become rather straightforward: either maintain a reactive strategy, giving ground only incrementally and only when forced to do so, or seize the opportunity to forge a more proactive approach that takes account of the new global political, economic, and technological realities and the actual sources of threat (both current and prospective) to U.S. national security. There is no turning back in any case, because the old circumstances and leverage simply cannot be recaptured.

To let this historic opportunity pass by—and with it perhaps the possibility of continued effective multilateral export control coordination—would likely be viewed in the future as a policy failure of monumental proportions and long-standing consequence.

NOTES

1. Ch. 10, 6 Stat. 411 (1917), as amended, 50 U.S.C. App. Sec 1–44 (1964).
2. Export Control Act of 1949, Ch. 11, 63 Stat. 7, as amended, 50 U.S.C. App. Sec 2021–32 (1964).
3. U.S. Congress, *Senate Report* 31, 81st Congress, 1st Session, 23 (1949).
4. Joint Resolution of May 16, 1951, Ch. 83, 65 Stat. 43.
5. 22 U.S.C. Sec. 1611 et seq. (1970).
6. Lord Ismay, *NATO—The First Five Years 1949–1954* (Bosch-Utrecht, 1958), p. 93.
7. 50 U.S.C. App. Sec. 2023(a) (1964), as amended (Supp. I, 1965).
8. U.S. Department of Defense, Office of the Director of Defense Research and Engineering, *An Analysis of Export Control of U.S. Technology: A DoD Perspective* (Washington, D.C., U.S. Government Printing Office, 1976).
9. U.S. Central Intelligence Agency, *Soviet Acquisition of Western Technology* (April 1982) and *Soviet Acquisition of Militarily Significant Western Technology: An Update* (September 1985).
10. Executive Office of the President, "National Security Information," Executive Order No. 12356, *Federal Register* 47, no. 66 (April 6, 1982), pp. 14874–14880.
11. See Protection of Trading Interests Order, 1982, "Complaint for Declaratory and Injunctive Relief," *Dresser Industries, Inc. v. Balridge*, 549 F. Supp. 108 (D.D.C. 1982) (Exhibit 2). Also, "France Defies the U.S. Ban on Gear for Soviet's Pipeline to Europe," *Wall Street Journal*, July 23, 1982, p. 20.
12. See National Academy of Sciences, National Academy of Engineering, and Institute of Medicine, *Balancing the National Interest: U.S. National Security Export Controls and Global Economic Competition* (Report of the Panel on the Impact of National Security Controls on International Technology Transfer, Committee on Science, Engineering, and Public Policy) (Washington, D.C.: National Academy Press, 1987), pp. 116–117.
13. See Paul M. Kennedy, *The Rise and Fall of the Great Powers* (New York: Random House, 1987).

Judicial Review Under the Export Administration Act of 1979: Is It Time to Open the Courthouse Doors to U.S. Exporters?

Franklin D. Cordell for John L. Ellicott

Covington & Burling

In 1945, the United States had in place an extensive system of controls on the export of goods that had been imposed, temporarily it was thought, to prevent U.S. goods and technology from aiding the Axis Powers. However, the Cold War emerged from the ashes of World War II without any meaningful hiatus, and the export controls developed during the war became a fixture in U.S. trade law. At present, a number of federal statutes and administrative regulations control the export of various types of U.S. technology, goods, and services. Perhaps the most important statute governing the export of U.S. products is the Export Administration Act (EAA) of 1979.[1]

The EAA places restrictions for reasons of national security on the export of so-called "dual use" technology—that which has a legitimate civilian purpose but also can be used militarily. It also restricts exports for a variety of "foreign policy" reasons and to protect commodities in short domestic supply. The Commerce Department is charged with the administration of the EAA. The EAA, alone among the major export control statutes, exempts actions taken by the Commerce Department from the judicial review provisions of the Administrative Procedure Act (APA).[2] Thus, until only recently, Commerce Department action in this area has been nearly impossible to challenge effectively in court. The Omnibus Trade and Competitiveness Act of 1988[3] amended the EAA so as to provide some limited judicial review to exporters against whom Commerce had successfully brought enforcement actions. Nevertheless, opportunities for aggrieved exporters to obtain judicial review of Commerce actions taken pursuant to the EAA remain extremely limited.

The recent transformation of the East European states, the thawing of relations between the United States and the Soviet Union, and the evolutionary changes in the world economy all have prompted a reassessment of the effectiveness of the current export control regime in the United States. One focus of this reassessment has been whether, or to what extent, exporters should be able to obtain judicial review of Commerce Department action taken under the EAA. Some have argued, in Congress and elsewhere, that the extremely complex system of export controls places U.S. exporters at a competitive disadvantage vis-à-vis foreign firms dealing in similar or identical technology. Commentators and legislators recently have suggested that the Commerce Department on occasion has acted arbitrarily and has failed to comport with the intent of the Congress as expressed in the EAA, thus needlessly compounding the detriment to U.S. exporters.

Consequently, it has been argued that the EAA should be amended so as to eliminate the exclusion from the judicial review provisions of the APA, thereby allowing aggrieved exporters to challenge all final actions of the Commerce Department in federal court. Indeed, a bill to reauthorize the EAA currently pending in Congress, at the time of this writing, would so amend the EAA. This paper, after a brief examination of the extent to which judicial review currently is available under the EAA, evaluates whether increased review of Commerce actions is desirable.

The paper concludes that eliminating the EAA's current exemption of agency actions from judicial review under the APA would help ensure Commerce's fidelity to congressional intent as expressed in the EAA and would help prevent needless economic harm to U.S. exporters and to the competitiveness of U.S. technology on the world market. The benefits of increased access to judicial review clearly must be weighed against the executive branch's legitimate interests in preserving the value of export controls as tools for protecting national security and for promoting U.S. foreign policy goals. So long as judicial review of Commerce action under the EAA is limited to justiciable, nonpolitical questions, increased judicial review in this area is warranted and will imperil neither the national security nor the proper autonomy of the executive branch over questions of foreign policy.

AVAILABILITY AND EFFICACY OF JUDICIAL REVIEW UNDER THE CURRENT EAA

The present version of the EAA provides for judicial review of agency action only in limited circumstances. The starting point is Section 13(a) of the EAA,[4] which, with certain exceptions, exempts agency functions taken under the EAA from both the formal adjudication provisions and the judicial review provisions of the Administrative Procedure Act. Thus, Section 13(a) begins by depriving exporters of any review of adverse agency action, either judicial or administrative.

There are several exceptions, however, to the general unavailability of judicial review of Commerce actions under the act. The EAA itself provides for judicial review in certain narrow circumstances, and general principles of administrative law may allow for judicial inquiry into Commerce actions in a few instances. In general, it is far easier to obtain review of Commerce enforcement actions than of purely administrative decisions.

Review of Enforcement Actions

The 1988 amendments to the EAA created a limited opportunity for judicial review of Commerce Department civil enforcement action.[5] Section 13(a) of the EAA now provides that, when Commerce brings a civil enforcement action against an exporter for violation of the EAA or the Export Administration Regulations (EAR)[6] promulgated thereunder, the exporter will be entitled to notice and an opportunity to be heard before an administrative law judge (ALJ) as provided for in Sections 556 and 557 of the APA.

After the ALJ renders a decision, the secretary of commerce (or designee, usually the under secretary for export administration) will review the ALJ's findings of fact and conclusions of law. The secretary must, within 30 days of the ALJ's decision, affirm, modify, or vacate the decision. Section 13(c)(3) provides that the charged party may appeal the secretary's decision to the U.S. Court of Appeals for the District of Columbia Circuit, which "shall set aside any finding of fact for which the court finds there is not substantial evidence on the record and any conclusion of law which the court finds to be arbitrary, capricious, an abuse of discretion, or otherwise not in accordance with law."[7]

There is an alternative route for judicial review if a civil enforcement action results in a penalty determination. Since penalties are not self-executing, EAA Section 11(f) allows the Commerce Department to bring an action against an exporter in a federal district court to recover unpaid civil penalties ordered in a civil enforcement proceeding. In the judicial proceeding brought under Section 11(f), the reviewing court is empowered to "determine *de novo* all issues necessary to the establishment of liability."[8] Thus, if an exporter is assessed a penalty in a civil enforcement proceeding, the exporter will be entitled to *de novo* review of the enforcement judgment should the exporter choose not to pay the assessed penalty.

The Section 11(f) avenue to judicial review has existed for some years. It has become less important since the 1988 amendments to the EAA, which provide for limited judicial review of all civil enforcement decisions. In addition, Section 11(f) was never a particularly valuable means of obtaining relief from adverse agency action, because the Commerce Department could deny the offending exporter's export privileges if a civil penalty was not paid rather than go to court to collect the penalty.[9] As matters now stand, there seems to be little justification for retaining the Section 11(f) judicial review procedure.

Finally, Section 13(d) of the EAA provides for judicial review of the issuance of a temporary denial order that is similar to that available in the Section 13(c) civil enforcement setting.[10] Under Section 13(d), the exporter made subject to a temporary denial order is entitled, first, to appeal in writing to an ALJ, though in this setting a formal APA adjudication is not available. After reviewing the pleadings, the ALJ makes a recommendation as to whether the temporary denial order should stand. The secretary of commerce then may accept, reject, or modify the ALJ's recommendation. The exporter subject to the temporary denial order may appeal an adverse ruling of the secretary to the U.S. Court of Appeals for the District of Columbia Circuit. The standard of review in the D.C. Circuit here is the same "arbitrary and capricious" standard as is mandated in the civil enforcement setting.[11]

Review of Nonenforcement Actions

The 1988 EAA amendments do not affect the Section 13(a) preclusion of judicial review of nonenforcement, purely administrative actions, such as the denial of an export license. It has been suggested that there is a genuine need for judicial review of the day-to-day agency decisions that have a direct impact on all exporters of controlled goods and technology.[12] Review of such administrative actions currently is available only in extremely limited circumstances.

EAA Section 10(j) allows an exporter who has applied to the Commerce Department for a validated export license to file suit in federal district court to compel the agency to act on the application within the deadlines set out in EAA Section 10. However, even if an exporter is successful in compelling the agency to make a decision under Section 10(j), the agency may simply choose to deny the application or return it without action. Thus, the Section 10(j) route to judicial review does not provide an opportunity to challenge the legal correctness of the agency's decision. This section is of no value to the exporter seeking judicial review of a denial of a license application.[13]

"Ultra Vires" and Constitutional Challenges

There are two possible avenues to obtaining judicial review of agency action under the EAA that do not depend on the provisions of the EAA. These avenues of review should be available in the contexts of enforcement and other administrative actions of the Commerce Department. First, an aggrieved exporter may challenge an action of the agency or of the secretary as *ultra vires,* or as outside the statutory grant of power to the agency under the EAA. It now seems settled that an exporter can bring such an *ultra vires* challenge in federal district court despite EAA Section 13(a)'s apparent preclusion of judicial review of agency action.[14]

The leading case holding that EAA Section 13(a) does not preclude judicial review of agency action when that action is alleged to be *ultra vires* is *Dart* v. *United States.* [15] *Dart* involved a Department of Commerce enforcement proceeding against Dart, an exporter of electronic manufacturing equipment, for allegedly exporting certain restricted machinery to Czechoslovakia without obtaining the required export license. After a five-day evidentiary proceeding held pursuant to EAA Section 13(c), the ALJ determined that Commerce had failed to prove that Dart knew or reasonably should have known that an export license was necessary for the products in question, and on that basis the ALJ dismissed the charges against Dart. Commerce then appealed the ALJ's dismissal to the assistant secretary for trade administration as provided for in EAA Section 13(c).

As stated above, EAA Section 13(c) empowers the secretary of commerce (or a designee) to "affirm, modify, or vacate" the determination of the ALJ in an enforcement proceeding. In Dart's case, however, the assistant secretary *reversed* the ALJ's dismissal of the charges and imposed a fine of $150,000 and a 15-year denial of Dart's export privileges. *Dart* arose before the 1988 amendments to Section 13, and at that time Section 13(c) provided that the decision of the secretary would be "final and not subject to judicial review."[16] Notwithstanding Section 13(c)'s apparent preclusion of judicial review, Dart filed suit in the U.S. District Court for the District of Columbia, arguing, *inter alia,* that the secretary in reversing the ALJ had acted outside of statutory authority. The district court dismissed Dart's complaint on the ground that the EAA made the secretary's judgment final and unreviewable. Dart appealed that ruling to the D.C. Circuit.

In the D.C. Circuit, Dart argued that even if an enabling statute purports to make a particular administrative action unreviewable, that action must still be subject to judicial review if the action was taken outside of the agency's statutory grant of authority.[17] The court agreed with this argument and held that EAA Section 13 did not authorize the secretary to reverse the ALJ's determination, and therefore the secretary's action was *ultra vires* and reviewable under established principles of administrative law. The *Dart* court placed great emphasis on the "well-established presumption favoring judicial review" of agency action alleged to be without statutory authority.[18] According to the *Dart* court, "[a]bsent a clear indication to the contrary, the logical inference is that Congress expected courts to enforce this [statutory] limitation on administrative power. Especially this is so where the administrative power can destroy . . . an individual's livelihood."[19] Thus, the court held that the limitations on judicial review found in EAA Sections

13(a) and 13(c) were insufficient to overcome the strong presumption in favor of reviewability of challenges to the statutory authority of agency actions.[20]

Although *Dart* arose out of an agency enforcement proceeding, the court's rationale for allowing judicial review in *ultra vires* situations seems equally applicable to all administrative functions taken under the EAA. It appears that no court has had occasion to apply *Dart* in the context of a nonenforcement administrative action, but commentators have argued that the *Dart* holding should not be limited to the enforcement context.[21]

It is important to note the limits of the *Dart* holding. The court made clear that not every agency deviation from the provisions of its enabling statute will give rise to an opportunity for judicial review. Rather, review will be proper only when the agency has violated the statute "on its face," that is, "there must be a specific provision of the Act which, although it is clear and mandatory, was nevertheless violated."[22] Thus, judicial review on *ultra vires* grounds will not be available when the dispute is merely "over statutory interpretation or challenged findings of fact."[23]

Although it is likely that exporters may obtain judicial review of Department of Commerce actions when the actions in question were facially outside the statutory authority granted by the EAA, this form of judicial review is less valuable to exporters than one might expect. When a court determines that a particular agency action was *ultra vires,* the court will not grant substantive relief to the exporter by entering a final judgment on the claim.[24] Rather, the court will only remand the case to the agency with instructions to proceed within the bounds of the statute. Therefore, an exporter could wage a long and expensive court battle to have a Commerce decision vacated as *ultra vires,* only to have the agency again rule against the exporter, albeit in a different, procedurally correct manner.[25]

Finally, an exporter may be able to obtain judicial review of Commerce Department action despite EAA Section 13(a) by claiming that the agency action in question violates the exporter's constitutional rights. While Section 13(a) of the EAA precludes judicial review under the APA, the EAA does not purport to limit review under other statutes. Thus, it seems that the EAA would not prevent a constitutional challenge to Commerce action brought under the federal courts' statutory "federal question" jurisdiction.[26] Aggrieved exporters have raised constitutional challenges to Commerce enforcement actions on at least two reported occasions,[27] but no court has yet addressed those arguments.

The instances in which an exporter will be able to assert a constitutional challenge to Commerce Department action under the EAA will be relatively rare.[28] Because there is no general constitutional right to engage in international trade, and because agency regulation of commercial activity will seldom implicate individual civil liberties,[29] constitutional issues are most likely to arise in the setting of an enforcement action, when the potential for deprivation of an exporter's liberty or property interest could give rise to a due process challenge. But, as noted above, the 1988 amendments to the EAA now provide for judicial review of the secretary's judgment in civil enforcement proceedings.

POLICY AND LEGAL ARGUMENTS FOR AND AGAINST EXPANDED JUDICIAL REVIEW OF AGENCY ACTION UNDER THE EAA

The above discussion shows that, while exporters can obtain judicial review of Commerce Department action in certain limited circumstances, there currently is no way for an exporter to challenge in an impartial forum the broad range of administrative (as opposed to enforcement) decisions of the agency that directly and regularly affect the ability of U.S. exporters to do business. This situation raises the question of whether Section 13(a) of the EAA should be amended to allow APA judicial review of the day-to-day administrative functions of the Department of Commerce. There are several valid arguments for so amending Section 13(a), which will be discussed in turn. These arguments must, of course, be weighed against the countervailing interests of the executive in exercising discretion on matters that affect important national security and foreign policy interests and in not imposing on government resources the burden that an increase in litigation in this area might cause.

The primary argument for subjecting agency action under the EAA to APA judicial review is that the Department of Commerce on occasion has not always administered the export control regime in accordance with the provisions of the EAA and that, as a result, exporters at times have wrongly been denied permission to export goods or have been subjected to undue delay and expense in obtaining the necessary authorization. Although in certain egregious cases an exporter may be able to obtain some limited review under the *Dart* case, the day-to-day agency decisions that are most important to the exporter, such as licensing decisions, interpretation of the EAA, and determining whether a particular good is on the Commodity Control List, remain insulated from meaningful review.[30]

There is a good deal of at least anecdotal evidence that the Commerce Department has not always carried out its licensing functions as it should; the 1982 Soviet gas pipeline case and the more recent case involving wirebonders are two examples.[31] Allowing aggrieved exporters to seek judicial review under Sections 701–06 of the APA would go a long way toward preventing this type of administrative shortcoming and would help ensure agency accountability to congressional intent as expressed in the EAA.

A related argument for expanding judicial review in the export control setting stems from the changes that have occurred in the world economy since export controls were first introduced in the period immediately following World War II. During the early Cold War era, the United States was the dominant source for many types of technologically advanced dual use products. Consequently, export controls in that era at least arguably were effective in preventing or delaying Soviet bloc acquisition of these types of products. Thus, during this period the benefits conferred by the export control system arguably outweighed any detriment to individual exporters or to the U.S. balance of trade.

Today, however, the situation is not so simple. There is mounting evidence that the vast array of export controls that have developed over the years impose significant costs on the U.S. export industry and impair the ability of U.S. companies to compete in the world market.[32] Although these costs are difficult to quantify with precision, it seems reasonable to assume that they are sufficiently large to support an argument that export controls should be imposed only in the situations specifically mandated by Congress or the President, and that they should be administered correctly and as efficiently as possible. If the foregoing is true, then judicial review of the administration of the EAA is one means that may help to ensure that the controls are imposed in the least intrusive and most cost-effective way possible.

However, this clearly is not the end of the inquiry, for there are at least two government interests that must be considered. First, removing the EAA Section 13(a) exemption from APA judicial review undoubtedly would result in an increase in the costs of administering the EAA, for the Commerce Department would be forced to defend its actions in court more often than under the present law. The Commerce Department undoubtedly would raise the familiar "floodgates of litigation" argument against opening EAA administration to judicial review.

There are at least three responses to this argument.[33] The most straightforward response is this:

> The threat of judicial scrutiny of Commerce Department actions should encourage the Department to draft its implementing regulations more clearly and to document its administrative decisions more carefully. It would, at the same time, inhibit actions that are clearly inconsistent with the statute and the Commerce Department's own regulations.[34]

In addition, the well-established administrative law doctrines of standing, ripeness, and exhaustion of administrative remedies would limit the availability of judicial review to situations in which the administrative process has been effectively utilized and found wanting.[35] Finally, it bears mentioning that the high cost of litigation should have a deterrent effect on frivolous challenges to Commerce action.[36]

The second, and more substantial, argument against exposing Commerce Department action under the EAA to APA judicial review concerns the close relationship between export controls and the foreign policy and national security interests of the United States. The foreign policy judgments of the executive branch have long been afforded great deference by the courts. The executive branch, and the President in particular, are thought to be best equipped to act quickly and decisively in the international sphere, and courts are thought to lack expertise at deciding questions that are basically ones of policy.[37] The legislative history of the original 1949 Export Control Act reflects that this was at least a part of the rationale for exempting the EAA from judicial review.[38]

It seems indisputable that the fundamental decisions of foreign policy and national security entrusted by Congress to the executive branch should remain free from judicial oversight. However, this does not mean that judicial review of Commerce Department actions under the EAA could not be expanded without infringing upon the proper domain of the executive branch. An examination of other statutes that allow the executive branch to restrict exports for foreign policy or national security reasons shows that judicial review is not incompatible with effective conduct of executive branch authority.

First, the International Emergency Economic Powers Act (IEEPA)[39] provides the President with broad powers to restrict exports and to implement various other economic restrictions when the President has declared a state of "national emergency" as defined in IEEPA. The primary uses of the IEEPA powers thus far have been to respond to the Iranian hostage crisis and the Soviet invasion of Afghanistan; to suspend certain transactions with Nicaragua, South Africa, Libya, and Panama; to respond to the recent Iraqi occupation of Kuwait; and to continue the export controls of the EAA during periods in which the EAA has lapsed. Clearly, the purposes of IEEPA are as closely related to the realm of foreign policy as those of the EAA.

Unlike the EAA, however, IEEPA does not purport to negate the judicial review provisions of the APA. The court in *Nuclear Pacific, Inc.* v. *United States Department of Commerce*[40] confirmed that agency actions taken pursuant to IEEPA are subject to judicial review. *Nuclear Pacific* arose during a period in which the EAA had lapsed and the President had used his powers under IEEPA to perpetuate the Export Administration Regulations until the EAA could be reenacted.[41] The plaintiff in *Nuclear Pacific* was a manufacturer of radiation-shielding windows. The Commerce Department, acting under the temporary extension of the EAR under IEEPA, denied the plaintiff's application for a license to export windows to nuclear power plants located in India. The plaintiff brought suit in federal district court, claiming that the Commerce Department's denial of the export license was arbitrary and capricious and violative of the plaintiff's due process rights.[42]

The Commerce Department moved to dismiss the complaint, arguing, *inter alia*, that EAA Section 13(a) precluded judicial review of the denial of the license application.[43] However, the court held that, because the EAA had lapsed at the time of the suit, the reviewability of the agency's action was governed by IEEPA rather than the EAA.[44] The court went on to find that "IEEPA neither expressly nor implicitly grants the President the power to limit the jurisdiction of the federal courts."[45]

Perhaps more important, the court squarely rejected the Commerce Department's argument that action taken under IEEPA nevertheless should be immune from judicial review because of the "intimate relationship . . . between the control of exports and foreign policy and national security."[46] The court characterized this argument as simply raising the question of whether the challenged agency action constituted a nonjusticiable political question.[47] The court noted that the plaintiff merely was challenging the Commerce Department's interpretation and application of the EAR in its particular circumstances, and was not challenging any broad policy decisions of the executive branch. Consequently, the court held that the plaintiff's challenge did not raise a nonjusticiable political question and that the Commerce Department's action was reviewable.[48] The court did, however, emphasize that "in reviewing [the plaintiff's] claims the court will be careful to give appropriate deference to the policy questions [sic] which the legislative and executive branches have already made."[49]

Thus, the *Nuclear Pacific* opinion supports the argument that judicial review can exist in areas that are related to foreign policy or national security. The opinion is also significant because it suggests that the familiar "political question" doctrine should serve as the dividing line between reviewable ministerial decisions and unreviewable policy determinations. Although an extended discussion of the political question doctrine is outside the scope of this paper, the doctrine is set forth succinctly in *Baker* v. *Carr*[50] The *Baker* Court described the doctrine as follows:

> Prominent on the surface of any case held to involve a political question is found a textually demonstrable constitutional commitment of the issue to a coordinate political department; or a lack of judicially discoverable and manageable standards for resolving it; or the impossibility of deciding without an initial policy determination of a kind clearly for nonjudicial discretion; or the impossibility of a court's undertaking independent resolution without expressing lack of the respect due coordinate branches of government, or an unusual need for unquestioning adherence to a political decision already made; or the potentiality of embarrassment from multifarious pronouncements by various departments on one question.[51]

Thus, it is reasonable to argue that the political question doctrine, as set out in *Baker* and developed in the courts, could be applied as a principled means of preventing judicial infringement on the proper discretion of the executive branch.

Another example of a federal statute that has a function similar to the EAA's but does not exempt itself from APA judicial review is the Arms Export Control Act (AECA),[52] which authorizes controls on the export of defense goods and services. The AECA does not contain a judicial review exemption similar to EAA Section 13(a), and judicial review of executive action under the statute presumably is limited only by traditional doctrines of judicial restraint, including the political question doctrine.[53] It seems self-evident that the national security and foreign policy considerations involved in the administration of the AECA are at least as important and sensitive as those underlying the EAA.

A final argument for opening Commerce Department decisions under the EAA to judicial review under the APA despite the EAA's relation to foreign policy involves the standard of review of agency action under the APA. Section 706 of the APA governs the scope of review under the APA, and provides in relevant part as follows:

> To the extent necessary to decision and when presented, the reviewing court shall decide all relevant questions of law, interpret constitutional and statutory provisions, and determine the meaning or applicability of the terms of an agency action. The reviewing court shall—
> (1) compel agency action unlawfully withheld or unreasonably delayed; and
> (2) hold unlawful and set aside agency action findings, and conclusions found to be—
> (A) arbitrary, capricious, an abuse of discretion, or otherwise not in accordance with law; . . .
> (E) unsupported by substantial evidence in a case subject to Sections 556 and 557 of this title [formal rulemaking or adjudication] or otherwise reviewed on the record of an agency hearing provided by statute. . . .[54]

The "arbitrary and capricious" level of review set out in APA Section 706 is relatively deferential to agency action.[55] The deferential nature of the review should help to ensure that opening the EAA to APA judicial review would not significantly intrude into the discretion of the executive[56] branch except in the most egregious instances of agency error or neglect. In addition, the level of review of agency action under the APA has been developed over many years of experience under the APA and would be a familiar standard for most practitioners and judges in the administrative law setting.[57]

THE EXPORT FACILITATION ACT OF 1990

On June 6, 1990, the House of Representatives passed H.R. 4653, known as the Export Facilitation Act of 1990.[58] Section 118 of the bill would amend Section 13(a) of the EAA so as to remove the current general exemption from APA judicial review.[59] The only Commerce Department function that would remain exempt from judicial review under H.R. 4653 is "[a]ny discretionary determination of whether a good or technology should or should not be on the control list. . . . .''[60] All other final actions of the Commerce Department would be reviewable in court; enforcement actions would be appealed to the D.C. Circuit under EAA Section 13(c), and other actions would be appealable in federal district court under the APA.

Section 119 of H.R. 4653 relates to the judicial review issue as well. Section 119 would amend EAA Section 15, which governs the promulgation of regulations pursuant to the EAA. Section 119 provides that ''[t]he provisions of this Act shall be self-executing and shall be in effect whether or not implementing regulations are issued by the agency or department with responsibility to do so.''[61] This proposed addition to the EAA is intended to prevent the Commerce Department from frustrating the purpose of the EAA by failing to implement the specific provisions of the statute with appropriate regulations.[62] Although the necessity of such a ''self-executing'' provision seems questionable, this section nonetheless would serve to emphasize that the Commerce Department cannot lag behind Congress or the President in decontrolling certain goods or performing other functions under the EAA, as has occurred at times in the past.

The Senate currently is considering its own bill that would amend the EAA. At the time of this writing, this bill had been reported out of the Senate Committee on Banking, Housing, and Urban Affairs.[63] The Senate measure, however, does not contain any provision amending the EAA so as to increase the amount of judicial review available to exporters. Further, the Bush administration opposes H.R. 4653, in part because of the bill's judicial review provisions and their potential negative impact on the executive branch's autonomy over export control matters. Thus, it is particularly difficult to determine the likelihood that the sections of H.R. 4653 dealing with judicial review will become law.*

CONCLUSION

In its current state, the Export Administration Act provides exporters with a meaningful opportunity to seek judicial review of Commerce Department action only in the setting of a civil enforcement proceeding. Because there is evidence that exporters on occasion have been subjected to needless delay and expense due to failures in the administration of the EAA by the Commerce Department, there recently has been a renewed call for an increase in the availability of judicial review under the EAA. Eliminating the exemption of the EAA from the judicial review provisions of the Administrative Procedure Act likely would benefit U.S. exporters and would restore an important check on the power of the executive branch. These benefits must be weighed against

---

*Subsequent to the preparation of this paper, the Export Facilitation Act of 1990 was passed by the Congress but pocket vetoed by President Bush on November 16, 1990.

the executive branch interest in avoiding new burdens on the Commerce Department's resources and in retaining unfettered discretion as to fundamental questions of policy. This paper concludes that the benefits of subjecting Commerce Department action under the EAA to the judicial review provisions of the APA would outweigh the possible costs, so long as review is limited by the traditional constraints on court oversight of administrative actions.

NOTES

1. 50 U.S.C. App. 2401-20 (Supp. V 1987).
2. 5 U.S.C. 701-06 (1988).
3. Pub. L. No. 100-418, 102 Stat. 1361 (1988).
4. Export Administration Act of 1979, Pub. L. No. 96-72, § 13(a), 93 Stat. 503, 531 (codified as amended at 50 U.S.C. § 2401-20 (Supp. V 1987)). This paper refers to the EAA by its Public Law section number rather than as codified in the United States Code, because this is the convention among courts, commentators, and within the act itself.
5. See Omnibus Trade and Competitiveness Act of 1988, Pub. L. No. 100-418, 2428, 102 Stat. 1361 (1988)(amending, *inter alia*, EAA 13).
6. 15 C.F.R. 768-99 (1990).
7. EAA 13(c)(3). This standard of review is identical to that found in APA 706. However, under the APA judicial review provisions, appeals are to be brought in federal district court unless the enabling statute provides otherwise. See APA 703. The drafters of H.R. 4653, discussed infra, chose to retain the provision of the current EAA that places appeals from Commerce Department enforcement decisions in the Court of Appeals for the District of Columbia Circuit. See infra, pp. 331–332 (discussing H.R. 4653).
8. EAA 11(f).
9. See *Judicial Review Under the Export Administration Act*: Hearings on H.R. 4653 before the Subcommittee on International Economic Policy and Trade of the House Committee on Foreign Affairs, 101st Cong., 2d Sess., at 2 (1990) (statement of Grant D. Aldonas representing the American Bar Association; hereinafter Aldonas *Testimony*).
10. The issuance of a temporary denial order arguably is more in the nature of an enforcement proceeding than a purely administrative decision, as such orders are issued when Commerce believes an EAR violation is imminent.
11. EAA 13(d).
12. See Aldonas *Testimony* at 5–9.
13. See Aldonas *Testimony* at 2; Aldonas and Henderson, *Judicial Review Under the Export Administration Act: Section 13 and* the *Cost of Unreviewable Regulation,* in The *Law and Policy of Export Controls* 123–24 (1990) (forthcoming book from the American Bar Association) [hereinafter Aldonas and Henderson].
14. See Aldonas and Henderson at 124–25.
15. 848 F.2d 217 (D.C. Cir. 1988).
16. *Dart* v. *United States* 848 F.2d 217, 227 (D.C. Cir. 1988).
17. See Brief of Amicus Curiae American Bar Association at 12–20, *Dart* v. *United States,* 848 F.2d 217 (D.C. Cir. 1988) (No. 86-5715).
18. *Dart,* 848 F.2d at 221.
19. Id. at 223.
20. Commentators as well have argued that Section 13 of the EAA should not preclude judicial challenges to agency action on *ultra vires* grounds. See H. Moyer and L. Mabry, *Export Controls as Instruments of Foreign Policy: The History, Legal Issues and Policy Lessons*

of Three Recent Cases 132–36 (1988) (discussing presumption of reviewability in EAA setting); Aldonas and Henderson at 124–25 (discussing *Dart* and judicial review in *ultra vires* context). C.f. Murphy and Downy, *National Security, Foreign Policy and Individual Rights: The Quandry of United States Export Controls*, 30 Int'l & Comp. L.Q. 791, 832–34 (1981) (arguing that all EAA enforcement activities should be subject to judicial review).

21. See Aldonas and Henderson at 125.
22. *Dart*, 848 F.2d at 231 (quoting *Council of Prison Locals* v. *Brewer*, 735 F.2d 1497, 1501 [D.C. Cir. 1984]).
23. Id.
24. Id.
25. See Aldonas and Henderson at 125.
26. See 28 U.S.C. 1331 (Supp. V 1987) (federal question jurisdiction).
27. See *Dart* v. *United States*, 848 F.2d 217, 219 (D.C. Cir. 1988) (declining to reach exporter's due process challenge to secretary of commerce's enforcement action); *Dresser Industries, Inc.* v. *Balridge*, 549 F. Supp. 108, 110 (D.D.C. 1982).
28. See Aldonas and Henderson at 126.
29. But see H. Moyer and L. Mabry, supra note 20, at 119–28 (discussing possible constitutional challenges to agency action under the EAA, including first amendment, due process, and the export clause).
30. See Aldonas and Henderson at 130–34.
31. See P. Ray, *Export Controls* 7–10 (rev. ed. 1987) (describing Soviet gas pipeline case); *House Comm. on Foreign Affairs, Report to Accompany the Export Facilitation Act of 1990, H.R. 4653*, H.R. Rep. No. 482, 101st Cong., 2d Sess. at 17–18 (1990) (describing wirebonders case); Aldonas and Henderson at 131–34 (describing examples of executive branch maladministration of the EAA); Aldonas *Testimony* at 8–9 (same).
32. See, e.g., National Academy of Sciences, National Academy of Engineering, and Institute of Medicine, *Balancing the National Interest: U.S. National Security Export Controls and Global Economic Competition* 116–33 (1987) (describing competitive effects of U.S. export controls); H. Moyer and L. Mabry at 149–56 (discussing economic costs of export controls on country imposing the controls).
33. See Aldonas and Henderson at 135–36.
34. Id. at 136.
35. Id.; see also R. Pierce, S. Shapiro, and P. Verkuil, *Administrative Law and Process* 180–204 (1985).
36. See Aldonas and Henderson at 136.
37. See, e.g., *United States* v. *Curtiss-Wright Export Corp.*, 299 U.S. 304 (1936).
38. See S. Rep. No. 31, 81st Cong., 2d Sess. 7 (1949); Aldonas and Henderson at 128–29 (criticizing argument that relation between export controls and foreign policy provides basis for insulation of EAA from judicial review).
39. 50 U.S.C. 1701-06 (Supp. V 1987).
40. No. C84-49R (W.D. Wa. June 8, 1984) (order denying motion to dismiss).
41. See Exec. Order No. 12470, 49 Fed. Reg. 13, 099 (1984).
42. *Nuclear Pacific*, supra at 2.
43. Id. at 3.
44. Id. at 4.
45. Id. at 10.
46. Id. at 12.
47. Id., citing *Baker* v. *Carr*, 369 U.S. 186 (1962); *Sanchez-Espinoza* v. *Reagan*, 568 F. Supp. 596 (D.D.C. 1983), *aff'd on other grounds*, 770 F.2d 202 (D.C. Cir. 1984).
48. *Nuclear Pacific*, supra at 12.
49. Id.

50. 369 U.S. 186 (1962).

51. *Baker* v. *Carr*, 369 U.S. 186, 217 (1962); see also L. Tribe, *American Constitutional Law* 96-107 (2d ed. 1988); Redish, *Judicial Review and the "Political Question,"* 79 Nw. U.L. Rev. 1031 (1985); Aldonas and Henderson at 137–38.

52. 22 U.S.C. 2751-96d (Supp. V. 1987).

53. See P. Ray, *Guide to Export Controls* 50 (1987).

54. 5 U.S.C. 706 (1988).

55. See R. Pierce, S. Shapiro, and P. Verkuil, supra note 35, at 357–69 (describing standard of review of agency action under APA).

56. See Aldonas and Henderson at 136–37.

57. Id.

58. H.R. 4653, 101st Cong., 2d Sess., 136 Cong. Rec. H-3284-90; see also H.R. Rep. No. 482, 101st Cong., 2d Sess. 50-51 (1990).

59. See H.R. Rep. No. 482, at 50–51.

60. Id.

61. Id. at 51.

62. Id. at 18.

63. See Staff of Senate Committee on Banking, Housing, and Urban Affairs, 101st Cong., 2d Sess., Committee Print of A Bill to Amend and Extend the Export Administration Act of 1979 (July 12, 1990).

A Proposal for Increased Use of Industry Technical Expertise in the U.S. Export Control Process

Paul Freedenberg

Baker and Botts

This paper examines the mechanisms by which the U.S. government obtains technical advice on U.S. and multilateral export control matters, in particular advice from industry experts. The first three sections of the paper describe, respectively, how technical advisory committees, technical working groups, and technical task groups function. The final section discusses problems with the current technical advisory system and recommends changes in the system in order to increase the participation of industry experts in decision making on U.S. technology transfer policy.

ROLE OF THE TECHNICAL ADVISORY COMMITTEES

Section 5(h) of the Export Administration Act (EAA) of 1979, as amended, mandates the existence of technical advisory committees (TACs) and charges them with the task of advising and assisting the executive branch of the U.S. government in matters relating to export controls. The secretary of commerce can establish a TAC on receipt of a request for such a committee from substantial segments of an industry that produces goods or technical data subject to export controls. The TACs enable private individuals from industry to discuss their concerns directly with government officials and to attempt to provide some perspective on national security issues in light of U.S. worldwide competitiveness.

Currently, there are 10 TACs, as follows:

1. Automated Manufacturing Equipment (AMETAC)

2. Computer Peripherals, Components, and Related Test Equipment (CPTAC)
3. Computer Systems (CSTAC)
4. Electronic Instrumentation (EITAC)
5. Materials (MATTAC)
6. Biotechnology (BIOTAC)
7. Semiconductor (SEMITAC)
8. Telecommunications Equipment (TETAC)
9. Transportation and Related Equipment (T&RETAC)
10. Militarily Critical Technologies List Implementation (MITAC)

Each TAC consists of representatives of U.S. industry and government, including representatives from the Departments of Commerce, Defense, and State, the intelligence community, and, at the discretion of the secretary of commerce, other departments and agencies of the U.S. government. A large majority (about 90 percent) of the representatives on each TAC are from industry. No industry representative, however, may serve on a TAC for more than four consecutive years. Thus, in order to obtain broader participation, the benefit of experience and expertise is sacrificed.

TAC Responsibilities and Authority

As outlined in Section 5(h) of the EAA, the tasks of the TACs are as follows:

1. To provide advice and information with respect to questions involving technical matters related to the particular TAC's area of expertise.
2. To provide information on worldwide availability and utilization of production technology.
3. To advise with respect to licensing procedures that affect the level of export controls applicable to any goods or technology.
4. To assist in the periodic review of the Commodity Control List.
5. To play a role in the revision of qualification requirements for minimum thresholds for any goods eligible for export under a distribution license.
6. To review draft regulations prior to their issuance.
7. To assist in the review of export control regulations and the Commodity Control List in order to determine how compliance with their provisions can be facilitated by simplifying the regulations or the list.
8. To advise the President with respect to the likely effect of the imposition of export controls for foreign policy purposes.

The TACs are also involved in the review of applications for U.S. export licenses and applications for approval by the Coordinating Committee for Multilateral Export Controls (CoCom) of exports from other CoCom countries. Each of the 10 TACs focuses on products and technology falling within specified entries on the Commodity Control List. The procedures by which the TACs perform the functions listed above are somewhat informal; there are no published regulations describing, for example, the TACs' role in the interagency review of proposed regulations.

The TAC program is administered by the Office of Technology and Policy Analysis (OTPA) of the Department of Commerce's Bureau of Export Administration (BXA). The OTPA coordinates the activities of the TACs and assists them with administrative and secretarial support. In addition, an OTPA representative is assigned to each TAC to provide policy guidance.

The agencies of the U.S. government are under no obligation to adopt recommendations of the TACs. The role of the TACs is to inform policymakers fully on the technical aspects of a particular license or commodity list entry so that their decisions will be based on knowledge of all relevant facts. Consequently, policymakers are free to ignore the advice and even the factual findings of the TACs. This has led some TAC members to criticize policymakers involved in the export control process for failing to respect and reasonably adopt the recommendations and findings of the TACs.

Recently, however, steps have been taken to strengthen the role of the TACs in the export control process. It has clearly been the intention of Congress that the TACs have a central role in the formulation and application of the U.S. export control regime. For instance, amendments to the EAA contained in the Omnibus Trade and Competitiveness Act of 1988 attempted to increase and strengthen the role of the TACs in the activities listed above. Also, the TACs have been put under the control of the Office of the Deputy Assistant Secretary of Commerce, a move intended to give the TACs more visibility and prestige. In addition, the Department of Commerce is in the process of writing a TAC handbook, which will, for the first time, delineate the particular procedures that the TACs and other government agencies are to adhere to in implementing those provisions of the EAA that describe the duties of the TACs.

During 1989, the TACs began to become more involved in U.S. participation within CoCom. For instance, an industry representative from one of the TACs has been participating in CoCom negotiations in Paris. (This is such a new concept that travel reimbursement has not been authorized, and the industry representatives on a TAC must pay their own travel expenses.) The TACs are also involved in the U.S. review of particular license applications brought to CoCom by other governments.

TAC Meetings

Roughly 80 TAC meetings are held annually. Meetings are generally announced in the *Federal Register* at least two weeks prior to the date on which the meeting is to be held. These meetings are open to the public, except when the TAC is reviewing (a) specific applications for licenses to export from the United States; (b) specific applications that were brought to CoCom by a foreign government and are being reviewed by the U.S. government, or (c) confidential government proposals to decontrol certain technology. Most frequently, meetings are "partially closed." This means that the public may attend as much of the meeting as is concerned with matters other than a specific application or confidential government proposals; when the TAC members begin to discuss confidential matters, members of the public are asked to leave. Unless a meeting is "closed," the public is invited to participate in the meeting, and members of the public may present papers or comments during the meeting. Often, members of the public provide briefing papers that are distributed to TAC members prior to a meeting so that each TAC member can read and consider the paper prior to the scheduled meeting. As companies have become aware of the role of the TACs in export administration, and as the role of the TACs has continued to expand, representatives from the public have more frequently participated in TAC meetings.

The Militarily Critical Technologies List

The Militarily Critical Technologies List (MCTL) is an outgrowth of a recommendation made by J. Fred Bucy of Texas Instruments to the Defense Science Board in 1976. A Defense Science Board task force chaired by Dr. Bucy proposed that the Department of Defense maintain a list of strategically critical elements, such as arrays of know-how; keystone manufacturing, inspection, and test equipment; keystone materials; goods accompanied by sophisticated know-how; and items of intrinsic military utility.[1] Section 5(d) of the Export Administration Act of 1979 (as amended) provides the authority for the secretary of defense to maintain such a list. The basic concept of the list is to focus control on technology and critical manufacturing know-how rather than on finished products.

ROLE OF TECHNICAL WORKING GROUPS

Technical Working Groups (TWGs) were established by the Institute for Defense Analyses (IDA) under contract to the Department of Defense. The TWGs are composed of knowledgeable technical persons from various elements of the Departments of Defense, Energy, Commerce, and State, other governmental agencies, industry, and academia. Membership in the TWGs is about evenly divided between members of industry/academia and government. Each TWG is responsible for a specific category, or group of categories, on the MCTL and for identifying technologies of a militarily critical nature in its area of responsibility. The TWG's job is to ensure that timely recommendations are made to set in motion the process of bringing such technologies under export control or decontrol. The TWGs also assist in assessing foreign capabilities in the technologies they are charged with monitoring. Inclusion of industry representatives in the TWGs provides for an interchange between industrial experts and technical experts from the government.

Currently, there are 12 TWGs; their organization parallels that of the 12 technical task groups (discussed below) established by the Department of State. They are as follows:

- Chemical and Materials (TWG1)
- Transportation (TWG2)
- Telecommunications (TWG3)
- Avionics, Navigation, Naval Equipment and Identification (TWG4)
- Semiconductors and Electrical Components (TWG5)
- Instrumentation (TWG6)
- Computers (TWG7)
- Industrial Manufacturing and Process Control Equipment (TWG8)
- Systems and Munitions (TWG9)
- Foreign Capabilities (TWG10)
- Nuclear Energy Systems (TWG11)
- Biotechnology (TWG12)

TWG Responsibilities and Authority

Each of the TWGs is responsible for accomplishing the necessary analysis and actions required to update and implement the portions of the MCTL for which it is responsible. The TWGs as a body must also ensure that any actions taken that affect other sections of the MCTL are coordinated with the other TWGs concerned. Some of the specific TWG member responsibilities are as follows:

1. Provide analysis and technical assessment for use in drafting MCTL items, CoCom proposals, or language for Department of Commerce implementation of the MCTL in West-to-East or West-to-West regulations.
2. Prepare drafts of MCTL items.
3. Assist in drafting technical proposals for CoCom.
4. Assist in drafting Export Administration Regulations.
5. Review and assist in resolving user comments on draft documents.
6. Review proposals from other TWGs and committees.
7. Provide information on foreign technology and products.
8. Arrange for regular attendance at meetings. Recommend new members or alternates.

9. Assist, as requested by the chairperson, in acquiring information on subject matter or other technical areas within the member's organization or agency.

10. Provide notice of emerging technologies they become aware of during their normal course of work or research, to include a short summary of the technology of concern.

11. Act as technical advisors for Department of State list review meetings and CoCom sessions when requested.

12. Provide unique information and briefings to other committee members.

Each TWG is responsible for ensuring that action is taken to prepare and forward to the appropriate technical task group technical proposals that implement its portion of the MCTL.[2]

TWG Membership and Application Process

The chairperson for each TWG is appointed by the IDA director of critical technologies and has overall responsibility for the operation of that TWG and any subgroup or subcommittee formed to support it. This general responsibility entails many specific responsibilities, including staffing the TWG with knowledgeable and technically competent members from industry, academia, and the government. The size of each TWG and the makeup of the membership are the responsibility of each chairperson.

Members of the TWGs are selected for their high degree of competence in their technical areas. Each member must volunteer his or her services and agree to participate actively in the technical activities of the TWG. The members must also possess a Secret security clearance.

TWG Meetings

Meetings of the TWGs are usually held at the IDA facilities in Alexandria, Virginia. Occasionally, meetings are held at other locations in the United States. These off-site meetings facilitate attendance of technical experts who may be concentrated in a geographical area remote from IDA; they also give TWG members an opportunity to tour facilities where the technology or products under consideration are being developed, manufactured, or used. Detailed minutes of the meetings are furnished to all attendees and certain key government and industry management personnel. A meeting coordinator at IDA provides administrative support.

TWG meetings are normally attended only by TWG members who possess a Secret security clearance. From time to time, unclassified TWG meetings are held so that a wide range of U.S. personnel from academia and industry who do not possess security clearances can participate. On selected occasions, open meetings are held on such subjects as optics and computer software. Non-U.S. personnel in industry and academia are free to participate in these open meetings.

ROLE OF TECHNICAL TASK GROUPS

The technical task groups (TTGs), or their individual members, also assist in identifying technical experts or serve as technical experts to support the U.S. delegation to CoCom during negotiation of specific items. In addition, they participate in strategy sessions and assist in drafting statements, proposals and counterproposals, and other documents; participate and assist in list review follow-up actions; and track items of interest to ensure that CoCom decisions are subsequently reflected in changes to the appropriate U.S. export control documents. Some of the specific TTG member responsibilities are as follows:

1. Assist in establishing positions on appropriate CoCom Industrial List (IL), International Atomic Energy List (IAEL), and International Munitions List (IML) items and formulate recommendations.

2. Assist in drafting comparisons of proposals, and accompanying commentary as necessary, to facilitate consideration of current drafts of proposals.

3. Furnish technical advice during the consideration of proposals forwarded by other TTGs for coordination.

4. Review, evaluate, and make recommendations as to U.S. positions on proposals of other CoCom nations.

5. Review and resolve user comments on draft documents.

6. Evaluate IL and IML coverage of new and emerging technologies.

7. Assist in the preparation of an overview and substantive discussion memorandum for delegation members of items of TTG responsibility prior to each negotiating session.

8. Recommend technical experts and other support staff to be available to support the U.S. delegation during negotiations of specific CoCom items.

9. Participate in strategy sessions and assist in drafting statements, proposals and counterproposals, minutes and summaries, cables, records of discussions, and other documents as required.

10. Prepare and maintain during CoCom negotiations a current status summary.

11. Redraft and resubmit proposals as necessary in light of comments and concerns of other CoCom nations expressed during negotiations.

12. Participate in and assist in list review follow-up actions.

13. Track items of interest to ensure that CoCom decisions are subsequently reflected in changes to the International Traffic in Arms Regulations, the Commodity Control List, and the list of nuclear equipment and materials

controlled under the licensing authority of the Nuclear Regulatory Commission.

The TTGs are also responsible for evaluating coverage of new and emerging technologies on the Industrial List and for formulating recommendations for new or revised coverage as necessary.

TTG members are all government personnel; a chairperson is chosen from the participating government agencies and formally designated by the Department of State. Industry representatives may serve as advisors to TTGs at the discretion of the chairperson. Each TTG has an IDA-provided technical advisor to its senior Defense Department representative, who assists in preparation of U.S. proposals to CoCom, the defense of proposals during negotiations, and other secretariat functions.

DISCUSSION AND RECOMMENDATIONS

The MCTL became a useful guide to the strategic value of dual use technology and products. It is an encyclopedia of critical technology, substantially longer than the Commodity Control List it was designed to guide. The MCTL is less relevant today, however, in the wake of the June 1990 CoCom High-Level Meeting and the political decision by the President to reduce the CoCom list of controlled commodities to a bare minimum (i.e., a "core" list).

It would be useful for the TWGs to continue to meet from time to time to update the MCTL and to do whatever special studies of dual use technologies the Departments of State and Defense think appropriate. However, because of the need for clarity and predictability as to the appropriate place for industry technical input into the U.S. export control process, it should be made clear that the Commerce Department's TAC system is the appropriate entry point for industry input and advice on key policy issues, such as the technical parameters of the U.S. and CoCom control lists.

It is important not to have a situation in which there are dueling industry experts. As a consequence, the TACs must be the focal point for industry input into list formulation and advice on specific CoCom licensing cases. Other sources of expertise are available to the U.S. government, such as the scientists and technicians of the armed services and national laboratories, but there is no inherent value in spreading industry expertise throughout the U.S. government. This does not mean that the U.S. government should stop recruiting industry experts to participate in the TWGs, but it should be made clear that the key entity for industry input into the CoCom list review process is the TAC. That clarification will also raise the morale of TAC members, thereby aiding in the recruiting process for that advisory group.

The European system for drawing on industry expertise is far less formal than that of the United States. For more than a decade, Philips, the premier

Dutch electronics company, has provided a technical representative for the Dutch CoCom delegation. Similarly, Siemens of West Germany has long provided technical experts for the German CoCom delegation, and International Computers Limited (ICL) has furnished similar expertise to the British team at CoCom. Although the European system is far less formal and administratively less transparent than that of the United States, no complaints have surfaced from other companies in those countries that the firms have taken unfair advantage of their position. Such suspicions, however, have frequently been voiced by U.S. companies, who find it difficult to believe that Philips, Siemens, or ICL do not derive some benefit from insider information and special treatment.

Nonetheless, the U.S. government has had a long tradition of bending over backwards to avoid giving even the appearance of favoring one U.S. company over another. Obviously, the informal European system is fraught with the danger of at least the appearance if not the reality of conflict of interest. Since there are at least two or three, and many times a half-dozen or more, major firms doing business in each of the major categories of the Commodity Control List (computers, telecommunications, electronic components, machine tools, and so on), it would seem unfair and arbitrary to single out an expert from one firm to be the industry advisor to the U.S. government. In every major category, there is the danger of one firm seeming to gain an unfair advantage through participation in CoCom. That is why it was not until 1989 that TAC representatives were asked to participate in ongoing CoCom negotiations, and even then it was done under strict guidelines that kept them from learning individual firm identities in cases before CoCom and from dealing with specific foreign licensing cases.

It is possible for industry expertise to be provided during CoCom negotiations, but with the U.S. system and regulatory framework, such expertise has to be carefully circumscribed. The conditions for industry representatives' involvement, a clear and open process for nominating those individuals, and an explicit statement of the areas in which they cannot participate would facilitate the creation of a permanent industry advisory system at CoCom headquarters. After the establishment of such rules, utilizing TAC chairpersons (or their designees) with a Secret security clearance ought to be quite easy if there is the political desire and will to do so.

The TACs have been an important yet grossly underutilized asset of the Commerce Department. The major reason behind this underutilization is a problem of management. The TACs meet several times a year. They frequently come forward with detailed recommendations for changes in the CoCom control list or with recommendations regarding the determination of foreign availability. All too often their recommendations have, for all intents and purposes, been ignored. That is, either their recommendations for list changes have not been raised by the Commerce Department in interagency meetings, or their recommendations for change have been voted down. Sometimes their foreign availability recommendations have been sent back to the Office of Foreign Availability in the Commerce Department. There, they have either died a slow bureaucratic death of endless debate, or they have not been acted on in a sufficiently timely manner so as to demonstrate to the TAC members that their proposals (or opinions) had an effect on policy.

This nonaction, in turn, has led to a loss of morale, to a sense that the hard work and long hours went for naught. Inevitably, there has been a demoralizing effect on the entire process. Senior engineers and officials of high-tech companies are not likely to want to devote their time and effort to a process that has no visible result. Eventually, they drop out, or they recommend against TAC membership to their talented colleagues. Sometimes they will simply miss meetings, or they will not put in the effort necessary to construct quality recommendations. Whatever the mode, the TAC process is undermined and diminished. Perhaps these individuals should have been counseled to have patience and to keep plugging away. But most engineers and members of high-tech industries do not have the patience and tenacity necessary to operate at the slow pace of government decision making.

Some of the problem stems from the fact that during the 1980s, the U.S. government (or at least the Department of Defense) had decided, as a matter of policy, not to decontrol—or even downgrade the CoCom classification of—any product involved in the manufacture of semiconductors. That would explain why recommendation after recommendation for change in the semiconductor manufacturing equipment list was ignored or fell into the bureaucratic "black hole" of interagency review, never to be heard of again. The simplest solution to this problem would have been to communicate frankly with the members of the SEMITAC, to tell them that it was highly unlikely that their recommendations would be acted on. Instead, the SEMITAC met several times a year, took up the time and effort of some of the leading semiconductor engineers of some of the leading manufacturers in the country, such as Intel and Hewlett-Packard, yet failed to have any visible result in terms of either list revisions or foreign availability decontrols (with the notable exception of the famous silicon wafer saw decontrol in 1987).

Fundamental changes are needed in the way the Commerce Department manages and utilizes the TACs. First, the status of the TACs and the level of their interaction with officials of the Commerce Department must be enhanced. Currently, TACs and their chairpersons interact with mid-level staff of BXA's Office of Technology and Policy Analysis. By contrast, members of the President's Export Council, Subcommittee on Export Administration (PECSEA) have regular (at least quarterly) meetings with officials at the level of under secretary or assistant secretary in the Bureau of Export Administration. Frequently, equally high-level officials of the International Trade Administration (ITA) join the meetings. It would be difficult to have this level of interaction for every member of the eight TACs. But an umbrella—or super-TAC—committee of TAC chairpersons could be formed and could have the same interaction with BXA and ITA officials, as well as the secretary of commerce, who has traditionally addressed the PECSEA annually. Increased interaction and feedback would have the immediate result of raising morale. This, in turn, would help the recruitment process. It also would enable TAC members to get policy-level feedback (and, as appropriate, commitments) on their proposals, so that the unfortunate history of the SEM-ITAC would not be likely to be repeated in the 1990s.

With regard to middle management of the TAC process, a new position, director of the technical analysis division, should be established at the Senior Executive Service (super-grade) level. Until there is a senior executive with the responsibility for the overall Commerce Department positions on CoCom list review proposals, the TACs will not have the focus and the status they deserve. The current director of the Office of Technology and Policy Analysis simply has too many other responsibilities to devote the time and attention necessary to coordinate and integrate the TACs into the Commerce Department's CoCom list review process.

Once the new director is established, the top priority should be the integration of the TAC chairpersons into the drafting of the CoCom list review positions. This would include full participation in State Department TTG discussions. This happened in November and December 1988 and during the 1990 core list discussions, but it has not been institutionalized and there could easily be backsliding into nonparticipation once again.

At the same time that the status enhancement and integration of the TACs into the policy process are accomplished, it would also be appropriate to depoliticize and centralize the TAC nomination process. Although TAC members have historically been viewed as highly specialized technical advisors, TAC membership is sometimes the result of partisan political payoff. The TAC chairpersons, who must utilize the talents of committee members to formulate TAC positions, have virtually no role in the selection process. Almost as bad, the political clearance process slows still further an already long security clearance process.

If the TAC chairpersons are to be upgraded and integrated into the Commerce Department/BXA policy process and have a voice in the State Department list review process, it makes sense to retain the political clearance process for those individuals. The only justification for extending that political clearance to the other TAC committee members would be for the purpose of extending the number of political plums available to the victorious presidential party—hardly the sort of reasoning that should guide those concerned about improving the technical expertise available to the nation's CoCom team.

Finally, if the TACs do become an integral part of the CoCom list review process, full compensation should be arranged for all travel expenses, particularly to Paris to participate in CoCom deliberations. The next few years are likely to be a time of austerity with regard to government expenditures, but surely the government can ensure that those who volunteer their time and technical expertise do not also have a special tax placed on them instead of repayment for their expenses.

The changes that have been outlined above would be quite easy to implement. They are fully in keeping with the legislative intent of the Export Administration Act and the Omnibus Trade and Competitiveness Act of 1988 with regard to the consultation process for control list changes and CoCom list review proposals. There is likely to be resistance from other agencies, particularly the Defense Department, as the TACs are fully integrated into the process both in Washington and in Paris. However, it is clear that the current approach to utilizing the TACs has repeatedly failed. Indeed, it has alienated and, at times, infuriated members of the business community who have volunteered their time and effort to the U.S. government. The government should do better. The implementation of these proposals will start that process.

ALTERNATIVE MECHANISMS

Are there any better mechanisms for involving high-level industrial leaders in technology transfer policy decisions than through the current advisory process? The answer is "probably not." There is no reason to invent a new mechanism when all that needs to be done is to streamline, focus, and manage better the current technical advisory system. If the companies affected by export controls recognize that the participation of their high-level engineers has a measurable payoff in improving the export control system under which they operate, the top executives in those companies will authorize the funds and identify the appropriate individuals to participate in the TACs. The current TAC participation in formulating the core list of CoCom-controlled products and technologies, scheduled to be completed by Spring 1991, may very well convince key members of industry that TAC participation does make a difference. Such a positive experience should do more to enhance future participation than all the structural changes and promises the U.S. government could make. As suggested above, a number of key improvements in the technical advisory system should be made, but the key to a well-functioning system in the future is a genuine commitment on the part of the Commerce Department—and, indeed, the U.S. government—to involve industry representatives in the review process, to give them appropriate feedback on their advice and counsel, and ultimately, to act on their suggestions for improvements in the control lists and their implementation.

NOTES

1. U.S. Department of Defense, Office of the Director of Defense Research and Engineering, *An Analysis of Export Control of U.S. Technology—A DoD Perspective* (Report of the Defense Science Board Task Force on Export of U.S. Technology) (Washington, D.C.: U.S. Government Printing Office, 1976).
2. For more information, see U.S. Department of Defense, Office of the Under Secretary of Defense (Acquisition), *The Militarily Critical Technologies List*, Vol. 1, *List of Militarily Critical Technologies* (Washington, D.C.: U.S. Government Printing Office, 1989).

Some Details on the Proposed Method for List Construction and Review

Chapter 10 outlined a general framework for approaching the problem of list construction and review. It included the following basic elements:

1. Identification of items of potential concern.
2. A rank ordering and weighting of items in terms of the security risks posed by trade in each item, with careful consideration given to the controllability of items.
3. An approximate rank ordering and weighting of items in terms of the economic and foreign policy costs of restricting trade in each item of concern.
4. A policy judgment as to how risks and benefits should be balanced.
5. A comparison of benefits and costs and a sorting into controlled and uncontrolled items.

The panel did not consider it appropriate to make the detailed policy and administrative judgments that would be required to spell out all the operational details of such a system. This appendix, however, provides brief additional discussion of three issues:

1. defining an item-group;
2. the feasibility and necessity of rank ordering item-groups; and
3. the use of quantitative analysis to assist in list construction.

DEFINING AN ITEM-GROUP

To facilitate judgments about the need to control different items within a broad class of items (an internationally accepted standard category, for in-

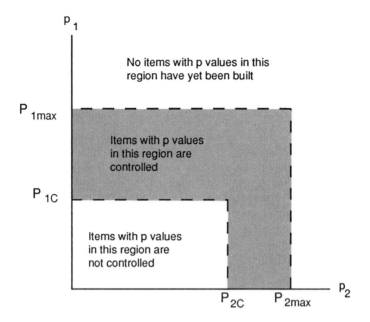

FIGURE J-1. Hypothetical parameter space for control of a particular class of items. In this example, the highest performance item of this class that is made has $p_1 = P_{1\text{max}}$ and $p_2 = P_{2\text{max}}$. Items with $P_{1c} > p_1 > P_{1\text{max}}$ and $P_{2c} < p_2 < P_{2\text{max}}$ are controlled. Items with $p_1 < P_{1c}$ and $p_2 < P_{2c}$ are not controlled.

stance, Harmonized System category 8471.91—processing units for computers), items should be sorted into item-groups.

In the current list, classes of items are controlled by specifying a set of performance parameters, such as bandwidth and operating frequency. Typically, items that have performance parameters above those thresholds are controlled, and all those lying below those thresholds are decontrolled. Suppose, for example, that for a particular class of items, I, two parameters are specified as important in making control decisions, p_1 and p_2. Items are controlled if $p_1 > P_{1C}$ or if $p_2 > P_{2C}$. Suppose that the highest performance version of I has $p_1 = P_{1\text{max}}$ and $p_2 = P_{2\text{max}}$. The situation is shown graphically in Figure J-1. The shaded portion of this figure represents the subset of items of type I that are subject to export control.

The objective in defining item-groups is to cluster items that lie in the shaded region into a finite number of groups. For example, if the controlled range of both p_1 and p_2 was divided into two equal intervals, the result would be the creation of the eight item-groups labeled I_1 through I_8 in Figure J-2.

To make the rank ordering and weighting process feasible, enough item-groups must be defined to allow distinctions to be made, but without over-

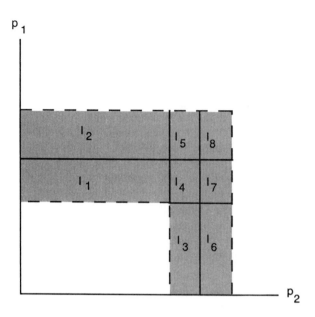

FIGURE J-2.   Hypothetical division of the parameter space into 8 item-groups, I_1 through I_8

whelming the sorting process. Also, items must be spread across groups with enough uniformity that "all the action" does not end up in a single item-group.

Item-groups could be defined in several ways:

- With fixed increments in the parameter values (e.g., every factor-of-10 increase in p_j defines a new item increment).
- By dividing according to natural "technological generations."
- By sorting specific products.

Specific definitions should be left to the technical working groups that possess this expertise. However, the procedure should lead to a sorting that has approximately the following characteristics:

1. Each Harmonized Custom code category used in the list should be divided into not fewer than 5 and not more than 20 item-groups.

2. Each item-group defined should contain at least one actual product on the market.

3. No item-group should contain more than 20 percent of the products or 20 percent of the annual sales by U.S. manufacturers in a custom code category.

4. New item-groups should be defined as needed to accommodate new higher performance items that cannot be appropriately included in the highest existing group. In doing this, boundaries around existing groups should not be changed unless required to remain consistent with the constraints outlined above.

5. As item-groups are decontrolled, boundaries around remaining groups should not be changed unless required to remain consistent with the constraints outlined above.

THE FEASIBILITY AND NECESSITY OF RANK ORDERING ITEM-GROUPS

In Chapter 10, the panel proposed that defense decision makers, with advice and assistance from the intelligence community, begin the process in the following manner:

• Place the entire list of item-groups proposed for control into rank order, from those item-groups judged to be in most critical need of control to those least in need of control.

• Allocate a finite number of points (e.g., 1,000) across the item-groups in proportion to the control desired.

Some may argue that such a rank ordering is not possible. The panel's judgment is that it is not only possible but necessary if a balancing of national interests is to be achieved. Such a weighted ordering might be done in a variety of ways. First, several broad categories might be constructed, based on the threat assessment, high-level policy guidance, and judgments of controllability. If it seems to be appropriate, a similar strategy can be adopted to achieve further refinements within categories, especially those that are most critical. Once the point is reached at which there is no clear preference between item-groups being compared, the process has gone far enough.

Details, such as selecting the kinds of analysis that could best support the necessary decision making, are best left to those who oversee the task. However, an intelligence-based analysis of Soviet weapons systems development could be useful.

USE OF QUANTITATIVE ANALYSIS TO ASSIST IN LIST CONSTRUCTION

In the list construction method proposed in Chapter 10, defense and intelligence decision makers identify dual use items of potential concern and then rank order them and assign weights to each item-group in terms of the security risks posed by trade to the targeted country.

For simple illustration, suppose that only five item-groups are of concern and the process of ranking and weighting has produced the following:

Item-group F	470 points
Item-group B	336
Item-group R	113
Item-group A	53
Item-group C	28
	1,000

The weights indicate an assessment of the relative cost to national security that would result from unlicensed trade with the targeted country in each of the item-groups.

As discussed in Chapter 10, a full weighted rank ordering of foreign policy and economic costs is not feasible. For purposes of illustration, however, suppose that it is. The communities concerned with foreign policy and international trade might produce a weighted list of the following sort to indicate their judgment of the relative costs of restricting trade in each item-group:

Item-group R	470 points
Item-group C	336
Item-group F	109
Item-group A	53
Item-group B	32
	1,000

If guidance provided in the national security directive on export controls led the decision makers doing the balancing to weight foreign policy and trade considerations with half the weight of national security considerations, the approximate net benefit of controlling each item-group could then be computed as follows:

Item-group F	$470 - (0.5*109)$	$=$	416 points
Item-group B	$336 - (0.5*32)$	$=$	320
Item-group A	$53 - (0.5*53)$	$=$	26.5
Item-group R	$113 - (0.5*470)$	$=$	-122
Item-group C	$28 - (0.5*336)$	$=$	-140

Comparing the order of this list (F, B, A, R, C) with the order of the original defense list (F, B, R, A, C), one of the important consequences of doing the full net-benefit calculation is that it can rearrange the order of items on the list. Thus, computing net benefit is not the same thing as simply deciding where to draw the line in the defense-ordered list.

Under the hypothetical circumstances illustrated here, item-groups F and B should be controlled, since the benefits of control clearly outweigh the costs. Item groups R and C should be decontrolled, since the costs clearly outweigh the benefits. Item-group A should be looked at with greater care before deciding whether to control or decontrol, since costs and benefits are fairly close.

Because the heterogeneity of foreign policy and trade interests prevents the costs of control ever being estimated with the sort of precision used in this example, such a complete benefit-cost calculation is not possible. Suppose, however, that it is possible to sort the foreign policy and trade costs of controlling item-groups into a small number of categories, such as the following (introduced in Chapter 10):

Category 1: trade with the Soviet Union in this item is of great importance to meeting U.S. foreign policy and/or trade objectives;

Category 2: trade with the Soviet Union in this item is of importance to meeting U.S. foreign policy and/or trade objectives; or,

Category 3: trade with the Soviet Union in this item is of limited importance to meeting U.S. foreign policy and/or trade objectives.

Then, foreign policy and trade decision makers might produce the following partly ordered list:

Item-group R	Category 1
Item-group C	Category 1
Item-group F	Category 2
Item-group A	Category 3
Item-group B	Category 3

Suppose again, for illustration, that guidance provided in the national security directive leads decision makers to assign no weight to any item-group ranked as category 3, and twice the weight to items in category 1 as items in 2. Continuing to weight foreign policy and trade considerations with half the weight of national security considerations, there are 500 points to be allocated across two item-groups in category 1 and one item-group in category 2. Under these conditions, each item-group in category 1 should be given a weight of 200, and in category 2 a weight of 100. A crude calculation of net benefit can then be performed as follows:

Item-group F	470	–	100	=	370
Item-group B	336	–	0	=	336
Item-group A	53	–	0	=	53
Item-group R	113	–	200	=	– 87
Item-group C	28	–	200	=	– 172

Once again, item-groups F and B clearly should be controlled, and item-group C should clearly be decontrolled. Because of the cruder nature of the estimate, the details of the case for item-groups A and R should probably be looked at more carefully before a final decision is made.

One would never want to make decisions slavishly on the basis of such quantitative evaluations of the net benefits of proposed control. However, as a "decision aid" to assist decision makers to regularize the list construction process and focus their attention on the decisions for which their powers of qualitative judgment are most needed, a quantitative approach, of the sort briefly illustrated here, could be very useful in supporting the implementation of a specific decision process within the general philosophical framework proposed in Chapter 10.

Glossary

5(k)   refers to Section 5(k) of the Export Administration Act, which requires preferential licensing treatment (''5(k) benefits'') for countries that promise to adopt the ''five essential elements'' defined by CoCom as constituting an effective export control program. The 5(k) benefits consist of the same special or general license practices that automatically apply to CoCom members.

Administrative exception note (AEN)   a CoCom term denoting the type of license that is approvable after review by national licensing authorities, without full CoCom review; also known as national discretion licensing.

Advanced materials   this category of materials covers powder metal alloys, composites, polymers, fibers, ceramics, aluminides, radar-absorbing materials, magnetic metals, and fluorinated compounds.

Australia Group   a group of 20 nations, under the leadership of Australia, that have taken steps to restrict, if not ban, the sale of chemical weapons precursors. The other members are Austria, Belgium, Canada, Denmark, France, the Federal Republic of Germany, Greece, Ireland, Italy, Japan, Luxembourg, the Netherlands, New Zealand, Norway, Portugal, Spain, Switzerland, the United Kingdom, and the United States.

China Green Line   the decision of the United States in the early 1980s to assist China with its efforts to modernize was reflected in a substantial relaxation within CoCom of the restriction on strategic technology exports to China. The level of technology approved for general licensing as a result of this relaxation is known as the China Green Line.

CoCom (Coordinating Committee for Multilateral Export Controls) a nontreaty organization that cooperatively restricts strategic exports to controlled countries. It consists of 17 member nations: Australia, Belgium, Canada, Denmark, France, the Federal Republic of Germany, Greece, Italy, Japan, Luxembourg, the Netherlands, Norway, Portugal, Spain, Turkey, the United Kingdom, and the United States.

Commodity in general parlance, any article, material, or supply. As used in this report, it refers to an item characterized by widespread availability and low cost; the term is used in association with the concept of controllability.

Core list the June 1990 CoCom High-Level Meeting produced a commitment on the part of the members to further reductions in the number of controlled-item categories. The result of this exercise is to be a sharply reduced list of controlled items.

De-Americanization the tendency of foreign companies to design-out U.S. products, components, or suppliers in order to avoid U.S. reexport controls.

Defense industrial base refers to the complex of industries, skilled personnel, and technologies needed to manufacture today's—and tomorrow's—sophisticated weapons systems.

Diversion shipment of militarily significant dual use items to unapproved end users, either directly, through the export of controlled items without a license (i.e., smuggling), or indirectly, through transshipment using a complex chain of untraceable reexports.

Dual use in the context of this report, items that have both military and commercial applications.

Eastern Europe in the context of this report, refers to the former Soviet allies in the Warsaw Treaty Organization.

Embargo a legal prohibition on commerce.

Enabling technology the data and know-how required to design and produce a product or its components. This includes knowledge regarding design systems, materials processing, manufacturing processes, or components thereof.

End use the purpose or application for which controlled commodities or technical data will be used by a consignee.

Espionage covert efforts to obtain illicitly—by theft, bribery, or blackmail—protected information or technology that is classified or of relevance to military systems.

Extraterritoriality in the context of this report, the assertion by the U.S. government that its export control regulations govern trade in U.S.-controlled commodities and technical data of U.S. origin outside the territorial boundaries of the United States.

Foreign availability   according to the Export Administration Act of 1979, a situation existing when an item comparable to a CoCom-proscribed item is available to adversaries, from non-CoCom sources, in quantities sufficient to satisfy their military needs. Foreign availability may apply to items that CoCom-proscribed nations manufacture domestically or buy freely from uncontrolled sources.

Foreign policy controls   restriction imposed on the export of items to a specified country (or countries) in order to further the foreign policy of the United States or to fulfill its international obligations (see the Export Administration Act of 1979, as amended).

General exception cases   approved sales of controlled items to CoCom-proscribed countries otherwise under general embargo.

General license   an export license established by the Department of Commerce for which no application is required and for which no document is granted or issued. General licenses are available for use by all persons or organizations, except those listed in and prohibited by the provisions of the Export Administration Regulations, Supplement No. 1 to Part 388. The licenses permit exports within the above provisions as prescribed in the regulations. These general licenses are not applicable to exports under the licensing jurisdiction of agencies other than the Department of Commerce.

Generic control indicator   an internationally standardized marking system (for example, a bar code) that might be used to identify the contents, origin, and destination of goods in trade.

Glasnost (openness)   the comprehensive strategy introduced by Soviet President Mikhail Gorbachev for political, economic, and social reform in the Soviet Union based on the democratization and decentralization of political and economic institutions; increased openness and public participation in decision making; modernization based on technological restructuring; and a new foreign economic strategy based on interdependence.

"High walls"   refers to certain end-use control techniques and to the items to which they apply. High-walls characteristics permit individual management of items and verification of their end uses. Among such characteristics are individual production and maintenance, large size and complexity, existence of internal performance tracking mechanisms, and ongoing vendor involvement in maintenance, repair, and resale.

Import certificate/delivery verification (IC/DV)   a procedure sometimes used by the United States, other CoCom countries, Austria, and Hong Kong to monitor the movement of exports of militarily strategic commodities.

Indexing a possible mechanism for review and modification of export control lists. It involves linking control thresholds with item performance characteristics so that controls on lower performance items are gradually relaxed as the performance of the item class increases over time.

Intelligence community a collective term denoting the director of central intelligence, the Central Intelligence Agency, the intelligence and counterintelligence elements of the Army, Navy, Air Force, and Marine Corps, the Defense Intelligence Agency, the National Security Agency, the intelligence elements of the Departments of Defense, State, Energy, and the Treasury, and the counterintelligence element of the Federal Bureau of Investigation.

Item in the context of this report, the units or entities subject to export controls. Items can be systems, individual products, critical components, unique or exotic materials, associated test and calibration equipment, software, and technical data and know-how.

Keystone equipment a term developed in the 1976 report of the Defense Science Board Task Force on Export of U.S. Technology, also known as the Bucy report after its chairman, J. Fred Bucy. The term is used to denote critical technological equipment, such as sophisticated machine tools, necessary to manufacture other products.

Militarily Critical Technologies List (MCTL) a document originally mandated by Congress listing technologies that the Department of Defense considers to have current or future utility in military systems. It briefly describes arrays of design and manufacturing know-how; keystone manufacturing, inspection, and test equipment; and goods accompanied by sophisticated operation, application, and maintenance know-how. Military justification for each entry is included in the classified version of the list.

National discretion item a level of CoCom control under which some items on the International Industrial List, as indicated in administrative exception notes, may be licensed for sale to proscribed nations by one member country without the approval of the others.

National security export controls procedures designed to regulate the transfer of items from one country to another in such a way as to protect militarily important technologies from acquisition by potential adversaries (see the Export Administration Act of 1979, as amended).

Neutrality Acts passed by Congress in 1935 and 1936, these acts forbade the sale of arms or their transport to warring countries once the President acknowledged the outbreak of war.

Nuclear Non-Proliferation Treaty (NNPT) a system of physical safeguards that help to prevent the diversion of peaceful nuclear energy technology into nuclear weapons programs.

Perestroika (restructuring)   an effort led by Soviet President Mikhail Gorbachev to restructure the Soviet economy from a centrally planned to a market-based system.

Proscribed countries   in terms of U.S. national security export controls, Albania, Bulgaria, Cambodia, Cuba, Czechoslovakia, Estonia, Hungary, Laos, Latvia, Lithuania, the Mongolian People's Republic, North Korea, the People's Republic of China, Poland, Romania, the Soviet Union, and Vietnam.

Reexports   the exportation of commodities or technical data from one foreign destination to another at any time after initial export from the country of origin.

Reverse engineering   obtaining design and manufacturing know-how and data on an item by study of the item itself.

Sunset provision   in the context of this report, a clause mandating the periodic review and automatic termination of an export restriction unless its continued inclusion on a control list has been rejustified and agreed upon.

Supercomputer Safeguard Plan   places restrictions on access to end use of supercomputers installed outside the United States, Canada, and Japan.

Technology transfer   in the context of this report, the acquisition by one country from another of products, technology, or know-how that directly or indirectly enables a qualitative or quantitative upgrading of deployed military systems or the development of effective countermeasures to military systems deployed by others.

Third countries   nonproscribed countries that are not part of CoCom.

Third Country Cooperation initiative   efforts made by CoCom countries, modeled on U.S. bilateral agreements, to convince third countries to cooperate with CoCom export control policies by preventing reexports of CoCom-controlled items.

Unilateralism   in the context of this report, refers to actions relating to export controls that are taken by only one nation.

U.S. Commodity Control List   the list of commodities under the export control jurisdiction of the Commerce Department's Bureau of Export Administration.

U.S. Munitions List   a list of defense articles and services developed by the Department of Defense and now maintained by the State Department with the advice of the Defense Department.

Weapons of mass destruction   weapons for use against large population concentrations, inevitably including both civilian and military personnel and facilities.

West-West trade   refers to trade between nonproscribed countries, including intra-CoCom trade.

Zangger Committee (the Nuclear Exporters Committee)   a group of signatories to the Nuclear Non-Proliferation Treaty that have agreed to prohibit the export of certain items to nonnuclear states without a pledge of "no explosive use" and acceptance of International Atomic Energy Agency safeguards. The committee takes its name from its first chairman.

List of Acronyms

ACDA	Arms Control and Disarmament Agency
ACEP	Advisory Committee on Export Policy
AEA	Atomic Energy Act
AECA	Arms Export Control Act
AEN	administrative exception note
ALJ	administrative law judge
APA	Administrative Procedure Act
ASIC	application specific integrated circuit
BMW	Bayerische Motor Werke
BXA	Bureau of Export Administration
CAD/CAE	computer-assisted design/computer-assisted engineering
CAD/CAM	computer-assisted design/computer-assisted manufacturing
CCL	Commodity Control List
CFE	Conventional Forces in Europe (treaty)
CMEA	Council for Mutual Economic Assistance
CoCom	Coordinating Committee for Multilateral Export Controls
COSEPUP	Committee on Science, Engineering, and Public Policy
CRS	Congressional Research Service
CSCE	Conference on Security and Cooperation in Europe
CWC	Chemical Weapons Convention
D-RAM	dynamic random access memory
DARPA	Defense Advanced Research Projects Agency
DEC	Digital Equipment Corporation
DoC	Department of Commerce

DoD	Department of Defense
DoE	Department of Energy
DTC	Defense Trade Controls
DTSA	Defense Technology Security Administration
EAA	Export Administration Act
EAAA	Export Administration Amendments Act
EAR	Export Administration Regulations
EARB	Export Administration Review Board
EC	European Community
ECA	Export Control Act
ECCN	export commodity control number
EC/PCC	Export Control/Policy Coordinating Committee
EDAC	Economic Defense Advisory Council
EFTA	European Free Trade Association
FRG	Federal Republic of Germany
G-7	Group of Seven (industrialized nations)
G-CEU	general license for certified end users
G-CoCom	general license for CoCom
G-Com	general license for CoCom and cooperating countries
GCT	general license for intra-CoCom trade
GATT	General Agreement on Tariffs and Trade
GDR	German Democratic Republic
GKNT	State Committee for Science and Technology (USSR)
GNP	Gross National Product
GRU	Chief Directorate of Military Intelligence (USSR)
IAEA	International Atomic Energy Agency
IAEL	International Atomic Energy List
IBM	International Business Machines Corporation
IC/DV	import certificate/delivery verification
ICL	International Computers Limited
ICT	intra-CoCom trade
IDA	Institute for Defense Analyses
IEEPA	International Emergency Economic Powers Act
IL	Industrial List
IML	International Munitions List
INF	Intermediate-Range Nuclear Forces (treaty)
ITA	International Trade Administration
ITAR	International Traffic in Arms Regulations
KGB	Committee for State Security (USSR)
LSI	large-scale integration
MCTL	Militarily Critical Technologies List
MITI	Ministry of International Trade and Industry (Japan)
ML	Munitions List

MOU	memorandum of understanding
MTCR	Missile Technology Control Regime
MTEC	Missile Technology Export Control (group on)
MTU	Motoren-und Turbinen-Union GmbH
NASA	National Aeronautics and Space Administration
NASP	National Aerospace Plane
NATO	North Atlantic Treaty Organization
NIC	newly industrializing country
NNPA	Nuclear Non-Proliferation Act
NNPT	Nuclear Non-Proliferation Treaty
NRC	Nuclear Regulatory Commission
NRL	Nuclear Referral List
NSC	National Security Council
NSD	national security directive
NSG	Nuclear Suppliers Group
NSWP	non-Soviet Warsaw Pact (countries)
ODTC	Office of Defense Trade Controls
OFAC	Office of Foreign Assets Control
OSTP	Office of Science and Technology Policy
OTCA	Omnibus Trade and Competitiveness Act
OTPA	Office of Technology and Policy Analysis
PC	personal computer
PC/AT	personal computer/advanced technology, a family of personal computers based on the Intel 80286 chip
PCC	policy coordinating committee
PDR	processing data rate
PECSEA	President's Export Council, Subcommittee on Export Administration
PEEK	polyetheretherketone
PM	Politico-Military Affairs Bureau (U.S. Department of State)
PRC	People's Republic of China
R&D	research and development
SEMATECH	Semiconductor Manufacturing Technology
SNEC	Subgroup on Nuclear Export Controls
SNECMA	Société Nationale d'Etude et de Construction des Moteurs d'Aviation
SSP	Supercomputer Safeguard Plan
START	Strategic Arms Reduction Talks
STEM	Strategic Technology Experts Meeting
SUB-ACEP	Sub-Advisory Committee on Export Policy
SUB-EDAC	Sub-Economic Defense Advisory Council
TAC	technical advisory committee
TCC	Third Country Cooperation

TDO	Table of Denial Orders
TTG	technical task group
TTIC	Technology Transfer Intelligence Committee
TWEA	Trading with the Enemy Act
TWG	technical working group
UN	United Nations
USSR	Union of Soviet Socialist Republics
VLSI	very large scale integrated circuitry
VPK	Military-Industrial Commission (USSR)
WTO	Warsaw Treaty Organization

List of Briefers, Contributors, and Liaison Representatives

BRIEFERS

MICHAEL ANDREWS, Office of Foreign Availability, Bureau of Export Administration, U.S. Department of Commerce

RICHARD BARTH, National Security Council, The White House

SUMNER BENSON, Defense Technology Security Administration, U.S. Department of Defense

ERIC BIEL, Mayer, Brown and Platt

EDWARD BLACK, Computer and Communications Industry Association

COLONEL EDWARD CAIN, Office of Proliferation, Bureau of Politico-Military Affairs, U.S. Department of State

JAMES CHAMBERLAIN, Office of Proliferation, Bureau of Politico-Military Affairs, U.S. Department of State

KENNETH CHARD, Center for Defense Trade, U.S. Department of State

WILLIAM CLEMENTS, Office of Technology and Policy Analysis, Bureau of Export Administration, U.S. Department of Commerce

RICHARD COOPER, Maurits Boas Professor of International Economics, Harvard University

TIMOTHY DEAL, Special Assistant to the President and Senior Director for International Economic Affairs, National Security Council

GREGORY DESANTIS, Defense Technology Security Administration, U.S. Department of Defense

SUSAN DRIANO, Office of East-West Trade, U.S. Department of State

CHARLES DUELFER, Center for Defense Trade, U.S. Department of State

JOHN ELLO, Office of the Under Secretary for Acquisition, U.S. Department of Defense

PAMELA ERNEST, Director of Federal Affairs, Honeywell Corporation

PAMELA FRAZIER, Center for Defense Trade, U.S. Department of State

PAUL FREEDENBERG, International Trade Consultant, Baker and Botts

HYUNG FUNG, Office of Foreign Availability, Bureau of Export Administration, U.S. Department of Commerce

FRANK GAFFNEY, Director, Center for National Security Studies

CHARLES GILBERT, Deputy Assistant Secretary for Defense Programs, U.S. Department of Energy

ROGER GROSSEL, Manager of Export Administration, Hewlett-Packard Company

VICKI HADFIELD, Chairman of the Operating Committee, Industry Coalition on Technology Transfer

EDWARD HEWITT, Senior Fellow, The Brookings Institution

DANIEL HILL, Individual Validated Licensing Division, Bureau of Export Administration, U.S. Department of Commerce

ERIC HIRSCHORN, Executive Secretary, Industry Coalition on Technology Transfer

CHARLES HOUGH, Director of Trade Administration, Honeywell Corporation

ROBERT DOUGLAS JENKINS, Central Intelligence Agency

LISA KJAER, Electronic Industries Association

GEORGE KOLT, Central Intelligence Agency

JOHN KONFALA, Defense Technology Security Administration, U.S. Department of Defense

GARY KRACH, Director of International Affairs, GTE Corporation

SCOTT KULICKE, President and CEO, Kulicke and Soffa Industries

JAMES LEMUNYON, Deputy Assistant Secretary, Bureau of Export Administration, U.S. Department of Commerce

O. M. LOMACKY, Office of the Under Secretary for Acquisition, U.S. Department of Defense

LEWIS J. LUDWICK, Central Intelligence Agency

JACK MARTENS, Office of Foreign Availability, Bureau of Export Administration, U.S. Department of Commerce

GEORGE MENAS, Strategic Policy Directorate, Defense Technology Security Administration, U.S. Department of Defense

VALERIE MOHN, Defense Technology Security Administration, U.S. Department of Defense

DAVID MOWERY, School of Business, University of California at Berkeley

JAMES NOBLE, Office of Nuclear Export Controls, International Environmental and Scientific Affairs, U.S. Department of State

BENJAMIN OBERHOLTZER, Office of Export Enforcement, Bureau of Export Administration, U.S. Department of Commerce

IRWIN PIKUS, Office of Foreign Availability, Bureau of Export Administration, U.S. Department of Commerce

ROBERT PRICE, Office of CoCom Affairs, Economic Bureau, U.S. Department of State

JOSEPH PUMPHREY, Office of the Secretary of Defense, U.S. Department of Defense

LARRY RADER, Office of East-West Trade, Economic Bureau, U.S. Department of State

VINCENT RADOSTA, Strategic Investigations Division, U.S. Customs Service

MICHAEL RITCHEY, Defense Technology Security Administration, U.S. Department of Defense

JOHN ROONEY, Office of Defense Programs, U.S. Department of Energy

ALAN SCHERR, Associate Director, Center for Foreign Policy Development, Brown University

JIM SCHLIEPPI, Manager of Munitions Licensing, Control Data Corporation

GLENN SCHWEITZER, Office of International Affairs, National Research Council

PETER SULLIVAN, Deputy Assistant Under Secretary, Defense Technology Security Administration, U.S. Department of Defense

GREGORY TAYLOR, Director of Public Affairs, AT&T

CARL THORNE, Office of Nuclear Export Controls, U.S. Department of State

TIMOTHY TYLER, Defense Security Assistance Agency, U.S. Department of Defense

DEBRA WAGGONER, American Electronics Association

ALAN WENDT, Ambassador and Senior Representative for Strategic Technology Policy, U.S. Department of State

CHRISTINE WESTBROOK, Research Associate, Center for Foreign Policy Development, Brown University

F. DOUGLAS WHITEHOUSE, Central Intelligence Agency

CONTRIBUTORS

JUDITH BROWN, U.S. Embassy; Bern, Switzerland

ROBERT BRUNGART, U.S. Embassy; Paris, France

ROGER CARIGNAN, U.S. Embassy; Bonn, Germany

CHRISTOPHER CARLE, Institut Francais des Relations Internationales; Paris, France

PAUL FREEDENBERG, International Trade Consultant, Baker & Botts

DONALD GOLDSTEIN, President, The Nomos Corporation

CALDWELL HARROP, U.S. Mission to the European Community; Brussels, Belgium

JOEL HELLMAN, W. Averell Harriman Institute, Columbia University

MARIE-HÉLÈNE LABBÉ, Consultant, Moquet Borde & Associés; Paris, France

HOWARD LEWIS, III, Vice President, International Economic Affairs, National Association of Manufacturers

WILLIAM J. LONG, Assistant Professor of International Relations, American University

DAVID MANASIAN, Business Editor, *The Economist*; London, England

JOAN PLOASTED, American Institute; Taiwan

KATHLEEN REDDY, U.S. Embassy; Brussels, Belgium

WOLFGANG REINICKE, Guest Scholar, The Brookings Institution

ALAN RIMAS, U.S. Embassy; Ottawa, Canada

REINHARD RODE, Peace Research Institute; Frankfurt, Germany

WILLIAM A. ROOT, Consultant, International Business-Government Counsellors, Inc.

NED QUISTORFF, Commercial Officer, U.S. Consulate, Hong Kong

VLADIMIR SAMBIEW, U.S. Embassy; Tokyo, Japan

ALAN B. SHERR, Director, Project on Soviet Foreign Economic Policy and International Security, Center for Foreign Policy Development, Brown University

ALLEN M. SHINN, Jr., Deputy Director, Office of Legislative and Public Affairs, National Science Foundation

SOLVEIG B. SPIELMANN, Chairman, International Business-Government Counsellors, Inc.

ZACHARY TEICH, U.S. Embassy; London, England

HEINRICH VOGEL, Direktor des Bundesinstituts fur ostwissenshaftliche und internationale Studien; Koln, Germany

CAROLINE WAGNER, U.S. Embassy; Seoul, Republic of Korea

HELGARD WEINERT, Directorate for Science, Technology, and Industry, O.E.C.D.; Paris, France

ROBERT D. WILSON, Wilson & Wilson

REPRESENTATIVE SPONSORS AND OTHER LIAISONS

SUSAN DRIANO, Office of East-West Trade, U.S. Department of State

VICKI HADFIELD, Chairman of the Operating Committee, Industry Coalition on Technology Transfer

ERIC HIRSCHORN, Executive Secretary, Industry Coalition on Technology Transfer

LISA KJAER, Electronic Industries Association

O. M. LOMACKY, Office of the Under Secretary for Acquisition, U.S. Department of Defense

ROBERT PRICE, Office of CoCom Affairs, Economic Bureau, U.S. Department of State

PETER SULLIVAN, Deputy Assistant Under Secretary, Defense Technology Security Administration, U.S. Department of Defense

MAUREEN TUCKER, Bureau of Export Administration, U.S. Department of Commerce

DEBRA WAGGONER, American Electronics Association

ALAN WENDT, Ambassador and Senior Representative for Strategic Technology Policy, U.S. Department of State

F. DOUGLAS WHITEHOUSE, Central Intelligence Agency

Biographies of Panel Members

ROLAND W. SCHMITT (*chairman*), president of Rensselaer Polytechnic Institute, brings to his role as panel chairman decades of experience in industry, academia, and government-related policy organizations. Before becoming the president of Rensselaer in March 1988, he worked for more than 37 years in R&D at General Electric, retiring as senior vice president of science and technology. He is a member and former chairman of the National Science Board, the policymaking body of the National Science Foundation; chairman of CORETECH, the lobbying voice of research and development in Washington, D.C.; a member of the National Academy of Engineering and former member of its council; past president and former board member of the Industrial Research Institute; and a member of the executive committee of the Council on Competitiveness. His activities related to export controls began a decade ago, when he served on a panel of the President's Foreign Intelligence Advisory Board that examined these issues.

WILLIAM F. BURNS (*vice chairman*) retired from the U.S. Army as a major general on March 31, 1988. He subsequently served as the ninth director of the U.S. Arms Control and Disarmament Agency (1988). During his 34 years in the U.S. Army, General Burns held a variety of important command and staff positions. From the inception of the talks in 1981 until November 1986, he represented the Joint Chiefs of Staff on the U.S. delegation to the Intermediate-Range Nuclear Forces negotiations. He also served as principal deputy assistant secretary of state in the Bureau of Politico-Military Affairs.

ARDEN L. BEMENT, Jr. was appointed vice president of technical resources at TRW in 1980 and was named vice president of science and technology in 1989. Prior to that, Dr. Bement became director of the Materials Sciences Office of the Defense Advanced Research Projects Agency in 1976, and in 1979 he was appointed deputy under secretary of defense for research and engineering. In 1990, the U.S. Senate confirmed Dr. Bement's appointment to the National Science Board for a term expiring in 1994. He is also chairman of the Commission for Engineering and Technical Systems of the National Research Council and the Statutory Visiting Committee for the National Institute of Standards and Technology.

ASHTON B. CARTER is Ford Foundation professor of science and international affairs and director of the Center for Science and International Affairs at Harvard's John F. Kennedy School of Government. He has worked at the congressional Office of Technology Assessment (OTA), the Office of the Secretary of Defense, and the Massachusetts Institute of Technology. In the Pentagon's systems analysis branch, his responsibilities included ballistic missile defense, MX missile basing, and various space activities. He coedited and coauthored *Ballistic Missile Defense* (1984) and *Managing Nuclear Operations* (1987) for The Brookings Institution and authored OTA's *Directed Energy Missile Defense in Space* (1984). He serves on advisory bodies to OTA, the Defense Science Board, the Joint Chiefs of Staff, and the American Association for the Advancement of Science.

KENNETH W. DAM is vice president, law and external relations, International Business Machines (IBM) Corporation. Before joining IBM, Mr. Dam served as deputy secretary of state from 1982 to 1985. From 1980 to 1982, he was provost of the University of Chicago. During the early 1970s, he served in several government positions concerned with national security and economic issues. Mr. Dam serves on the boards of a number of nonprofit organizations, including the Asia Society, the Japan Society, The Brookings Institution, and the Foreign Policy Association. He has written a number of books, including *The Rules of the Game: Reform and Evolution in the International Monetary System* (1982) and *Economic Policy Beyond the Headlines* (coauthored with George P. Shultz) (1978).

HERBERT M. DWIGHT, Jr. was the cofounder of Spectra Physics and served as its chief executive officer (CEO) from 1961 to 1988. He is currently CEO of Superconductor Technologies, as well as a member of the board of Applied Materials Inc., Applied Magnetics Corp., Trans Ocean Limited. Mr. Dwight received his BSEE and MSEE from Stanford University and is currently a member of the Stanford Board of Trustees.

JOHN LEMOYNE ELLICOTT is a partner in the law firm of Covington and Burling, where he has served (from 1986 through 1990) as chairman of the firm's Management Committee. He holds an LL.B. from Harvard Law School and an A.B. from Princeton University. Mr. Ellicott's law practice is predominantly in the field of export control regulation. He has served on the faculty of the Salzburg Seminar in Austria and as a professorial lecturer on law at The George Washington University Graduate School of Public Law.

LINCOLN D. FAURER is the president and chief executive officer of the Corporation for Open Systems. He retired from the U.S. Air Force as a lieutenant general after a 35-year career. General Faurer was a rated pilot and also served in the missiles and space field, but he spent most of his last 20 years of military service in intelligence. He retired in 1985 from the position of director of the National Security Agency, to which he had gone from successive assignments in Europe at U.S. European Command and NATO headquarters.

CHARLES GATI is a specialist on Central and Eastern Europe and the Soviet Union. He is a professor of political science at Union College and a consultant on Eastern Europe to the Policy Planning Staff of the Department of State. His latest book is *The Bloc That Failed: Soviet-East European Relations in Transition* (1990).

SEYMOUR E. GOODMAN is professor of management information systems and policy and director of the Mosaic Group at The University of Arizona. He served as chairman of the Committee to Study International Developments in Computer Science and Technology of the Computer Science and Technology Board of the National Research Council. This committee produced the 1988 National Research Council report *Global Trends in Computer Technology and Their Impact on Export Control*. Dr. Goodman has also served on advisory and study committees concerned with export controls and technology transfer under the Departments of Commerce and Defense and the Office of Technology Assessment of the Congress.

RUTH L. GREENSTEIN is the vice president for administration and finance of the Institute for Defense Analyses. Until May 1990, she served as vice president and general counsel for Genex Corporation. From 1981 until February 1984, Ms. Greenstein acted as deputy general counsel for the National Science Foundation. She is currently a member of the Committee on Scientific Freedom and Responsibility, American Association for the Advancement of Science, and the Advisory Board, Special Report Series on Biotechnology, Bureau of National Affairs, Inc.

BENJAMIN HUBERMAN is a consultant on technology issues. He has served as deputy director of the Office of Science and Technology Policy in the White House and in senior positions on the National Security Council staff, the Nuclear Regulatory Commission, the Arms Control and Disarmament Agency, and the Naval Reactors Branch of the Atomic Energy Commission.

RAY KLINE has been president of the National Academy of Public Administration since 1985. Prior to that he served as acting administrator of the U.S. General Services Administration (GSA) from 1984 to 1985 and as deputy administrator of GSA from 1979 to 1985. He went to GSA from the National Aeronautics and Space Administration, where he had been associate administrator for management operations since 1977.

ROBERT LEGVOLD is the director of the W. Averell Harriman Institute for Advanced Study of the Soviet Union at Columbia University, where he is also professor of political science. Prior to joining the Harriman Institute in 1984, he served for six years as senior fellow and director of the Soviet Studies Project at the Council on Foreign Relations in New York. For most of the preceding decade, he was an assistant, then associate, professor of political science at Tufts University. In recent years, he has appeared regularly on national network news programs, and for each of the past four U.S.-Soviet summit conferences he joined ABC's Peter Jennings in live commentary.

BOYD J. McKELVAIN is broadly experienced in the development and management of technology in both private industry and government. He has corporate responsibility for General Electric's export administration and previously was a member of the corporate staff with responsibility for science and technology policy and planning. Mr. McKelvain is chairman of the Department of Commerce's Technical Advisory Committee on Implementation of the Militarily Critical Technologies List. He formerly was a member of the Subcommittee on Export Administration of the President's Export Council, and was cofounder and chairman of the Industry Coalition on Technology Transfer.

JOHN L. McLUCAS, an aerospace consultant, is currently chairman of NASA's Advisory Council, and the NRC Air Force Studies Board. He is a member of the Stafford Committee on the Moon-Mars Initiative and the National Academy of Engineering Council. He also served as chairman of the board for QuesTech, Inc., from 1986 to 1990. Dr. McLucas was executive vice president for COMSAT from 1983 to 1985 and president of COMSAT's World Systems Division from 1980 to 1983. In addition, he served as an administrator of the Federal Aviation Administration from 1975 to 1977 and as secretary of the U.S. Air Force from 1973 to 1975.

M. GRANGER MORGAN is head of the Department of Engineering and Public Policy and professor of engineering and public policy, electrical and computer engineering, and urban and public affairs at Carnegie Mellon. He holds a BS from Harvard, an MS from Cornell, and a Ph.D. in applied physics from the University of California at San Diego. Since 1970, Dr. Morgan has been involved in research and teaching on a variety of problems related to technology and public policy, focusing on that subset in which technical issues play a central role. Much of his work has focused on risk analysis and on the problems of dealing with uncertainty in quantitative policy analysis.

WILLIAM J. PERRY is chairman of Technology Strategies & Alliances and a professor in the School of Engineering and codirector of the Center for International Security and Arms Control at Stanford University. He was under secretary of defense for research and engineering from 1977 to 1981 and president of ESL, Inc., from 1964 to 1977. He is a trustee of the MITRE Corporation and the Carnegie Endowment for International Peace and a member of the National Academy of Sciences' Committee on International Security and Arms Control, the Carnegie Commission on Science, Technology, and Government, the President's Foreign Intelligence Advisory Board, and the Defense Science Board. Mr. Perry is also a director of FMC Corporation, Science Applications International Corporation, and several private companies.

O. M. "Rusty" ROETMAN recently retired after a 47-year career in aviation, 22 of which were spent on active duty in the U.S. Navy as an officer and aviator. On retiring from the Navy, Mr. Roetman spent a year in Washington, D.C., working in a law and engineering consulting role. He joined the Boeing Company in early 1966 and, during his 24-year career with Boeing, served in a number of senior positions. Assignments within the Commercial Airplane Group included vice president for international sales and vice president for contracts. At the time of his retirement from Boeing, he was serving as corporate vice president of government and international affairs. Mr. Roetman's extensive international experience involved him in a variety of activities associated with the export of high-technology products. His formal education includes an undergraduate degree from the University of Minnesota, an aeronautical degree from the U.S. Naval Postgraduate School, a law degree from The George Washington University, and a year of study at the U.S. Naval War College.

GASTON J. SIGUR is currently distinguished professor of East Asian studies at The George Washington University. His government service includes positions as assistant secretary of state for East Asian and Pacific affairs from

1986 to 1989 and special assistant to the President for national security affairs from 1982 to 1984. He served as director of the Institute for Sino-Soviet Studies at The George Washington University from 1972 to 1982, and he held numerous positions in the Asia Society throughout the 1960s. He received a Ph.D. in history in 1957 from the University of Michigan.

JOHN D. STEINBRUNER has been director of foreign policy studies at The Brookings Institution since 1978. His areas of expertise include East-West relations, national security policy, the strategic balance, and foreign policy in general. Prior to joining Brookings, Dr. Steinbruner was an associate professor in the School of Organization and Management and in the Department of Political Science at Yale University from 1976 to 1978. From 1973 to 1976, he served as associate professor of public policy at the John F. Kennedy School of Government at Harvard University, where he also was assistant director of the Program for Science and International Affairs. He has held the positions of executive director of the Research Seminar on Bureaucracy, Politics, and Policy at Harvard's Institute of Politics, and assistant professor of political science at the Center for International Studies at the Massachusetts Institute of Technology. Dr. Steinbruner is a member of the Council on Foreign Relations, the International Institute of Strategic Studies, and the Committee on International Security and Arms Control at the National Academy of Sciences. He received his A.B. from Stanford University in 1963 and his Ph.D. in International Relations from the Massachusetts Institute of Technology in 1968.

PAULA STERN is president of The Stern Group, an international trade advisory firm; a fellow at The Johns Hopkins School for Advanced International Studies; and a speaker and media commentator on U.S. trade policy and global competitive challenges facing American firms. From 1984 to 1986, Dr. Stern chaired the U.S. International Trade Commission (ITC), and she served as a member of the ITC from 1978 to 1986. She is the author of *Water's Edge—Domestic Politics and the Making of Foreign Policy* (1979), a study of the politics of U.S.-Soviet trade that summarized the congressional-executive debate over the Jackson-Vanik amendment. East-West trade and U.S. attempts to apply economic leverage on other nations are two policy arenas about which she has written extensively and delivered congressional testimony.

MITCHEL B. WALLERSTEIN, who directed the study, is also the deputy executive officer of the National Research Council, which is the research and action arm of the National Academies of Sciences and Engineering and the Institute of Medicine. In 1987, he directed the previous National Academies' study on national security export controls, the report of which was entitled *Balancing the National Interest: U.S. National Security Export Controls and Global Economic Competition* (also known as the Allen report). Previously, in 1982, he played a principal role in another related Academies' study on *Scientific Communication and National Security*, often referred to as the Corson report. Dr. Wallerstein holds a Ph.D. from the Massachusetts Institute of Technology, where he served on the faculty for five years. He is a member of the Council on Foreign Relations and the author or editor of numerous books, articles, and monographs dealing with various aspects of science, technology, and international affairs.

Index

A

Administrative due process, 148-149, 193
Administrative law judge, 94-95, 323-325
Administrative Procedure Act (APA), 101,
    148-149, 312, 321, 323, 324, 326-331,
    333
Administrative reforms
  alternatives for consolidating agency
    functions, 144-146, 179-180
  changes in agency and administrative
    authority, 146-147
  need for consolidated functions, 143-144
  recommendations for, 190-191
Advanced materials
  control/decontrol of, 204-206
  relationship to militarily critical weapon
    systems, 202-204
  report of subpanel on, 199-221
Advanced materials industry
  effect of export controls on, 20-22, 202
  in Taiwan, 289
  U.S. export controls and, 20-22, 200-202
Advisory Committee on Export Policy, 82
Afghanistan
  foreign policy export controls, 314
Aircraft industry. *See* Commercial aircraft and
    jet engine industries
Allen, Lew, Jr., 6, 318
Allen panel, 6, 10-11, 28n, 100
Allen report (*Balancing the National Interest:
    U.S. National Security Export Controls
    and Global Economic Competition*), 6,
    10, 153, 318
Antiterrorism controls, in Export
    Administration Regulations, 78
Argentina

cooperation on export controls with U.S.,
    123
  nuclear facilities in, 56
Armenia, 55
Arms Export Control Act (AECA) of 1976,
    62, 77, 104, 114, 146-147, 313, 330-331
Asia fact-finding mission
  general issues, 286-288
  Hong Kong meetings, 291-293
  Japan meetings, 296-299
  Macao visit, 293
  Republic of Korea meetings, 293-295
  Taiwan meetings, 288-291
Atomic Energy Act of 1954, 70, 95, 104
Australia Group
  British membership in, 270
  core list developed by, 77, 98
  export of chemicals to members of, 85
  as members of Missile Technology Control
    Regime, 129-130
  purpose of, 71, 135, 136
  Swiss membership in, 286
Austria, 67, 124, 125
Azerbaijan, 55

B

*Balancing the National Interest: U.S. National
    Security Export Controls and Global
    Economic Competition. See* Allen report
Battle Act (Mutual Defense Assistance Control
    Act), 62, 311, 314
Belgium, fact-finding mission to, 282-285
Biological weapons
  biological organisms, 79
  efforts to limit proliferation, 89

need for changes in access to, 107
proliferation of, 2, 59
Brazil
cooperation on export controls with U.S., 123
nuclear facilities, 56
Bucy, J. Fred, 28n, 339
Bulgaria
change in relationship with Soviet Union, 43-44
economic aid for, 50
Bulk licensing, 109
Bureau of Export Administration (BXA), 79-80, 94, 95, 146, 191, 338

C

Cambodia, 72, 78
Canada fact-finding mission
general issues, 299-300
meeting with government officials, 300-301
meeting with industry representatives, 302-303
Canadian Aerospace Industries Association, 303
Canadian Export Association, 302
Canopies for jet fighter planes, 21n
Carter, Jimmy, 314, 316
Center for Information on Strategic Technology, 298
Center for Study of Relation Between Technologies and Strategies (CREST), 276
Central America, regional conflict in southern, 55
Chad, 57
Chemical weapons
availability in countries in Middle East, 55
foreign policy controls and, 116
license processing for items related to, 83
need for changes in access to, 107, 108
problems in monitoring, 35-36
proliferation controls, 2, 71, 77, 79, 89, 132, 135-136, 178
proliferation of, 57-59
Chemical Weapons Convention (CWC), 71, 135-137, 185
China. See People's Republic of China
China Green Line, 51, 65, 279, 281
CoCom. See Coordinating Committee for Multilateral Export Controls
CoCom countries. See also Coordinating Committee for Multilateral Export Controls (CoCom); individual countries
access to export control information in, 20
differences in control practices vis-à-vis U.S., 19, 101
interest in changing dual use item restrictions, 107
opposition to extraterritoriality, 317
prevention of reexports of CoCom-controlled items, 30
Third Country Cooperation initiative, 66-68, 122-126, 171, 176
trade between European Community

members of, 120-122
CoCom High-Level Meeting (June 1990)
redefinition of control levels for computers, 25
results, 20, 67, 96, 126, 343
CoCom Industrial List, 3, 75, 87, 95, 118, 121, 175, 192, 242, 302
Cold War era, 310-312, 321
Commerce Department, U.S.
as chief export control administrative agency, 145-146, 180
enforcement procedures of, 150
involvement in judicial review, 101-102, 321-333
involvement in National Security Council meetings, 153
licensing responsibilities, 79-86
problem of overlapping jurisdictions facing, 94-95
study on emerging technologies, 21, 200
technical advisory committees established and administered by, 102, 103, 195, 336, 338, 343-347
Commercial aircraft and jet engine industries
Airbus Industrie, 23, 227
effect on U.S. economy and national security, 225
effectiveness of controls based on structure of, 240-241
export control problems related to, 241-243
features of, 224-225
foreign partnerships, 226, 246
impact of export controls on, 22-23, 222, 238-239
major companies, 223
nations with heavy maintenance capability, 226, 247
purchase orders, 244, 245
report of subpanel on, 222-247
Soviet, 234-238
technologies critical to military lead of West, 230-231, 234
technology components, 228-230
trend toward globalization and foreign competition, 225-228
U.S. vs. Soviet technologies, 236-238
Committee on Science, Engineering, and Public Policy (COSEPUP), 5-7, 6-7, 306-307
Commodities
characteristics of, 252
computer products classified as, 256
definition of, 163, 164
Commoditization of products, 250
Commodity Control List (CCL), 72, 73, 77, 80, 95, 190, 192, 241
analysis of selected entries, 207-213
application of risk/opportunity formula to items on, 200, 214
controllability of items, 172
Computer industry
controllability issues in, 251-253
export controls, 23-25, 256-261
and foreign availability assessments, 255-256

international issues, 261-265
means of control and decontrol in, 253-255
report of subpanel on, 248-265
in Taiwan, 289
trends, 249-250
Computer networks, 258-260
Computer software
  export controls, 163, 260-261
  military-use, 260
  over-the-counter, 249, 260-261
  sunset provisions, 254
Conference on Disarmament, 71
Congressional Research Service (CRS), 87,
  171
Control identifiers, 122
Control list construction (U.S.)
  comparing benefits and costs, 159-160
  defining item-groups, 349-352
  development, 20, 155
  identifying economic and foreign policy
    costs, 158-159
  identifying items of concern, 156-157
  identifying security risks, 158
  quantitative analysis used in, 352-355
  rank ordering of item-groups, 352
  recommendations regarding, 147-148, 188,
    192
Control list management
  administrative problems, 223
  and foreign policy controls, 76-77
  industry participation, 103, 176
  integration and review, 147-148, 160
  jurisdictional disputes, 87, 147, 148
  national security priorities, 73-76, 162
  periodic reconstruction, 161-162
  single agency authority, 144
  sunsetting, 160, 161, 184, 248
Control lists
  characteristics of CoCom, 3, 65-66, 73, 75
  characteristics of U.S., 72-73, 172-173
  controllability aspect, 162-164
  policy and procedures established by
    national security directives, 142-143
  problems with established system, 39, 52,
    95-98, 154-155
Controllability
  of computer technology, 248, 251-253
  list, 162-164
Coordinating Committee for Multilateral
  Export Controls (CoCom). See also
  CoCom countries
  administration and management, 126-128,
    176-177, 187
  British views of, 268-269
  characteristics of control lists, 3, 65-66, 73,
    75
  as coordinator of nonproliferation efforts,
    131, 177-178
  development and strategy, 3, 64-65
  effects of borderless trade within European
    community on, 120-122, 175-176, 186
  establishment, 62, 311
  involvement of TACs in, 338, 339
  involvement of TTGs in, 342, 343
  licensing and enforcement standards, 67-69,

127
  list development, 24, 52, 65-66, 73, 97-98,
    126, 156, 157, 159-164, 347
  list review in 1990, 138, 154
  meeting of panel fact-finding delegation and
    U.S. representatives to, 275
  objectives, 118-120, 175
  outdated export controls used by, 39, 95-98
  recommendations on, 120, 123-124, 126-
    128, 185-187
  relaxation of restrictions, 2, 51, 52, 107,
    249
  and third country cooperation, 66-67, 122-
    126, 176
  U.S. representation, 151, 194
Copyright protection, software, 261
Corson report (Scientific Communication and
  National Security), 6
COSEPUP. See Committee on Science,
  Engineering, and Public Policy
Crime control, in Export Administration
  Regulations, 78
Cuba
  Canadian trade with, 300
  export controls targeted against, 72, 78
Czechoslovakia
  change in relationship with Soviet Union,
    31-32, 43, 47-48
  economic aid for, 50
  economic change in, 49
  export regulations for, 65, 93

D

De-Americanization of foreign-made products,
  115n, 280, 317
Defense
  deficiencies in industrial base, 10
  impact of export limitations of advanced
    materials on, 21-22
Defense Advanced Research Projects Agency,
  41
Defense article, 87, 190
Defense Department, U.S.
  as chief administrative agency, 145, 179
  influence on U.S. and CoCom policy, 127
  involvement in technical advisory
    committees, 195
  jurisdictional problems involving, 93
  licensing responsibilities, 80, 81, 83, 316
  May 1989 report on militarily critical
    technologies, 41
Defense industrial base, weakening of U.S.,
  42
Defense Science Board Task Force report on
  Export of U.S. Technology (Bucy
  Report), 28n, 234, 314
Defense Technology Security Administration
  (DTSA), 316n
Departments, U.S. government. See
  Commerce Department, U.S.; Defense
  Department, U.S.; Energy Department,
  U.S.; State Department, U.S.
Detente era, 312-313
Differentiation policy

British view of, 269
French view of, 273, 274
German view of, 279, 280
Dispute resolution
  deadlines, 148, 190
  inefficient, 98-99, 173
  jurisdictional, 87, 93, 147, 148, 172
  national security directives regarding, 143, 188
Diversion, technology acquisition through
  British view of, 269
  East European-Soviet cooperation regarding, 44
  searches for patterns of, 133
  as technology acquisition method, 30, 31, 167-168
Diversion-in-place protection, 253, 257
Drug Enforcement Administration, 150, 180
Dual use products/technologies
  development of standards for, 190
  European support for controls on, 52, 62
  export control of, 80, 87, 100, 101, 132, 137, 191, 217, 242
  jurisdictional problems, 147
  methods of acquisition, 32
  military benefits provided to adversaries, 128-129, 134, 156-157
  possibility of assurances with Soviets regarding nondiversion of, 45
  restriction changes, 107, 111, 118, 120, 182
  for Soviet Union and Eastern Europe, 50, 52, 107, 108, 156-157, 169, 183, 250, 314
Due process, administrative, 148-149, 193

E

EAA. See Export Administration Act (EAA)
East Germany. See German Democratic Republic
Eastern Europe. See also Warsaw Treaty Organization (WTO) allies
  computer industries in, 24
  economic and political changes in, 2, 10, 13-14, 16, 27-28, 43-46, 166, 181
  economic exchange with West, 49-50, 169
  goods eligible for export to, 93, 185
  intelligence services of, 28, 44
  need for changes in export controls for, 111-112, 118, 120
Economic aid, to Soviet Union and Eastern Europe, 50
Economic challenges, of United States, 14-15, 40-43, 165
Economic Defense Advisory Council (EDAC), Working Group I, 75-76
Embargoed countries, in Export Administration Regulations, 78-79
Embargoes
  as form of export management, 109, 132
  toward Iraq, 72
Enabling technology, 231n
Encryption technology, 260
End-use controls
  explanation of, 162

need for CoCom to revise guidelines on, 164
  properties of items for, 163
  published standards for, 186
  risk reduction through, 248, 253-254
End-use verification, 119-120
Energy Department, U.S.
  jurisdictional problems, 93
  licensing responsibilities, 83, 84
Enforcement of export controls
  British views regarding, 271
  in Japan, 297-298
  judicial review of Commerce Department, 323-324
  overlapping, 94-95, 172
  recommendations regarding, 94, 149-150, 193-194
  responsibilities, 150, 180
  of sanctions, 85-86, 94-95, 149-150, 180
Espionage, technology acquisition through, 28-29, 167
Europe fact-finding mission to
  general issues covered, 267-268
  meeting with European Parliament, 284-285
  meetings in Belgium, 282-285
  meetings in Federal Republic of Germany, 276-282
  meetings in France, 273-276
  meetings in Great Britain, 268-273
  meetings in Switzerland, 285-286
European Atomic Energy Community, 283
European Bank for Reconstruction and Development, 50
European Community (EC)
  delegation meeting with Commission of the, 283-284
  German view of, 278
  trade within, 120-122, 175-176, 186
European Parliament delegation meeting, 284-285
Export Administration Act (EAA)
  authority to maintain list of strategically critical elements, 339
  control list management under, 73, 75-76
  foreign policy export controls under, 76-77
  industry participation provisions, 102, 336, 337
  judicial review under, 101-102, 321-333
  objectives and purpose of, 62-64, 104, 312-313, 321
  and overlapping jurisdiction, 94, 95, 146-147
  renewals and revisions, 313, 314
  on specific export restrictions, 71, 72
  time limits on case review, 82
Export Administration Amendments Act (EAAA) of 1985, 64, 317, 318
Export Administration Regulations (EAR), 77-79, 93
Export Administration Review Board (EARB), 81-82, 84, 99
Export Control Act of 1949, 61, 62, 309n, 310, 312
Export Control Policy Coordinating Committee (EC/PCC), 140, 141, 189, 191

Export controllability. *See* Controllability
Export controls. *See also* Foreign policy export
   controls; National security export controls;
   U.S. export control policy; U.S. export
   controls; individual countries
applicability to control of proliferation, 132-
   133
in changing global environment, 165-166,
   174
on computer technologies and products,
   256-261
controllability issues, 162-164
economic and foreign policy costs of, 158-
   160, 318
forms of, 109-110, 132
impact of aircraft industry structure on
   effectiveness of, 240-241
problems related to commercial aircraft
   industry, 241-243
Export Facilitation Act of 1990, 331-332
Export/Import Permits Act (Canada), 300
Export management mechanisms, 108-110

F

Fact-finding missions
   Asian, 286-299
   Canadian, 299-303
   European, 267-286
Farewell affair, 33, 315
Farewell papers, 33
Federal Republic of Germany (FRG). *See also*
      German Democratic Republic (GDR)
   aerospace industry in, 22-23
   economic aid for former GDR, 50
   economic outlook for, 41
   effects of unification, 43, 44, 49, 169
   fact-finding mission to, 276-282
   involvement in Libya's chemical facility, 57
Fibrous and filamentary materials
   export controls on, 210-211
Finland, 67, 124, 125
Force multiplier strategy, 62, 312
Foreign availability, 75, 162-163
Foreign availability assessments, 96-98, 248-
   249, 255-256
Foreign policy
   and economic costs of export controls, 158-
      160
   national security as goal of U.S., 115, 154
Foreign policy export controls. *See also* U.S.
      export control policy
   and control list management, 76-77
   effect on aircraft industry, 22-23, 222, 239,
      242
   explanation, 1n, 63-64, 114n
   Japanese, 298-299
   license processing, 83-85
   limitations on types and uses, 115-117, 175
   recommendations regarding, 116-117, 183-
      184
France
   aerospace industry, 22-23
   fact-finding mission to, 273-276
   as missile technology supplier, 57

French Institute of International Relations, 276

G

General Accounting Office, 150, 193
General Agreement on Tariffs and Trade
   (GATT) talks, 215
German Democratic Republic (GDR). *See also*
      Federal Republic of Germany
   dissolution of, 32
   export control system for, 277-278
Germany. *See* Federal Republic of Germany;
   German Democratic Republic
*Global Trends in Computer Technology and
   Their Impact on Export Control* (National
   Research Council), 7, 24, 250, 257-259,
   261-264
Great Britain. *See also* United Kingdom
   aerospace industry in, 23
   fact-finding mission to, 268-273
   view on economic aid to Soviet Union and
      Eastern Europe, 50

H

Harriman, Averell, 311
High-walls principles/products, 251, 257, 297
Hong Kong
   concern regarding China, 287
   export control program with United
      Kingdom, 123
   fact-finding mission to, 291-293
   industrialization of, 41
Hungary
   change in relationship with Soviet Union,
      31-32, 43, 48
   economic aid for, 50
   economic change in, 49
   export regulations regarding, 65, 93

I

Illegal sales
   technology acquisition through, 29-30
India
   conflict with Pakistan, 55, 57
   export controls for, 113
   as missile technology source, 134
   nuclear weapon capabilities, 56
Indonesia, 123
Industry. *See* U.S. industry
Industry advisory committee, 151-152
Industry representatives, meetings with during
      fact-finding missions
   British, 271-273
   Canadian, 302-303
   French, 274-275
   German, 279-282
Institute for Defense Analyses (IDA), 75, 152-
   153, 195, 339, 341
Intelligence community
   explanation, 26n
   implications of evidence regarding
      technology acquisition, 36-37
   recommendations for monitoring computing

technologies, 264-265
recommendations regarding monitoring of
    technology acquisition, 37-38, 182-183
role in export control policy process, 36,
    168
Intermediate-Range Nuclear Forces treaty
    (1987), 45, 112
International Atomic Energy Agency, 287
International Atomic Energy List (IAEL), 65,
    119-120
International Emergency Economic Powers Act
    (IEEPA) of 1977, 71-72, 115, 117, 184,
    329, 330
International Industrial List (Industrial List)
    (IL), 65, 119-120
International Munitions List (IML), 65, 119-
    120, 242
International Trade Administration, 94, 345,
    346
International Traffic in Arms Regulations
    (ITAR), 77, 80, 93, 114, 242, 251, 258-
    260
Intra-CoCom Trade (ICT) working group, 69
Iran
    chemical weapon capabilities, 71
    export controls targeted against, 85
    war with Iraq, 56, 57
Iraq
    chemical weapon capabilities, 71
    conflict with Israel, 57
    decision to invade Kuwait, 53-54
    export controls targeted against, 85
    nuclear weapon capabilities, 56
    war with Iran, 56, 57
Ireland, 120
Israel, 56, 57
ITAR. See International Traffic in Arms
    Regulations (ITAR)
Item-groups for lists
    method of defining, 157, 349-352
    rank ordering of, 352
    use of quantitative analysis, 352-355

J

Jackson-Vanik amendment to Trade Reform
    Act of 1974, 313
Japan
    aerospace industry, 23, 227
    competition in supercomputer industry, 25
    as economic rival of U.S., 286-287
    fact-finding mission to, 296-299
    position in advanced materials technology,
        21, 200
    technological and manufacturing advances,
        41
    U.S. withdrawal of forces from, 55
Jet engine industry, 231, 233-234. See also
    Commercial aircraft and jet engine
    industries
Judicial review
    availability and efficiency under current
        EAA, 322-327
    background information, 321-322
    and Export Facilitation Act of 1990, 331-

332
    insufficient, 101-102, 148-149
    policy and legal arguments regarding
        expansion of agency action under EAA,
        327-331
    recommendations regarding, 173, 193

K

Kennan, George, 310
Kennedy, John F., 56
Keystone equipment, 28n
Kirghizia, 55
Korea. See North Korea; South Korea
Korean Institute for International Economic
    Policy, 295
Kuwait, invasion by Iraq, 53-54

L

Legal sales, technology acquisition through, 31
Libya
    chemical weapons capabilities, 57, 71, 112
    export controls targeted against, 78, 85
Licenses/licensing. See also U.S. export
    licenses/licensing
    bulk, 109
    CoCom standards, 29, 67-69, 127
    elimination between CoCom partners, 121,
        122
    third country comparisons, 123-125
    transactional, 109
Lists. See Control list construction; Control list
    management; Control lists; individual lists
London Suppliers Group. See Nuclear
    Suppliers Group (NSG)

M

Macao, 293
Machine tool industry, Taiwanese, 289
Malaysia, 201
Microelectronics industry. See Computer
    industry
Middle East, 8, 55. See also Persian Gulf
    crisis
Middle-ground products, 252-253
Militarily critical products
    in advanced materials industry, 203-204
    in computer industry, 251
Militarily Critical Technologies List (MCTL),
    73, 75, 95-96, 172, 339, 341, 343
Militarily related technologies. See also Dual
    use products/technologies; Proliferation
    technologies
    of commercial aircraft and jet engine
        industry, 231-234
    Soviet utilization of, 33-35
Military procurement process, 10
Military-use software, 260
Missile delivery systems
    availability to countries in Middle East, 55,
        57
    need for changes in access to, 107
    proliferation control of, 70-71, 79, 89, 134-

135, 178
threat posed by proliferation of, 57-59
Missile technology
under foreign policy controls, 116
license processing for items related to, 84-85
Missile Technology Control Regime (MTCR)
annex to, 76-77, 98
British view of, 270
effectiveness, 134-135, 137
establishment, 70-71
membership, 129, 137, 185, 282
Missile Technology Export Control (MTEC)
group, 85
Mongolia, 48
Most favored nation (MFN) trade status, 313
Multilateral export controls. *See also*
Coordinating Committee for Multilateral
Export Controls (CoCom); Proliferation
controls
and CoCom administration and
management, 126-128
need for collective proliferation controls,
128-136
objectives of CoCom, 118-120
political and economic changes affecting
operation of CoCom, 120-126
Multinational firms
export control problems created by, 40
sale of small U.S. companies specializing in
advanced materials to, 200-201
U.S. advanced materials companies bought
by, 21
U.S. compliance requirements faced by, 93-94
Munitions List (ML), 72, 77, 80, 87, 192, 242
function of, 73
jurisdictional problems of, 87, 147, 148,
190
Mutual Defense Assistance Control Act (Battle
Act), 62, 311, 314

N

National Defense Act, 153
National discretion (administrative exception
controls), 101, 127, 128
National Munitions Control Board, 309
National Science Park (Taiwan), 290
National Security Act of 1947, 139-140, 187
National Security Council (NSC), 139-140,
153, 189, 191
National Security Decision Directive 189, 6
National security directives (NSD), 140-143,
157-159, 187-189
National security export controls. *See also*
U.S. export control policy
on commercial aircraft and jet engines, 222,
242
control list management and, 73-76, 158.
See also Control list management
elimination of unilateral features, 19-20
explanation, 1n, 12n, 63, 114n
industry participation, 102
interagency groups, 141-142, 189

international conditions impacting, 106
license processing, 79-83
limitations on types and uses, 114-116, 175
matrix of, 86, 88-89
new targets for, 112-114, 174-175
outdated, 39, 106-110
policy mechanisms, 140-142
presidential role, 139-140, 187-188
recommendations regarding, 116-117
National security interests
and changes in sources of threat, 43-59, 170
changes in Soviet Union and Eastern Europe
impacting, 43-46, 168-169
economic and technological challenges, 40-43
and economic exchange with East, 49-50, 169
economic factors in formulation of, 43, 168
export control policy and, 140
findings and recommendations concerning
traditional threat, 52-53, 181-182
and People's Republic of China, 50-52, 170
proliferation threat, 2-3, 170-171
shifts in, 15
Soviet defense doctrine and military force
deployment impacting, 46-49
studies, 5-6
NATO. *See* North Atlantic Treaty
Organization
Netherlands, the, 285
Neutrality Act of 1935, 309
Newly industrializing countries (NICs)
growth, 41
participation in Third Country Cooperation
initiative, 122
Niobates, 212-213
Nixon administration, 313
Non-Soviet Warsaw Pact (NSWP) countries, 32
Nonenforcement, judicial review of, 324-327
North Atlantic Treaty Organization (NATO)
espionage as concern of, 28
establishment, 310
force deployment by, 47
meeting of fact-finding delegation with, 285
strategy, 61-62, 311, 312
North Korea
export controls targeted against, 72, 78
nuclear weapons and facilities in, 55-57
viewed as threat, 287, 293-294
Nuclear Non-Proliferation Treaty of 1968
(NNPT), 57, 69-70, 73n, 76, 113, 129,
134, 136, 185, 270, 282
Nuclear Referral List (NRL), 72, 73, 76, 84,
98
Nuclear Regulatory Commission, 84
Nuclear Suppliers Group (NSG)
lists maintained by, 76, 98
purpose of, 70
view of dual use items, 134, 137
Nuclear weapons/materials/technologies
under foreign policy controls, 116
license processing for items related to, 83, 84
need for changes in access to, 107
proliferation controls, 69-70, 76-77, 79, 88,
134, 177-178
proliferation of, 2, 56-59. *See also*

Proliferation technologies

O

Office of Defense Trade Controls, 80
Office of Defense Trade Policy, 80
Office of Export Enforcement, 150, 172, 180
Office of Technology and Policy Analysis,
190, 338, 345
Omnibus Trade and Competitiveness Act of
1988
and companies exporting without a license,
29-30
export control provisions, 319n
foreign availability assessments under, 96, 97
judicial review provisions, 101, 149, 321
Section 2433, 5, 7, 304-305
Over-the-counter software, 249, 260-261

P

Pakistan
conflict with India, 55, 56
nuclear weapon capabilities, 56
Panel on the Future Design and
Implementation of National Security
Export Controls
charge to panel, 7-9
establishment of, 6-7
focus of study, 9-10
key findings and conclusions, 165-180
scope of work, 8-9
summary of recommendations, 181-195
summary of recommendations of. See also
Policy recommendations
Panel on the Impact of National Security
Controls on International Technology
Transfer (Allen panel), 6, 10-11, 28n,
100, 318
People's Republic of China (PRC)
British policy toward, 269
China Green Line, 51, 65, 279, 281
as controlled destination, 51, 65
efforts to deny access to militarily relevant
technology to, 106
export restrictions following Tiananmen
Square demonstrations, 72
as missile technology source, 57, 134
as national security threat, 50-52, 170, 287
need for changes in export controls for, 111-
113, 170-171
need for participation in efforts to reduce
proliferation, 2, 58, 171
technology acquisition by, 26, 27
Perle, Richard N., 313n, 314n, 316
Persian Gulf crisis
as source of physical threat, 40, 53-54
and Soviet-Western cooperation, 14, 55
trade embargo against Iraq during, 72
Poland
change in relationship with Soviet Union,
31-32, 43, 48
economic aid for, 50
economic change in, 49
export regulations regarding, 65, 93

martial law in, 316
Policy Coordinating Committee on Non-
Proliferation (PCC), 83, 85
Policy recommendations. See also U.S. export
control policy; U.S. export control
proposed reforms
in response to changes in traditional threat,
52-53, 181-182
on administrative due process and judicial
review, 102, 148-149, 193
on borderless trade within European
Community, 122, 186
on CoCom, 120, 123-124, 126-128, 185-187
on computer equipment/technology controls,
264
on enforcement issues, 94, 149-150, 193-194
on foreign policy export controls, 116-117,
183-184
on industry participation, 151-153, 194-195
on intelligence community, 37-38, 182-183
on national security export controls, 116-117
on policy execution, 143-146, 190-191
on policy formulation, 140, 187-190
on proliferation controls, 58-59, 114, 131-
133, 136-137, 182, 184-185
on structure and format of control lists, 147-
148, 188, 192
on technology acquisition, 37-38, 182-183
on third country cooperation, 126, 186
Polycarbonate sheet, 211-212
Polymeric substances, 208-209
Postexport recordkeeping, 110
PRC. See People's Republic of China
Preexport notification, 110
President
authority during World War II over exports
of militarily significant goods, 309
role in formulation of export control policy,
139-140, 184, 187-188
President's Export Council, Subcommittee on
Export Administration (PECSEA), 345,
346
Proliferation
as national security threat, 10-11
U.S.-Soviet cooperation regarding, 111
Proliferation controls
British approach to, 270-271
chemical, 2, 71, 77, 79, 89, 132, 135-136,
178. See also Chemical weapons
coordination of, 129-130, 177-178
in Export Administration Act, 115
German approach to, 278
missile, 70-71, 79, 89, 134-135, 178. See
also Missile delivery systems; Missile
technology
need for applicability of export controls to,
132-133
need for high-level leadership and policy
coordination to deal with, 130-132
nuclear, 69-70, 76-77, 79, 88, 134, 177.
See also Nuclear weapons/materials/
technologies
problems existing with, 2-4, 128-129
recommendations regarding, 58-59, 114,
131-133, 136-137, 182, 184-185

Proliferation technologies. *See also* Militarily
related technologies
acquisition of, 35-36
attempts to limit, 69-71
country-specific objectives, 71-72
regional instabilities exacerbated by, 54-56
threat posed by, 56-59, 170-171, 182
Publicly available software, 260-261

Q

Quantitative analysis, 252-255
Quartz crystals, 208

R

Reagan administration, 314-317
Recordkeeping, postexport, 110
Reexport controls
barriers in Eastern Europe to supply for
Soviets, 32
CoCom authorization requirements, 171
CoCom participation in, 30, 66, 100
effect on computer and microelectronics
industries, 24
U.S. authorization requirements, 66, 100-
101, 171
Regional conflict
overview of changes in, 54-56
as source of physical threat, 8, 14, 53-54,
112
Regional stability controls, in Export
Administration Regulations, 78
Republic of Korea. *See* South Korea
Research and development (R&D)
aging U.S., 41
export restrictions on advanced materials
limiting incentives for, 21, 201
Romania, 43-44

S

Samsung plant, 295
Sanctions
enforcement, 85-86, 94-95, 149-150, 180
use of trade, 99
for violations of international agreements or
norms of behavior, 3, 108
Scientific Communication and National
Security (Corson report), 6
Selective activity prohibitions, 109, 132
Selective export prohibitions, 109, 132
Singapore
industrialization of, 41
national security export controls with U.S.,
123
third-country licensing comparisons, 124, 125
Software, computer. *See* Computer software
South Africa
export controls toward, 79
nuclear weapons capabilities, 56
South Korea
business practices, 294-295
economic growth and industrialization of,
41, 286-287

fact-finding mission to, 293-296
national security export controls with U.S.,
123
third-country licensing comparisons, 124,
125
U.S. withdrawal of forces from, 55
Soviet Acquisition of Western Technology
(U.S. Central Intelligence Agency), 315
Soviet aircraft technology
status of, 234-236
U.S. vs., 236-238
Soviet military
defense doctrine and force deployment
changes, 46-49
influence on design philosophy of aircraft
industry, 235
internal and external changes affecting, 43-
46, 170
Soviet technology acquisition
changes since beginning of 1990, 31-32, 36
methods prior to 1990, 27-31
policy recommendations regarding, 181
role and implications of intelligence
evidence on, 26-27, 36-37
U.S. efforts to limit, 3, 12, 52-53, 88, 106,
314
and utilization, 33-35, 46, 315
Soviet Union
computer industry/technology in, 24, 261-
264
determining items acceptable for export to,
93, 156-159
economic and political changes in, 8, 9, 13-
14, 16, 43-46, 49-50, 52, 154, 159, 166,
181, 250
export control changes needed for, 107,
108, 111-112, 118, 120, 161, 171
human rights issues, 313-314
intelligence services of, 28
as missile technology source, 57, 134
need for participation in efforts to reduce
proliferation of weapons, 2, 58, 113, 171
policy recommendations for dealings with,
181-183, 185
Reagan administration view of, 314-316
regional conflict in, 14, 55
South Korean concern regarding, 293
strategic offensive capability in Central
Europe, 2
technology denial strategy used against, 311
threat presented by, 39-40, 51-53, 158, 165,
181, 267, 287
U.S. controls on oil and gas equipment to,
72, 115, 316-317
Space launch technology, 36
State Department, U.S.
as chief administrative agency, 145, 179
as coordinator of nonproliferation efforts, 131
involvement in technical advisory
committees, 195
licensing responsibilities of, 80, 81, 83, 84
Strategic Arms Reduction Talks (START), 45,
48
Strategic Technology Experts Meeting, 127,
128, 187

Subgroup on Nuclear Export Coordination
(SNEC), 84
Subpanel on Advanced Industrial Materials,
20-22
Subpanel on Advanced Industrial Materials
Report
executive summary, 199-200
recommendations, 206-207
relationship of advanced materials and
technology to militarily critical weapons
systems, 202-204
review of control/decontrol of advanced
materials, 204-206
U.S. advanced materials industry and U.S.
export control, 200-202
Subpanel on Commercial Aircraft and Jet
Engines, 22-23
Subpanel on Commercial Aircraft and Jet
Engines Report
civil aircraft industry, 223-225
examination of Western and Soviet
technology, 228-238
impact of export controls on U.S. firms,
238-239
influence of industrial structure on control
effectiveness, 239-241
major findings of, 222-223
problems with export control system, 241-243
trend toward globalization and foreign
competition, 225-228
Subpanel on Computer Technology, 23-25
Subpanel on Computer Technology Report
executive summary, 248-249
export control of specific technologies and
products, 256-261
foreign availability assessments, 255-256
industry information, 249-251
international issues, 261-265
issue of controllability, 248, 251-253
means of control and decontrol, 253-255
Sunset provisions
procedures, 160, 161
recommendations for use, 184, 254-256
risk reduction through use, 248
Supercomputer Safeguard Plan, 251, 257
Supercomputers
effect of export controls on, 24-25
export controls on, 257-258
as high-walls product, 251
Supercritical technology, 214n
Switzerland
licensing benefits, 67
panel fact-finding mission to, 285-286
third-country licensing comparisons, 124, 125
Syria, 71, 85

T

TACs. See Technical advisory committees
(TACs)
Taiwan
economic growth and industrialization, 41,
286-287
fact-finding mission to, 288-291
interest in establishing export controls with

U.S., 123
third-country licensing comparisons, 124, 125
Tantalates, 212-213
Technical advisory committees (TACs)
establishment and function, 75, 102, 336-337
financial responsibility and coordination for,
152-153, 195
meetings, 338-339
recommendations regarding, 343-347
responsibilities and authority, 337-338
role in construction of CoCom core list, 103
Technical task groups (TTGs), 75, 342-343
Technical working groups (TWGs)
establishment of, 75, 339-340
meetings, 341-342
membership and application process, 341
recommendations regarding, 343
responsibilities and authority, 340-341
Technological challenges, of United States,
14-15, 40-43, 165
Technology. See Militarily related
technologies; Proliferation technologies
Technology acquisition
changes in nature and patterns since
beginning of 1990, 31-32
and implications of intelligence evidence,
36-37
panel examination of, 26-27
of proliferation concern, 35-36
recommendations regarding, 37-38
and role of intelligence community, 36, 168
Soviet. See Soviet technology acquisition
Technology acquisition methods
diversion, 30, 31, 44, 133, 167-168, 269,
288
espionage, 28-29, 167
illegal sales, 29-30
legal sales, 31
Technology transfer
Allen study on, 6, 10
by multinational firms, 40
with Soviet Union and Eastern Europe, 2,
262-264
Technology Transfer Intelligence Committee
(TTIC), 27-28, 36
Terrorism
impact of trade restrictions on state-
sponsored, 55
as source of physical threat, 54, 112
Third countries
control program, 66-68, 122-126, 171, 176
explanation, 28n
policy recommendations regarding, 126, 186
technology acquisition through, 30, 31
Third Country Cooperation (TCC), 30, 66-68,
122-126, 176
Third Country Cooperation Working Group, 66
Titanium-based alloys, 213
Toshiba-Kongsberg case, 29, 33, 64, 296-298,
318-319
Trade
as catalyst for change in Eastern Europe and
Soviet Union, 50
within European Community, 120-122
impact of export control policy on U.S.,

107, 108
importance to U.S. economy, 42
Trade Reform Act of 1974, 313
Trading companies, 292-293
Trading with the Enemy Act of 1917, 71, 72, 78-79, 95, 104-105, 308-309
Transactional licensing, 109
Transborder data flow, 258-260
Treaty of Rome, 121, 271, 284
Treaty on Conventional Forces in Europe (CFE), 1-2, 34, 45
  limitations imposed by, 52
  on-site inspection regimes in, 112
  terms, 48
Trigger lists, 70, 76
Truman, Harry, 310-311
TTGs. *See* Technical task groups

U

Uncontrollable items. *See* Controllability
Unilateralism, of U.S. export policy, 19-20, 167, 173
United Kingdom, 123. *See also* Great Britain
United Nations, 131
United Nations Conference on Disarmament, 58
United States
  aircraft and jet engine industry, 223. *See also* Commercial aircraft and jet engine industries
  economic aid to Soviet Union and Eastern Europe, 50
  economic and technological challenges, 14-15, 40-43, 165
  economic cost of export controls, 154, 318
  efforts to deny Western technology to Soviet Union and its allies, 12
  as missile technology supplier, 57
  recommendations regarding national security policy, 181-182
  Soviet military-related technology vs., 33-35
U.S. Chamber of Commerce
  fact-finding meeting in Frankfurt, 280, 281
  fact-finding meeting in Hong Kong, 292-293
  fact-finding meeting in Taiwan, 291
U.S. Customs Service
  function of export policy enforcement, 85-86, 150, 180
  overlapping jurisdiction problem, 94-95, 172
U.S. distribution licenses, 119
U.S. export control policy. *See also* Foreign policy export controls; National security export controls
  adverse effect on competitive position in international trade, 107
  and balancing national interests, 317-319
  changes related to proposed reforms, 146-151, 178-179
  and CoCom involvement, 64-69. *See also* Coordinating Committee for Multilateral Export Controls (CoCom)
  containment policy during Cold War, 310-312
  control list management, 72-77
  early history, 61-64, 308-309

economic and technological impact of, 10
effectiveness of traditional, 113
European concern regarding, 268
execution of, 143-146
future opportunities for, 319-320
impact on U.S. industry, 18-25, 166-167, 202, 222, 239, 317
industry participation in, 102-103, 151-153, 173-174, 180, 194-195
mechanisms studied by panel, 108-110
organization and objectives of, 1, 3, 4
process goals, 138-139
promotion of trade and national security during détente era, 312-313
Reagan administration influence on, 314-317
redefinition of, 15-17, 165-166
regulations, 77-79
role of intelligence community in, 36
unilateral nature of, 99-101, 173
U.S.-Soviet relations and, 313-314
U.S. export control problems
  exercise of export control authority, 99
  industry participation, 102-103, 173-174
  ineffective dispute resolution, 98-99, 173
  insufficient judicial review, 101-102, 173
  jurisdictional disputes, 87, 93, 147, 148, 172, 190
  licensing complexity, 93-94
  multiplicity of statutes, agencies, and regimes, 86-92, 171-172
  nature and extent of unilateral controls, 99-101, 173
  outdated and confusing control lists, 95-97, 172-173
  overlapping enforcement, 94-95, 172
  severity of restrictions, 215-216, 220, 221
U.S. export control proposed reforms. *See also* Policy recommendations
  administrative due process and appropriate judicial review, 148-149
  changes in agency and legislative authority, 146-147
  enforcement issues, 149-150, 180
  increased industry participation, 151-152, 336-348
  integration and review of control lists, 147-148
  munitions and dual use item standards, 147
  policy execution, 143-146, 190-191
  policy formulation, 139-142, 179, 187-190
  time limits and dispute resolution, 148
  U.S. representation at CoCom, 151, 194
U.S. export controls. *See also* Export controls
  enforcement, 85-86, 94-95, 149-150, 180
  impact of industry structure on effectiveness, 240-241
  impact on U.S. economy, 158-160, 318
  limitations on types and uses, 114-116, 175
  proposal for decision making, 216-221
U.S. export licenses/licensing. *See also* Licenses/licensing
  authority for, 144
  complexity of regulations, 93-94
  dispute resolution, 98-99
  impact on manufactured exports, 318

improvements, 29
national security directives and, 143, 188
national security license processing, 79-83
requirements, 176
time involved to obtain, 23, 93, 123
U.S. distribution, 119
U.S. industry
advanced materials, 20-22, 200-202
commercial aircraft. *See* Commercial aircraft
and jet engine industries
computer. *See* Computer industry
concerns regarding export controls, 19-20,
167
effect of export controls on, 18-25, 166-
167, 202, 222, 239, 317
participation in control list management,
103, 176
participation in export control policy, 102-
103, 151-153, 173-174, 180, 194-195
proposal for use of technical expertise in
export control process, 336-348
U.S. Table of Denial Orders, 95
Uzbekistan, 55

V

Vietnam
export controls targeted against, 72, 78
U.S. trade with, 292

W

Warsaw Pact. *See* Warsaw Treaty Organization
(WTO)
Warsaw Treaty Organization (WTO)
change in relationship with Soviet Union,
44, 168
dissolution of, 1-2, 32, 48, 168
establishment, 61-62, 311
force reduction by, 48

Warsaw Treaty Organization (WTO) allies.
See also Eastern Europe
British policy of differentiation toward, 269
commercial aircraft and jet engine exports
to, 236n
economic and political changes in, 8, 13-14,
39-40, 43-46, 166, 267
efforts to deny access to militarily relevant
technology to, 106
technology acquisition by, 26-31
technology acquisition since beginning of
1990, 31-32
Weapons. *See also* Biological weapons;
Chemical weapons; Nuclear weapons/
materials/technologies
efforts to limit proliferation of, 89
exports from EC members, 121
of mass destruction, 54
need for international attention to trade
issues, 128
U.S. export control policy objectives
regarding, 3
West Germany. *See* Federal Republic of
Germany
World War II, 309
WTO. *See* Eastern Europe; Warsaw Treaty
Organization; Warsaw Treaty
Organization allies

Y

Yugoslavia, economic aid for, 50

Z

Zangger Committee
formation of, 70
membership and function, 129-130
trigger lists, 76, 98
view of dual use items, 34, 137, 185